Alex has a successful career in the professional services industry, which he took time out from to travel and write his first book, *The Weird Way Round*, a travel story written in the style of his literary idol, Bill Bryson. Alex lives in Sydney, his home since moving from the UK to Australia in 2006.

Alex Maycock

THE WEIRD WAY ROUND

Backpacking Through a Midlife Crisis

To Jackee,

Thanks for starring in my book!

Enjoy

Alex

AUSTIN MACAULEY PUBLISHERS™
LONDON • CAMBRIDGE • NEW YORK • SHARJAH

Copyright © Alex Maycock (2021)

The right of Alex Maycock to be identified as the author of this work has been asserted by the author in accordance with section 77 and 78 of the Copyright, Designs and Patents Act 1988.

All rights reserved. No part of this publication may be reproduced, stored in a retrieval system, or transmitted in any form or by any means, electronic, mechanical, photocopying, recording, or otherwise, without the prior permission of the publishers.

Any person who commits any unauthorised act in relation to this publication may be liable to criminal prosecution and civil claims for damages.

A CIP catalogue record for this title is available from the British Library.

ISBN 9781528974752 (Paperback)
ISBN 9781528974776 (ePub e-book)

www.austinmacauley.com

First Published (2021)
Austin Macauley Publishers Ltd
25 Canada Square
Canary Wharf
London
E14 5LQ

Prologue

And so there I was, seated on the pavement in a gated residential community somewhere in Guatemala City, tying my shoelaces and adjusting my hastily thrown on outfit. Glancing at my watch, I saw it was just after eight in the morning. Sunday, I think. Did I get all my clothes out of the house? Did I leave anything in her car? I couldn't say for sure, but I wasn't going to get a chance to get them if I had, so those questions were a bit irrelevant really. There were questions I did need answers to though. It was no good, I was going to have to send her a message to ask.

A – "Maria, I don't know where I am. Can you tell me somewhere I can go please?"
M – "Are you still outside the house? You need to go! He's coming!"

But wait. I'm getting ahead of myself. Let me take a moment to explain who I am, and how on earth I came to be sitting here with just two bags of travel luggage for company and a mildly neurotic date-gone-wrong urging me on my way.

I'm Alex, and I am an accountant. Cue sympathetic applause from the group and earnest attempts to make some reassuring eye contact to break the tension of the uncomfortable moment. I have been an accountant for coming on for 19 years or 228 months, and the chips are weighing heavy in my pockets. The problem is, I'm not sure I really am an accountant – sure, that's what it says on my business card, and that's what I get paid to be, but is that what I am meant to be doing with my life? Is being an accountant my destiny, my purpose even? While that sounds more like a punishment than a purpose, it's a fact that in society, someone has to add stuff up – I get that. But is it meant to be me? Or have I been falsely imprisoned in a pair of chinos and a checked shirt that was intended for someone else?

I have started with a lot of questions. Relax, I'm not expecting you to have the answers – there won't be a test. We are not calling it a crisis – actually, 'we' are not doing anything, as this is not a two-player game – that's just me hiding behind the shield of the first-person plural for some imaginary support. So let's put that shield down – dammit, I'm at it again…

I'm not calling it a crisis. But it kind of is. Let me be more brave and use the whole sordid expression – I'm having a mid-life crisis. I have recently turned 40 so feel entitled to use the phrase, though in honesty it's been brewing for a little while now. I have been with my wife for twelve years and married for nearly eight, but we have been stumbling towards divorce, via a separation and unsuccessful reconciliation for the last two. And last month we decided it was time to call it a day. I won't be going into the details as to the why, as that's not the best subject matter to go to for humorous content. But it's definitely needed for context – so consider yourself sufficiently briefed on that topic for now.

So the crisis in a nutshell – misgivings on my sense of purpose at work, the breakdown of my marriage and my arrival back on the singles market, which now seemingly includes 'swipe right' and other terrifying procedural developments (of which I am yet to learn) since my last visit there many years before. And while that probably doesn't sound that interesting as the starting point of a book – and in truth, it may well prove not to be 'that' interesting, or even interesting at all, but here's the thing – the next bit hasn't happened yet, so at this point, the rest of the story is a mystery to me and you both.

That said, I can tell you roughly what I think is going to happen. With the combination of the relationship breakdown and work misgivings described above weighing on my mind, I decided it was time for a break, and my employer has very kindly agreed to allow me to take six months off work. I am going to spend four months of that time doing some travel with the aim of seeing a bit more of the world while also using the time to re-establish my individual identity and to get back into the rhythm of single life, after a hiatus of about fifteen years.

In recent years I have found myself yearning for a creative outlet outside of work and found the first steps towards that goal in an unusual place – writing match reports for my football team, the 'Mighty Rozelle Dads' Over 35 Division 7 team. These reports were less about the actual events of the game and more about drawing out the humour of the moments we shared as a great group of friends before, during and after the games. Through the power of Facebook, the audience for these reports grew to a broader network of friends and relatives, and each week I felt that my story-telling was bringing just a few moments of joy to those people that they may not have experienced if I had not put pen to paper – and I found that quite a heart-warming feeling. That had been the extent of my writing to date, but I am thinking that perhaps a random, largely unplanned jaunt around the globe will bring new adventures, experiences and stories worth sharing, and at the very least is an interesting idea to explore as I make my way.

Before I take you on the journey to Guatemala and beyond, I want to share a little bit of history on my historical travel experiences and to give some context as to the person behind the pen (or the warrior behind the keyboard, as I'm currently typing this madly on my iPad, seated in the departure gates in Toronto Pearson International Airport). Bear with me, it won't take long.

Born and bred in the UK but now happily residing in Sydney Australia since relocating in 2006 aged 28, most of my travel has taken place since the move to the southern hemisphere. This relocation was a catalyst for many changes in my life, but I think the one that stands out most is the change in my attitude to travel. The short version of my childhood travels is that they were relatively limited, comprising annual iterations of the same holiday in Cornwall (albeit a very pleasant one), a trip around Scotland in a motor-home and a handful of overseas trips to Germany, Portugal and Florida, as my parents spent their money on more worthy pursuits than overseas travel, like my exorbitant school fees for example. I didn't make much more progress in my teen years, didn't have much spare cash during university for travels and then before I knew it, I was preoccupied with getting ahead with my career. In short, I had laid no foundations to build an interest in travel, and holidays were just something I looked to fit in at the best time so as to not compromise my career progression.

I had no plans to work overseas, and I hadn't given a lot of thought to more extensive travel until my hand was forced in 2006 when my then Australian girlfriend received the bad news that her father had some serious, potentially terminal health issues. Six months later, after quickly packing up my current life, I was off to the other side of the world. In a story for another day, the Australian girlfriend ended up being superseded soon after by an English girlfriend (later wife, later still ex-wife), but after that initial break-up, I had already decided Sydney was an exciting place and that I would stay for my two years nonetheless.

The planned two-year time frame on my stay in Australia ended up kick-starting my interest in travel, as faced with a country more than thirty times the size of the UK with interesting-looking places to visit in all corners of it, we decided we had better get on and see some of it. With neither of us having families in the country that required periodic visits and having only a small network of friends, we had lots of time for travel and booked long weekends away to whatever cities had cheap flights on any given week, and generally had a good look around. Before long we had amassed an impressive list of places we had been, eliciting surprised responses from the Aussies we worked with, some of whom would say things like "Really? I have only been out of New South Wales twice!" (My smugness here is qualified by the fact that many of the other Aussies had been to Prague, Barcelona, Madrid, Warsaw and maybe ten other European cities I had not bothered to visit in my 28 years in the UK).

When September 2008, my scheduled return date to the UK, came around, there was something called the GFC going on, and it's fair to say my employer was not knocking down my door to make me come home. So two years became three and a similar economic climate the following year led to three years becoming four. With that extra time and Australia largely 'done', the travel expanded into the local region, taking in New Zealand, Malaysian Borneo, Hong Kong and some long-haul trips back into Europe and suddenly travel for me, had become the activity I was working to pay for, not just something that filled the brief periods of work downtime.

And so to the present, and the destinations on my planned route. I am struggling to recall what my logic was in planning the said route, or in fact if there was any, as looking now at the expected weather conditions in some of the countries which I am due to visit, it seems there is a high probability I will be getting quite wet. That said, the route appears to make geographical sense and includes lots of places I have never been to, so the plan is to just make the best of whatever comes my way. I won't spoil the surprise by telling you where I am going; let's just say I will need four languages which I don't speak, a wardrobe to cater for temperatures from -6 degrees to 45 degrees Celsius and the courage to eat various unrecognisable foodstuffs…

Peru
An Incan Introduction

So, what was I doing at Toronto Pearson Airport? Well, I was drinking a coke and a glass of pinot noir and eating a horribly overpriced sandwich ($49 for those three items?), but the more important point was that I was waiting for my connecting flight to Lima, having arrived from London Heathrow. If you think that sounds like an odd route to take, then I agree with you – but it came up as the cheapest option on Skyscanner and given I wasn't in a hurry I thought I would take the scenic route.

For the majority of my trip, I was going to be doing independent travelling, which loosely translated means making it up as I go, but Peru was one of the two stops where I had decided I would join a tour group. Earlier in the year I had taken some 'regular' annual leave and had gone to walk the Annapurna Circuit in the Himalayas in Nepal, a 15-day trip. That tour was booked with Intrepid Travel, an Australian based company, whom I had been impressed with by both the organisation of the trip but more importantly the demographic and mindset of other travellers they seemed to attract. I made some good friends on that walk who I have kept in touch with since (some of whom will crop up later in the book), and so, using that trip as a barometer for future bookings I decided to book with them again for this one.

The end of my relationship and the ensuing decision to take time off had happened in an impetuously short period of time at the end of May 2018, with my leave starting only four weeks later, so I was booking stuff at relatively short notice. This maybe should have triggered the thought that I would be unlikely to get on the Inca Trail, one of the most popular walks in the world for long-distance travellers, but it didn't, and I charged ahead and booked my 'Inca Express' tour for July. It was only when I picked up a voicemail the following day asking if I wanted to do the 'Quarry Trail' or 'take the train option' that I realised it was time to read the itinerary for the tour and find out what either of those were. It turned out that there were only a limited number of Inca Trail permits available at any point in time (of course), and the next availability was for November. That wasn't going to work for me, and I wanted to walk, not ride a train, so the Quarry Trail it was. I still didn't pay that much attention to what that meant, figuring it would all become clear when I got there, so I made sure I had all my walking gear packed and off I went.

While we are on the subject of bags and packing, you might be wondering how or what one packs for a four-month trip around the world, covering various climates and activities. I don't like to refer to it as a backpacking trip as, well, I felt like I was too old for that – and the main bag I had was an 'expedition bag' not a backpack. However, putting the semantics aside, I carried it using its backpack straps, so I guess that does make me a backpacker. Anyway, for your mental picture, it was a red, cylinder-shaped bag with a nameplate capacity of 60 litres – converting that into real money, once I had stuffed it as tightly as possible with clothes, it weighed 15 kg exactly according to the airport scales. For completeness, I also had a 28-litre daypack filled mostly with electronics and cables and other random stuff, for about another 3 kg. And that was it. For four months. Laundry stops along the way were clearly going to be important…

Apart from packing my bags and doing some clearly reasonably superficial reading about the itinerary ahead of me, the only other preparation I had done for the trip was a half-hearted attempt to learn a bit of Spanish. At school, I spent many years learning French and am fairly confident in following what's going on when someone speaks to me in French, but Spanish, not so much. In the second year at 'grown-up school' (so age fourteen) we had to choose between Spanish, German, Geography or Greek – per my earlier comments on trivia, it was always going to be Geography for me, so when it came to Spanish speaking ability, I had nothing. Nada. Fortunately, there is an app for everything these days, and the most popular one for learning a language is 'Duolingo', which has courses in all the obvious languages you can think of and even a language from Game of Thrones, High Valyrian. Apparently, they do speak this language in some rural parts of Venezuela (ahem…) but I wasn't stopping there, so it was just Spanish I would need for South and Central America.

The guidance on the Duolingo app suggests you should do at least one class a day, which takes a couple of minutes and also recommends that you make the effort to maintain the discipline of doing your daily learning as long as possible. In the lead, up to my trip, I had proudly managed to string together a '50-day streak' which you would think would leave me well equipped for my travels. Unfortunately, there were two issues, the first being that I had only retained about 30% of what I had learnt, and the second being that it seemed to be teaching me a lot of content that appeared to be largely useless. Some favourite examples that I remembered from this category included 'No, he is not the Colonel' and, even more bizarrely, 'No, my cat does not wear trousers'. So long story short, I was arriving in a Spanish-speaking continent with my ability to converse in the local language best described as 'underdone'. But in the words of Baldrick, I had a cunning plan – when commencing any conversation, I would lead with "Hablar Ingles?" ('Do you speak English?'), they would smile at my genuine attempt to learn their language, respond with "Of course sir, how can I help you today?" and we would be all good. Fool proof.

And so, begins the Peru leg of my adventure, arriving at Lima airport at about 1 am, with the tour kick-off meeting due to take place that afternoon at the hotel in the Miraflores district. I had arranged to stay at the hotel for the night before the tour and had the foresight to email them to organise a driver to collect me from the airport, so as to avoid any holiday disaster stories occurring before the holiday had even begun. This plan was going well until we got to the hotel, the driver asked me to pay him, and I didn't have any cash. I had assumed it would go on my hotel bill, and there had been no ATM's between me picking up my baggage and the driver meeting me 50 metres further on. Never mind, after a quick trip round the block to the ATM we were sorted – except we weren't quite done. The ATM had offered me the choice of USD or Peruvian Soles, and I had selected USD as the price for the cab had been stated in dollars ($30), and the machine gave me a wad of $20 notes. Back round the block to the hotel, I handed him $40, and he said, "Don't you have any change?" I'm not sure where he thought I was going to magic change from, but anyway, the answer was no, and his next question was then, "Is change in Soles okay?"

Given that was clearly one of those questions where there was only one answer available, I said "Yes," and he pulled out the calculator and typed in '10*3.2' to get the answer that he owed me 32 Soles. Maybe I am being harsh, as I am a 'numbers guy', but that has to be the least necessary use of a calculator I have seen. And to top it off he only gave me 30 anyway!

Sixteen hours of travel completed and with the clock now showing it was two in the morning, it was time for bed. Buenos Noches.

After waking the next day and having a bit of clean up, I decided I had better charge my phone, which was not really being used as a phone but had a more important role as my only piece of photographic equipment for the trip. It was at this point that I realised that one day into the trip I had already lost something – my universal adaptor plug that all of my USB connected devices (phone, watch, power bar, iPad and Kindle) relied upon. How can you have lost that already, I hear you say! Well, remember that overpriced glass of wine and sandwich at Toronto Airport? Right, so we all know where my adaptor is – or was. And the USB to micro-USB socket that was connected to it…

Ironically, I had bought that adaptor on my last overseas trip while in Manila in the Philippines, having lost the one before – and had paid an exorbitant amount of money for it, after failing to negotiate the dual challenges of a language barrier and melting in the heat. And here I was again, off to buy an adaptor in a foreign country, no doubt also for a King's ransom. After a bit of Google Maps research, I decided the fancy-sounding shopping mall on the side of the cliff in Central Miraflores was my best bet, and sure enough, I found myself an electronics shop where I could see a number of suitable looking adaptors and cables, but they all had security locks on them so I couldn't pick up the ones I wanted. I was going to have to ask for help…

Me – "Buenos dias, hablar Ingles?"

Shop assistant – "No."

Ah.

I hadn't prepared for needing Plan B this early in the trip. From my limited number of conversational Spanish words, I somehow needed to come up with the following sentence translated into Spanish:

"Hello, I would like to buy a universal plug adaptor that I can plug USB cables into, and I also need a USB to micro-USB cable, and no, I don't mean the USB to lightning cable that you are bound to insist is the one I actually want to buy."

Well, that wasn't going to happen, so I went for the only other strategy available – a combination of pointing and miming, and also throwing in the odd English word spoken in a foreign accent. It was tough going, but we got there, and the lady put the two items I wanted on the counter. But we weren't done yet. I was the first customer of the day, and they hadn't fired up the computer that they needed to use to facilitate the transaction. After the longest Windows boot-up process you have ever seen, and two tech-support phone calls, the content of which I am unable to relay for obvious reasons, they finally got it working, and I was able to stop pretending I was interested in their selection of headphones and camera memory cards. But still, we weren't done – in that time period, the lady had come up with some Samsung adaptor and cable thing that would give me the same as my two items but for less money – at least I think that's what she said. Anyway, this sounded sensible, so I bought that one (for $51!) and scurried back to the hotel after binning all the packaging en route. And the bloody thing wouldn't work! The only thing it would charge was my watch, so she must have sold me the lowest powered power accessory on the market. There was no chance I was going back to the shop again though, so I decided I would work out my next move later on, after my tour meet and greet, and try to conserve what power I had left in the meantime.

Before the adaptor cock-up, I also realised that I had forgotten to bring one reasonably important item – sun cream. So I wandered into a pharmacy and searched around for the exact bottle of Factor 30 Nivea sun cream I always buy and presented it to the lady at the counter, who then started rattling off at me in Spanish. I looked at her blankly, and she went and picked up a different brand of Factor 50, which she waved at me and rattled off some more, a bit more insistently this time. I managed a "*No, gracias*" and bought the one I wanted, but having seen my change and the receipt, I think what she was saying was:

"That one in your hand is $40. This one is $2.75, you should buy this one. And you will burn yourself to shit with your fair skin with Factor 30."

Anyway, I promised you a meet and greet, so let's get to that. Arriving in reception, I bumped into someone who had the air of a tour guide, and sure enough, he was. John Smith was his name, perhaps a bit confusingly given, he was a local Peruvian and looked and spoke the part, but what can I say, that was his name. And he was a bit precious about it, as revealed by his later introductory statement, "Don't call me Juan as that is not my name. My name is John." Got it, John.

In total there were seven of us at the initial briefing, myself, two Canadian girls called Sonia and Carly who looked like they were just out of school but who turned out to be on a 30th birthday trip, a married couple from Australia, Ben and Bec, and their friend Graham, and Rachel, a lady from the States who was a little bit older than me and had three old-ish kids, but who was flying solo on this trip. Another couple, Alex from the UK and Siri from Norway were to join us later in the evening when their late connection from the Galapagos arrived.

Siri. I've not met anyone with that name before, but it's one of those names that her parents couldn't have known would take on a different kind of meaning later in her life. Every time there was a roll call, I was half expecting at least three of the group's mobile phones to spring into action and get started on whatever she was being asked to do next.

But I digress. John gave us an initial briefing on the order of events for the tour, explaining that his role was limited to hosting this meeting, taking us on a walking tour of Lima in the afternoon and then dropping us off at the airport in the morning for our flight to Cuzco, where we would be collected by another guide called Armando, who would run the rest of the show. As it turned out, John was a bit of an acquired taste, or 'a character' might be another code word I would use in this circumstance, so we weren't too sad that his role in proceedings was but a cameo.

And so to the walking tour, which actually began with a bus ride. Lima is absolutely enormous, so to do a walking tour in the historic centre meant we first had to ride a bus for about 40 minutes from Miraflores. The traffic was insane, even at 3 pm, but the magic of the bus plan was that they get an express lane to themselves (to compensate for the fact there is no metro rail system), and after a bit of time, we were at the main square. John's tour involved taking us to maybe three or four spots in the city (max) and then delivering a lengthy sermon at each on the detailed history of the country and city, breaking only to take exception to anyone who raised any pieces of info they had heard which he disagreed with. I can't tell you what he taught us as my attention span for such talks is about three minutes, so instead, I will give you the first of what might be a regular fixture of city/country fast facts.

Peru is a country of about 33 million people, with a large proportion of those living in Lima and surrounding areas. The favelas (unplanned shanty towns) make it difficult to state a reliable figure for Lima's population, but it's roughly nine million, which, according to Wikipedia makes it the second biggest 'city proper' in the Americas, behind São Paulo in Brazil. I was going to write that it is a predominantly Catholic country, but John took exception to the use of that word, saying the correct word to use was Christian, but whatever, I can tell you they are definitely not Buddhists. Peru is one of a small number of countries that has the three vastly different ecosystems of coastal, highlands and jungle within its borders, and I would be spending nearly all of my time in the highlands. Lima, in contrast to the highlands, is considered to have a desert climate, and

John claimed it had an annual rainfall of just 11mm a year. This sounded ridiculous, so I checked online, and while there was a range of numbers cited, 11mm sat about in the middle of them – that's about ten minutes of rain on a bad day in Sydney! The other reason I didn't believe him was that since I had arrived the skies had been grey with clouds and I, along with many of the group, had come out for the walk in a rain jacket – appearances can be deceptive when it came to Lima weather it seems. My key takeaway from my time with John was that it was never a good idea to mention anything to do with Chile, as I could immediately see his blood pressure rise each time. In his defence, I got a similar reaction from others later in the tour, so obviously, the bad blood from Chile's historical interactions with Peru must still run deep. The one point he was most definitive about was that the pisco sours I had drunk many years before in Chile were not worthy of the title, that the drink had been invented by a Peruvian, and that only Peruvians knew how to make it properly. This was the kind of history that I was more interested in, and I made a mental note to make sure I explored the quality of the pisco sours later in the trip, though perhaps not when at altitude on my walk.

As darkness fell on the end of the tour, it was time to head back to the hotel, but this time we were taking cabs rather than the return bus, and I was with the Canadian girls. The traffic was absolutely horrific, and we took a good hour to get back, including a fifteen-minute period stationary at a traffic light attempting to cross the main road – what kind of place has traffic lights that are red for fifteen minutes? The journey was lightened, however, by the radio that the cabbie had on, which seemed to be firmly rooted in the 1980s. I very much enjoyed the juxtaposition of the sights of the historical buildings in Lima's centre with Bonnie Tyler's *'Total Eclipse of the Heart'* – who doesn't love a singalong to that? When we finally got back to the hotel, the loosely planned group dinner evaporated when John smoke-bombed and the Canadians also disappeared off somewhere. I had no idea where the other cab was, so I took myself to a place down the road, realised I hadn't eaten all day, and put away half a chicken and some unspecified other 'anticucho' skewer (maybe heart?) in about seven minutes. And so to bed.

***

Passing through the airport en route to Cuzco the next morning, I found myself in a newsagent staring at adaptors and cursing my misadventures from the day before. The prices were even more ridiculous here, but I couldn't bear the thought of a) having to go through the charade again in Cuzco or b) them not having any, so I clenched my teeth and handed over my card to be relieved of $80 for my new favourite adaptor. On the plane, I sat next to Bec and Ben and had a good chat with them to find out what they did for a living. Bec was in marketing, working for a not-for-profit FMCG company that gave their profits to worthy causes, Ben was in 'sports apparel and performance apparel' (compression shorts, tights etc.) and their friend Graham was a pilot. It didn't take more than about ten minutes of discussion to determine that we had similar senses of humour and as the conversation flowed freely, I knew I had identified my 'gang' for this trip, and Intrepid had delivered the goods for me again. As luck would have it, we were also the only four of the nine who were making the Quarry Trail, with the Canadians taking the 'train option' and the others on the Inca Trail. As promised, our new guide Armando collected us at the airport, and we took a 20-minute ride in a minibus to our hotel on the edge of the historic centre of Cuzco. Cuzco is a city in south-eastern Peru, in the highlands near the Andes mountain range and has a population of around 450,000 people. It was the historic capital of the Inca Empire from the 13th century until the Spanish conquest in the 16th century, and in present times is the most famous tourist destination in Peru, with nearly two million visitors from all corners of the globe coming to marvel at its rich Incan history and the nearby towns and ruins which also formed part of the historic empire. And that's why I was here too.

The city was spectacular, with beautiful squares surrounded with cathedrals and other old buildings, all with the backdrop of the hills rising up around the city with their patchwork of buildings, and a cloudless blue sky framing the scene. Amazing. Armando also went on a bit with his history chat, but it was easy to tune out and just take in the sights and the energy of the place while catching your breath after feeling the impact of the altitude during any uphill walking. One thing that did catch my attention were the flags that we saw all over town, usually hanging as a pair comprising the Peru flag and a rainbow flag. Armando asked us if we knew what the rainbow flag was to which three people immediately said, "It's the gay pride flag" – except it wasn't. The Cuzco flag is also, by coincidence, a rainbow, but is distinguished by the fact it includes all seven of the recognised colours of the rainbow, whereas the gay pride flag only has six colours on it. It has always bugged me slightly that they gay pride 'rainbow' flag didn't have the seven colours I recalled learning at infant school, so it was nice to see they were doing it properly here!

After the main squares, we then went around the central market, always my favourite part of a tour of a new city. This was a great example, with row after row of stalls selling fresh juices, fruit and vegetables, meat, spices, pulses, cheeses and clothes and souvenirs. Armando had been joking that we would be trying guinea pig cheese, but after some discussion on the logistics of milking a guinea pig, he came clean that it was really just cow's milk. Guinea pigs, if you were not aware, are a popular delicacy in Peru, having been eaten there since Inca times, and the tension of this practice with the Western World's adoption of them as household pets made it a topic of discussion that would come up a lot over the course of the trip!

Back at the hotel we split into our subgroups and met the remainder of the group for the Quarry Trail walk. So, joining myself and the three Aussies, we had a couple from Canada, Dan and Nancy, a couple from London, Kamal and Brigal and a Swiss chap called Felix. Some guide, who wasn't Armando and who wasn't going to be leading our tour gave the briefing of what the Quarry Trail was with the use of a map that he handed out, but which was impossible to correlate with what he was describing. Anyway, who cares I thought to myself, we were going on a walk, someone would tell us which way to go, and we would see stuff along the way which they could explain at the time – easy.

That said, now is probably the right time to explain the Inca Trail versus Quarry Trail distinction. The Inca Trail as understood by hikers today is a trail that runs from a point 82 kilometres from Cuzco on a four-day hike through to the sun gate at the entrance to Machu Picchu, 42 kilometres further on. The Quarry Trail does have similarities with the Inca Trail in that it is a multi-day walk that goes over mountain passes and visits historical Inca sites, but the differences are more marked. The Quarry Trail runs largely over farmland tracks and paths (in contrast to the broken rock path of the Inca Trail) and is in a location some distance from Machu Picchu, starting near Ollantaytambo and following a big circuit to arrive back in the same town. From Ollantaytambo, it's a 90-minute train ride up to Aguas Calientes, which is the town at the bottom of the mountain that Machu Picchu sits on. So the bad news was that we didn't get to walk through the sun gate to arrive at Machu Picchu, but the good news was that we had one less night of camping and would be able to arrive at Machu Picchu clean and well-rested, and actually earlier in the morning than the weary Inca Trail hikers.

The next day's itinerary saw us heading to Ollantaytambo, with a visit en-route to a local community, where we would get a bit of a flavour of the traditional life. What that was going to involve I didn't really know, but after turning off the main road and travelling down a bumpy dirt road for another half an hour, a posse of about twenty ladies in local dress dancing to music from a small band seemed a pretty big clue that we had arrived. On arrival, we were presented with flower necklaces, and the dancing ladies took us each by the hand and walked/danced us into the main grassy forum that was the centre of their town. My lady was about 80 years old (no exaggeration), so it was more of a walk for me, but that was just fine. A quick admission at this point; I usually hate these kinds of local community shows that are often transported to five-star hotel lawns around the world, as they tend to feel staged and generally awkward. That said, this did feel a bit different, first of all, because we were visiting their actual home and secondly because I was feeling energised by the buzz generated with their grand welcome, and by what looked like their genuine joy welcoming us to spend a few hours with them.

It was harvest time, and most of the men of the village were out in the fields, save the two lucky gents who got to stay behind to bang their instruments for a few minutes for this introduction, and then just hang out with the 'chicas' for the rest of the visit. So the responsibility for the presentations fell to about ten of the ladies of the village, and I use the term presentation advisedly as that's what happened once we were all lined up on the grass – each of the ladies introduced herself in their native Quechua tongue, and Armando translated into English for us. The standard format was as follows:

"Hello, my name is Maria. I am 29 years old, I am married, and I have three children. My husband is a farmer."

And so on for each lady in the line, with a slightly embarrassed giggle by a couple of younger ladies after they had declared their single status, and then it was our turn, with the same content requested, with the addition of what our job was. I was about tenth in line so had time to plan but was immediately stumped by the marital status question, as thus far I had only explained my current situation to Ben and Bec and could foresee that giving the honest answer of 'married' was going to elicit a number of questions from others. This issue was compounded by the first few exchanges, which involved follow up questions from the ladies for more details about the length of marriage and child ages and the like. Finally, it came to my turn, and I kicked off with:

"Thank you very much for welcoming us into your community today," and before I could continue, Armando jumped in and translated that bit, resulting in smiles and nods. I then quickly blurted out, "I'm Alex, I'm 40, and I'm an accountant," smiled at the ladies, and immediately looked to the next person in line to indicate they should take their turn. The plan worked – no follow up questions. Phew.

My favourite response in the introductions was from Ben, who launched into what, in his defence, was a wholly accurate, if slightly overcomplicated, answer, given the audience:

"Hi, I'm Ben, I'm 31 and married to Bec, and I work in sports and performance apparel."

I can't tell you what Armando translated for them but looking at the line of ladies in their traditional attire, I'm fairly confident they were unlikely to be sufficiently regular purchasers of compression tights to understand his vocation. Anyway, it made me chuckle.

The next few hours passed by partaking in activities such as bean shelling, textile demonstrations where we saw first-hand the magical ways they turn sheep into those beautifully coloured Peruvian clothes (by hand), and of course a lunch prepared by the locals. Having said our farewells, we were finally sent on our way with a song by some of the ladies and hit the road to Ollantaytambo, arriving in the early evening at our hotel, where there was time to sit in the deck chairs out the front and enjoy the sunshine. As it turned out, the main attraction wasn't the potential for tanning, but rather the comedy troupe of four resident alpacas that were roaming around, occasionally sparring with each other, spitting and generally providing excellent entertainment for us in securing the perfect alpaca selfie.

During the evenings walking tour, Armando filled our heads with historical facts, and this may be time to disclose that due to my previously mentioned short attention span, I can't tell you much about what Armando told us – in any case, Wikipedia can sort you out if you feel you need to know some history. What I can tell you is that he told us about the local drink, chicha, or corn beer, an alcoholic drink that the locals all drunk whenever the opportunity arose, and which it was even standard practice to give to your children apparently. Armando had just finished telling this tale while standing in one of the narrow alleys in the town, when from up ahead a local gentleman came stumbling towards us and passed through the middle of the group, occasionally steadying himself on the walls on each side before continuing on his way, swaying as he went – we could not have wished for a better illustration of the powers of this mystical local brew.

Walking through one of the alleyways and into one of the tiny stone cottages, we found ourselves with 30 or 40 guinea pigs scurrying around our feet. Armando explained that they had been eaten since Inca times and their popularity had survived the arrival of the Spanish (and their more refined ways) and endured through to the present day, where they are still a popular special occasion meal. Another walk guide, Julio, raved about his love for the guinea pig, saying he could eat two whole ones himself – they really do love the things. Just in case you were going to read ahead, I can save you the trouble – I didn't end up eating one, so I can't tell you what they taste like. The safe money would say probably 'a bit like chicken'…

The abiding memory of the dinner that followed was not the food, but rather the entertainment. About half an hour into the meal (well, actually, half an hour into the wait for the meal – food doesn't happen fast in Peru) a man walked in dressed in the full local gear, pulled out a guitar and a set of panpipes and launched into his set. To start with, it sounded like he was playing some local music, but then I started to recognise some tunes and could tell he was actually doing covers. The first one I could identify was a Spanish tune whose name I don't know, but which I recognised as the tune behind the football ground chant of 'Score in a minute! We're gonna score in a minute!' which made me smile. A more mainstream reference for you that followed was his reimagining of Simon and Garfunkel's *'Sound of Silence'* – which was very relaxing but not what I was expecting to be hearing from his pan pipes! He finished his set, asked if anyone wanted to buy one of his CD's (no), and the group conversation moved on to memories of CD's, Minidiscs (remember them?), cassettes and making mixtapes off the radio. Nostalgia.

***

And so, seemingly an age into the chapter about my walk in Peru, we finally arrived at the start of the walk to meet with our guide Julio, and his assistant Katia. The format of the walk was that we would be camping for the next two nights, so we also had a load of equipment to carry – mercifully the support team included five horsemen, a chef and an assistant chef, and thirteen horses, who between them would be lugging the majority of the tents and food and toilets for us, leaving us just with daypacks – hurrah! Also joining us at this point were Dean and Lucy, a couple in their mid-40s from Bromley in Kent. Lucy had one of those very distinctive Essex/Kent female accents that I didn't hear so much of anymore in Australia, and it was immediately obvious she had a bubbly personality, so I looked forward to hearing more out of her along the way. This took our group size to eleven, with double tents for the four official couples, a double tent for the scratch pairing of Graham and Felix, and a single tent for me.

Why did I have a single tent? The answer is that I had chosen to pay a single supplement and the reason I had done that was on my trip to Nepal I had chosen not to do so and had been paired up with an English gentleman in his mid-60s called Robin. Robin was a lovely chap, a retired teacher who knew a lot about a lot, and apart from a slightly annoying habit of asking lots of questions about laundry facilities and how much to tip, seemed a solid enough roommate. And so it was for a couple of days until one night I was awoken by a violent thunderstorm – which was actually Robin snoring. It was incredible – booming volume, noises on both the inhale and exhale, and extraordinary stamina, extending for unbroken periods of over an hour at a time. I didn't feel like I knew him well enough to beat the shit out of him to make it stop, so I just endured it and didn't sleep much until we finally got to a hotel where there were enough rooms for us not to share. I wasn't running the risk of that happening again, so single tent it was.

At the start of the walk, Julio, who was a genuinely lovely happy-go-lucky guy (and perfect tour guide) asked us all to introduce ourselves with name, age (an acceptable question to ladies in Peru it seems) and what we were most scared of, with the presumed aim that he would look to put us at ease about those fears. I was only third in line this time so didn't have much time to think anything up – spiders went early, so I went for snakes, but the majority of people seemed scared of altitude sickness or not completing the walk. For context, we were starting the walk at about 2,800 metres and would be climbing to about 4,300 metres at the highest point. Anyone who has spent time at that kind of altitude will know it's reasonably hard work getting your body to do simple things (like breathing) when you are getting a significantly reduced amount of oxygen. The worst-case scenario is that your body can't cope with it and you get altitude sickness, which comes in two forms, neither of which are particularly enjoyable and both of which will likely land you in hospital. So it's a fair thing to be worried about. A lot of people try to remedy the issue by taking a drug called Diamox, which about half of the group was taking. I haven't used it before, but the well-documented downside is that you spend an inordinate amount of your day going to the toilet, which none of the people in the group who were currently experiencing these symptoms seemed that pleased about.

The best exchange on this round of introductions was yet to come – I forget who said it, but someone said they were most afraid of getting old. Quick as a flash, also bearing in mind this was in his second language, Julio quipped:

"I'm a tour guide, not a genie."

Gold.

After the introductions we were off, taking a gentle climb through farmland with the occasional pig and cow sighting, kicking off the initial exploratory chats with our fellow walkers, and getting the leg muscles ready for the tougher tests ahead. My initial expectations for Lucy's banter were soon rewarded when she mentioned the guide in Cuzco, who had given their intro meeting, talking about the recent cold weather they had been having.

"They were saying that there was going to be snow up there that we were going to have to walk through and I nearly turned around and said well, in that case, I'm not going as no one said anything about that when I booked it."

Fortunately for us, Lucy had bitten her tongue and her and Dean had gone out and found some cheap warm jackets and gloves to buy and were ready for whatever lay ahead. As it happened, it was looking like the bad weather had passed, as we were walking beneath beautiful blue skies and getting a little bit cooked by the sun, so the snow threat appeared unlikely to be a problem after all. The first stop of the day was by an empty school after a few hundred metres of ascent, where we took the opportunity for a snack break. After being there about five minutes, a scruffy chap in sportswear wandered over with a carrier bag, from which he pulled a traditional Peruvian poncho and hat and a flute and launched into a few tunes to try and land a few Soles. I did give him a couple of coins for his efforts but, if I had the Spanish, I would probably have advised him to do the carrier bag bit around the corner first next time.

Along the way, Julio shared various stories and nuggets of info about Peru to keep us entertained and distracted from the gradual uphill slog. One worth sharing was about the various llama and llama-like animals indigenous to the country, and how each of those converted into the quality of wool and corresponding prices for the scarves and jumpers that were for sale everywhere in Cuzco and Lima. The ranking apparently goes like this – llama is the bottom rung of the ladder, then you move up to alpaca, and then it's baby alpaca. Baby alpaca, however, does not mean toddler alpaca hair, it is a term that refers to the first shearing of the animal, which doesn't happen until they are about two years old. Top of the pops goes to the vicuña, which commands top dollar in the fancy boutiques – but most of the street salesmen were trying to push their baby alpaca wares. Julio had a word of warning for us here:

"If someone is saying they want to sell you a baby alpaca jumper for $20, that is not baby alpaca – that is 'maybe alpaca'." Touché.

The terrain started to get a bit steeper, and we could see some Inca ruins gleaming up at the top of a cliff way up above, which it transpired was the destination just before our lunch break. By now, subgroups had formed according to relative walking speeds, and with my competitive nature, I was up the front with the Aussies, followed by the main 'peloton', less Kamal and Brigal who were bringing up the rear. Kamal was already having some trouble getting his breath on the climb, so it was looking like a long day for him, and a potential job later on for one of our 'emergency horses'.

After a brief stop at a lookout over the valley that we had spent the morning walking up, we arrived at the Inca ruins site at Qorimarca. The light falling on the site was perfect, and I scrambled up the hill to take in the view from above of the ancient stone buildings against emerald green lawns and the amazing blue sky above the valley tumbling away below. After some time to walk around all the buildings, we had another half an hour of flat walking to our lunch stop, which was also our campsite for the evening – meaning we were done for the day and our legs could take a well-earned rest.

Around the lunch table, Ben kicked off a discussion for everyone to share what they did for a living. We had a few teachers, Kamal was a tax advisor, Dan was a fireman, and there were general polite nods in response to the answers until Graham revealed he was a pilot. There was a collective 'ooh' around the table, and I could sense the ladies in the group were picturing Graham in his captain's outfit, striding through the airport like Leonardo Di Caprio in *'Catch Me If You Can'* – I know I was. After the awe subsided, I got in first on the 'questions I always wanted to ask a pilot' – mine was about when you are on board a plane waiting for the final people to board and the public address system comes on and the steward says, "If Ignatius Fortescue-Smythe (or something equally preposterous) is on board, can you please press the call button" – how do they not already know the answer given the process we have all just been through having our boarding passes checked. The answer is that they are 99% sure that they are 'NOT' on the plane, but they are just double-checking there wasn't a scanner error or similar if they did get on. Which put my mind at rest. The next question was the old favourite about why you have to put up the window shades for landing – if you don't already know that one, the answer is so if there are any mechanical issues while coming into land, the flight crew are able to easily look out the window to check for engine shutdowns or fires or the like. So there you go.

Oh, and also, Dean's answer was that he worked for the UK government, but couldn't tell us any more than that. So he either had a really cool James Bond kind of job or a really dull one that he didn't want to admit to. I'm going for the former.

Something I had been a bit apprehensive about was the toilet tent arrangements, after hearing horror stories about human waste issues along the Inca Trail. But I wasn't on the Inca Trail, and the horsemen were carrying chemical toilets for us that had their own tents, so that meant everything was going to be fine right? Wrong. After we had been briefed on the respective gents and ladies toilet tents (one receptacle for 'ones' and one for 'twos') I decided I was brave enough to go in for a 'wee' and was immediately faced with a scene of horror. I didn't stay long enough to work out exactly what had happened, but I only saw one toilet, which seemed to have what I will just describe as a scene of uncontrolled discomfort in it. I backed out swiftly and upon exit shared a few knowing looks with Ben and Graham who had also been in there and walked briskly away from the campsite to wee in a bush. The strategy for 'number twos' could wait – but I told myself I wasn't going back in there again, whatever happened.

Later on, we regrouped for dinner, played a bit of UNO (how good is UNO?), it got dark, and we went to bed to prepare for the big day ahead, which would comprise fifteen kilometres of walking and scaling two mountain passes at an elevation of about 4,200 metres over the course of an estimated ten-hour day.

Having slept surprisingly well in the tent, we were pumped full of carbs at breakfast to fuel the day ahead and off we went, but it was slow going. Our day one campsite was at 3,700 metres, so we were already at a pretty decent altitude and the steep incline for the first hour was hard going for many. At that point, we stopped for a break, and sadly, it was time for me to concede that the number two situation could be delayed no longer. I headed into the nearby bush to find a suitable spot, only to find that each time I looked around to check I was hidden, I was still in plain sight – which was always going to happen given I was walking uphill with only short bushes for cover. Anyway, eventually, I found a hidden lair, did my first ever 'second-grade nature business', felt a Bear Gryll's like the sense of manly accomplishment and returned to the group, just slightly elated in the knowledge I wouldn't need to use the chemical toilet.

Feeling substantially lighter on my feet, I pushed ahead up the next hill with the Aussie speedsters and enjoyed the growing expanse of valley views and distant mountain peaks as we ascended. At the rear of the group, things weren't going so well for Kamal, and it wasn't too much of a surprise when later in proceedings he passed us going up the hill on a horse, with the obligatory slightly embarrassed look that is reserved for those kinds of situations. After about four hours of an uphill slog, we were richly rewarded, coming over the final crest of the hill at 4,200 metres to reveal a panorama of snow-capped mountains ahead of us, falling down to the distant valley below, all in clear sight under the cloudless skies. Magnifique!

As I mentioned, we were walking under clear skies with the sun beating down, and as I walked into the lunch tent, Nancy said, "Alex, I think you need some sun cream on your face, you are looking pretty red." Damn that Lima pharmacy soothsayer! As it happened, some of the red was exertion-related, and it wasn't the disaster it could have been, but I would be dishonest with you if I said I wasn't burnt.

Traversing a reasonably barren mountaintop plateau we reached the next pass at 4,250 metres, where we celebrated raucously (well, a bit) that we had finished the last uphill of the day. But what goes up must come down, and the next section was a steep downhill Having walked for fifteen days in Nepal with my walking poles only having come out of my bag once, I had decided not to bring them this time, but looking at the descent ahead, and everyone else getting out their poles I was slightly regretting that decision. Walking down the hill at the back of the group at a snail's pace, waiting for the inevitable slide and hamstring tweak, I decided there had to be a better way, and started jogging down. It was bit haphazard, it wasn't completely controlled, but it seemed to work, and so I jauntily worked my way through the group and kept on going until the gravel slope finished half an hour later, ignoring the fact my quads were by now on fire. I had a sit down for ten minutes before the Aussies caught up, and Julio decided we could do the rest of the walk at our own pace rather than wait for the rest of the group. Graham and I needed no second invitation and tore off into the distance, both with half a mind that we would get to camp first before anyone else had visited the freshly erected toilet tent...

Now I don't like to overdo the toilet stories, but I feel it would be remiss to skim over what happened after I went to bed, so apologies in advance – this will hopefully be the last mention in the book. Two hours after I had fallen asleep I woke up with my stomach absolutely churning – after a brief failed attempt to meditate it away, it was apparent action was going to be required in a hurry, so I reached for my head torch with a sense of urgency – and couldn't find the bloody thing! With panic levels increasing that a sorry fate was about to befall my sleeping equipment, I fumbled around but to no avail – seeing my iPhone was the best light source I was going to manage, I grabbed it and ran. I made it into the toilet tent, established which receptacle was which and jumped on. It was at this point I realised the two receptacles set up was designed for a controlled visit, which this clearly was not – cue jumping between the two in an inelegant fashion, trying my best not to create any horrors for later users. I just about managed it, but it was traumatic. And a final confession – when I had regained my composure and stepped out the tent, I realised in my panic I had run into the ladies' tent – sorry girls...

Day three of the walk was pretty 'cruisey' in comparison to the previous day – eight kilometres of mainly gentle downhill to the end destination of Ollantaytambo, with a stop along the way at the eponymous Quarry. The quarry was pretty impressive, with tales of the giant stones being transported down hills and across vast distances to build temples, much like the stories you might have heard about the Pyramids or Stonehenge, that are simply mind-boggling to contemplate in the absence of the assistance of modern technology. After reaching the town we had a quick pit stop for lunch, and then it was on to the station to catch the 90-minute train up to Aguas Calientes, and time to ignore the spectacular views and play more UNO – again, how good is UNO? This time round, we were teaching Armando how to play, who was clearly right into it, and got very excited when he put down his final card thinking he had won. Except he hadn't, as he hadn't realised what the 'Pick Up 4' card that had just been played meant, which we all roared at him and laughed. The whole of the rest of the carriage stopped what they were doing and gave us dirty, disapproving looks, and we looked sheepish and quietly played out the remainder of the game.

The evening in Aguas Calientes was spent packing in several activities that would make the Inca Trail group, who were about to have their third day of camping, as jealous as possible the next day. So the Aussies and I had an awesome shower and wash up (in our respective rooms), went and got massages, ate a hearty dinner and drank pisco sours and wine. And slept fabulously well. In truth, the fabulousness was short-lived, as we had to get up at 4:30 am (4:30!) to have breakfast and get to the queue for the buses to Machu Picchu at 5 am). It is a measure of the tourist appeal of the place that there was already a massive queue there when we arrived – this was low season, but people still start queuing at 3:30 am! It took about an hour for us to get onto a bus, and the thirty-minute journey winding up switchbacks meant we arrived at the site for about 6:45 am, with the sun yet to rise above the surrounding mountains. I'm not going to try and fully describe the scene as words really can't do it justice – you will probably have seen photos of the place, but it was quite special standing in front of that scene as the sun crept over the hills and the light falling on the city evolved minute by minute. And the Inca Trail walkers would not walk through the sun gate for another hour yet…

During the site visit, I learned Machu Picchu was built back in the 15th century, over a period of around 40 years, as an estate for the Incan emperor of the time, *Pachacuti*. The estate remained incomplete at the time of the Spanish invasion, and the Incans abandoned the site, which the Spanish explorers never ended up finding. It was only many hundred years later that the site was re-discovered by the American historian Hiram Bingham, covered under a thick covering of vegetation, which over the years after this discovery was cut back to reveal the outrageous beauty of the site that will be familiar to many from postcards and photos. Julio's also advised us on the correct way to pronounce the place name as Machu Picchu ('picku'), not Machu 'pitchu' as most people refer to it. The proper pronunciation translates in the local dialect as 'Old Mountain', whereas (according to Julio) the incorrect version translates as 'old penis' – good to know!

It would be remiss not to share that there are tonnes of tourists and it does feel like a bit of a zoo – it's a shame, but if there is something this awesome to see, lots of people are going to want to see it. How they deal with the numbers continuing to rise, I don't know, but hopefully, someone has a solid long-term plan to preserve the magic of the place.

The zoo-like feeling also extended to the queues for the buses back to catch the train, which was just mental, and people were trying every trick in the book to cut in, with zero success. One lady in her early thirties took one look at the queue, and you could see she had no intention to wait in it, and we watched her try to jump in at four different spots, arguing with the security guys at length to push her claim. When we finally got on our bus 45 minutes later, we took much pleasure from seeing her standing at the back of the line having admitted defeat and adding thirty minutes to the journey time she would have spent, had she just queued properly in the first place. Ha!

Joining back up with the Inca Trail group, who looked absolutely wrecked, we smugly enjoyed a beer and lunch, which was backed by the music floating up from downstairs…would you believe the panpipe rendition of *'Sound of Silence'*. That evening, it was time to check out Cuzco's nightlife, and we managed to rouse all eleven members of our tour group to some closing drinks at what sounded like the noisiest bar on the square. Most of the group called it a night around 12 am, but the Aussies and I pushed on, heading upstairs to the club, which was playing highbrow music including the Grease Megamix and *'Wannabe'* by the Spice Girls, perfect fodder for a bit of dance around. When we were in Lima, John Smith had said that after four pisco sours, most people were on the floor, which Graham had scoffed at, saying he thought he could do eight. He was, therefore, less than impressed when we finally called it a night from the club at around 2 am and he had got through seven, agonisingly short of his target. So on we went to another bar, he drank two more, and we all went home happy. And shitfaced. Apart from Ben, who was a lifelong non-drinker…

Next day it was time to move on for me – Ben and Bec had one more day in Cuzco before going to Cartagena in Colombia, but I was off to Panama, via Bogotá. As it happened Graham had also decided to go to Colombia and was booked on the same flight as me, so we went to the airport together. Which meant he was there to witness me realising, as I approached the security scan, that I had left my sun cream in my hand luggage, and also to witness the nearly full bottle being confiscated. $40!

Summary – Peru

Kilometres travelled (air) – (Inc. Syd to Lima) 29,590
Kilometres travelled (land) – 200
Number of items confiscated or lost – Two
Number of effective conversations in Spanish – None
Number of photos with llamas posted on Instagram – Two

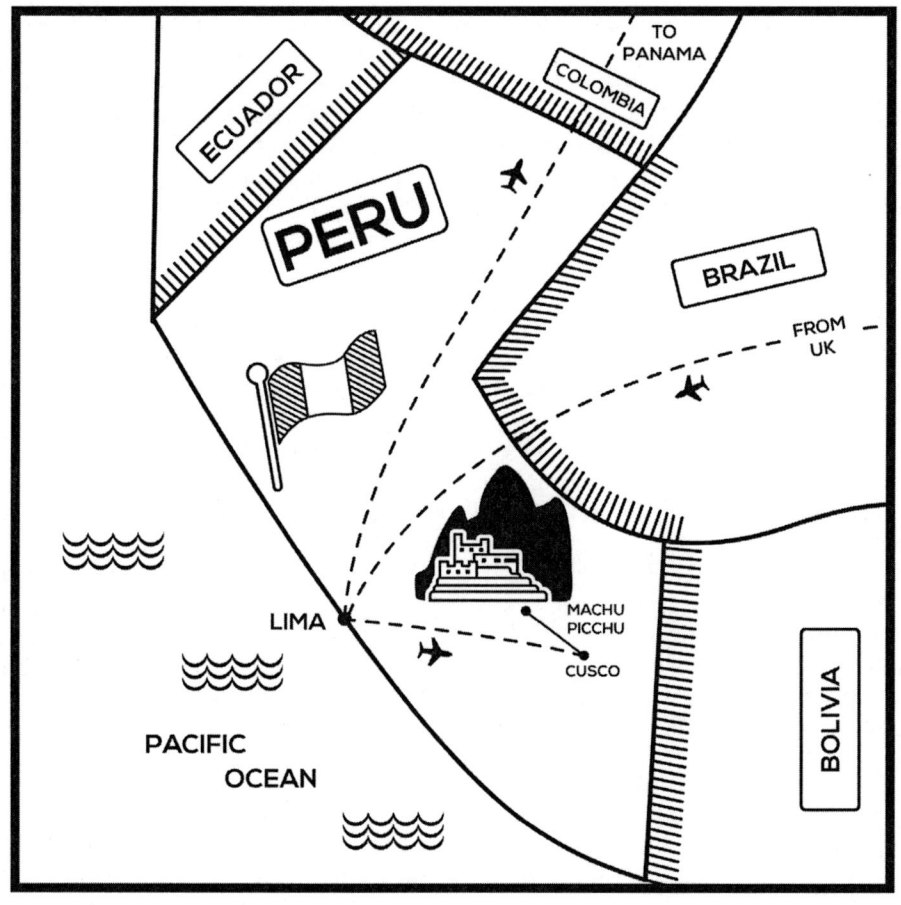

Panama
Adventure Planning-on-Sea

And so, after a brief transit stop in the seemingly never-ending international terminal at Bogotá airport, I arrived at my first Central American country of the trip, Panama. When I had checked in at Cuzco, there had been a fair bit of questioning about my onward travel plans, and the lady had said I wouldn't be allowed into Panama unless I could prove I was going to leave again. This had resulted in a quick hunt around Cuzco airport for some decent Wi-Fi, so I could book a cheap shuttle bus from my end destination in Panama over to Costa Rica, which I could easily cancel if required. I had also read that to enter Panama from Peru I would need the yellow booklet that proves you have received the yellow fever vaccination – this jab, and a typhoid shot, had set me back a princely $250 in Sydney shortly before I left, but needs must, and I was all set for my immigration interrogation and document check as I walked up to the lady on the booth.

"Hola, blah blah blah…?" (Her, not me)

"Perdon?" (Me)

"How many days are you staying?"

And that was it. She stamped the passport and waved me through, with no requests to see anything else. That said, it was one in the morning, so she was probably in a hurry to get out the door. This theory was validated when I arrived at Customs and handed over the form where I had ticked 'yes' to one of the questions you know is always going to cause problems, 'Have you been near farmland and horses etc.?' I was all set to get my hiking boots out to be taken away and washed, but the guy barely even looked at the form and waved me straight through. Which would never happen in Sydney.

This reminded me of arrival back into Sydney from a trip to Chile and Argentina, which had involved a large amount of hiking in rural areas. As expected, the hiking shoes were whisked away for a wash, and I waited patiently for their return, the final hurdle before getting home for a shower after the fourteen-hour flight. After what felt like about fifteen minutes, the guy trotted out with my shoes in a carrier bag and apologised for taking so long, explaining that there was some stuff really well stuck on, which had taken a lot of effort to get off. It was only later in the day when I opened the bag and looked at the shoes that I discovered the 'well stuck on stuff' was a grippy plastic part of the sole itself, which he had kindly removed from both shoes. Straight in the bin.

I had taken the cheat's option and organised a guy to pick me up from the airport, and as soon as I connected to the airport Wi-Fi, I saw I had a new WhatsApp buddy called Alcibiades, who had messaged me to say he was waiting for me outside. The drive to the area I was staying took about half an hour, and we had a stilted conversation in Spanish for a few minutes before he had to pass me his phone with Google Translate open so he could follow what I was asking. Having overcome the language barrier, we were firm friends by the end, and I told him I would message him about taking me to my next airport in a few days' time.

So where was I staying? This is the point in the story where I reveal one of the core building blocks of my plan to travel around the world in countries where, in most cases, I could not speak the local language – Airbnb. I'm not sure where I got the idea, as before this trip I had never booked one, but I decided that if I stayed in Airbnb's, I would immediately have someone who hopefully spoke a bit of English, and who could give me a bit of a steer on what I should do in that place, and perhaps also help me with things like onward planning. And so outside of a couple of organised group trips I intended to take, the plan was to book the rest of the trip's accommodation in Airbnb's. I did a bit of research before I left to check coverage in all of my intended destinations, and it looked like there were loads of options everywhere. With this knowledge, I decided I would book my accommodation in a given country from the country prior on my itinerary, by which time I should have a good feel for planned timing and towns to stay in. So before I left Australia, the only thing I had booked was the Peru trip, flights to Panama, and accommodation for two days in Panama City – the rest of the trip, flights, accommodation and timing was all still to be worked out.

My first Airbnb didn't quite conform to this plan, as I had booked a stand-alone apartment as opposed to a room in someone's house – I don't recall that being deliberate, so I think it was just the best option in the area I wanted to stay, Casco Viejo. Actually, I have a confession here; this Panama City apartment was not my first Airbnb. I had spent a week in the UK prior to commencing my travels proper and had stayed at one in the Bristol area and one in Richmond, just outside London. In Bristol, I was hosted by a lovely lady called Delyth in a 'room in house' scenario, which was very stylishly decorated and probably nicer and better equipped than most hotel rooms. The Richmond one, however, did come with a funny story, and given that's the business I'm in, that one definitely merits a few column inches (or whatever the book version of that expression is).

Check-in at the Richmond property was at 3 pm, but I was due to arrive in London on a train from Bristol at about 12 pm, before meeting an old friend for lunch in Clapham Junction. Rather than having to lug my bags to lunch, I thought I would see if I could drop my bags off in Richmond so I messaged the host, James, the night before to see if that would be possible. He had been quite responsive on the email exchanges when I was making the original booking, so I was bit surprised when I hadn't heard from him by the time I got the train the next day. I still hadn't heard back by the time I arrived at London Paddington, so I went straight to lunch instead. After finishing up at lunch, I found my way back to Richmond and did the ten-minute walk to the flat, still having received no response or any instructions on how to get in, which is the usual Airbnb modus operandi. With no other way forward, I rang the doorbell and was greeted by a slightly flustered looking guy wearing just a towel.

Me – "Err, Hi, I'm looking for James?"

J – "Yes, I'm James."

Me – "Err, I think I'm staying here today?"

J – "Today? No, that's on the 19th."

Me – "Err, today is the 19th."

He grabbed his phone to check his diary and realised that it really wasn't the day he thought it was. Luckily, it turned out he had a boat nearby that he also lived on, but as he was looking a bit hassled, I suggested that it might be best if I came back a bit later. We agreed that seemed a sensible way forward, and I disappeared back up the road to a pub for an hour and a half while he got his shit together. I was slightly troubled by what he was doing in a towel in 'my' house at four in the afternoon, but I tried to let that thought pass. When I returned, and James had disappeared after tidying the place up, it was worth the wait, a lovely little flat that even came with its own house cat, Samson. My new feline friend arrived through the window about an hour after I had arrived, saw me watching TV and walked straight up and sat on my lap – I do find cats quite presumptuous sometimes.

Back in Panama City, my apartment was hosted by a gentleman named Mauricio, who I didn't end up meeting, wearing a towel or otherwise. We swapped a few messages on logistics, but that was the extent of our relationship, so Alcibiades had a pretty untested run to the accolade of my best Panama City buddy. I was staying in a part of the city called Casco Viejo ('Old Quarter'), which was first settled back in 1671 and had been the centre of the city for many years before falling out of favour and subsequently falling into disrepair. The area had roared back into fashion in recent years, had been designated a UNESCO World Heritage site in 1997 and was seeing many of its old buildings being carefully restored. The slightly dilapidated look of the place and restoration works reminded me of the following exchange from a guilty pleasure film of mine, *'A Good Year'* (the film version of Peter Mayle's excellent book *'A Year In Provence'*), between Max Skinner, who has just inherited an old estate in Provence he immediately wants to sell, and his real estate agent, Charlie Willis:

Charlie: (calling from London) "How's the house, Max? Is it gorgeous?"

Max: "Well, to tell you the truth, Charlie, it's a little shabby."

Charlie: "We don't say 'shabby' Max. We say, 'filled with the patina of a bygone era'."

While it was a nice area to spend a day or so, the Panama City stop was only really intended to break up the travel from Peru through to my principal destination in Panama, an archipelago of islands on the Caribbean coast in the north-west of the country called Bocas del Toro. That said, I felt duty-bound to have a bit of a look around, so took a walk around Casco Viejo, finding a friendly coffee shop lady nearby to test my Spanish on and learn how to say 'to go' ('para llevar'), and then heading in the direction of the fish markets. Along the way, amongst the succession of grand old buildings in the course of being restored to former glories, I found that elaborate graffiti was a popular pastime in the area – graffiti is perhaps doing the art a disservice – they would be better described as murals, rich in colour and character, providing something engaging to look at around many corners. Unfortunately, when I got to the fish market, it was a bit of a disappointment, one smallish room with about 30 stands selling a similar range of fish at each. I have high standards for such outings as Sydney Fish Market, while a bit grotty from the outside, is wonderful inside, with colourful spreads of prawns, crustaceans and an array of whole fishes of all shapes and sizes – this one wasn't really in the same league.

The other activity that I felt obliged to do while in town was to go and visit the Panama Canal – apart from hats, that's probably the first thing that comes to mind when Panama is mentioned, so I thought I should go take a look. The Miraflores Locks is one of the three giant sets of locks that facilitate the transfer of ships through the canal from the Caribbean to the Pacific and vice versa. Miraflores Locks is about fifteen kilometres from Casco Viejo so after establishing, to my delight, that my Uber app worked in Panama, I took the 25-minute trip out there. At the moment I arrived, two giant vessels (car transporters) were passing through the locks, so I was advised to join the throng of tourists watching the nearer ship crawl through into the second lock. It was obviously impressive from a scale perspective, but in a practical sense, it was the same as watching any boat go through a set of locks, as I had done at the Kennet and Avon canal near Reading as a child. I don't recall being that excited about that spectacle, and I was feeling similar emotions in response to this one – perhaps if I had more interest in engineering marvels, the sight would have got me in more of a lather. But it didn't. The highlight was probably when the captain let rip on the giant horn as he passed the spectators and we all cheered and waved at him waving at us. And then it stopped moving as they drained the lock, and the crowd quickly dispersed to find a coffee or an empanada.

I was more engaged; however, by the video that I watched afterwards which talked through the history of the canal, much of which I was unfamiliar with. It had been obvious to explorers of the area that a link through the country between the Pacific and Caribbean Oceans would have a massive impact on world trade, and it was the French who had begun work on the canal back in 1881, but after many years of toil, engineering issues and high worker mortality from the tropical diseases of the area they finally had to admit defeat in 1894 and give up. The US took over the project in 1904, and the canal was finally officially opened to vessels in 1914. The US managed the canal until the 1977 Torrijos-Carter Treaties provided for the gradual hand over of control to Panama, with Panama assuming full control in 1999. Watching the video that captured these moments in history, it was clear that the canal is a source of great national pride in Panama, and they have gone on to complete a major upgrade in recent years to help accommodate the larger and heavier vessels seeking passage through the mighty system of locks.

Back in Casco Viejo, I had done a bit of Lonely Planet research and identified a rooftop bar which sounded like THE place to go to watch the sun go down over the city and work through some mojitos and a couple of Balboa's, the rather good local lager. It was at this point, quietly enjoying my beer alone amongst the early evening couples' get-togethers, that my thoughts started to turn to another, as yet unknown, the quantity for the trip ahead – where or how I was going to find some romance. As I alluded to the right at the start of my story, things on the dating scene had moved on quite a lot since I was last single, about fifteen years earlier, and it was clear I had some learning to do on what it all meant for me. When I first started planning where I was going to go in my trip, I had vague visions of going into bars and clubs, striking up a conversation with some easy on the eye ladies and taking things from there. It was now, as I thought through how this 'straw man' would be progressed to an actual real-life plan that I realised there were a few flaws with this plan:

- I didn't speak any Spanish.
- Going to a bar or club on your own and working out who to talk to, and how, isn't easy.
- I was never any good at it back in the day, even when I did speak the relevant language.

I didn't have the answers as I sat there that evening, but I knew I was going to need to work something out, if nothing else, to help me make some more travel buddies on my way round (apart from Airbnb hosts and taxi drivers).

***

The flight to Bocas the next day was on a small Fokker propeller plane and took a shade under an hour, the highlight of which was the 'inflight meal' of a bag of Doritos-like corn chips (local brand), which, actually, was just what I fancied. Arriving in Bocas Town, the largest settlement on the islands and tourist centre, to gloomy skies, I had the shortest transfer to one's accommodation on record, stepping out the exit of the terminal building to see the gate to my accommodation, 'Stay Bocas'. Given there were only about four flights a day, this location was not as bad as it sounds, and my room was excellent.

My host here was Jorge, the owner, but he was away for a few days, so I was expertly taken care of during the day by a supercool gentleman called Raul, and at breakfast by the lovely Elli.

So, let me briefly introduce you to the region. Bocas del Toro comprises a relatively small area of the mainland, nine main islands and a number of smaller islands and coral cays and the like. The whole area has a population of only around 130,000, though that number swells considerably when you add in the number of visiting tourists at any point in time. Christopher Columbus explored the area way back in 1502 (he got about didn't he?), and the area has been claimed by both Colombia and Costa Rica over the years, until landing up as a province of Panama. I was due to stay here for a relatively extensive stay of five nights, the logic at the time of the booking being that I would be ready for a bit of a beach chill out after the rigours of the Inca Trail. So that left me plenty of time to work my way round a good number of the islands, which I kicked off that evening with a walk around Bocas Town, the main town on Isla Colon.

The West Indian influence was clear to be seen, with the familiar red green and yellow livery scattered around various buildings in the town and a number of Rasta's manning the shops and tour offices, but the whole town was a riot of colour, with blue, green, orange and yellow buildings and colourful bicycles, the preferred form of transport, parked around all the streets. The demographic of the tourists was a mix of young European backpackers, surfers and holidaying families from the US and further afield, and the place had a buzzy, friendly feel about it.

In my airport reading, I had established there was a yoga studio in town, and so the next morning, I took the short walk to join the morning drop-in class. One of my other aims for the trip was to make the most of the time away from sitting at my desk to have a good go at getting in really decent shape fitness-wise, and I had decided that as I have some of the tightest hamstrings in Sydney yoga should play a role in this. 'Bocas Yoga', is owned and run by an American ex-pat called Laura, who had just turned 50 and, from reading the info on her website blog was clearly a colourful character. You would need to go and read the entries yourself to get the full picture, but I think the potted summary was that she was a bipolar, ex-addict, LSD enjoying free spirit who had realised later in life that she was a lesbian. It was basically just Laura, myself and four ladies who it sounded like were all waitresses or cooks at restaurants in the town, and it was a fun class, with the real-life Laura delivering a bubbly rendition of her online persona – and I started my day feeling filled with virtue.

Suitably loosened up, and seeing the blue skies overhead, I decided I would double down on the exercise and take one of the rental bikes from the hotel for a ride to the far north-west of the island, where there was a popular tourist spot called Playa Estrella, which promised pretty starfish in the sea just off the beach. The guidebook said most people got a van or boat there, but I am not most people, and I had read that the 16-kilometre ride was quite hilly, but 'challenging and rewarding'. I have recently discovered the pleasures of road biking and had bought one for myself for Christmas and had got into taking long rides, so this sounded like an excellent opportunity to remind my legs what it was all about. I should note for non-bike riders that there is quite a difference between riding a super-light carbon road bike with 18 gears, and riding a 'Bocas cruiser', which had one gear, no brakes (pedal backwards to brake) and which weighed about the same as a small hatchback car. Undaunted, I packed my beach gear into a bag and put it in the basket (yes, it had a basket) and set off, wearing shorts, a t-shirt and my flip flops.

The first few kilometres took me out of town, passed alongside some pretty looking beaches and were completely flat, but soon I was at the first of the promised hills and life started getting harder. The sun was beating down, I was sweating like a drain, but I was feeling good about my progress up the hill, satisfied that, come to the end of the day, I would be able to smugly report I had conquered the challenge with little difficulty. And then it started going wrong. Stamping hard on the pedals to maintain momentum up a hill, I hit a pothole in the road, and the chain fell off. I'm not sure conceptually how that happens on a one-gear bike, but it did, and I couldn't get the bloody thing back on the rear cog. After sweating even more copiously while I worked on the bike, I finally got it back on and was about to turn it back over and get away from the scene of the crime when I saw my efforts had taken the chain off the front cog – and no matter how hard I tried, I couldn't find a way to get it back on. Luckily, a man in a passing van stopped, and he managed to get it back on – it did take him about five minutes though which made me feel a bit better. When I reported this incident on Facebook later in the day, Rachel (from my Peru trip) commented that failing to get a chain back on a bike was a 'man card violation'. Probably fair.

Anyway, finally, I was back on and moving again, looking more cautiously at potholes when the next disaster hit – one of my flip flops decided the hill-climbing was too much and snapped (I believe the Australian translation of this event would be that I 'busted a plugger'…) After a brief pause for thought to consider my options, the main one being to abort and chuck the bike in a passing truck and head back home, I deemed a failure as being an unacceptable option, put both flip flops in the basket and powered on barefoot – given I was only five kilometres in at this point, this was a bold call. As the Aussies say, I decided it was time 'to drink a cup of cement and harden the f**k up', and with just a handful of spots where I had to get off and push, I made it to my destination and gave my aching feet some respite on the sand. After a pit stop at a beach bar for a Corona, a Coke and the bag of Gummi Bears I had decided were the best athlete food in town, I made the short final walk to the starfish beach, to find the hundred people already there who had taken the more sensible transport options of a boat or a taxi. Fortunately, it was a long stretch of beautiful sand, so it didn't feel too crowded, and there were plenty enough starfish to go around. They were quite a sight indeed, a vivid red colour, hanging out in the shallows in twos and threes and making a great photo against the still glistening waters and the blue skies above. Their numbers have apparently depleted significantly in recent years due to tourists handling them – sadly, another example in the long list of natural attractions threatened by too much demand and not enough common sense.

After a very pleasant walk around the shallows, it was time to walk back to the bike and make my way home. In the blog I had read about the bike ride, the writer had recommended just doing the ride one way as 'there were loads of cabs around there which you could chuck the bike in the tray in the back and travel home in comfort'. Except there weren't any there. And I was being British, which meant I couldn't ask any of the people hanging around how to organise one. So I rode all the way home as well, with a bit more pushing uphill, another chain falling off episode (which I did fix this time) and a decent amount of pain. Fair to say I was pretty happy when I made it back to the hotel and collapsed in a sweaty mess. There was a reward waiting for me on my return to the hotel, in the form of a bin liner full of clean, ironed and folded clothes, something of a transformation from the stinky bag of Peru trip clothes I had meekly handed over the day before. This was quite a relief as I was down to the last few garments already – thinking about it when I gave you the overview of my baggage I never explained what made up the 15kg, so perhaps now is a good time for that. For my four months of travels, I had the following:

- Four pairs of shoes – hiking shoes, trainers, loafers, flops (so at this point in time, make that three pairs of shoes.)
- Four pairs of trousers – jeans, chinos and two pairs of walking trousers that converted to shorts as required.
- Four pairs of shorts – one smart-ish, one for sports and two pairs of swimming shorts.
- Three jumpers.
- Three shirts – one smart-ish, two more casual/Hawaiian.
- Two raincoats, one down jacket, one gilet.
- One pair of waterproof trousers.
- Eight T-shirts.
- Beanie, gloves, head torch, neck warmer.
- Seven pairs of boxer shorts, seven pairs of socks.

That sounds like a lot now I list it out, but it didn't feel like I had much – and as of the day before, I had been at critical levels for the bottom line items, so this was a well-timed mercy drop indeed.

I was a bit tired to do much in the evening but made it out to a Japanese restaurant for some pretty good sushi and a beer or two. I was now into the swing of eating as a solo traveller which basically involves ordering your food, getting the Wi-Fi password and then cluster bombing your WhatsApp contacts to find one on the right time zone to 'hang out' with you for a bit. That, and posting the day's photo selection on Instagram. I was taking the opportunity to check in with various friends from the UK who I had not been in touch with for a while as a result of the awkward UK/Australia time difference, so it was great to 'dine out' with them in such fine surroundings (well it was for me, anyway). The people on the other end were probably not quite so excited about hearing about my endless holidays, but they did seem to be enjoying the photos. For the time being anyway.

This was also the evening where there was a development in the romance-planning mission I outlined for you back in Panama City. I had decided I needed some expert input on the topic, so had checked in Emily, my ex-EA turned firm friend, turned life coach. Emily, or Em as everyone else apart from me managed to call her (I struggle with nicknames and shortened names – don't ask), was a fresh-faced 27-year-old youngster, which meant she knew how dating apps worked. She had assured me that Tinder was a safe learning environment and that I should download it and 'get involved'. I was advised I 'wouldn't have to go out with anyone I didn't want to' and with that reassurance, I took the plunge, downloaded the app, took an awkward selfie to put on it, and had a look who was on there. Not many people as it turned out. Obviously, Tinder isn't a big thing in Bocas, at least not for the age group I was looking at, as after saying no to about four people a screen came up saying no one else was around. And that was it. Without wanting to jump ahead in the story, the same thing happened each time I looked while in Bocas, and I left still waiting for the first person that I could click on the green tick for.

***

The next day at breakfast I gave Elli the debrief on my action-packed bike ride, and she helpfully pointed me in the direction of the biggest general store in town where she said I could get some new flip flops for $2 – it turned out I actually had to pay $10 for them, but I was back up to my full complement of four pairs of shoes and couldn't have been happier about that.

The day's activities involved a boat tour around the islands, and although the weather was looking a bit menacing as we set off in the boat, we started off well by ticking off the dolphin spotting at the aptly named Dolphin Bay off the coast of Isla Cristobel – though we only managed to see two of them and one of them had most of its fin missing, so it was hardly National Geographic worthy material. The next stops, at Crawl Cay and Cayo Zapatillo, were meant to involve lunch and a relaxing sunbathe, but this wasn't quite how events played out. A storm rolled over, and a downpour of biblical proportions lashed the boat in which you literally could not open your eyes there was so much water. Finally, it started to relent, and we arrived at the 'sunbathing' spot, sodden and a little bit shivery. Sunbathing was clearly off the menu, so the guide suggested we go take a walk on the path through the island – I managed about five minutes of walking through puddles before reaching the point where that path was currently closed. For the first time on the trip, my state of mind would best be described as grumpy.

But as is often the way, things didn't take long to turn around. All of the people who had arrived on the island on their respective tours had done the usual trick of not venturing more than 50 metres from their boat before setting up camp. Setting off for a walk along the beach, it was only about five minutes before I was on my own, strolling through the surf and dodging palm trees that had fallen across the beach – and the sun had come out at last! Proper Robinson Crusoe scenes. I found a tree to hang my sodden clothes on to dry a bit and then amused myself by slowly edging myself along a fallen palm tree that went right out over the sea, where I bounced around merrily for a little while to soak up the desert island vibe. I had just finished the shuffle back along the tree trunk in time to see my t-shirt blow off its branch and land in the sandy swell by the shore – not quite the plan I had in mind. My sense of humour had by now returned, so it was no big deal, and I hopped back onto the boat to head for the snorkelling stop.

I have done a fair bit of diving in my time so am reasonably comfortable floating around with a snorkel and mask, but it seems this isn't the case for everyone, as lots of the group started pulling out a weird plastic face mask things with a built-in breathing outlet, adorned with flashes of pastel colours like turquoise and magenta that made them look like they were made by Tomy. I had to make some WhatsApp enquiries in the evening as to what on earth had been going on, but apparently, they are made by Decathlon and aimed at people who can't manage to snorkel the old-fashioned way. I suppose it's fair enough that everyone should have a way to be able to have a go but just to let you know if you do have one of those, you look like a bit of a ninny.

In the afternoon we made a couple of stops to look at wildlife, the first to see starfish, which I paid a bit less attention to given my previous day's activities, and secondly to Sloth Island, and you can probably guess what we saw there. I assume they were sloths, but they were quite far up a tree and just looked like a hairy bowling ball, much like nearly all of the wildlife photos I have taken of various animals on previous trips. Having learned from this frustration, I know better than to try and take photos in this situation now (especially just using an iPhone), so I just enjoyed the scene with my eyes, knowing I could find a vastly superior photo of what they looked like up close on Google Images another time.

I had also set my sights on conquering another of the extremities of Isla Colon, this time the north-east point, where there were a number of popular surf beaches, ending up at one called Playa Bluff, which was about ten kilometres from my hotel. So the next morning, following the now daily routine of briefing Elli on my plans to walk to Playa Bluff, she seemed to think it a vast improvement on the bicycle escapade but said it was quite a long way and I should probably get a cab or a 'collectivo', which is a shared minivan, for the return journey. Pah!

So off I went. The other relevant context for this walk story is that it was absolutely pissing it down, and I had gone for a raincoat, shorts and trainers outfit, making it two out of two on poor footwear decisions for Bocas outings, as the trainers were soaked through after about fifteen minutes. I didn't see much for this first section as I had my hood up to deflect the rain and was mostly just looking down at the asphalt, but when I got to a big hostel/beach club place called 'Scully's', the road turned into a sandy track running along the back of the beaches, providing a bit more reward for lifting your eyes. A bit further on I passed by Paki Point, which apparently was an acceptable place name here, and it was then about another four kilometres of slightly undulating dirt road before I reached Playa Bluff. I might pause there for a racism-related tangent that has just come to mind, which you might find interesting. In Peru, we had seen lots of banners and wall paintings for candidates for the upcoming elections, and one of the names we kept seeing was 'Chino'. Armando explained to us that this meant 'Chinese', and was referring to a candidate of Asian background who went by that name – did you notice he said 'Asian' and not 'Chinese'? Well, apparently it is common practice in Peru to call an Asian person Chino, regardless of which country they are actually from. This casual racism extended as far as a previous Peruvian President, Alberto Fujimori, who clearly was of Japanese descent, but who was still referred to as Chino. I retold this story later on my trip to Costa Rica, and apparently, it's also standard in Central America. The mind boggles.

Back on the walk, I had arrived at Playa Bluff, having seen a total of zero other walkers braving the rain. Having grown up on rainy Cornish holidays, this kind of walk was bread and butter to me, but most of the other tourists were probably doing more sensible things like watching Netflix and waiting for the rain to stop and were nowhere to be seen. On the beach, which was spectacular even though draped in storm clouds, there were three people who had arrived on bikes with their surfboards on the back, sitting on beach chairs under a tree on the fringes – I am not a surfer, but I could see conditions were not suitable to surf, so that was looking like a wasted trip for them. But that was fine because that left the whole of the beach to me, a load of crabs popping in and out of holes in the sand, and the music of Paul Oakenfold (on my iPhone). I'm not a spiritual person, but as I walked along the vast expanse of golden sand on my private beach, bordered by palm trees and tropical vegetation, with occasional thunderclaps and flashes of lightning, listening to a particularly good psytrance track at full blast, it really felt quite special, and I felt completely content and at peace with myself. Sounds wanky, but that's what I felt. And I don't mind admitting I had a little bit of dance and threw a few shapes – or 'did some backstroke' as one unkind observer had previously described my dancing style.

I was also reminded at this moment of a book (and later a Sean Penn directed film) I had read by the American journalist/adventurer Jon Krakauer, called *'Into the Wild'*, which tells the story of a young American guy, Christopher McCandless, who, after graduating, donated all his money to charity and set off on a trip across America, without telling his family, to live simply on the land, alone. Krakauer pieces together his movements from the interactions he had with people along the way until he ends up getting into trouble and meeting a sad demise in rural Alaska. Why am I raising this? Two reasons, firstly because I am recommending it for you to read, but secondly because of a quote they found he had written in his journal after he had been on this epic solo journey, which said:

"Happiness is only real if it is shared."

This quote had resonated with me at the time I had read the book, during an initial period of separation from my wife, as I had taken a holiday on my own and found that the happy moments I had experienced along the way felt just a little bit empty alone – and I also felt an overriding emotion back then that the best way to make yourself happy was to make someone else happy. But now, about eighteen months after feeling that way, I stood on this beach and felt a completely different emotion, one that made me feel that I didn't need anyone there with me to validate my happiness at the moment, and I also didn't need to share it with anyone to make it real – well apart from me telling you now that is. And posting photos of it on Instagram…

Back in Bocas Town in the evening, I took myself out for a quick bite at a food truck kind of place which I had already been to earlier in the week, which was knocking out ceviche and very tasty burgers. As on my previous visit here, I was eating on communal tables with the younger backpacker crowd here, but unlike the previous visit, where there had been a couple of guys strumming guitars and singing to provide the soundtrack, this time the musical entertainment was provided by a roving Mariachi band – who proceeded to launch straight into 'Score in a minute!' Hilarious. I was able to use my fast-developing social media app skills to get some video footage of this and send it to my Aussie Peru trip buddies – too good not to be shared.

***

My mission for my final day in Bocas del Toro was to get a boat to take me over to Isla Bastimentos, an island with a few settlements and no cars, whose headline attraction for me was 'Red Frog Beach' which was meant to be one of the prettiest in the area. After the boat had navigated a small maze of mangroves to the shore to drop me off at the jetty, it was a short walk through the light forest to the beach on the other side of the island, and it was spectacular. As I arrived, I could see there were several people on the stretch of beach to the south, where the bars and restaurants were located, so I set off instead to the deserted end to the north. Similar to the day before it was desert island beauty kind of stuff, and I really won't do it justice with my words, so you must take a look at some photos online – my Instagram account is a great place to start…

While planning my day out, I had been reading up on Isla Bastimentos and had found there were two ways to get to Red Frog Beach, the first being the way I had gone, and a second cheaper option, where you took a shorter boat ride to Old Bank, the main village, and then walked along a wooded track across the island to Wizard Beach, where you then joined another track to Red Frog Beach. However, the blogs I had looked at had several references to muggings taking place on that track at machete-point, which didn't sound like an experience I needed, so I had decided to go the other way. On my return home I decided to read more about these crimes and found out that in February 2017 there had been a murder on the track. A 23-year-old solo traveller from the US, Catherine Johannet, had gone missing after taking a water taxi to Old Bank, and her remains, which were later found near the track, indicated that she had been hit with a rock and strangled. A local man had later been charged with the murder, but in the press coverage I found from the time shortly after the murder, before this arrest, there had been speculation of a link to another crime in the area from a few years previously.

In April 2014, two Dutch tourists, Lisanne Froon and Kris Kremers had been declared missing after going hiking near the tourist town of Boquete on the El Pianista trail between Chiriquí and Bocas del Toro, about 40 miles away from Isla Bastimentos. What fate ended up befalling them, is unclear, but eight weeks after their disappearance, five small bone fragments, which were confirmed as being the remains of the two women, were found. The case is shrouded in suspicion as there were documented signs of bone bleaching on the remains, and also evidence found in a backpack belonging to one of the victims, that was found on the banks of a river near Boquete, which included two cell phones and a camera. These cell phones were covered in fingerprints that didn't belong to either girl, and there were other oddities in the evidence and its condition when recovered. I found an excellent series of articles on the case by a journalist called Jeremy Kryt on the Daily Beast website and I wouldn't want to steal his thunder, so you should go and have a read of that if, like me, you are intrigued by a good unexplained death mystery.

Before I finish on the crime tangent, this research also threw up another interesting crime story from the area, involving an American expat by the name of William Dathan. William or 'Wild Bill' was sentenced to 47 years in prison in 2017 for robbing and killing five other Americans in Bocas del Toro in a period spanning 2007 to 2010. In a scarcely believable story, he befriended a man called Michael Brown who he suspected was an ex fugitive after finding out he had large amounts of money in his bank accounts. He proceeded to murder Michael and his wife and 17-year-old son in 2007, burying them on their own property, which he then assumed as his own by taking possession of the title documents, and got by using money drained from Michael's offshore bank accounts. Having grown tired of living in the remote location where the house was located, in 2010, he killed another man, Bo Icelar and a lady, Cheryl Lynn Hughes, who were both looking to sell properties which he had his eye on for his next home. Again, lots more info on this story available on the net if you are interested – a genuinely fascinating read about the rather unconventional way some people choose to conduct their lives and the lengths they will go to in satisfying their criminal urges.

Next morning it was time to say farewell to Panama and head overland and cross the border into Costa Rica. The drive was unspectacular, but as I looked at the simple breeze blockhouses and muddy yards that lined the roads, it was a bit of a reminder, having come from the colourful tourist town of Bocas Town, that I was visiting a relatively poor developing country, with scenes and living conditions very different to the ones I take for granted at home. The Panama side of the border was a fairly painless process, and after getting a stamp on my passport with no questions asked, I was ready to walk over the bridge to Costa Rica. At the bridge, a guard armed with a large automatic weapon stopped me and asked to see my passport. This was fairly confrontational, and I waited nervously, while he flipped opened the passport to the page which had my Nepali entry visa and stamps on it, read that page attentively for a few seconds before deciding he was happy with whatever he was pretending he was reading and waved me on my way.

I took the first few nervous steps over the bridge before gaining in confidence and striding faster, never once looking behind me or dwelling on the horrors I had endured over the last week, making my way through the light mist and reaching the other side of the bridge where the welcoming arms of Costa Rica embraced me, and I was finally, once again, a free man. Or something like that.

Summary – Panama

Kilometres travelled (air) – 3,120 (Inc. Cusco to Panama)
Kilometres travelled (land) – 65
Number of busted pluggers – 1
Number of world-renowned engineering marvels belittled in my write up – 1
Number of internet dating registrations – 2

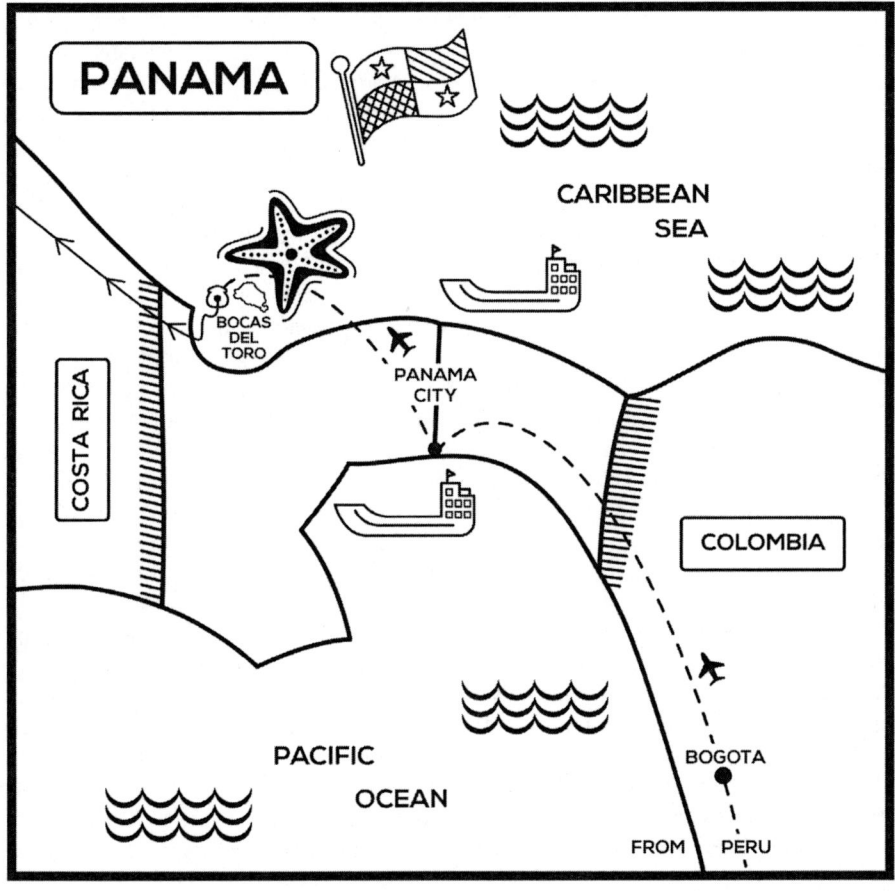

Costa Rica
Sloths, Monkeys and Sex Tourism

In the border entry of Costa Rica, I found my attention drawn to a girl standing two people ahead of me in the queue, who had a funny looking tattoo of a person on the back of her leg. I was thinking to myself that whoever it was a picture of, they looked a bit like Garth from *'Wayne's World'*, so I started fumbling around to get my phone out to capture this likeness for posterity. However, as the queue moved forward slightly, the other leg came into view and what do you know, if she didn't have a tattoo of Mike Myers as Wayne on the other leg – it actually was Garth! I got my photo of the full glory of both legs, but then it got even better when she raised her shorts a bit to reveal a quote above Wayne's head which said, "Party on Wayne!" The auditor in me immediately wondered whether that quote would have made more sense on the 'Garth leg', but regardless, it was wonderful. She also had a bunch of other bizarre tattoos that were visible – I dread to think what else she had lurking under her garments.

This was a cracking start to my Costa Rica stay, and a few minutes later I got to the immigration guy, who opened my passport to a clean page, hovered over it with the stamp and then looked blankly past me to watch something going on outside for about thirty seconds before finally stamping it and sending me on my way; I'm sure the speed of his work had nothing to do with the length of the queue. My Airbnb in the beachside town of Puerto Viejo de Talamanca was a place called 'Hidden Jungle Retreat', which was just on the edge of town, up a small track from the main road that ran alongside the beach. I had faffed around and left the booking quite late so had ended up with a small single room, which was nonetheless perfectly functional. I was quietly amused to see a very young-looking backpacker had a superior looking double room next to mine – I said a polite hello, attempting to maintain my 'fellow young backpacker' disguise, and sat down to work out a plan of attack.

Puerto Viejo (Old Harbour) is a small town that, from my reading, appeared most famous these days for having the biggest and most powerful wave in the country, known as the Salsa Brava. The other main draws for tourists were the strip of beautiful beaches from the town until the end of the road, thirteen kilometres further south at Manzanillo, and a Jaguar Rescue Centre, also found on that road. The town was indeed pretty small, a selection of restaurants, shops and souvenir stalls along the main road, which didn't take long to look around, so I was soon on the road out of town to find the other beaches. I hadn't checked the map to see how far the next beach was, but the walk was taking longer than I had expected and as the coast was lined with trees and vegetation, I couldn't actually see much. I carried on gallantly, overruling about three self-imposed 'I'll turn around if it's not around the next corner' edicts, before eventually, well, turning around after the next corner, having not reached my destination. I decided I would return under bicycle power the following day to deal with this unfinished business…

After a wash-up and a nap and a cursory look around for one of the sloths that allegedly lived here (unsuccessful), I headed back into town to find a drink or two. I was looking for the bar that Lonely Planet had recommended going to for a sundowner, but was having trouble finding it, as it didn't appear to be where Google Maps said it was. After doing a few laps of the area from both the beach and roadside I gave up, cursing the Lonely Planet for not keeping their publication up to date, before realising it was the giant yellow bar right in front of me, exactly where Google Maps said it was. And it was closed, which probably explained how it had managed to remain invisible to me. I found a spot at a bar nearby instead, which was still quite pleasant, just off the beach with a great view of the impending sunset, and it was happy hour, and some live music was about to start. Result.

In Bocas Town, when I had been in the bars for Happy Hour, and it was two-for-one drinks, they had very sensibly adapted the system for a solo traveller and brought the beers one at a time to keep them cold. Assuming this common-sense approach would have made its way over the border and along the coast, I decided to go nuts and order a cocktail, opting for something with a fancy name I forget (something dreamy), which was ostensibly a rum and pineapple juice. Unfortunately, it turned out to be a very long drink, and both glasses of it were brought out at the same time, meaning I was faced with about two pints of boozy juice with fast-melting ice cubes. Worse things happen at sea, I thought to myself and piled in. It actually turned out to be a blessing in disguise as when the live music started, it was apparent that being a bit merry was a prerequisite for enduring it – judging by the state of some of the local ex-pats who had come along to listen and dance wildly (at 6 pm), this was already a well-tested strategy. The music was being performed by a couple of old guys on guitars and a lady singing, all of whom I think were expats from the States. The lady had a strange style of dancing, where each appendage seemed to be operating independently of the others, and her singing also had quite a unique style; to be fair she could hold a tune, but for those of you familiar with the comedy game show *'Shooting Stars'*, she was very much from the Vic Reeves style of jazz singing which, combined with the jerky dancing was quite a sight to behold. Certainly entertaining though. To help you better immerse yourself in the experience, the songs sacrificed at her altar included *'Fever'*, *'Ain't no Sunshine'* and a version of *'Back to Black'* that I think would have had Amy Winehouse turning in her grave. The small crowd of (hammered) locals seemed to be enjoying themselves though, so I guess that's what counts.

One thing I forgot to mention in my potted summary of the town was that there was a fairly noticeable smell of cannabis in the air, particularly after dark, and no shortage of willing salesmen. While walking through town to not find the bar I was after, I was serenaded by a barrage of different gentlemen all saying in not very hushed tones:

"Bro! Bro! Smoke? Bro! Smoke? Bro!"

And it was the same at this bar, with several gents coming up to make sure I was enjoying my evening, before quickly cutting to the chase with their offers – as if a prospective buyer of weed would not have been able to find some on the road without this additional table service. I had discovered early in my university life that smoking cannabis dulled my senses to the extent that I (and these were my words at the time) 'lost my competitive edge', something that was clearly inconsistent with my life mantra, so I had never gone back there, and these salesmen were therefore on to a loser with me.

After drinks, I went for a wander around some streets off the main drag to find a local Jamaican restaurant I had read was the place for authentic cheap local food. There was only one other couple eating there, who looked like European backpackers, but I decided to turn a blind eye to the tumbleweeds blowing through the restaurant and eat there anyway. The menu was in Spanish, and I ordered what I thought was a starter and a main, but it all ended up coming at once, so who knows. I would later learn this was my first 'Casado' which is a simple 'tipico' meal found all over Costa Rica which comprises rice, beans, cheese, usually meat of some description, sometimes a bit of salad and some fried plantains. It was a massive plate of food, but I had developed a superhuman appetite on the trip for mealtimes (probably due to not snacking at all) and devoured it, feeling that I was right in character, eating my cheapo dinner with my fellow backpacker diners. Those comrades spoiled that moment by getting up to pay, and then walking out of the restaurant, getting into their rental 4x4 which was parked outside and driving off, probably to their resort hotel – charlatans!

My WhatsApp correspondence for the evening included a conversation with Emily, who was intrigued as to how my book was shaping up, as at that point I was still being a bit vague on the details as to what I was going to write – on account of not knowing this answer myself. I told her it was going to be a travel story of some description, to which I was offered the following guidance:

"Please don't do the boy version of Eat, Pray, Love – not unless Tinder features heavily."

The next morning was an early-ish start, firstly as I wanted to get the bike ride out of the way before it got too hot and secondly, so I could have a look around before too many other people had surfaced. The road was reasonably quiet, and it was a somewhat sedate ride for the thirteen kilometres to Manzanillo where I had read there was an impressive reserve. At the far end of Manzanillo, the road ended, so I locked up the bike and set off on foot over a footbridge that led into the reserve towards the lookout. The view from the lookout was indeed spectacular, with waves crashing against a rocky outcrop directly in front of the point, and the coastal views extending from the barren coast to the south around to the palm tree-fringed beaches to the north which arced around to form a crescent-shaped coastline.

After a stop for a cooling paddle, it was back to base camp for a lazy afternoon away from the heat of the early afternoon sun. I decided it was going to be an exercise doubleheader and walked down the road to a yoga place I had read about. The centre was up a hill on the edge of the town and had an open-air studio that looked over the vegetation and town below with a view out to the sea. It was a beautiful setting, but an open-air studio at 5 pm in the tropics had one downside – the sticky heat. Having done a fair bit of hot yoga in the past I was used to sweating during class, but this was crazy – twenty minutes in I was holding my 'down dog' (well, more trembling) as sweat poured off my nose onto the mat in a persistent stream. After half an hour I could hardly hold a pose it was so slippery – a bit of a gross story this one I know, but I'm trying to help you live the experience, and this was mine. I say mine, as I appeared to be the only person of the class of six who was sweating at all – I must have some kind of design flaw.

I was planning on going straight on for food after the class, but that was clearly off the cards, so after heading home to clean up, I was back out on the hunt for dinner. I had asked Vanessa for a recommendation, and she had suggested a restaurant that served local food. It was actually also the nearest place to my accommodation but having seen it and thinking it looked a bit sketchy I walked on. However, it quickly became apparent that I was in one of my moods where I am incapable of making a decision, so I walked around nearly every street in town, coming up with reasons why each place I found was not suitable, and twenty minutes later found myself sat in the restaurant I had definitively decided I wouldn't go to – I am a mystery even to myself some days.

The next challenge was that the waitress only spoke Spanish, and there was no menu. There was a cat sat by my table, and I was confident that my Duolingo tuition would mean I could entertain some conversation about its attire, or lack of, but that wasn't going to help get me fed. After racking my brains for some inspiration, I managed to get the word 'Pescado?' out and nodded politely at whatever she said next and waited for my fish surprise to arrive. Which took ages. And here's the next reason why I shouldn't have come here – the restaurant was situated down a small slope by the river at the entrance to the town, and it was dusk. One word – mosquitos. I hadn't put on repellent and soon saw there was a fair bit of excitement under the table around my ankles. I turned to put my legs out in the open as if that would shake them off the scent, but when that had no impact, I had to do a quick mime to get hold of some repellent from the waitress. I think she actually gave me some kind of mosquito aphrodisiac, as that just got them more excited, and I shuffled around uncomfortably, mumbling under my breath, 'Come on, come on!' to encourage the food to arrive, as I felt the bites accumulating. And still, it didn't. By now the mumbling had progressed to a despairing 'Please!' and that seemed to do the trick as the food finally arrived – a plate of fish, rice, black beans and plantains which disappeared in the blink of an eye, and I raced up to the counter to pay the bill and escape. The meal cost me 4,000 Colones or approximately 10 Colones per mosquito bite…

***

Next morning I was on my way to San Jose, resisting the urge to do the asking for directions joke that had been circling in my mind for the last two days, and taking my seat on the bus next to a local lady for the four-hour ride south-west to the country's capital city. After the first big town of Limon, the logistics industry scenery there was replaced by miles and miles of banana palms, the bunches of bananas hidden under plastic bags, something I later read is proving a bit of an environmental issue, part of the broader plastic pollution disaster which is currently exercising minds around the world.

My sustenance for the bus trip included a cereal bar and the internationally recognised breakfast item of a small box of sour cream and chive Pringles. This experience was all the more pleasurable for me as I had already discovered earlier in the trip that South and Central America had not been hit with the awful decision to reduce the diameter of the Pringles tube, presumably made elsewhere in an attempt to squeeze out a few more cents of profit, dressed up as being in the name of 'healthy eating'. In a similar vein, while in the UK a few weeks before I had bought a Yorkie bar and was astonished at how small they now are – I actually felt a bit sorry for it as it must have been quite a fall from grace to go from being the strongman of chocolate bars to ending up there. And don't get me started on Toblerone. I digress – but anyway, I could get my whole hand into the Pringles tube, and that brought a little ray of sunshine to my bus journey morning.

Disembarking into the bus terminal in San Jose, we were almost forced back onto the bus by the scrum of taxi drivers looking to secure our business. My host at the place I was staying in San Jose, Scott, had already tipped me off that the best way to get around was Uber, so I skipped past them, finding Jessica, my driver ready to whisk me away as if out the back door of a venue after a celebrity appearance and away from a paparazzi throng – or at least this is how I imagine that might be anyway. 'Scott's Place', is actually marked as such on Uber and Google Maps, which I thought was eminently sensible. Scott was an artist, whose main business was currently painting murals, including the ones that brightened the walls of his property, and he also ran a walking tours business aimed at his guests and other tourists. Scott was a gay man in his 50s at a guess, from Indiana in the US originally, but his work had taken him around the globe, staying in places including Italy and my hometown Sydney, before settling in San Jose. He had started with a couple of rooms for rent on Airbnb but had expanded to take the lease of the floor below his apartment, so he now had four rooms, plus two pairs of hammocks in the living areas on each floor which could also be used if group sizes required it. The apartment was decorated with lots of Scott's art, including both paintings and photos, and had a warm, welcoming feel to it. I was in San Jose for just a day and had booked his walking tour, and after a coffee with Scott on the balcony, overlooking the hustle and bustle below, we set off for a walk.

San Jose is the largest city in the country with a population of about 350,000 and is laid out in a grid pattern, so it was fairly easy to get your bearings. The place doesn't get much love from the guidebooks, and it was not difficult to see why, as it comprised an unremarkable city centre area, with the handful of old characterful buildings which still remained, rather hidden by the modern concrete blocks which had grown up around them. That said, once we made our way round to one of the more affluent suburbs, Barrio Amon, there was quite an elegant feel to the place, with neat and colourful residential buildings interspersed with coffee shops, restaurants and arts venues. There were signs of some money arriving in town with smart new apartment developments springing up around the skyline, but Scott pointed out a number of no-go areas right by where we were walking, troubled by drugs, prostitution and other crime, and the centre of town had an uneasy feel. A feature that did fascinate me was the train tracks that ran straight through the middle of town. Every ten minutes or so a massive train hauled by old diesel locomotives would roll through, using the same road as the cars, signalling its presence with a deafening horn, as there were no barriers, level crossings or any other safety features we are used to seeing. Another oddity of the place was the fact they have no address system here – if you wanted mail, you got a box at the central post office, and none of the houses had numbers, with people relying on descriptions like 'it's 200 metres south of the big blue building' – ridiculous!

Scott's tour was light on the history of the place and more about the here and now, which was ideal for me given my previous comments about my retention of historical information. He was quite upfront about this and told a funny story about a previous tour where an American lady had grown increasingly frustrated at his not being able to answer questions on matters of historical detail. This had culminated in a Scott telling her, mid-tour, that he didn't think he was the guide for her and leaving her there while he went home to watch Netflix! Apparently, the negative review she posted about the experience had resulted in an uptick in business for him, so he was understandably relaxed about the incident. As we made our way around I was a little bit taken aback by how many of Scott's stories ended up with references to hookers – he had pointed out areas they frequented, he had shown me bars and hotels where they worked, and also educated me that any establishments which had the words 'Sports' or 'Lodge' in the title would have hookers hanging out in them. It was only later in the evening when I was reading about the place that these references made more sense, as it turns out prostitution is legal in Costa Rica, and the country is a popular sex tourism destination, particularly for American men of advancing age, with the activities mostly found in San Jose and the Pacific coast-side resort town of Jaco. A Google search enlightened me that the Hotel del Rey in the middle of town was the infamous centre of said activities but, before you ask, no, I didn't feel the need to visit to further my research on the topic.

In the evening, after Scott's less than glowing review of the city after dark, I decided I didn't feel comfortable in straying too far from the apartment but fortunately managed to find a quite lovely Argentinian restaurant just a few blocks away. It was in the top ten restaurants for the city on TripAdvisor and was rammed. I got myself a seat at the bar to eat and soaked up the atmosphere, before remembering I should probably check in on Tinder. In contrast to my previous experience in the small towns I had been staying in, I was astonished by the number of ladies now coming up, and after a couple of minutes of trying to carry out the task discreetly, I decided this probably wasn't the best place to be browsing, so put it away for later. Dinner was wonderful – a giant steak and a glass of Malbec, a welcome change from the meals of recent days, and I went home well fed and watered – and then spent about forty minutes completing the earlier Tinder task, from which I think I managed to identify three yeses – a landmark for me in my internet dating personal development.

The next morning, I was woken at 4:30 am by that train horn I was talking about. Did I mention the train went right past Scott's house? No? Well it did, and after that first horn, which was incredibly loud, they continued every 20 minutes or so, and I figured it was time for an early start to the day. The plan for the day was to get to La Fortuna, a resort town at the foot of Volcan Arenal, the top tourist destination in Costa Rica, where I planned to do some walking, hopefully up, the volcano. En route to the bus station my Uber driver gave me some helpful language tips, including the most important expression in the country, which is 'Pura Vida', or 'pure life'. This saying is used in response to a 'How's it going?' question and is a way of expressing their joy for their way of life – which I thought was a refreshingly positive mantra. Bus ticket in hand, I checked, double-checked and triple checked that I was in the queue for the right bus, also checking with the driver and ticket collector as I boarded. My point of reference from popular culture for taking bus trips in Central America was one of the favourite films of my childhood, *'Romancing the Stone'* – those of you familiar with that film will know that bad shit happens when you get on the wrong bus, and I was keen to avoid a similar fate. On the point of detail, I think Joan Wilder might have been travelling in Colombia in that film, not Central America, but for the purposes of my analogy, I think that's near enough.

Fortunately, I was on the correct bus and arriving at La Fortuna, the volcano, or at least what I think was the volcano, was completely shrouded in cloud, leaving a glimpse only off its lowest flanks. I was reminded of a previous experience at the Tongariro National Park, near Lake Taupo on New Zealand's North Island, where I had gone to do the 'Tongariro Crossing'. Due to the rain clouds, the views were completely obscured, and the walk ended up being delayed, but the following day, we were rewarded with cloudless skies and hauled our crampons up to the snow-covered saddle and epic views between Tongariro and Ngauruhoe. I told myself now that this dramatic turnaround in the weather would also happen here, with the skies clearing to reveal the majesty of Volcan Arenal for the eight-hour hiking excursion I had booked for the following day.

Back in reality, it was not a nice day, and I had taken an immediate dislike to the town of La Fortuna, which was a collection of scrappy looking buildings with travel agents and tour guides as far as the eye could see, looking for takers for their zip line tours, rafting trips, hikes, nature reserves, hot springs – the list went on. I probably should have expected this from the top tourist town in the country but, coming from the sleepy Caribbean towns I had been staying in, it was a bit of an assault on the senses. I made the short walk across town from the bus station to my accommodation, which was akin to a motel room, in a block of four rooms that an enterprising local family had built in the grounds of their family property. My host here was Greivin, their son, who I was guessing was in his late twenties, and who ran the business. The room was actually really well-appointed, a large room with a king-size bed, a sight not yet seen on the trip, and a bathroom with a cracking shower, both of these raising my spirits from the initial disappointment of the arrival in the town. Those spirits then took an immediate downward turn when I had to pay Greivin for the tours he had organised for me ahead of my arrival, comprising my day hike the next day and my transfer the day after to the next town. On impulse, I also signed up for a night wildlife tour for the first evening as I was growing frustrated at not having properly seen a sloth yet and thought there would be other cool stuff to see alongside that, presumably guaranteed sighting.

Almost as soon as I booked the wildlife tour, I was regretting it – while I do enjoy seeing animals in the wild, I wouldn't call it a passion of mine, and I had found several previous similar tours quite disappointing. And as it turned out, my pessimism was indeed well-founded. After arriving at the tour location, meeting the group and getting armed with our flashlights, we walked down to the start of the park area with dusk falling and the guide started looking up a tree, pausing, getting another vantage point, pausing again and repeating the cycle. There was a sloth up there apparently. Well, we craned our necks looking for it for fifteen minutes and saw nothing – and then it started to rain. Leaving the non-sloth in peace, we went and looked at three crocodiles, which I will concede were quite cool, with one of them over 50 years old, but the rain had been building and all of a sudden a massive thunderstorm descended on us. I had my rain jacket on, so was ready for it, while the rest of the group fumbled around trying to find the head hole in their ponchos, and we then had to take cover from the storm, looking around the indoor snake and frog exhibits for the remainder of the two hours. Again, some interesting stuff there, but not quite what I had in mind for the evening. Just when I thought the experience couldn't get any worse, the guide started talking about armadillos, an animal that I am quite fond of, or was, until he forever sullied their standing with me by telling us that you can catch leprosy from them. Gracias, mi amigo.

***

Putting that experience behind me, the next morning, I was ready for a grand day out for my volcano hike. The itinerary for the trip was a one hour bus to the walk start, three hours walking to the lunch spot, then another two hours of walking to the Volcan Observatory, where we would be back on the bus to go to a 'hot river' near La Fortuna, where we would enjoy a soothing muscle soak and a cocktail. Sounded like an excellent way to spend the day to me. Back on my *'Romancing the Stone'* references, I knew appropriate footwear was important for a walk in the forest, so I had left my heels at home and put on hiking shoes – as often happens on these tours, not everyone had been through this thought process, and I would see when we started walking there was the usual selection of tennis shoes being worn by some of the youngsters – they made it round, but those shoes will never be the same again…

But wait, we haven't got to the walk yet, as something happened on the drive to the start – we saw a sloth! The eagle-eyed guide spotted one in a roadside tree, and as we stopped for a closer look, it was near enough that you could see its face and watch it eating food off the tree. Seeing an active sloth is quite unusual apparently, though I should maybe have realised that would be the case for an animal that sleeps 18 hours a day, about the same as a koala. Koalas sleep that much because they spend all (of their awake) day eating their sole food source, eucalyptus, which contain toxins that they have to use a lot of their energy to digest, leaving only enough left to sleep – I didn't feel the need to read up on sloths to find out what their excuse is, and was happy instead to just assume they do it because they are lazy.

When we did get going on the walk, it was another cloudy day, and there was still no visual confirmation of what I was thinking at this stage was more of an alleged volcano. The walk started off as a gentle stroll through the woods but quickly got harder, with lots of short sharp ascents and descents, navigating around giant tree trunks and trying to avoid the frequent patches of deep boggy mud. It was quite a big group for the walk, and something of a United Nations, with a group of four Americans in their mid-

20s, a French family of four and then about eight other younger backpacker types, from Germany, Spain and the Netherlands. The up and down continued to get more advanced after we had crossed an old lava flow, with fixed ropes coming into play to assist the climbing up and rappelling down. I got talking to one of the American group who was a bit cagey about his work, finally admitting he worked in defence but that he couldn't tell me any more than that; these secret ops professions were becoming a recurring theme of the trip. One of the young Germans managed to highlight why we were walking with guides when he strayed off the path and found himself up to his knees in a muddy bog. He was pulled out to safety, leaving his trainers still in the bog, with one of the guides having to rescue them, which he only narrowly managed to do, so deep were they buried.

After ascending a hill, we arrived at a Mirador (lookout) from where you could see the full glory of Lago Arenal, the largest man-made lake in the country and major source of hydroelectric power. Except we couldn't see this because we could only see the cloud. Fortunately, after a ten-minute stop there for a drink break, the clouds did part to give us a glimpse of what I am sure would be an epic view on a clear day. As we continued on, I got talking to one of the guides, Daniel, and when I told him I had been in San Jose before, the discussion quickly turned to the Hotel del Rey and prostitution, a topic which Daniel, a father of two, seemed genuinely disgusted about until he let his cover slip by saying, "I would never sleep with one of those prostitutes! Well, apart from a couple of times that I did in Jaco."

The walk carried on for the remainder of the budgeted three hours to the lunch stop, which we took on the banks of a river, me, hood up on my rain jacket as the rain became more persistent. After lunch, we traversed five more ravines along the side of the volcano, with the up and down continuing to get more challenging and more rope dependent. I was reminded of the climb up Mount Gower on Lord Howe Island, which is the best walk you never knew you needed to do, on an island you have probably never heard of. The island is about 700 kilometres off the coast of New South Wales and is tiny, with only 380 permanent residents, but with extraordinary scenery, not dissimilar to the Hawaiian Islands. Mount Gower is the highest point on the island, affording spectacular views back across the other mountains and the beaches below. It's a pretty tough eight hours up and down, traversing a cliff path with a sheer drop to the sea below, and then scaling rocks with the help of ropes to get to the summit. The first time I did it, there was a group of ladies climbing with us, maybe late 40s, looking absolutely pristine in what looked like brand-new hiking outfits and wearing full makeup and fashion sunglasses. When I got to the bottom, my hair and clothes were soaked through with sweat, and I looked broken – these ladies looked exactly the same at the end as they had at the start. Amazing.

Back on Arenal, we had just about made it to the end of the walk when the heavens opened, and we were drilled with torrential rain for fifteen minutes. I was completely saturated and squelching along in my hiking shoes, pretty much ready to call it a day. We arrived at a spectacular waterfall where we had been promised we could swim and climb behind the cascade, but I couldn't face the prospect of putting all my wet clothes back on after this swim, so decided I would wait for the hot springs, but amazingly nearly the whole of the group piled in, leaving me to stand and watch for fifteen minutes with one other non-participant, while they all judged the two of us for being pussies. After arriving at the Volcan Observatory centre a bit later on, there was one more cool sight for the day, with spider monkeys swinging through the trees in the distance. As I walked on towards the van, I found a bigger group and spent a captivating few moments watching them swing off one by one in the direction of whatever party they were on their way to.

The final stop of the day was at the 'hot river' – there are a number of high-end hot springs resorts in the area, but as I was on the cheapo tour, we weren't going to any of those, instead just parking up by the side of the road and getting into a river, where there was a clearly well-established haunt for evening drinks, a large pool in the middle of some gentle cascades. The river temperature was about 37 degrees, so it was a very relaxing spot for a post-walk soak while we drink our 'cocktails' which were basically vodka and old fashioned lemonade in plastic cups; they tasted great though, and I enjoyed a couple while waiting for my volcanic soil face mask to work it's magic (yes, really). I should have been exhausted after all that, but I wasn't for some reason, so instead of sleeping, I stayed up until three in the morning booking flights and accommodation for later destinations on the trip so as to make some productive use of my time.

Given I had managed only a few hours of sleep, I was actually feeling not too bad when I was collected the next morning for my transfer to Monteverde, a town further into this mountainous corner of northwest Costa Rica. While only about 80 kilometres away from La Fortuna as the crow flies, the road between the two, which passed around Lago Arenal, was in very poor condition, and the bus trip between the towns was a bumpy six or seven-hour journey. Luckily there was a better option than that, described as the 'Jeep-boat-jeep' route, which comprised a 45-minute road transfer from La Fortuna to Lago Arenal, a one-hour boat across the lake, and then a further 90 minutes or so for the final road leg to Monteverde. It would have been better described as the 'minibus-boat-people carrier' route for me, but the Jeep one has a nicer ring to it so let's stick with that.

In the people carrier, I was seated next to an American couple who, by coincidence, I had also sat next to on the bus from San Jose to La Fortuna, and upfront, there was a family of four (two girls) from Derby in the UK. I found the two topics of conversation when people of those two nations met, are generally, "How on earth did Donald Trump get elected?" and "Can you believe what happened in the Brexit vote?" On the latter topic, I was on holiday in the Dolomites on the border of Italy and Austria back in 2016 for the week of the vote, and any time I found myself near another English holidaymaker, and they heard my English accent, they wanted to get my opinion and debate the topic. A comment I particularly enjoyed in one of those discussions went, "I just can't understand it – no one at my sailing club voted 'Leave'," presumably taking that the sentiment of the said club was a reliable bellwether of how the majority working-class population would land.

And it was a bit more of the same here, as one of the girls, who would have been all of about nine years old turned around in the car and said to me, "It was because all the old people voted to leave, and they are going to be dead soon anyway!"

My accommodation in Santa Elena, Monteverde, was at the delightfully named 'Sloth Hostel', and this was the first real backpacker kind of place I had stayed. That said, while the youngsters were packed into dorm rooms downstairs, my room upstairs had two beds in it and an en-suite bathroom, so I still wasn't completely slumming it here. The place appeared to be deserted as I waited to check-in, so I had to shout 'Hola' around the property until a cleaner appeared and went down the road to find the man, Mauricio, who would check me in. My Airbnb booking here also qualified me for an included breakfast, which was signified by a green wrist band which Mauricio slapped on my wrist before I had the chance to ask if I really had to wear that for the rest of the day for a meal that was nearly 24 hours away. Never mind, it was a handy accessory for adding credibility to my backpacker disguise.

Before tackling the action of Monteverde, I think it's an appropriate time to introduce you to another feature of Airbnb travel that you may not be aware of, and that's the end of stay review. Given that online reviews are pretty much a feature of everything these days, I had assumed I would be writing reviews of the places I stayed. What I didn't realise was that the hosts you are staying with are also asked to give a review on how you were as a guest – presumably with the aim of alerting other hosts to guests whose business they might not want. I haven't mentioned this feature thus far in my story, as up to this point the reviews of me had been fairly standard stuff – 'Alex is friendly, Alex is a considerate guest, it was a pleasure to have Alex stay' etc. However, our friend Greivin from back in La Fortuna – his review was, as they say in the north of England, 'different gravy!' I won't try to explain it and will instead just hit you with it in its full glory:

"Alex is a really nice person. He is so friendly and communicative. Also, very educated and clean. It was a pleasure meeting and having such a beautiful person here. I highly recommend him as a future guest!"

Educated and clean – I don't think I have ever felt so humbled. The only sad thing about this review was that I suspected it represented a high watermark in the review process that would never be surpassed, but each time I read it, it makes me laugh, so I think I can live with that lingering sadness.

A little bit of bad news coming out of Australia had hit my socials, my football team, the Mighty Rozelle Dads, had fallen at the semi-final stage of the end of season playoffs. Having won our league for the last two seasons this was clearly a bitter blow, as described in the match report I received on WhatsApp, currently being written by a guest editor in my absence. The vibe of the report was very much in the vein of 'we tried our best, never mind boys, we'll do it next season' kind of stuff until I got to the final line which read:

'PS – We all agreed that it was Alex's fault that we lost this year (you have to blame someone) and that hopefully his career break in South America setting up a drug trafficking cartel goes well for him!'

To which I replied as follows:

'Hard luck, gents. I'll take that final comment as a backhanded compliment – I think. I have found out there is more money in Costa Rica in organised prostitution than drugs, so I am focusing my business development activities there instead.'

***

The bed in my room was not very comfortable as a result of either the mattress or the frame being strangely warped, and I woke up feeling like I had been lying on a hole on a crazy golf course. I was down at breakfast at 7 am on the dot as I was aiming to get the first bus to the Monteverde Cloud Forest Reserve, which was due to leave at 730. Breakfast was scrambled eggs, and a dish of rice and black beans, which I later learnt was 'Gallo Pinto' (which translates literally as 'spotted rooster'), the national breakfast dish in Costa Rica – though apparently, Nicaragua thinks they thought of it first. Tread carefully if you find yourself in a discussion on that, in the same way, you would approach an argument as to whether Australia or New Zealand invented an item (e.g. lamington, Pavlova, Crowded House etc.). The Monteverde Cloud Forest Reserve was founded in 1972 and covers over 10,500 hectares of cloud forest with an extraordinary level of biodiversity which includes over 2,500 plant species, 100 species of mammal, 400 bird species and 120 reptilian and amphibian species. The area that is open to the public, which consists of a small visitor centre and a network of walking trails covers only 3% of the total area, and I had read that the majority of the animals had the sense to go and live undisturbed in the other 97%, so my expectations were suitably managed ahead of my visit. On arrival, there were a number of private tour buses starting to appear, so I decided I would make a quick break for the furthest corner of the park where I hoped it would just be me and the forest. And sloths. So off I went down the trail called the 'Sendero Bosque Nuboso', and for an hour the walk was quite magical, a narrow winding path through the vegetation with just the odd bird call and the sound of rain landing on the canopy above to keep me company, and an array of plants of all shapes and sizes, and trees covered with their own ecosystem of other mosses and plants to peer at along the way. I reached the furthest corner having only seen two people, enjoyed another classical Costa Rican non-mirador, and then set a course for the most photographed sight in the park, the red hanging bridge that spanned a ravine, with trees growing up to it from the valley far below. Which is where things started to go wrong, as there were about thirty people there, blocking the path and generally spoiling my serenity. From then on, every trail I went down was infested with large tour groups crowding around a guide with a scope to pick out the wildlife for them, and it soon became more of a brisk walk workout for me than the forest immersion experience with which I had begun my day.

My competitive spirit meant I felt compelled to make sure I made it round every one of the trails before I left, something that took a little bit under three hours. If you were taking your time and walking round with one of the guides I suspect you could spend more than double that time taking it all in, but three hours was plenty enough for me (and it was raining again of course), and I headed for the exit. En route, I was called into action to take a photo of a happy couple standing at the foot of a giant tree – I was finding this was a regular request of a solo traveller, but I had by now embraced the opportunity and had perfected my 'Uno, dos, tres, QUESO!' lead up to taking these photos, which the recipients loved. I think.

As I arrived at the road, the weather had started to clear and given I had several hours back in my day I decided I would walk back to Santa Elena, which was about six kilometres away, nearly all downhill. As I started down the road, there was a man walking up the hill towards me with his dog, a small mongrel, running a little way behind, and I said "Buen Dia" to him and waited for his dog to catch up and pass too. Except it wasn't his dog, it was a stray, which greeted me in an excited fashion and then turned on his heels to accompany me on my walk down the hill. On a trip to Salta in Northern Argentina, I had had a similar experience, where one of the many street dogs there had joined us on a walk up to a viewpoint over the city. At this viewpoint, there was a gondola back down to the centre of town, and this dog had jumped in for the ride and continued to walk with us around the shops in town. We finally parted company when he ran off with another group of tourists heading in the other direction – given the bond we had developed by that point, I don't mind telling you I felt quite used as he cast us off for his new friends.

But my companion here today, let's call him 'Monty', seemed a much more loyal sort, continuing with me along the road while sometimes breaking off to bark and run aggressively straight at passing bikes and police cars, but still coming back to my side after he had calmed himself, and the smile had returned. He stayed with me for about five kilometres, by which time I had the theme tune to *'The Littlest Hobo'* firmly embedded in my head – it was quite hot and sweaty, and I think his little legs had gone as far as they could, as that was when he finally disappeared. I finished the last kilometre or so alone, stopping briefly at the bus station to proudly order my ticket for the next day in Spanish, before returning home for yet more travel booking. I had found that a few places did not have suitable Airbnb options (or they were already booked) so I had gone a bit off-piste and started looking on booking.com for those places, which were mostly in the Canada section of my itinerary. I don't often book on that site as I get a bit annoyed by the comments they put against the options like:

'Selling fast!' – 'Ten people looking at this offer.' – 'Last room available!'

These comments annoy me, not because they are most likely not true, but because even though I KNOW they are most likely not true, I feel powerless to resist them and find myself rushing into book the first thing I see, 'just in case'! Which is what I did. I was also a bit bored of this process now and just wanted it done, so booking.com was the lucky recipient of several bookings that, on another day, I would probably not have made.

Back in Santa Elena, I had achieved what I wanted from this leg of the trip and had a quiet evening catching up on some WhatsApp. One of these exchanges was with my friend Louise from the Nepal trip and, after telling her that I was currently staying at a backpackers and doing my best to blend in, she responded,

"Little do those other backpackers know how much wisdom you carry around with you – the Gandalf of backpacking!"

I enjoyed this response somewhat more than one I received from my old friend Richard in a similar discussion. He, like several others thus far, had sent me a message to get an explanation for my endless posting of photos from far-flung destinations, and had correctly assumed that I was 'having a mid-lifer, and had put on a bag and left'. When I told him that my youthful appearance meant I was able to blend in well with the backpackers, his response was,

"Smells a little sex pesty."

***

I filled in time on the bus journey to Jaco, finally learning how to lock the screen on my smartwatch. I had owned it for about four months and had been getting increasingly frustrated at it randomly deleting stuff off menus while it was hidden under my sleeve – how ridiculous, I thought, that you couldn't lock it. Well, of course, you could, and thankfully I now knew how. I had experienced similar technological incompetence with my Kindle, owned for a similar period of time, on which I had been incapable of working out how to change the font size until a few days prior to this bus ride. So for months, I had been reading books on the setting designed for elderly people with failing eyesight – while thinking it was strange that they had fixed the font size so large. To summarise, I have been highly deficient in common sense for many years now, most likely since birth.

My nourishment for this journey comprised a bottle of water and two of the smallest cereal bars you have ever seen in your life. Having found a box of ten cereal bars that looked similar to the ones I would buy at home, I got to the checkout and found it was '20% off everything' day, so this was scoring as a highly successful outing – until I got home and opened the box. The bars looked nothing like the picture on the box and were absolutely tiny, not even big enough to fill the wrappers they were in – like four or five squirrel bites worth. '20% off everything' day apparently also applied to the size of the products you were buying. So today, having eaten those two bars in the first twenty minutes, I was already ravenous.

Jaco is a large beachside town on the Pacific coast. You might recall previous mentions of this place but, if not, we were back in sex tourism land, with Jaco taking second place for such pursuits in the country, after San Jose. My accommodation here was a spare room in a family house, and as the hosts were out, the mother-in-law let me in, using her limited English effectively enough to show me to the room and give me the Wi-Fi password. It was stinking hot out, and I had lugged my bags a bit further than necessary after missing my bus stop, so I had a quick clean up before heading back out for a walk on the beach.

The beach was pretty enough, but of course, paled in comparison to the idyllic beaches I had seen on the Caribbean coast. As I walked down to the water's edge, I could hear the familiar cry of '*Amigo! Amigo!*' and knew someone was on their way to sell me something. I had seen enough tour salesmen in the last four days, so didn't turn around and walked into the sea, with the intention of waiting out there, 'paddling', until he gave up and left. But he didn't. He just stood there waiting for me. It wasn't that warm in the sea, so five minutes later I turned and tried to make a diagonal escape down the beach, but he cut me off. It was surf lessons he was selling, and to be fair he didn't hassle me after I said, "No gracias," and I continued on my way, maybe just slightly admiring his patience in the name of potentially making a sale.

The beach went on for what must have been a couple of kilometres, and as I took in the scene, I found myself reflecting on my journey so far and my thoughts turned to my friend Dorion, who I had met in Bali earlier in the year and become 'message buddies' with. Dorion is a Canadian ex-pat living in Bali, yoga teacher and general free spirit, the type of person I didn't meet that often in my work and home life circles. Dorion had travelled quite extensively and had loads of interesting stuff on her Instagram, vibrant scenes from far-flung communities around the world, and her intro on her profile had her mantra of 'Travel. Ponder. Repeat.' which I had found intriguing back when I had read it, but even more so now as I had been effectively living it for the last few months. Six months off work was a wonderful enabler for travel, but it was the almost limitless time for pondering which I was feeling most grateful for at this point in time, and the lack of any pressure for that pondering to get to any answers. At least for now.

On the return walk, I was reflecting on the alarming statistic that as many as eight in ten of the women found in certain bars in town were prostitutes, and I found myself wondering if I could tell which of the ladies walking around town were part of that 'gang' and which were just 'regular' ladies, perhaps on holiday with their partners or friends. As I walked past 'Cheerleaders', a bar at my end of town, a lady shouted across at me to ask if I wanted a blow job, and I immediately remembered there was a pretty easy way to tell which ladies were which. 'Cheerleaders' had a giant logo out front which said, 'Sports bar and pleasurable stuff' – this 'pleasurable stuff' wasn't the kind of romance I was searching for, so I hurried on to the safety of my adopted family's home for a lazy afternoon and a peaceful night's sleep.

It was the Manuel Antonio National Park that had drawn me to Jaco, as it seemed a sensible place from which to make a day trip, but at 6:15 am standing on the roadside waiting for a bus, I could not recall why I had ruled out just staying in Manuel Antonio village. Although, I felt a bit better about not staying in the area when the bus pulled into a touristy road crammed with accommodation, hot dog, burger and pizza restaurants and another one of the fancy Selina hostels I saw everywhere on my travels. My smugness at arriving 'early' at 8:30 am to beat the crowds quickly dissipated when I arrived at the entrance to the National Park to find a sea of people waiting to get in. The length of the queue was actually due to the bag check process that was being carried out to make sure people didn't have any food in their bags. Sandwiches were allowed, but nothing else, including crisps and biscuits and the like, were permitted in the park, presumably to avoid a rubbish problem. After a twenty-minute wait, it was my turn, and she had a quick look through my bag and sent me on my way, failing to find my two cereal bars – though to be fair, even with an infra-red scanner she would have struggled to detect those sorry little biscuits.

Manuel Antonio National Park is actually the smallest of the national parks in Costa Rica, covering barely 2,000 hectares, but it punches well above its weight as a result of its picture-postcard beaches and the wide variety of wildlife that can be easily viewed within the park. The animals that live in the park include both varieties of sloths found in the country, as well as three of their four monkey species, the mantled howler monkey, the white-headed capuchin and the Central American squirrel monkey. The beaches, where the rainforest meets the sea, which sounded a lot like the Daintree in Far North Queensland, were also claimed as some of the finest in the country and having seen the quality of the beaches up north, I was excited to see if this was true. So into the park, I went and was disappointed to find that this was the biggest tourist zoo of the trip so far, with hundreds of people crammed onto the walkways to catch a look at the wildlife and ugly concrete paths running all around the public area. It was also tipping it down again, and I was starting to feel like maybe I had had enough of the nature spotting part of my trip, which was effectively the majority of my Costa Rica visit. Putting these feelings aside, I again headed for a far corner of the park and found some solitude in the corner of a beach that would have looked perfect were it not shrouded in driving rain. I sat there for a while before the arrival on the other side of the beach of a family in banana yellow ponchos signalled that it was time to move on. As I passed this group at the exit to the beach, I saw another family to my right, all in swimming costumes and applying sun cream before heading out for a swim – the contrast between these hardy souls and 'family poncho' was quite delightful.

 I'm happy to report things started to improve at this point. I took another path, which led up to the highest part of the park and (of course) a mirador over the coast to the north. While it was still raining, you could see a bit of a view, but the more exciting development was as I looked out to sea, a large group of squirrel monkeys arrived in the branches overhead and spent the next ten minutes climbing and swinging over the deck upon which I was standing. After deciding that show was over, I walked back down the path to another lookout area and, almost on cue, a group of howler monkeys started passing at eye level, not far from the platform. I got a few 'monkey blob' photos, but then managed to get some decent video of the scene, including a mother carrying a tiny little baby monkey on her back. Finally, some wildlife spotting success! Shortly after it was three from three, as at my next stop, I saw a sloth up a tree in fairly clear view – and there was the Derby family from the Monteverde transfer taking pictures. I caught up with them briefly, talking mostly about the weather (as you do) and then continued on with my walk around the park, which was now taking in the main tourist populated beaches. The rain was pretty heavy now, and I was soaked through and once again back in Cornwall holiday mode – except there was no nearby National Trust stately home where I could seek refuge.

 I was about done with all the trails and thinking it was time to start heading towards the exit when I chanced upon the scene of a raccoon and a capuchin monkey walking up the path towards me. I quickly grabbed my phone, only to find the screen was wet and I had no part of my body or clothes that was not also wet, meaning I couldn't unlock my phone to get the photo, no matter how much I contorted myself in my attempts to do so. By now the monkey was practically riding the raccoon, but still, I was unable to capture the moment and eventually conceded defeat, trudging off in a squelchy mess towards the exit. After dodging coconut water and hammock sellers outside the gates, I repeated my morning's bus journey in reverse and was back in Jaco for a late lunch. When I got back to my house, my lovely hostess Alexandra had done all of my laundry and left it neatly folded on my bed, for no charge. I could have kissed her, but Carlos, her husband, had finally appeared on the scene so I decided that maybe would not be appropriate.

 It was Mother's Day in Costa Rica the following day, which they celebrate with a public holiday. I had read previously that Costa Rica has historically done a commendable job on equality for women and general respect for their standing in society, and an interesting aspect of this was that women keep their maiden names when they marry, with their children taking both surnames, a system I had not heard of elsewhere. My memories of the two-hour ride included the plethora of roadside rambutan stalls, football pitches absolutely everywhere (no coincidence Costa Rica punches above its weight in world soccer), and my favourite sight, a local man dropping off his family to catch the bus while holding in his hand a giant fish he appeared to be taking for a walk – well, why not!

Arriving back in San Jose that evening, I made a return visit to the Argentinian restaurant and remembered I should check back in on Tinder when something amazing happened – I got my first match! Veroni from Brazil looked really rather attractive in her pictures, so this was exciting news, save for two problems, the fact I was getting a plane the following day at 5 pm and, more bizarrely, a premonition that Emily had shared with me before I left. This premonition was that I would return home to Australia at the end of my trip with a Brazilian wife, who I would then also end up getting divorced from – so we hadn't even had a date yet, and we were already doomed. Nevertheless, unperturbed by these dual challenges, I sent Veroni a message back, explaining my movements and asking if she wanted to meet for lunch tomorrow anyway. And then had three glasses of Malbec to celebrate before returning home to retire for the evening.

The next day I was getting organised to head to the airport at 2 pm when I looked at my phone and saw a red blob on the Tinder icon and realised I had missed a message from earlier – "Hello Alex…morning. It would be great to have coffee with you today." Dammit! I wasn't sure what the etiquette was here but decided I would send her a note with my apologies, saying I was sad I didn't get to meet my first match, and wishing her all the best for her time in Costa Rica, which she seemed to like. But dammit!

Costa Rica had delivered rather a lot of rain, a lot of amazing scenery and wildlife, and I had eaten my body weight in 'Casados', dodged prostitutes in San Jose and Jaco and started to show a few glimmers of being able to speak a bit of Spanish. Most of all, though, I had got a bit of a feel for why the Ticos and Ticas are so proud of their country and their 'Pura Vida' outlook to life. Next stop Guatemala…

Summary – Costa Rica

Kilometres travelled (air) – None
Kilometres travelled (land) – 950
Number of sloths seen – Two
Number of successful sloth photos – None
Number of volcanic formations – 121 (Seven active)
Number of volcanic formations seen – None

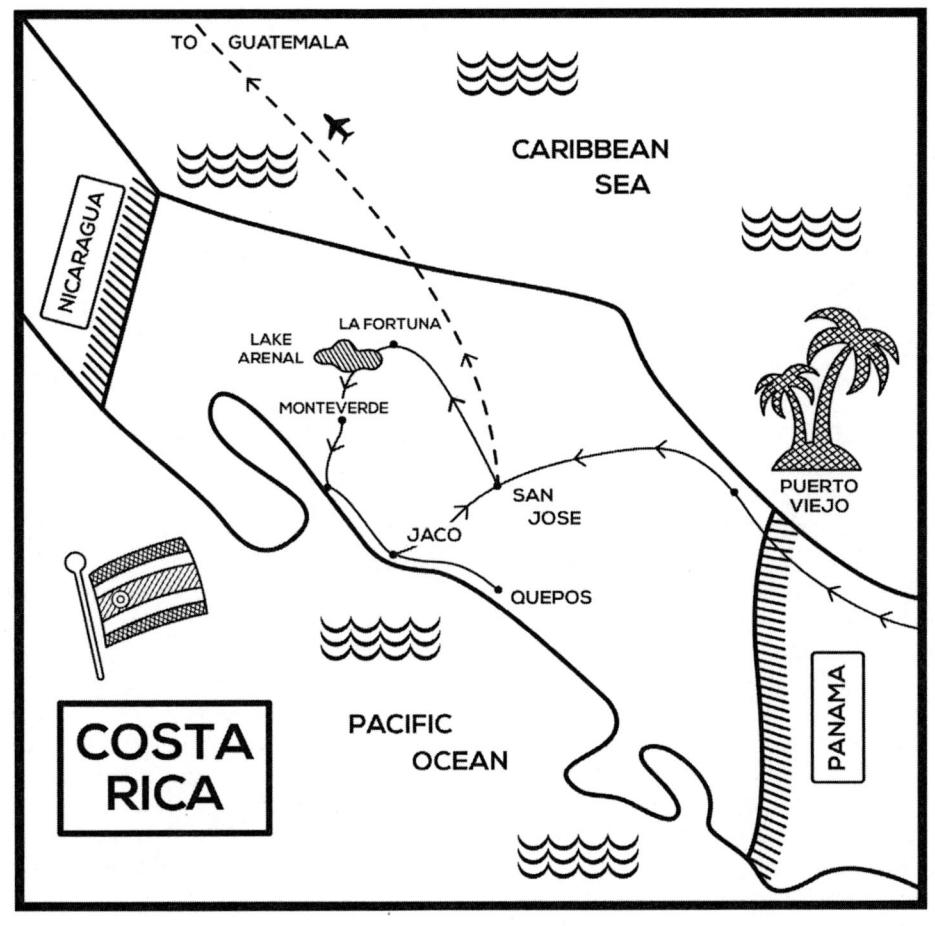

Guatemala
Volcanoes, Lakes and a Plastic Bag

It was just a 75-minute flight from San Jose to Guatemala and with about ten minutes to go to landing I looked out the window and was delighted to see in the failing evening light the clear outlines of the monstrous volcanoes which surround the city. I was in the aisle seat so was having to steal glances across the Japanese gentleman sat in the window seat, who was pretending I wasn't annoying him by doing so but anyway, the view was awe-inspiring, and I had a real sense of excitement about the days ahead. The travel plan was to spend three nights in Antigua, primarily as a base for climbing one of the nearby volcanoes, followed by four nights at Lago de Atitlan, 90 kilometres to the west, before returning to Guatemala City to get a flight over to Flores in the northeast, where I would spend a couple of days seeing Mayan ruins before continuing overland to Mexico.

After collecting my bag and dodging a lady trying to hard sell me a trip to Antigua in a 'collectivo' van, I found myself an Uber, established the driver had zero English, and settled in for the silent one-hour trip to the city of Antigua. As we arrived at the cobbled streets at the entrance to the city, even in the dark, I could make a sense it was going to be an awesome place as we passed neat terraces of coloured houses, interspersed with ruined buildings in varying states of disrepair. In keeping with these surrounds, on arrival I could see the place I was staying was equally impressive, making my way through the double-width wooden front door to reveal original stone floors, a partially open atrium in the middle looking up to a roof terrace, and exposed brickwork throughout and wooden rafters above. Evelyn was my host here and given the hour, we just exchanged brief introductions, and she showed me to my room where I was almost ready to bed down for an early night. There were a couple of jobs to deal with first though, the first of which was to gently encourage the two cats who had wandered into my room to find alternative sleeping quarters, and secondly, given I was in Antigua for a few nights, a Tinder check-in seemed sensible.

As in San Jose, this was clearly a popular place for it, and as I swiped through, I was pleased to see that there were a couple of women who I liked the look of, and on the second one, I got the happy news – 'It's a match!' Controlling my excitement, I decided I should finish the run-through, so I went back to the list and found another that I liked – and it happened again! Confusingly, both women had the exact same name (Maria), but before I had time to dwell on that, I received a message from the first Maria asking how I was – now what? I had a quick look back at her profile which said, she was an 'adventurer', so I confidently wrote back 'I see you are an adventurer – would you like to climb one of these volcanoes with me?' to which I got a 'Ha, we'll see!' and some other general banter. After this success I thought I should message the other Maria too and looked up her profile for a clue on what to write, but found there was no blurb, meaning I didn't even know if she spoke English. Now brimming with confidence, I decided to write my introductory message to her in Spanish, something along the lines of 'Hello Maria, how are you? I don't speak much Spanish, but I am trying!' To my horror I saw this Spanish message go on to the bottom of the English message chain I had just had with the first Maria – I had mixed the two up, and the initial message exchange had not been with the adventurer, but from the one with no blurb. Realising my error, and the now fortunate name coincidence I quickly typed another message, 'Practicing!' – which she thought was hilarious – what a save! I then managed to successfully message the second Maria, who replied and seemed to have potential too, and I left both conversations that evening with the next steps to be determined.

In the morning I woke at about 630 and could see around the edge of the curtain that it was a lovely start to the day out. I positively leapt out of bed, grabbed my phone and set off to get some photos of the sights around town in the morning light before the other tourists were there to pollute my snaps. And what a place it was. The centre of the town is laid out in a classic grid formation, with seven main 'avenidas' running north to south, intersected by nine 'calles' which run east to west, and every corner you walked around to the next block, there was some kind of new wondrous sight to behold. In the morning light, I could now properly see the terraced houses, a bright patchwork of colours dominated by mustard yellow, terracotta red, burnt orange and sky blue that combined to give the place a warm, welcoming feel. Nestled amongst these houses were ruins every two or three blocks, ranging from buildings and churches which were still sufficiently intact to show their original form, to some which were little more than just moss-covered piles of ancient stone. In the main squares stood more significant two or three-storey buildings, housing museums and administrative buildings, some of them spanning entire blocks, with their ornate structures looking down over the neatly maintained squares, with small areas of grass and flowers everywhere. The highlight of the walk, and the hero of many a photo of the city was the Arch of Santa Caterina, which spans Avenida 5, framing a beautiful vista looking south, of the city falling away in the distance to the foot of the imposing Volcan Agua, which towers over the city at over 4,000 metres. There was barely a soul or car in view at this early hour, just the beauty of the buildings and their natural surrounds and thousands of cobblestones. The place was simply incredible.

Returning back to the house, I had breakfast around the communal table in the kitchen, Evelyn whipping up a mean omelette for me and the other guests, who comprised a lady from Poland, a man from Peru and an old retired couple from California who were staying for a month to practice their Spanish, an annual routine for them. Over the course of the breakfast conversation, the guy from the States made some comment about 'people my age' and, as usual in these (regular) situations I decided not to tell him his estimate of my age was probably well off and that I was, in fact, 'old enough to know better'. And besides, I was eager for a more comprehensive walk around town so didn't want to be drawn into the chatter. The highlight for me (as always) was the main market which sprawled across a large complex of buildings, housing clothes, souvenirs and cooked and fresh food. The food stalls were watched over by ladies in beautifully coloured Mayan dresses, who were transporting the fruit and vegetables between the stalls in bowls carefully balanced on their heads, a sight I would see many times in my travels in Guatemala over the next week or so. My main business for the day was to confirm my hike for the next day, an ascent of the nearby Volcan Acatenango, which looked back over the town and which sat directly alongside the active Volcan Fuego. I had paid a deposit the week before with a local company called Ox Expeditions, but the trip was subject to them finding their required minimum of three climbers. When I dropped into the office they hadn't yet found the two others, but good news arrived later in the day when they emailed me to confirm we would be doing the climb, starting with a 5 am meet the following morning.

After a brisk climb to the lookout over the town provided a light warm-up for the following day, I went and had lunch at 'Rincon Tipico', a place recommended by Evelyn. It was a stone building with high ceilings, crammed full of wooden benches that were nearly all taken when I arrived. At the entrance, there were three ladies with a large basket of tortilla dough, which they were moulding together with their hands and cooking on the hot plate in front of them (a sight I would see repeated in shop fronts and house doorways absolutely everywhere), while at the back a large rack of chickens cooked over a giant wood fire, which heated the whole dining room. I opted for the chicken option, which came with the tortillas, new potatoes and salad and which replenished my energy levels from the morning's walking for about $5; I came back here to eat a further two times while I was in Antigua it was so good. I had established a good rapport with Maria #1 and thought that with the exchange of messages, she seemed to be shaping up as a strong candidate for Tinder date number one. She was busy that evening but suggested I should visit a bar, El Barrio. The bar was actually a large complex that had five separate bars, but it was pretty empty, so I decided to park myself in the bar at the front, the intriguingly named 'Ocelot Bar'. I got talking to the barman who, during the conversation, explained that the hospitality market had been changing in recent years following the arrival of some 'super hostels', which were able to house large numbers of travellers in modern, relatively luxurious, facilities and which had in-house bars and even clubs, making sure all of the travellers' cash was ending up in their tills. The leading player in this new category was an organisation called 'Selina', and I was intrigued to learn more about them, as I had seen them absolutely everywhere I had been – Bocas Town, Isla Bastimentos, Puerto Viejo, San Jose, Jaco, Manuel Antonio and now here too. The barman told me the business had been set up a few years previously by three 30-something Israelis backed with family money and had been expanding aggressively since. I read online they had recently secured $95 million of venture capital to drive this rapid growth further, based on a business model of acquiring existing large properties and repurposing them as 'traveller communities', with rooms at all price points and facilities like co-working spaces and entertainment facilities. According to their president, Yoav Gery, this 'created a more holistic program for the traveller – everything that they might want'. Who knows whether they were making decent money alongside this breakneck pace of investment, but it certainly looked an impressive new business idea to the untrained observer.

After we had been talking about this for a while, a man came and sat next to me and introduced himself – after a brief chat it transpired this was Shaun, originally from Bridgend in Wales, now living in Antigua with his Guatemalan wife and three children, and the part-owner of El Barrio. His bar ownership journey had started in 2004 when he had arrived in the country and bought into a bar which was up for sale for $12k, but which he had negotiated to buy for $10k, the limit on his credit card, which he had used to finance the purchase – a gamble that looked to have paid off! Over the course of the conversation I told Shaun he owed my business to a recommendation from a girl I was due to have a Tinder date with the next day, and I then mentioned the story of my initial messaging gaffe with the two Marias to which he commented he knew a few Marias and wondered if he knew her. Around the same time, I was receiving some messages from Maria #1, and I wrote back to say I had gone to the bar she had recommended and was chatting to the owner, to which I got the response:

"Oh, is it Shaun?"

Doh! I shared this information with Shaun and suggested he maybe didn't repeat the 'two Maria' story next time he saw her. By that point in the conversation, he had already given me the advice of 'Don't marry the first person you kiss after a divorce', something he said he saw several regrettable occurrences of, and this is advice we will come back to later in my story. After drinking four more beers than planned, the energy of the place (and probably date excitement) was clearly having a big impact on me, and it was time to return home.

***

It was back to an early start the next day for the Acatenango volcano climb at the Ox office where I met my guide (who I am going to refer to as Chino, as that is what the other guides we met later called him) and shortly after, my solitary fellow walker, Lindsay, a lady from the US. It was a 50-minute drive to the hike start point, which was at an altitude of about 2,400 metres, stopping en route to get a coffee from a roadside vendor in a small town. Lindsay, who had good Spanish, organised things, translating the question as to whether I wanted milk, to which I said yes. The guy then ladled almost a whole cup of milk into my Styrofoam cup and topped it with a light coffee glaze – the wrong answer, I guess. I had a bit of an intro chat with Lindsay with much of the discussion focusing on how I could possibly have six months off work, and the contrast to the meagre holiday allowances people get in the States, starting at two weeks annual leave, a fact that I had been horrified by when I first heard it, and which I still struggle to comprehend. Lindsay worked for 'US Aid' and was currently in Guatemala doing work in connection with the Zika virus which had been found in the country, and which the US was quite keen to keep out of the US – foreign aid, or self-serving investment? You decide.

And so, to the walk. On my Nepal trip earlier in the year, I had made friends with an English guy called Sunny, who worked as a travel agent, specialising in high-end travel in South and Central America. He had waxed lyrical about an amazing day walk he had done scaling Acatenango and then coming down and climbing Fuego as well, a gruelling 16-hour walk he had described as the most challenging of his life. This had sown the seeds in my mind for some volcano hiking, and while his double hike sounded awesome and I was in good shape, I decided one volcano was enough and messaged him to tell him this, but he was still pushing me to double up and do Fuego as well:

"Come on, Alex, it's the attitude, not the altitude!"

As we say in Australia, "Yeah, nah!"

The walk started with a decent uphill gradient right which didn't relent until you reached the top. Chino was in training for an ultra-marathon and Lindsay was a keen half marathon runner, so I had my dream walking group. About an hour into the walk, Chino told us of the local legend that there were spirits who lived on the volcano and, when pushed, launched into a story about why he believed these stories. He had been climbing Acatenango with a couple of girls from Australia, and as they approached the area where they would camp for the night, a storm came rolling in. Chino quickly started putting up the tents as the rain started but was halted when one of the girls was suddenly in a panic, saying she had felt the electricity from the storm, with her hair apparently standing on end. Chino tried to calm her, saying camping there was the best plan but shortly after felt a numb feeling in his arm and realised the same had happened to him. Now quite concerned, he quickly packed the tents, and they descended quickly into a forest area below to seek cover. Ahead of them down the track they could hear voices through the dark and Chino walked on to try and find the people who were talking, to warn them of the storm danger – except he couldn't find anyone there. And no one else was walking on the volcano that day. The girls said nothing about the noises as they carried on down the mountain until they got to the safety of the bottom and asked about the voices, to which Chino had no answer.

After this eerie tale, I was glad we were walking up in bright sunshine and doing a day walk that would not require me to camp near the forest he had just described. The landscape we were walking through passed through three clearly identifiable phases, starting with farmland, then rising into the cloud forest and then higher into a pine forest, with each section taking a bit under an hour to ascend. On the way up, we enjoyed wonderful clear views of the other volcanoes, the towns in the valley below as well as Antigua in the distance. Agua, the largest of the nearby volcanoes was sadly closed for climbing due to regular robberies with machetes by people who apparently lived in a village at the bottom of the trail – which was a shame as the views from the top are apparently incredible. From the lookout, we turned off onto a steeper path for the last ninety minutes to the summit, and the path gradually turned into large sections of loose volcanic soil and gravel, a part of the walk known as 'La Maldita', or 'cursed trail'. With each step we took forward, we slid back down the hill about half the distance – a bit frustrating, but my legs were feeling strong, and I pressed on, eager to get to the top before the clouds rolled in. After just over four hours of climbing, we made it to the summit, and I ran excitedly along the crater path to the side where we could see Volcan Fuego. I had just finished taking a video of the panorama from the top when I looked back at Fuego, which was mostly obscured by cloud, to see plumes of volcanic ash coming out the top of the cloud as it erupted. Incredible awe-inspiring sight of Mother Nature turning it on, and a great reward for the efforts of the climb.

Fuego is one of the most active volcanoes in the world with almost constant small eruptions, but on Sunday June 3 2018, pretty much as soon as I had put a visit to Antigua to climb volcanoes onto my itinerary, it erupted in a major way, and two villages, which Chino showed us from the summit, were completely buried. The death toll on Wikipedia is 'at least 159', but Chino said he believed the government had suppressed the real toll, as the villages that were buried housed about 6,000 people, with only about half that amount fully accounted for from refuge centre arrivals and other confirmed sightings. It was a sobering reminder of the power of these mighty forces of nature, and with this knowledge, I felt a tinge of silliness taking selfies with the eruption behind. The day before Fuego erupted, a man had died on the walk to the summit of Acatenango, and six of Chino's friends were on the mountain recovering the body when the neighbouring volcano erupted, filling the air with ash and gases and showering them with flying rocks. As they desperately attempted to descend from the danger, the situation was apparently so dire that a number of them made phone calls to say goodbye to their loved ones but, mercifully, they all made it to safety.

As we watched Fuego continue to erupt in small plumes of gas, Chino took the opportunity to try and beat his personal best time for running around the path that circled the crater, arriving back a few minutes later, gasping for air but looking pretty happy with himself – nutter. As the cloud and wind rolled in, the temperature dropped about ten degrees in as many minutes, and it was time to make a move. We paused briefly to read the memorial at the summit for six local climbers who had frozen to death near the summit the year before after being caught in a storm, another reminder of the danger all around, and it was then downhill all the way for the next couple of hours. The descent was actually a lot of fun, running down the loose soil of La Maldita in about a tenth of the time it took to go the other way and keeping a brisk pace for the remainder, stopping only to make room for the large groups of ill-dressed young backpackers who were heading up for the overnight camping experience – two of them were even wearing jeans!

And with that, we were at the bottom – as Lindsay neatly summarised, "What a lovely way to spend a Saturday."

***

Returning to Antigua it was time to get ready for my date, and I texted Maria to ask 1) whether people dressed up in Antigua and 2) whether we needed to make reservations given it was a Saturday night. The reply I got did not address 1), saying just,

"You only need to make reservations if you are going for a date in a restaurant."

This sounded fairly close to what I thought was about to happen, so gave me pause for thought before I sent my considered reply,

"What are *we* doing?"

Apparently, it was up to me what we were doing, so I suggested a wine bar, and we agreed to meet there at 8 pm. At 7:40 pm (I have always been an early arriver), seated at the bar enjoying a crisp glass of Torrontes, I started getting messages saying there was nowhere for Maria to park her car. These messages continued for a while, I had another glass of wine, and then at about nine, I received instructions to go to El Barrio (again) instead, which I did. Maria was there with some friends, and it later transpired this was a deliberate move to have some security/backup for meeting random Tinder guy for the first time – I hadn't really considered this (not for meeting me, surely!), but on reflection, it was eminently sensible.

So what can I tell you about Maria? Maria was 36, born and raised in Guatemala City but had been living in Switzerland for a few years until she returned home earlier in the year following the end of the relationship that had taken her there in the first place. Probably the main point to note upfront was that she had a 13-year-old daughter and she lived in her childhood family home along with her slightly younger brother. Family was clearly important to her, and her main focus in life was, understandably, providing for her daughter, or 'douter' in her Spanish English accent. While we are on the subject, her accent was quite hypnotic to me, whether speaking English or breaking into Spanish while speaking to her friends. It was music to my ears, and a couple of times I realised I was lost in her accent, not actually paying attention to the words that were coming out and staring just a bit too long, a couple of times prompting the response, "Why you lookinadme that way?" which just served to further entrance me. Maria was about 5'6 with piercing blue eyes, long brown hair and a beautiful, slightly mischievous smile, and looked in real life every bit as good as her profile pictures, which was quite a relief. When I had told my friend Richard ('a bit sex pesty') I was going to give Tinder a go, his helpful advice was 'Watch out, most will be bat shit cray-cray!' – while it was quite possible this was true, after a few hours chatting with Maria I was feeling reasonably confident that she was one of the minority of sane romance seekers.

In the messages we had exchanged during the days before the date, I had established that she had quite a promising sense of humour. She had asked about funny stories from my trip to date, and I had sent her the Wayne's World tattoo photo, and in response, she had immediately sent me a photo of someone she knew in the city who had what appeared to be a My Little Pony tattoo on his lower back, right above his backside – someone with the foresight to capture that moment for posterity was surely a worthy sparring partner for me. Maria was a real estate agent, working for one of her cousins (she had 40!), which she seemed to really enjoy but I don't recall much work chat after that which was a relief, as it meant I didn't have to bore her explaining what I did for a living. The discussion was more about other passions, including travel, dogs and music, where we seemed to have a number of shared favourites, including my brave early confession to be a fan of musicals – it was risky, but it landed. I was also interested to learn that one of the main reasons she had swiped on my profile was because of the beard I was sporting, a look that I had tried for the first time this year, and which I had been umm-ing and aah-ing on whether to keep. Based on feedback from my Tinder polling group, sample size one, I would definitely be keeping it for now.

We quickly hit it off, with loads to chat about and mutual enjoyment of each other's company – we shared a laugh at her friends mocking me for buying a 'pussy drink' (gin and tonic), and the drinks flowed. Maria claimed this was only the second time she had been on a date with a random from Tinder, and the other guy sounded like a bit of a dullard. This, coupled with the fact her recently terminated long term partner didn't sound like he had much chat either, meant I was on a good wicket, scoring highly just by being able to sustain a conversation for several hours – AND cracking jokes too! At this moment, on my first date in many a year, kissing before I had even left the bar and still elated from my earlier volcano climb, I couldn't have been happier!

The evening got rowdier and, as last drinks at 1 am arrived, it had descended into a bit of group karaoke, working through the classics like AC-DC's *'Thunderstruck'* and Bon Jovi's *'Livin' on a Prayer',* with Shaun proudly displaying his Welsh heritage, ripping into Bonnie Tyler's *'Total Eclipse of the Heart'* – yep, that song again. Maria's friend Ramon was very drunk when I arrived and had been deteriorating over the course of the evening, and Maria said she was going to have to drive him home but wanted me to go with her. Given I didn't have other plans that sounded fine to me, and apparently, we could also stay there – even better! So at about 1:30 am, off we went, stopping at a petrol station on the way to buy Ramon more beer and cigarettes, which for some reason I was apparently financing – given they were about $3 I decided I could live with that. Shortly after we arrived at Ramon's house, and this is when things started to get bizarre. Ramon, who was forty-something, still lived with his parents (and grandma) and had managed to lose his keys, so had to wake his mother to let us in, who didn't seem pleased by this, nor in meeting me or Maria, saying something in Spanish which Maria reacted strangely to, before going back to bed. It turned out that she had said to Maria, 'You are the devil!' apparently in reference to previous high jinks involving Ramon, which had been blamed on her influence. Meanwhile, Ramon had cracked open a beer and put on some music, which started with *'Careless Whisper'* by George Michael and then Ramstein and Napalm Death – really, I couldn't make this up. He also wanted to show us his dog, which was a conspicuously overweight St Bernard and after saying hello to us in the kitchen, it thundered off into the house, hopefully not up to the mother's bedroom.

Anyway, Maria had decided she didn't want to stay here after the devil comment, which seemed fair enough, so we left Ramon to his mid-90s death metal and the fourteen remaining beers, and it was off to another random friend's house, 20 kilometres away from Antigua. Apparently, she had a provisional arrangement that she might stay here, as she didn't want to go back to her own house, where we might run into her brother or daughter. I was going to leave the story of the evening's events here as what happened next was moving towards the kind of R rated content I wasn't planning on writing about, but having told the initially omitted part of the tale to several people, all of whom said I simply had to include it, here it is. Things had heated up to the point where Maria asked if I had a condom. My answer to this was 'unfortunately not', which you might say was a rookie error, but then you have to remember this was my first 'first date' in many a year, and while I had thought about it beforehand, I had decided that it would have been presumptuous to rock up for a first date with a condom. Anyway, it wasn't this poor planning that was the reason for me sharing this part of the story, it was the question that Maria asked me in response to this admission.

"Shall we just use a plastic bag instead?"

I was a little bit taken aback by this question and wasn't really sure logistically how that would work; in any case, I was in Guatemala for a while longer and thought I would get another opportunity, so I politely declined, suggesting that the proposed course of action didn't sound very romantic. When I have re-told this story to people, I have found that, without fail, it has prompted detailed analysis of what she actually meant by her question, and the comments and discussion have gone something like this:

'A bag? A bag? What kind of bag? Did you ask her what kind of bag she meant? Did she mean a shopping bag? No, she can't have meant a shopping bag – that would be quite painful, I think. Did she mean a freezer bag? Maybe she meant a freezer bag, like one of those zip-lock bags? That might have worked – did she mean that? Or what about Glad wrap – did you think about Glad wrap? Did you ask her about that?'

To the folks who asked me all of that, and to you as well if you have similar questions, I repeat, no, I did not ask her what she meant, and my final resting place for the night was the sofa at 4 am. After 24 hours awake, an epic volcano climb and this crazy date safari it had been a very tiring, but amazing day out!

Waking at 6:30 am with a cat on my chest, I scanned the room and had that alarming 'where the hell am I?' feeling before I remembered and was briefly calmed. However, I also remembered that Maria had said that her friend had three kids, and I was feeling very uncomfortable about them coming down and discovering a random man on their sofa. Looking out on the street I saw there was a park at the bottom of the road and texted Maria to say I was not comfortable in the house and would be waiting in the park until she was ready to take me elsewhere. After about an hour there I got a voice message from Carolina, the friend and owner of the house, who very nicely said I was welcome in her house and that I should come back, which I did. Maria was feeling sorry for herself and was incapable of movement, but said if I waited for a bit, Carolina would drive me to a petrol station where I could get an Uber home. Apparently, I couldn't do this from Carolina's as the house was in a security-controlled estate and so I waited patiently as the three kids finally appeared for their breakfast, offering awkward waves and '*Holas*'. After what seemed like an eternity, the family was finally ready to go out for their day, and they all piled into the car, with me as the random gringo in the front seat. I agreed with Maria that we would meet up again in a few days when she could get time off work and waved goodbye. Carolina drove around the corner, took one turn, went through the security gate and turned onto the petrol station forecourt right outside and stopped for me to get out.

Me – "Oh, I could have walked here."

C – "Yes, I thought that too, but Maria was worried you would get lost."

***

Having said my goodbyes over my shoulder to the still bemused children, my Uber arrived quickly, and I had another silent ride for the 40-minute drive home. This unexpected night safari meant I was now a bit behind schedule to organise and get to my next destination, Panajachel at Lago Atitlan. Given the hour, I only had the option of shuttle departures scheduled at either 2:30 pm or 4 pm, so I made a booking with a travel agent for the 2:30 pm shuttle. The agent confusingly wrote 12:30 pm on the ticket, so I reminded her I wanted the 2:30 pm service, to which she nodded (no English), and I headed back to the hotel to collect my luggage and from where the shuttle would collect me. At 2:15 pm, I was on the street with my bags waiting for the shuttle, with the odd tourist walking past on their way to a lookout up the road. A family walked past, and the dad started talking to me in Spanish, asking what I assumed was whether I could take a photo of them, so I offered to take the camera. But no, he wanted me in the photo, in the middle of his family photo, with arms on shoulders across the group – err, okay! My survival training kicked in, and I made sure I had all my valuables and could see my bags, but apparently, he really did just want me in the shot. I would be fascinated by how that shot was explained in the holiday photo rundown – hopefully, I made the album.

With the time now approaching 3 pm it was clear something was amiss, so I phoned the travel company, to be told, 'No, you booked the 12:30 pm, it says so on the ticket.' I should have seen that coming. After a few more calls and me patiently (ish) explaining I booked the shuttle at around 1 pm and could not have wanted to book a shuttle that took place in the past, they worked out a Plan B; a van would pick me up at 3:30 pm which was going to San Pedro (another town on the lake), and I would get out along the way and get a cab for the last leg to Panajachel. Phew. And that's what happened – the bus drove at breakneck speed along winding roads through the mountains until I decided it was best not to watch the manoeuvres he was making, and I subsequently transferred to my cab and arrived at the outskirts of Panajachel. Along the way, Maria had been sending me a load of photos of family, friends, pets past and present – less than 24 hours after the first date we seemed to be going through the gears quite quickly but I was still basking in the glow of the previous day so that all seemed rather thoughtful, and I was looking forward to meeting again. Dusk was starting to fall as we descended the hill to the town, but there was enough light to see the silhouettes of the three volcanoes which circle the lake, Toliman, Atitlan and San Pedro, and I had the same feeling of excitement about the view the sunrise the next day would bring that I had felt when I arrived in Antigua. I was met at the entrance to my lodgings by Tomas, a lovely old local man with three teeth, who gave me a warm greeting and showed me to my room, giving me the usual Spanish intro where I followed just enough to know about keys, Wi-Fi and – no, that's it actually, just keys and Wi-Fi.

Despite the failing light, I decided I would go out for an evening walk to get my bearings and a bit of a feel for the place, though as it turned out, I managed to achieve neither of these objectives. As I got to the top of the road, the dark streets were filled with a strange sound, music that reminded me a bit of Level 42, with the 80s sounding synth and bass guitar, but with someone singing painfully off-key over the top. As I walked past I could see it was a church and as I walked further, I saw a few more churches, also with music blaring, which I would later read were evangelical Christian churches, a form of religion very popular in the local area. Continuing on, I saw the obligatory scenes of ladies making tortillas in small shop fronts and then was amazed to see an Internet cafe, something I hadn't seen in a long time. I was going to make a joke here about checking for its heritage listing, but I saw loads more in the coming days and realised I had been a little naive to assume that the spread of mobile devices familiar to the Western world, which has all but killed off Internet cafes, would have also already played out in this relatively poor developing country.

I should probably explain something at this point – wherever I am, whether at home abroad, I really like walking, often ignoring cheap, convenient alternatives, like the tuk-tuks here, to do so. I haven't owned a car since I have lived in Sydney and have always lived centrally, so I am in the habit of walking whenever I have the time. When I was in Bali earlier in the year, I walked up to the reception at my hotel and said I wanted to go for a walk to buy sun cream (sound familiar?) and could the man tell me where the nearest shop was. He looked at me like I was on something and said,

"Walk? Sir – we can drive you to the shop. It's really quite far."

I assured him I was happier to walk, got my directions and set off for the shop. It really wasn't quite far, fifteen minutes in fact, but when I arrived back, a walking fountain of perspiration, I could maybe understand why people don't walk around much in Bali. Well, mostly it's the heat, but also the fact most of them are lazy Australian holidaymakers. But to return to my point, in summary, I like to walk.

Back in the darkness, I had not learnt from my mistakes and had turned off the simple route to the lake for a more scenic route – well, it looked scenic on Google Maps. Soon I found myself walking down a barely lit road with no shops or restaurants, which then became a dirt track running alongside what seemed to be a fly-tipping area. I was starting to feel a bit uncomfortable now as there was no one else around so quickened my stride, but some relief came a bit later when I was passed in the other direction by a young couple out on a walk who, presumably, were navigating with a copy of the *'Alex Maycock Guide to Walking in Panajachel'*. Finally, the surface improved to paving stones and I arrived at a load of restaurants – all of which were closed. I continued on and at last arrived at a street with open restaurants, though all of these were completely empty with small groups of waiting staff at the door of each, waiting for someone to arrive to give them something to do. I didn't want to eat on my own in an empty restaurant, so carried on for a while to find somewhere with some more life, before running out of enthusiasm and stopping at an empty taco restaurant to eat on my own. The tacos were great to be fair, but it had been a long day, powered by minimal sleep, and after successfully navigating the short route back to my room I settled in for a long sleep.

Except it wasn't a long sleep, as I was unceremoniously awoken at 4 am (still pitch black) by an over-enthusiastic rooster (or 'Gallo', or 'fucker') outside my window which then carried on crowing every five minutes thereafter. Looking to get some benefit from this interruption of my slumber, I eventually got up at about 5:20 am and set off down the road for sunrise over the lake, followed by a Pied Piper-esque procession of street dogs who I guess were also fans of the view at first light. And what a view it was. I walked down to the docks to find there were no boats there at all, so the view in front of me was a row of rickety wooden jetties spearing out into the lake, some of them painted in light shades of blue, some of them just left as untreated timber, and a shimmering expanse of millpond still waters stretching until the far side of the lake where the three volcanoes loomed large on the skyline. I sat on the end of one of the jetties, no one else around saves a few early rising boatmen preparing for the day ahead, and drank in this scene as the sun rose over my left shoulder, throwing beautiful orange and red hues across the sky.

A while later, having triumphantly achieved booking a boat tour in Spanish, and waiting for its departure, a boatman shouted at me, asking if I wanted to go to San Pedro – spotting a perfect opportunity to use my favourite nonsense Spanish expression I replied quickly, 'No gracias, mañana,' which he nodded at knowingly and moved on to look for other customers. 'Mañana' in Spanish means both 'tomorrow' and 'morning' – exactly the same spelling and accents, which I thought was really weird, and had noted as such to Maria in conversation – the reply I had received was along the lines of 'you are the weird one', which I would concede was probably true. But still, exactly the same word! My boat tour would visit three towns around the lake, San Juan, San Pedro and Santiago Atitlan, spending about an hour at each, before returning to 'Pa-na-ha-chell' (as I kept saying to myself to try and finally say it right).

In the introduction to Lago Atitlan in the Lonely Planet, they reference a quote from a nineteenth-century traveller called John L Stephens who, in *'Incidents of Travel in Central America'*, called the lake 'the most magnificent spectacle we ever saw'. Let me rephrase that in less eloquent terms, this place was the Italian Lakes on acid; below the blue skies with their smattering of cotton wool clouds, the beautifully serene (at this moment) lake was hemmed in on all sides by green hills and volcanoes rising steeply up the sides with the lower levels of the hills studded with towns. The still surface of the lake was broken only by the lanchas hurrying between the towns with their cargo of eager tourists and the simple wooden canoes nearer the shores, in which solo fishermen tended to their nets and pots. It seemed every place I had visited seemed to be more amazing than the last, and I decided Guatemala is a blessed country, at least with regard to its natural surrounds.

San Juan, the first stop, was a small town, more of a village really, and this place was all about the art. A steep hill rose up from the jetty to the town, with galleries lining both sides crammed with paintings and a lesser number of other souvenirs. A lot of the paintings had a similar style with a bright palette of vivid rainbow colours in the background lighting up the subject – I read later that this was a local style called the '*Tz'utujil*' oil painting, which was celebrated here and in a handful of other nearby towns. It was quite striking, but when I saw a painting at a shop near the top of the hill with Lionel Messi at the centre, I knew the pieces on display perhaps weren't as authentic as they might have been. Around the town, away from the tourist hub, the passion for art continued with impressive wall paintings on some of the buildings, and regular use of stencilling to help depict whatever a particular shop sold, whether it be scissors and comb at the barbers or crayons at the art shop for example. And there were the Mayan ladies once again in their colourful dresses, this time carrying firewood and flour for the tortillas in the bowls balanced on their heads. The prescribed hour there passed all too quickly, but nevertheless, I was quite captivated by San Juan.

From San Juan, it was just a five-minute hop across to San Pedro. I was going to be coming back to San Pedro the next day as I was staying a night there with the intention of climbing Volcan San Pedro, so I knew I would have more time to explore here and therefore didn't feel the need to rush around town. This place reminded me a bit of my earlier stops in the Caribbean, as the familiar green, yellow and red colouring was everywhere, from the tuk-tuks' paint jobs to shop colours and statues around town and as in those previous places, these colours seemed to instil a vibrant, welcoming feel to the place. At the street market, the colours were complemented by rainbow-coloured umbrellas that lined the stalls of fruit and vegetables, which I had a good nose around before getting a bit lost and finding myself at the cemetery. This was a fascinating place, as it was filled with rows of concrete stacks which, rather than going down underground as I was used to, rose up, like a high-rise building of coffins interred in the cement blocks. While the blocks were a dull grey cinderblock, the ends of the tombs were painted in bright colours, and most of them included high definition photos of the person buried there, doing something they loved, like riding horses or just surrounded by their family. It was quite an arresting sight and seemed a much more joyous way of celebrating lives past than the more morbid cemeteries I was used to, back in the UK and Australia. I got a little bit more lost before recovering my bearings and getting back to the centre of town via a maze of random alleyways through the buildings. Shortly before I got back to the jetty, I stopped at a stall, which just comprised two elderly Mayan ladies, a basket of green oranges and a citrus press. I handed over my five quetzales (about 70 cents) and got the sweetest, most thirst-quenching freshly squeezed orange juice I can recall drinking – perfection.

The final stop on the tour was Santiago Atitlan, a much bigger town which I didn't really warm to, though that could also have been because I had probably had enough for the day. I wandered around, got lost (again), and after getting back on track, found a coffee shop to pass the time until the boat for home. One sight I noted down from the town was that I was quite taken by the ice cream men, who I had seen in each town so far, who travelled around, either on foot or riding a bicycle, carrying their box of ice cream and their cones, and ringing a hand-bell to alert the kids (and big kids) of their arrival. My first thought when I heard this was that it was their version of the ice cream van music from UK or Australia, and I thought it was great that ice cream the world over gets to have this unique calling card that everyone instantly recognises. My second, darker, thought was that I was reminded of the child catcher from *'Chitty, Chitty, Bang, Bang!'*:

'Lollipops! Lollipops!'

While reading in the afternoon, I learnt that Lago Atitlan goes through cyclical changes in its water levels, which no one seems to quite be able to explain. It's currently in a rising phase and has apparently risen five metres since 2009, which sounds extraordinary to me, but there you go – it means Panajachel currently no longer has the beach it used to have, and some pieces of infrastructure have disappeared into the waters below. Let's hope it starts going down again soon as the place is far too pretty to be swallowed up by the lake! The more worrying information from my reading was some recent TripAdvisor write-ups of the climb of Volcan San Pedro, which my Airbnb host had told me I could do without a guide without any problem. These reviews painted quite a different picture, referencing two armed robberies on the trail, one with a machete and one with a machine gun – a machine gun! This was disappointing news as that was my sole reason for staying there, but I wasn't going to do a walk that could end that way, and I had already done a sensational volcano climb, so I didn't feel too bad about missing out – I could just find some other productive activity, like drinking, to do instead.

***

My mate, the rooster, was on even more absurd form the next morning, this time starting at 2:30 am, so I didn't get the best sleep ahead of my boat ride to San Pedro. Having seen the hills there the day before, I had decided I would get a tuk-tuk to my accommodation, but when I arrived at the jetty, a man asked where I was going and said I should walk there, before rushing off to get a map for me to help (which of course also advertised all of his tours). This map was quite hard to follow, and I got lost. This time I was less amused by my incompetence as it was about 30 degrees and I was lugging all my stuff. Once I got to the right place, I realised he was right to have recommended walking, as the correct route included none of the crazy hills I had just been up and down. My host wasn't ready for me, so I dumped my bags and headed to the dock to get a boat to San Marcos, the one remaining town on the shores of the lake that I wanted to visit. San Marcos was a 'hippy' town, and it did appear to live up to this billing, with places advertising yoga, massage, wellness, spiritual learning and vegan facemasks (I made up one of these...) I walked straight past all of that as I needed to satisfy my current addiction for walking up hills, and I could see there was a cracker up to the old village. I powered up that and carried on into the undergrowth to a place called the *'Yoga Forest'*, which was some kind of residential 'immersive' experience. I knew I wouldn't be able to go in there without ending up with a henna tattoo, braided hair, or both, so I got my breath back and headed back down for a better look around the tourist bit. Before deciding I couldn't be bothered with that, and instead heading back to the dock to get the boat back – I was ready for a sit-down.

Arriving back I found the place I was staying was one of those places that looked nothing like the advertised picture, comprising seven rooms in line with windows onto a central corridor, and no window on the external wall – it felt bizarrely like a prison cell, particularly given the bunk bed in the room. I wasn't impressed. It wasn't until the next day that I discovered there was a really pleasant roof terrace that ran the length of the complex, one floor up, which is where I could have been sitting, and not down here in lockdown. It didn't take long for me to decide to go out and find alcohol, and on my way out, I saw a lovely Dalmatian sitting on the floor near the gate. I bent down to say hello, and it leapt up at me and almost bit my hand – the place wasn't growing on me. I went for a walk around the area and for the first time in a while I managed to locate my intended destination (not at the first attempt though…), a hotel with a beautiful roof terrace overlooking the lake and volcanoes, which Maria had recommended as the best spot on the island.

As I sat enjoying my evening beers in front of this epic view, it started to dawn on me that there was a bit of a flaw in my romance plan for the trip. I wasn't staying in any one place for more than four or five days at the most, which meant that unless I managed to talk someone into joining my further travels (and they were free to do so), I was going to be spending no more than a few days with them before moving on, not to be seen again for another few months at best or, more likely, never. I have never really been a 'fly-in, fly-out' kind of guy, as I am more interested in the lengthy conversations, email or text exchanges where you can really get a sense for what a person is about – find out what makes them happy, what makes them sad, what weird habits they are brave enough to admit, and work out if the person behind all of that is someone who I think I might be able to really connect with. In truth, it's probably the exact opposite of the more superficial approach which was probably better suited to my travel plan, sure, connecting at some level, but not really getting into the details to the extent that you realise you are already a little bit emotionally reliant on someone.

And that was where I found myself – I had only met Maria once, and we had spent little more than twelve hours together, but through all of the messaging, both in the build-up to meeting and the days that had followed, I already felt that the bond we had formed was one I wanted to last beyond the end of the week. I wasn't so naive as to not remind myself that a common-sense check was needed at this point – the first new person to show an interest in me for a long time was always going to seem very exciting, given they were responsible for unearthing powerful emotions not felt for a while, whoever they were. So I paused for thought but decided I was satisfied with my gut feeling that I had a genuine connection here. This might all sound a bit serious in comparison to the light-hearted journey we have been on until this point, but I wanted my story to be about the whole experience and right now I found myself confronting the reality that I had moved from 'happy place' to 'uneasy place'. As I pondered these thoughts, watching the fluttering of children's kites in the beautiful light of the evening skyline, a party boat came sailing past blaring out 'Barbie Girl' to rather ruin the moment, and I concluded it was a sign it was time to move on.

I found a Mexican place around the corner from my prison for dinner and enjoyed a few more beers and an enormous plate of fajitas while listening to an eclectic soundtrack, which included *'Zombie'* by the Cranberries and then *'Hotel California'* by the Eagles. There is a town in Baja California, Mexico, called Todos Santos, where I had been on a previous holiday, and there is a pub there called the Hotel California, which I remember at the time was making some loose claim to be the inspiration for the song, presumably to help sell their branded merchandise. I was reminded of this place now and Googled it to see how they were going – it seems The Eagles didn't appreciate their name association shenanigans and had been involved in a long-running court case with them on the matter, though the most recent update said the case had been settled and they were allowed to keep trading under the name. I enjoyed the rendition here, as each chorus was followed by a Spanish-accented echo of 'such a lovely place!' from the small group of local gents at the bar.

***

After returning to Panajachel the next day and having let things pass for a day or so on the dating front, I decided it was probably time (it was now Wednesday lunchtime) to be brave and ask if we were still going to be meeting up on a Thursday, to which I got the reply,

"Hola Guapo. I do not know yet because I have many things to do."

Which sounded a lot like a no. My theories on this were, a) that she did indeed have many things to do, b) she didn't want to see me again, or c) she did want to see me again but didn't think it was a good idea given my impending departure. For the sake of my ego, I decided it was probably c) and then tried to get back to writing my book to save stewing on it. I wrote back to her to say I didn't want to leave without seeing her again, however much or little time together that might mean, and left it there. And went back to stewing on it.

I soon got my answer though as she messaged me on the drive back to Antigua, and apparently, it was answer a) 'many things to do', and she was still keen to meet up – but tomorrow was looking unlikely. In any case, good news, I thought. That said, this is the point in the trip where I (briefly) started to lose control of things. I was due to fly to Flores, in the east of the country, on Friday evening, so with the news that the Thursday date wasn't going to happen, that didn't leave much time to do anything on Friday, so I messaged Maria to say that if she could tell me she would definitely be free on Friday or Saturday, I would change my plans. Apparently, Saturday worked, and by coincidence, it was Ramon's (him again) birthday, and he was having a big party at his house (yes, that house again), which she would take me to. That sounded like a fun plan, so I went ahead and moved the Flores trip back two days, also cancelling the first two days of my stay in Tulum, Mexico. I say I lost control of things because I also now had some extra days in a place where I had already achieved what I wanted to and found myself passing the time by writing (fine) and going for random walks to non-tourist parts of town (not so fine). One of these random walks took me to a small town right next to Antigua called Jocotenango, where there was a spa that Chino, from my volcano hike, had recommended for a massage without paying Antigua prices. So that's where I went.

On arrival, I established it was a 'no hablar Ingles' place, but I managed to book in for a one-hour massage, with the lady asking me to wait for fifteen minutes. At the appointed time, a guy walked through the front door with a pushbike and said something to me that I deciphered as meaning that he was there to give me a massage. Interesting. I have got quite into massages (mainly post sport) in recent years but hadn't had one from a man before, so this was uncharted territory for me. He asked me to follow him and led me past smart-looking massage rooms and opened the door to what looked like a men's changing room. The walls of the room were made of sky blue and white tiles up to a couple of metres in height with red brick above, and the room had cubicles and showers on the far wall – it wasn't like a changing room, it 'WAS' a changing room. I then looked at the other wall and saw there were three massage tables in a row in the middle of the room, and the two outside ones had middle-aged, reasonably overweight gents sat on the edge of them in their pants. Are you with me? Anyway, the masseuse showed me where the lockers were, I stripped down to my boxers and then had to lie on my back on the middle one, with none of the usual towels to cover your malarkey, while the guy got the oil out and got cracking. With the other gents just seated there having a good old gossip across me throughout the whole massage! I tried to keep my eyes shut and think of other things, but lying prone on the table with an unknown conversation going on around me and a stranger rubbing what smelt like marzipan oil all over my body was not the most relaxing experience. When he got to my head, he kept forcing my eyes open with the massage motion and actually I was super relieved when it was finally time to turn over. I couldn't tell you what kind of massage it was – maybe Swedish – but it included some of that weird karate chop percussion stuff. Whatever it was, it was an experience that's for sure.

The following day I was back on the dating trail as Maria was free to come to Antigua for the evening, so I met her for drinks at, you guessed it, El Barrio, and met some of her friends, including a girl called Monique and a very sharply dressed man called Marcus ('Marrrcuuuuuse') who was the mayor of Jocotenango of all places, so I complimented him on his town's massage facilities. It was soon 1 am kick out time and, given we were meeting the next day again for the party, I didn't feel compelled to go on another late-night magical mystery tour and left Maria to drive back home with her friend – to wherever it was they lived.

And so, to the party the next day which, without wanting to jump ahead, was a bit of a disaster. We had swapped some messages in the morning, the details of which I won't dwell on, but the general gist of my side of the exchange was that I would be leaving the next day to continue with my travel, which I had said was going to be the case all along, but I could sense this hadn't gone down very well. I hadn't booked anywhere to stay for the evening yet, but we had loosely agreed I would get a hotel near her house, or near the party. So I packed my things, taking an Uber to another random petrol station in between Antigua and the town where the party was, where she picked me up and took me to Ramon's house. Maria had previously said there would be more than a hundred people there which had allayed my concerns about speaking any Spanish, as I figured I would be able to blend into a crowd that size, but when we arrived, there were literally twelve people there. I got a drink and sat at the table and smiled politely as two or three Spanish conversations took place around me, none of which I could understand. Maria was chatting away to a friend and leaving me to it, so I could tell she had the shits with me, but I sat there, with all my bags in her car outside, in the realisation that I was really rather stuck. I played with the St Bernard a bit, which by this stage I had already seen eat five tortillas, but the lack of conversation was a bit hard going. As the evening moved on, a few more people arrived, and I managed to find a few guests who had some English who I quickly latched on to, and five or six drinks later, it was just about bearable again.

Then the tequila came out, and things started to go downhill. Ramon, who was even drunker than the last time I had seen him and who had a reputation for getting out of control, was well on his way but was celebrating the fact that at least he didn't have to worry about getting home. I was reminded of a party I had been at once where I had found myself in a state of some merriness, spinning around on a barstool at the kitchen bench at about two in the morning, declaring that I was having such an awesome time but that I had no idea how I was going to get home – when someone reminded me the party was actually in my own home. Proud moment. Anyway, after the tequila shots, it started raining and the remaining guests crammed into the living room where music videos were blaring from a giant TV, and everyone was dancing to what I think is called 'Reggaeton' music – it was a new one for me, but I will dance to anything when inebriated, so I was getting into it anyway. This went on till it was quite late, and there were only about ten people left when there was an almighty crash – Ramon had fallen through a plate glass window into an internal courtyard and was bleeding from various parts of his anatomy, though they luckily all looked like minor cuts. What was more worrying was his mother (her again), who had arrived on the scene and was going absolutely 'troppo' – clearly it was time to leave.

After a terrifying car journey home which I won't dwell on but which thankfully ended without incident, I found myself staying in another random spare room, with another fake cover story of why I was there – this not being able to behave like a grown-up was now getting tiresome! I was by now also slightly regretting my answer to the 'bag question' the week before as my window of opportunity had clearly now passed – an outcome which I had predicted as inevitable from the moment I had gone out to buy condoms. This state of affairs got worse in the morning when the father of the girl whose house I was at was apparently about to arrive and would not be tolerant of finding a stranger in the house. So I literally got the bags on the street treatment!

And that was where you found me back at the very start of my story, seated on the pavement in a gated residential community somewhere in Guatemala City, tying my shoelaces and adjusting my hastily thrown on outfit. After the less than sympathetic encouragement from Maria to quickly leave the area, I found my way out onto the main road and, once again, waiting at a petrol station to catch yet another Uber after a chaotic final date and decisive end to the relationship. It was all a bit of a shame really, as Maria was quite lovely and we got on really well, but it was a bit of a wakeup call for me that I probably shouldn't be wandering in and disrupting people's lives while I was on a bit of a jolly – not unless they properly accepted upfront the limitations of the potential relationship.

***

Next stop Flores – the gateway to the majority of the best Mayan ruin sites in Guatemala, including the most famous, Tikal. My plan was to see Tikal one day, probably some other ruins the next day, and arrange a transfer for the following day that would take me out of Guatemala and through Belize to my next destination, Tulum in Mexico. To organise all of this I needed a travel agent and as I stepped off the coach at 6 am, bleary-eyed, there was an enterprising salesman (of course there was) waiting to help me with all of the above. I knew from my research that the prices he was quoting were higher than what I could probably negotiate elsewhere, but he was right in front of me, and I was tired and not too fussed about the $20 or so extra he was taking me for. So I booked in for a 10 am trip to Tikal that day and organised the Mexico transfer, leaving just the middle day to sort out at a later point.

He also gave me a free lift to my hotel, so that won him further points. When I said where I was staying, he asked me to clarify the exact name twice and then on the way there said, "Did you book online?" in a tone of voice that immediately told me I had booked into a shithole. And so I had. It was about one kilometre away from the pretty, lake encircled, town of Flores, on the main road, and looked quite run down. You will recall I had cancelled a booking in Flores and then had to replace it with this – well the first place was in Flores and looked nice – this was neither. The guy on the front desk had zero English, and I struggled through asking if I could drop off my bags and have somewhere to get changed, given check-in was not until lunchtime. He finally seemed to understand what I was looking to achieve and put my bag in a room near reception, but still stood there looking at me; I told him to give me five minutes, quickly got changed and then came back out to ask where to leave my bag. It was only then I realised this was my room, and he was giving it to me already – I meekly went back into the room, got undressed again and had a cold shower, before heading into town to join my tour.

I was now back into full backpacker disguise mode, on a bus tour of about 20 youngsters. On the road to Tikal, I saw what I thought was a novel sight of a pig running across a football pitch at full pelt, but as we passed through small villages, there were pigs and piglets everywhere, faithful friends and future meals I would assume. After half an hour we passed through the village of El Remate, which sat directly on the main lake of the area, Lago Peten Itza. With the blue skies overhead today, this place was straight out of a postcard, with wooden jetties running out into the lake and disappearing into the azure blue waters, some of them with decked platforms at the end, sheltered by thatched roofs where people sat and revelled in the view.

Arriving at Tikal, we began the walk through the trees, and already there was plenty of wildlife to see, with literally thousands of army ants going about their business on the ground while spider monkeys passed by overhead, and after about ten minutes we got out first look at the amazing temples that the park is famous for. Some of the monuments on the site date back to 400BC, but the main period of occupation was between 200 and 900AD when it is estimated the population was as high as 90,000 people, spread across the vast area of buildings, with a survey of the city estimating there were as many as 3,000 structures. It's one of those places where you look at the scale of the structures, in what seems to be the middle of nowhere and marvel at how it could have been possible for them to be constructed. In truth, it didn't seem possible to me, and I suspected alien involvement, but I couldn't find anything on Wikipedia to support my theory.

The nanny state has not yet arrived in Guatemala so you could climb up the majority of the temples to reach a number of amazing vistas of other temples and, on the taller ones, views that extended over the top of the tree canopy and out to the horizon, broken only by the taller greystone structures poking out the trees and reaching up to the skies. The soundtrack for today's adventure was provided by the many howler monkeys that live in the area, and it was mating season, so they were even more boisterous than usual, filling the air with a cacophony of their cries. These cries were apparently used by the makers of Jurassic Park as one of the main components of the T-Rex roar, which gives you some feel for the power of these monkeys' lungs. One more popular culture reference for you at this point – if you saw a picture of the place, you might well recognise Tower IV, one of the larger structures, from *'Star Wars Episode IV'*, in which Tikal doubled as Yavin 4, site of the hidden military base of the Rebel Alliance. Definitely, some alien business going down here. Timing is everything, and walking down from the tower, I somehow managed to take a photo of a monkey that could actually be clearly identified as a monkey – as it leapt from one tree to another, with the treetops and a tower in the background – my work for the day was done!

While walking around the remainder of the site, I learned from one of the information boards that 'the monkeys like to defecate on the heads of people below to show their presence' – who doesn't like to do that every once in a while? The complex of ruins was spread over a large area and, as I walked around, I saw a few temples in the further reaches with no one else around, which made a refreshing change from some of the places I had visited earlier in the trip. I also read that they estimate only ten per cent of the buildings at Tikal have been uncovered – and this is just one site of many in the El Peten area, so there just isn't the money or manpower to be able to do it all. At this site, and another one the following day, I walked past mounds of earth of all shapes and sizes which were covered by vegetation, but which the archaeologists had determined to hide all manner of buildings beneath, from when the site was abandoned at the end of the 10th century – it's quite mind-boggling to contemplate. This is another place that I can't do justice with words, but Google Images will help you picture it, and then you just need to put on Jurassic Park in the background, and you are there. Kind of.

After I posted my photos for the day, I got a message from my friend Jane, asking me to bring her home a spider monkey, which was sounding challenging as my bag was looking quite full given I think I was already on a promise to pack a sloth for Emily. After a bit of chat about how I was getting on, we established that I was going to be in Japan later in my trip at the same time as Jane and this provided a solution to a logistical issue I had yet to overcome. My travel in Japan was to be mainly conducted on the bullet trains, and Japan Rail offered a great value travel pass for this, with the only issue being you had to have it delivered to an overseas address before you arrived in the country. I had contacted a couple of my future Airbnb hosts to ask if I could have it mailed to them, and both had declined, saying they didn't like getting random mail as if I was going to send myself bomb-making equipment, or anthrax or something. Anyway, I agreed with Jane that I would get it mailed to her instead and she could bring it with her to Tokyo – result. Her only request for this arrangement was as follows:

'Please don't send anthrax in the same envelope as the spider monkey – I don't want to open the parcel to a deceased monkey – it would really ruin my day…'

And so Jane joined a growing list of my friends who were unwittingly qualifying as a character in my book, on the basis they had said something funny enough to merit inclusion.

Returning to my hotel I decided this was the sort of place where people would bring their Tinder dates to murder them, and I unwittingly contributed to this mental image by accidentally leaving some bloodstains on the towel from some mosquito inflicted damage. Despite the grim surrounds, I managed to have a surprisingly good night's sleep and was back on the road in the morning to another nearby ruins site. This one was called Yaxha (awesome Scrabble word), and the tour had a scheduled run time from 12 pm to 8 pm, which would allow us to watch the sunset from one of the towers. The route was similar to the previous day, but the weather was not so glorious, and El Remate looked absolutely miserable as we passed through this time, before forking off on a different road. I had read in the Lonely Planet that the final eleven kilometres to the site were on an unpaved road, but I think they had been a bit remiss in not also disclosing this was eleven kilometres of the worst unpaved road you could imagine, and this road/track was completely unsuited to our barely roadworthy minivan. After about one kilometre of being thrown around in the back, the driver managed to break the catch to the boot, with a giant water bottle, some boxes and people's bags getting expelled out the back of the vehicle and onto the road. He quickly recovered the situation by pulling out a length of rope and securing the door with a taut line tied around a hook on the floor by our feet, a manoeuvre that seemed way too slick for it to have been the first time he had been required to do it.

After 25 minutes of the bumpy ride, which resulted in a few green looking passengers, we arrived at another vast site where an even lower percentage of the buildings had been uncovered than at Tikal. The focus of the main buildings here was for 'astronomical observation', which I thought would probably be more accurately described as 'alien communication', and one of the main features of this site was that many of the buildings looked down over a beautiful lake below, further adding to the mystique of the place. Walking between these buildings, our guide Saul found some spider holes, and we watched in amazement as he used a small twig to lure a tarantula out into the open, which he then picked up and offered around for photos. After letting two other people go first, I decided this looked safe enough and took my turn to hold it while Saul took some photos, which I was already chuckling about posting on Instagram when I got home later. There were lots of howler monkeys here too, and we also got a fleeting glimpse of a toucan (or 'flying banana' apparently) flying through the trees in front of us. The remoteness of this site meant there was just a handful of groups there, though this did include a large group of Dutch male youths who I had also seen in Antigua, Lago Atitlan and nowhere. They were easy to spot as most of them wore short pastel colour shorts and partially buttoned-up, light fabric shirts and looked like they were on a Grand Tour of Europe – think Jude Law as Dickie Greenleaf in *'The Talented Mr Ripley'*. I mentioned to a young English lady in my group that I kept seeing them, and she explained they were 'a Dutch sorority on an exchange program with a Guatemalan sorority' – I didn't correct her – I knew what she meant.

After climbing several, really quite steep, temples (with no safety protections) the tour culminated at the top of the highest temple, watching the fading light over the buildings below and the lake that stretched out into the distance. There was more unexpected entertainment for me here as I sat down next to an American family of birdwatchers (apparently a thing) who were up there with a local guide, armed with binoculars and listening intently for bird noises. Each time there was a bird call, the dad, let's call him Brad, would turn to the guide and excitedly tell him what kind of bird it was – except he got them all wrong. This sequence of events repeated a few times and was then replaced by a new approach, whereby the guide jumped in first with the correct name, which Brad then immediately repeated and nodded knowingly as if he was just about to say that. Love your work, Brad.

The following day it was time to bid a fond farewell to Guatemala. Right from the start, I had been wowed by the magnificence of the natural beauty of the place, and it had ended up being quite an adventure, what with the volcano climbing, epic lake scenes and romantic escapades, and I was genuinely a bit sad to be moving on. That said, it was comfortably my favourite country of the trip so far, and I was certain I would return – hopefully before I did so, my Spanish would indeed have improved…

Summary – Guatemala

Kilometres travelled (air) – 850 (Inc. San Jose to GCY)
Kilometres travelled (land) – 1,100
Number of volcanoes conquered – One
Number of self-guided walks I got lost on – All of them
Number of Uber petrol station visits – Three
Number of days of amazement – Twelve (of twelve)

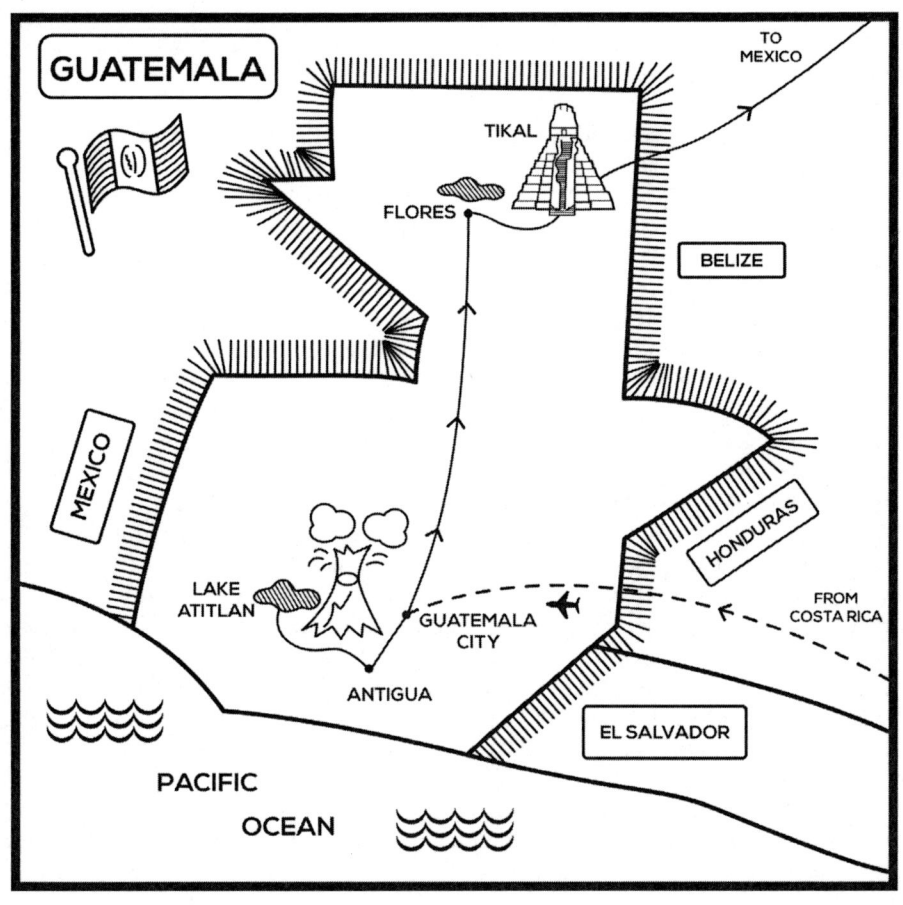

Mexico
Mayan Monuments and Taco Trauma

My first stop in Mexico was Tulum, where I finally ended up at my lodgings, Saul and Giselle's house, thirteen hours after I had started the journey in Flores that morning. The house was in the middle of an estate of houses which all seemed to be in a state of mid-construction and Saul's one was no exception, with my room (and bathroom) being the only completed room on the partially built second floor – which was perfect as it was completely private for me. Suffice to say that after a fairly epic day of travel, I slept rather well that night.

Tulum was spread over a fairly large area, with the 'town centre' area, where the bus station and most of the shops and restaurants were, and where I was staying, a few kilometres from both the ruins and the beaches. The place was almost completely flat though, meaning those distances could be quickly eaten up by pedal power, which was my plan for the morning as I set off on my free loan bicycle from the house. I decided I would head for the ruins first of all to get my usual head start on the crowds, but the morning's lie-in (relatively speaking) meant there were already quite a few people there when I arrived. The Tulum ruins are unique in that they are the only Mayan ruins which are located right on the coast, with the grand buildings, which are still in good shape, sitting atop small cliffs overlooking the beaches below. As you can imagine, this scene is highly photogenic and its proximity to a strip of beautiful white sand beaches and associated resorts makes it quite a draw for the tour groups. That said, at that time in the morning it didn't feel too crowded, and I was able to have a good look around the whole of the site in an hour or so, escaping before the morning sun got any more punishing. I had read that the beaches in the ruins complex were quite spectacular, so was surprised when I walked down the steps to the main beach to find only a few people, and not much evidence of a beach – the reason for this would become apparent later in the morning.

By now I was getting quite hungry (following the previous day's meal count of nil) so I got back on the bike and continued on a couple of kilometres to the first of the strip of beaches just south of the ruins, Playa Santa Fe. The sand was beautifully fine and deep and felt wonderful underfoot on the short walk to a place that seemed a fine candidate for breakfast, with a handful of small plastic tables and chairs shaded by Corona umbrellas right on the sand. I was the only customer, and I tucked into my scrambled eggs, rice, beans and tortillas with considerable glee in view of the sight before me, boats bobbing just offshore, my feet buried ankle-deep in the sand, and the fact I was finally having a meal. The tortillas here were really thin, and it was only now that I registered how different the ones in Guatemala had been, big thick ones that you pulled pieces off like you might eat a naan bread at an Indian restaurant, not suited to making your own 'wraps' as I did now with these Mexican ones. This was actually as good as this scene got, as after I had finished eating and gone for a walk on the beach, it became apparent that all was not well in paradise.

As I approached the sea, I could see it was separated from the sand by a thick, wide deposit of seaweed that ran as far as the eye could see – and the stench was almost eye-watering. My plan had been to walk the length of the beaches before retracing my steps to my bike and, never one to abandon a plan lightly, I set off on my walk anyway, taking care not to breathe through my nose. A few boat trips were going out with snorkelers and divers, but there was literally no one swimming in the sea and the sun loungers that lined the beaches all lay empty – it was a bit of a sad sight, to be honest. The only people on the beach were the small gangs of labourers standing out in the stinking piles of seaweed with pitchforks, throwing it back to a tractor, which was taking away truckloads of the stuff, without appearing to make any real dent in improving the scene. The offending item was 'sargassum seaweed', which had been an increasing issue in the area over recent years, but from my reading of online forums, it seemed that 2018 was the worst year yet, with the seaweed having been a permanent fixture along the whole length of the Playa Riviera since February, ruining many a 'dream vacation' here. I found a news article that referenced an amount of four million cubic feet of the stuff having been removed from Quintana Roo beaches between June and August, which sounds like an extraordinary amount, and the article also noted that they were experimenting with offshore barriers to try and prevent future build-ups. Many of the theories on the causes of the problem were blaming global warming – if that is the case, then the issue is likely not going away, so hopefully, they find a solution to stop losing holidaymakers to other beach destinations in future years.

I just about completed my intended walk but I certainly wasn't going to linger long with that smell and took myself back home for a break before lunch, and one of the fifteen showers per day that appeared to be required to survive in this climate. I was back into the pages of the Lonely Planet for a lunch recommendation, and this sent me off to the other end of town, this time on foot, to a favoured seafood restaurant called 'Las Aguachiles'. I was soon regretting leaving the bike behind, as I hadn't paid attention to the scale of the map, and a two-kilometre walk in the sun at 1 pm was right in 'Mad Dogs And Englishmen' territory, and I was absolutely wiped out by the time I got there. Fortunately, it was completely worth the walk, as I put away some awesome shrimp tacos and an absolutely giant plate of ceviche – it's a mystery to me why we don't eat more ceviche at home, as it's such a simple meal, full of fresh flavours and tonnes of fish, which we are all told we don't eat enough of. Superb. Even better than the fish was the drink – the waiter had a bit of a glint in his eye as I ordered and managed to sell me something called a 'mezcal pepino' to go with my Corona. That translates roughly as 'cucumber flavoured local grog', and it was served in a glass with a rim of some kind of chilli and salt combination – it was beyond amazing, and half an hour later, after two of those and two Coronas, I was feeling distinctly wobbly for the walk back across town.

I noticed I saw a lot of old VW Beetles around the place and my thoughts turned immediately, of course, to Herbie, and more specifically the fourth instalment, *'Herbie Goes Bananas'*, which my distant childhood memories told me was set in México. After consulting the third-best Internet resource, IMDB, I confirmed my hunch was correct and was reminded of the harrowing scene where Herbie ends up getting dumped off the side of a ship off the coast of Mexico – before later emerging from the sea to live another day and continue his 'madcap' antics. I was disappointed to read that this Lazarus like revival had actually been a fraud, and that the car they had dumped in the ocean for that scene had actually just been left to sink and never recovered – they killed Herbie! IMDB also reminded me that this film was actually quite shit, so I didn't feel the need to watch it again for further research for the book – for the record, Herbie Goes to Monte Carlo will always be my favourite instalment – you just can't beat a car romance storyline…

After sobering up a bit, it was back home for another three showers, and a bit of travel admin, including trying to decipher my recent online banking transactions, of which there was a multitude from the storm of bookings I had made a few weeks prior. I was somewhat mystified by a charge on there of about $1,200 from Jetstar, given I had not booked any flights with them, so my thoughts turned quickly to card cloning and online fraud. I spoke to my bank, NAB, to ask them to look into the transaction, and the man suggested I deactivate online transactions on that particular card but leave it available for me to use as a physical card, which sounded sensible, and which I did. Secondly, I messaged Jetstar on one of those online chat things, who also said they would look into it, but only once I could provide a credit card statement proving the charge, which I wouldn't get for about another three weeks' time. I never understand in those situations why they can't just look at their 'cash in' breakdown to see (immediately) that they have my money, rather than the burden of proof falling on me, but I couldn't be bothered to argue further, so left them to work it out.

My boozy lunch had exhausted my cash reserves, so first stop for the evening's outing was the ATM where, as you have probably guessed, my card no longer worked – thanks NAB guy. Luckily, I had one other card with me, so after finding some Wi-Fi to go online and transfer money between accounts, I was able to use this card to restock my beer money. Mojito money might be a more apt description, as my destination for the evening was a 'Mojito and Guarapo Bar' called 'Batey's', which Saul had included in a very comprehensive list of recommendations he had sent me earlier in the day – legend. This place had live jazz playing when I arrived and had a great vibe, so I got myself a spot near the bar and settled in. Saul had mentioned they were all about the freshness of the ingredients here, and this was fantastically illustrated by the way they produced the sugar syrup that the cocktail aficionados amongst you will know is a crucial ingredient in a decent mojito. In the middle of the bar, they had a converted VW Beetle (him again) which had a wooden bench across the back half of the car, with a giant hand-operated mechanical press on it, which one of the barmen was feeding whole sugar canes through and collecting the juice in a tray at the back of the car. I mean, seriously, does it get any cooler than that? They were making a number of different flavoured mojitos with this syrup, and I had one with ginger, prickly pear and some other morsels of genius – it was delicious.

My drinks and dinner later were punctuated every ten minutes or so by the arrival of the now regular sight of street vendors wandering the streets, restaurants and bars with the tray of goodies they had strapped to their person, a walking shop front. Picture the lady with the sweets and ice creams in the interval at the cinema or theatre (older readers maybe…), but instead with a tray of sweets, crisps, drinks, biscuits and cigarettes. Lots of cigarettes. I haven't mentioned this yet, but everywhere I went in Central America, everyone seemed to smoke, quite a contrast to the amount you see it these days in Australia and the UK. I haven't had a cigarette in about fifteen years, but I have to confess while I was in Guatemala, I was the proverbial bee's dick from having one, as everyone else chain-smoked around me. The higher take-up of the pursuit over here probably had a fair amount to do with the fact they cost $3 a pack (versus $40, I think, in Australia) and they didn't have graphic photos of cigarette induced disease on them – they have that (the photos, and the disease) to look forward to I suspect.

***

The following morning, I was off out on the bike again to go and visit my first Cenote. Cenotes are limestone formations that are found all over the peninsula, which are basically large holes in the ground in the form of beautiful natural swimming holes, often adorned with stalactite formations and caves. Given the oppressive heat of the place, these cenotes provided a great place to take a cooling dip. I was heading to Gran Cenote, about four kilometres outside of Tulum, and one of the most famous in the area, and I had timed my arrival to make sure I was first through the door when it opened, with just a handful of other couples and a small Japanese tour group in attendance. I got down to the swimming area, put my stuff in a locker and was in the Cenote for a good ten minutes on my own while the rest of them faffed around. I say I was on my own, but I am just referring to humans here, as the pool was full of small fish and a large group of turtles, who looked a little bit perturbed by the arrival of a wild-man to break the peace of their morning swim. Swimming past this open area, where the morning sunlight was shining down and reflecting off the waters to create some stunning aquamarine colours against the bright yellow of the rock walls, I entered a cave area where, overhead, literally hundreds of small bats were hanging from the ceiling.

As I swam through the cave to another area which was open to the skies above, the bats started to fly around not far above my head, which was a little bit unnerving, as all I could think about was the fact I had left my pre-trip vaccinations too late to include rabies shots. I was sure a major tourist attraction was not going to be serving up rabies to unsuspecting swimmers, but nonetheless, I set a course for a spot back out in the sunshine away from this potential flying cloud of disease, where I floated around and enjoyed the warming morning rays. Over to my left, the serenity of the scene had been broken by the Japanese group finally getting in the water, a human flotilla of orange life preservation vests, filling one of the caves with their excited babbling. By now lots more people had also started to arrive, and I had swum around all of the available areas, so I got out and retrieved my stuff, pausing briefly to get someone to take some photos of me which I knew would stimulate some discussion on Facebook later as my beard, which had been left to do its thing for two months now, was really starting to look quite wild.

I spent the morning doing some laundry, and the machine did that thing where it says it will take one hour and fifteen minutes but then actually takes over two hours. What is the point of those timers? Back in my regular life, while waiting impatiently to go out, I have watched my machine at home take eight minutes to complete its final 'minute' – surely someone at the manufacturer has done that on purpose just for their own entertainment? When the machine was finally done, and I had hung my laundry up on the baking hot roof terrace, I was back into town for lunch, visiting 'the best taco place in town', *'Taqueria Don Honorio'*, where I had four tacos with 'cochinita pibil', or marinated pork, and some seriously frigging hot sauce. They were delicious, and the total cost, including my drink, was $5; amazing. I spent the afternoon writing, and also working through the array of comic reactions to my 'clickbait' swimwear photos from earlier in the day. On two of the photos people had posted a photo of Tom Hanks in *'Castaway'*, and I had received two other 'Where's Wilson' comments on WhatsApp, so that seemed the most popular likeness comparison, though I also got 'a bit of Conor McGregor' and Bear Grylls, all of which I quite enjoyed – and it was warming to know I was bringing a bit of humour to my various Facebook and Instagram friends across the globe.

The beard had made its first public appearance in Bali earlier in the year, a visit I have referenced a couple of times already in my ramblings, and which I think merits some further coverage now. The occasion for my visit, which directly preceded my Nepal hike with Intrepid, was the 40th birthday of Cyrus, one of my oldest friends from my school days. Cyrus was one of thirteen in my year group in my house at school and, since school, had always prioritised the finer things in life, in his case surfing, ladies and partying, usually in that order. When we were at school, his family lived in Indonesia, and he always had an affinity with South East Asia, and pretty much since university he had lived and worked in Hong Kong, also owning a villa in Bali where he tried to spend as much time as possible. Cyrus is one of those people who makes new friends very easily and is also very good at maintaining those networks. It was those two factors (I think) which meant when he announced he would be having a 40th birthday party in Bali, he managed to get more than 150 people from all corners of the globe to say they would come and stay – for what ended up being a five-day-long party, based out of a beautiful beachside villa he had rented. Cyrus was, like me, also currently having something of a midlife 'hiatus', having recently finished up with the hedge fund he had worked with for many years and doing not a lot currently, other than surfing and looking after his recently adopted stray dogs that he had found near his villa in Bali. Cyrus's wide travels with both work and play meant the invitees included a wide range of people, many of whom had not met each other before, but with a core group of his network of friends who currently, or had previously, lived in Hong Kong.

The day before the main party, some of that core group had been amusing others with a video that had gone viral recently in Hong Kong. The video showed a gentleman walking through central HK in the middle of the day, right outside the lobby of the International Finance Centre (IFC) complex, completely butt naked but striding purposefully in a slightly odd bolt upright fashion amongst the businessmen milling around the city in their suits and ties, as if he knew exactly where he was going, but clearly under the influence of something or other. This video was hilarious, and was doing the rounds amongst the other party guests and was being explained to late arrival to the party, an American guy called Brian who Cyrus had met on a surfing holiday, who had a reaction to it that surprised everyone:

"Err, that's me!"

And sure enough, Brian was random naked guy! He had indeed been at a party, had taken some regrettable cocktail of mind-altering substances, and not remembered much else until he came around at the police station. The police had been surprisingly calm about it apparently, retracing his steps to find his neatly folded pile of clothes and shoes around the corner from IFC, which they reunited him with, before giving him a warning and sending him on his way. He was in the process of locking in a new job in Hong Kong, so was understandably a bit concerned to hear the video was again doing the rounds on the internet (this was the third time apparently), but he was a lovely bloke and seemed to think the whole episode was basically hilarious – which it was.

Another point of note from the party was that one of the other guests was Josh Lewsey, who Cyrus had made friends with after meeting in Hong Kong, and who many readers will recognise as a member of England's Rugby World Cup-winning side of 2003. I had recognised him as the guy built like a brick shit house, who was lifting bikini-clad ladies on his shoulders in the pool and also doing push-ups on the side of the pool – with a bikini-clad lady lying on his back, while Cyrus shouted at regular intervals, 'For God's sake Lewsey, put a shirt on!' Josh was now a partner at a 'Big 4' accounting firm, and after talking him to him at length, appeared to be one of the biggest overachievers I have ever met. After graduating from Bristol University, while also playing professional rugby for Bristol, he found the time to graduate from the Royal Military Academy in Sandhurst and was commissioned as a troop commander into the Royal Artillery. He was in the army for another two years, while also playing rugby for London Wasps, before deciding that was maybe a bit much, concentrating on rugby and picking up the World Cup winners medal shortly after. He had also found the time to write two books and get a PhD and spoke with genuine passion about the work he did, which he described to me (and I heard him tell many others) as 'driving meaningful change in businesses'. This articulation of his work stood out for me, as I could feel this was exactly the kind of passion for one's work that I felt that I did not currently have. Oh, and he was also working towards a wine qualification and teaching himself how to play the guitar – seriously, how is it possible to have that much drive? Cyrus had told me that Josh had asked him what his three goals for the year were and Cyrus had just laughed – Cyrus really wasn't a development goals kind of person! In conversation with Josh, I mentioned I was going to Nepal shortly to walk the Annapurna Circuit, which I think he thought was maybe more adventurous than it actually was, because he then started telling me about the time he had climbed Mount Everest, and asked if I would be interested in going on an expedition with him to climb Mt Denali in Alaska, or Mt Vinson in Antarctica. Given Josh's expedition on Everest nearly cost him his life, and I had read a Jon Krakauer book on climbing mountains in Alaska where he almost met a similar fate, I knew these trips were just a bit above my ability level, and I politely declined. I can report, however, that I got to ride on the back of his scooter when the remaining group went out for dinner later that evening, so I think I will just put that accomplishment/life event on my Wikipedia instead.

Back in the present in Tulum, I was awoken in the middle of the night with a cramping sensation in my stomach that told me all was not going quite to plan with the digestion of my previously reported 'amazing tacos'. I gingerly walked to the bathroom, trying to decide what end the impending assault was going to arrive from, as the combination of cramps, nausea and sweating suggested it might be both at once. I guessed correctly initially and sat down but could feel we weren't done yet and it seemed to becoming the other way so I quickly swung around to get ready to wear the porcelain collar, only to find I had called it wrong and I now had an unwanted surprise on the bathroom floor. Thankfully it was a tiled floor and, after I had finished losing the rest of my guts, I was able to effect a swift clean-up operation and then crawl to lie in the foetal position under the cold shower for a while, until I had recovered from the loss of dignity and felt settled enough to go back to sleep.

***

I was still feeling quite delicate the next morning, which was a slight worry as I had a two-hour bus ride ahead of me at 12:30 pm, but with my facilities seemingly under control I got a cab to the bus station, only to find the bus was fully booked, as was the next one, so I wouldn't be leaving till 2:45 pm instead. Spirits further deflated, I found somewhere nearby for lunch and a two-hour hangout and picked gingerly at some food while drinking every available liquid I could get my hands on. Tulum felt like a slight failure on my part, having missed the first two days and then not getting to as many sights as I had planned, but I was finding the heat really quite draining and concluded I needed to be more realistic in my expectations for the remainder of the Mexico stops, which I took the time now to give a bit more thought to. I had chosen to stay a few days at my next stop, Valladolid, to make the trip to Chichen Itza more bearable, as I had read you needed to get there early to avoid the crazy crowds at what one of my Facebook friends referred to as 'the Mayan Disneyland'. Chichen Itza would be the second 'Wonder of the Modern World' of my trip, after Machu Picchu, and while we are on that topic, I might explain how they came to inherit such a title. You will probably be familiar with the 'Seven Wonders of the Ancient World' from school (and pub quizzes) but not from visiting them, given the Great Pyramid at Giza in Egypt is the only one of the seven that still exists today. Perhaps inspired by that modern-day lack of sights to visit, an enterprising Canadian gentleman started a campaign to choose a contemporary version of the list, which were to be called the *'New 7 Wonders of the World'*. The way the poll was run caused a fair bit of controversy, due to a lack of controls to prevent multiple repeat votes through the telephone system, but that's basically history now, as they whittled down a shortlist to the seven winners listed below, alongside honorary member, the Great Pyramid of Giza:

- Great Wall of China.
- Petra, Jordan.
- The Colosseum, Rome, Italy.
- Chichen Itzà, México.
- Machu Picchu, Peru.
- Taj Mahal, India; and
- Christ the Redeemer, Rio de Janeiro, Brazil.

Of this list, I had only seen the Colosseum previously, so this trip was providing a huge step forward for my percentage completion. Having seen Ricky Gervais's deadpan sidekick Karl Pilkington take a thoroughly miserable trip to the Taj Mahal on his hilarious show, *'An Idiot Abroad'* I feel I will probably manage to get by without needing to go there or complete the full set, but if you are a bucket list kind of person, there's some more food for thought for you.

After killing enough time reading for it to finally be bus time, I survived the two-hour journey to Valladolid without incident, and also successfully negotiated the ten-minute walk from the bus station to my Airbnb, this time hosted by a bubbly American lady called Sara and her local partner Mauricio. They lived at the back of the house, and there were two guest rooms and a bathroom in the front half, but no one else was staying so I had the run of the place to myself, which was lovely. My first impressions of the town were positive – it was a small, grid layout town centre, which still showed plenty of the Spanish colonial influence, and as with many of the places I had been of late, there was plenty of colour.

Arriving at Chichen Itza the next day I paid my entry and walked down the short avenue which leads straight to the most famous attraction, the towering main pyramid of El Castillo, which is the image you will probably have seen at some point. In my reading from the previous day, I had learnt that climbing of the pyramid had been prohibited since 2006, when an 80-year-old lady, Adeline Black from San Diego in the US, slipped and fell to her death from the 46th of the 91 steps, about 18 metres above the ground. So, unlike Guatemala, where you could pretty much clamber over everything, this site was more of a two-dimensional viewing experience. After having had a good look at the pyramid from all angles, I set off to take in as much of the site as I could before the hordes arrived, which included some more temple complexes, the largest 'ball game' court in Mexico, a large area of neatly organised columns and a couple of cenotes. In totality, it was undeniably an impressive sight, but I think I had already been a bit spoilt in Guatemala as I couldn't help feeling that I had been more wowed by Tikal, probably because of its more spectacular forest setting and elevated viewpoints. The other factor working against Chichen Itza was the small army of vendors who lined almost every path around the site with their stalls of local textiles, wood carvings, t-shirts, 'Day of the Dead' skulls and an array of other trinkets and ornaments. I was early enough that they weren't really ready to pester me, but I could see how this had probably contributed to the previously noted 'Disneyland' assessment of the place. After a couple of hours, I was satisfied I had covered the high points and made a run for it, escaping past the swarm of tour groups now arriving at the entrance. I have said at many points on the trip so far that it was hot out, but at just 10:30 am in the morning this was feeling like the warmest yet, and to illustrate the point, the print was melting off the front of my t-shirt in the heat. I was going to wait for a collectivo back, but I didn't want to wait around, so extravagantly got a taxi back for nearly ten times the cost of the collectivo ride – I justified this to myself (yes, I felt I needed to…) on the basis that the average cost for the two trips combined was still pretty cheap!

Sunday evening in Valladolid is dancing night, and ahead of these festivities, the main square was full of people sitting and chatting, being entertained by various street acts and buying food from the many stalls. These were serving a range of food including fresh corn, nachos, tamales, tacos, flavoured ice and churros, but the focus of my attention was the 'Marquesitas' stalls, which Sara had raved about and told me I must try. Marquesitas were thin waffle-like pancakes which the vendors cooked up from their batter mix on gas-fired waffle press, before adding various fillings, including cheese, fruit and chocolate spread, and rolling them up into a giant long cigar shape. Sara had told me the best flavour to have was the grated cheese (which, bizarrely was Edam, or 'queso de bola' as they called it) and Nutella, which just sounded wrong to me. Anyway, I hovered around three different stalls, but I just didn't have the courage to try one, in view of the parlous state of my innards – without spoiling the story, I would manage one at a later date, so watch this space for the verdict.

By now it was dancing time, and that was great fun – on the side of the square was a large cobbled area in front of a long three-storey historical building of some sort, and under the arches of the open ground floor, there was a twenty-piece band of old Mexican gents, with plastic chairs set out around the dance floor for people to watch. The band was really quite loud, with a dominant brass section and an extravagant conductor running the show, which was, I assume, 'Mexican big band and dance favourites'. They were just a few bars into their second song when the first dancers hit the floor, a tiny lady who would have been in her seventies, being twirled around carefully by a slightly younger man who clearly knew his stuff – this couple danced on their own for a while in a touching little cameo, but when the band kicked into a more up-tempo number, the chairs emptied and suddenly there were about 50 people moving around in various fashions, from the slight shuffle on the spot, right through to the budding Strictly Ballroom youngsters. The energy was fantastic, and on a warm Sunday evening on the cobbles, with the cathedral at the end of the square lighting up the night sky, it was a truly joyous sight.

***

The view from the window of the coach for the journey to Mérida was the same as all the other bus rides in Mexico, wide concrete freeways with trees on both sides and nothing else really visible. Putting the views aside, I was really quite impressed with the coaches in Mexico, which were clean, comfortable, always on time and excellent value for money – I think I had been expecting a somewhat more chaotic experience, so it was a welcome surprise every time I spent a relaxing few hours on one. My Airbnb in Merida was a fair way from the bus station, and this was my first clue that I was in a large city for the first time in a little while, with Merida's population totalling roughly 900,000. My host, Albany, a photographer, was out when I arrived so her exclusively Spanish speaking boyfriend Juan gave me the intro; this place was a bit more basic than the last one, with dubious looking insect screens, a point Juan reinforced when handing me a giant tin of mosquito repellent and saying (I think) – 'It's necessary!'

Albany had sent me a message earlier in the day with a recommended place to go to for lunch, and when I got there, it seemed to be a bit of a cross between an English pub and a Mexican sports bar, with three sides of the large square bar lined by Mexican gents eating their lunch and having a bit of a chinwag. The place seemed to be something of a shrine to Corona, with a three-metre high poster of scantily clad ladies in 'underboob' revealing Corona branded 'football kits', and a giant trophy cabinet next to my table filled only with six rows of Corona longneck bottles. The sport on the screens over the bar was the US Open tennis, which was a welcome distraction from the poor food order I had made. In the advert break I saw one of the upcoming feature games was a football match between Azerbaijan and Kosovo – I think you would know you are having a slow day if you were to find yourself watching that clash of the titans. A brief post-prandial stroll later I found myself nervously entering a barbershop to get something done about the unkempt mess on my head and face, though was soon slightly more at ease when I found the guy had some English. He asked where I was from and he excitedly asked if I knew about kangaroos and koalas, before revealing a bit later that Nicole Kidman was his favourite actress – thankfully the chat ended after that, and he concentrated on the task in hand. This was the first time I had been for a beard trim, and I didn't really know how to describe what I wanted – but I can tell you that what he ended up doing was not what I had in mind. Loads more came off than I had expected, and he then spent about twenty minutes at the end, when I thought we were already finished, doing what I can only describe as a bit of a 'Craig David' on me (or a 'Jason Derulo' for my younger readers), all sharp lines and the like. I couldn't really ask him to put it back on so I grinned and bared it, resolving I would need to stay in hiding for the next month before it had grown back to respectability. And there would likely be no dating.

I did pluck up the courage to head out in public in the evening and headed for a bar called La Negrita, which was apparently a good place for live music. It was only 7 pm, and I was a bit apprehensive having sat in a number of empty bars in Tulum at that hour – and it was Monday. So imagine my surprise when I got there, and the place was absolutely heaving! The front bar area was full, and I walked through to the area where I could hear the music coming from, to find a rear bar and aircraft hangar (maybe not that big) sized covered beer garden/patio full of people eating, drinking and enjoying the music. There were no tables free at all, but that was fine with me as I took a spot at the bar, right next to the band. The band was a five-piece outfit, comprising a double bass, a violin, two guitars and a piano accordion, and they were playing an up-tempo range of what I think was Cuban music. Two of the guys were also singing, and the energy in the place was infectious, with a few people twirling around at the front. I decided I would have a mojito and saw on the drinks list the cocktails came in two sizes, 350ml or 950ml…950ml! Looking around the bar, I saw most of the tables had people drinking from these giant mason jars, and it was quickly apparent why the place was so lively so early. I wasn't out for a massive one, so I just got the regular sized one and was feeling quite smug about having only paid $3 for the pleasure when I had a read of the small print on the menu; what's better than a mojito for $3? How about two mojitos for $3? Yep, Monday and Tuesday were two-for-one on mojitos all night, which meant I could get my sugar allowance for the month of September out the way in one sitting and also get a bit merry at the same time. The band finished up with a cracking finale of *'I Wanna Be Like You'* from *'The Jungle Book'*, with monkey noises and everything, and I finished my drink and stumbled home – an excellent start to life in Merida.

***

After a second day enjoying the sights and finally recovering my intestinal composure it was time to move on, and I caught a bus back across to the coast at Playa Del Carmen. The place I was staying there, the front room of my host Cassie's house, was just five blocks from the bus station and when I got there, I was greeted by 'Cassie's Mum' who also lived there – I write it that way as that is how she introduced herself, so I never learnt her actual name. I also saw on the Airbnb reviews that she always seemed to be referred to as such, so maybe she just doesn't like her actual name. The place was a fairly new condo, and I had a big room with an en-suite, so Playa del Carmen was looking quite encouraging at this stage, an initial view that firmed after a delightful lunch at a Venezuelan restaurant called Festival Kaxapa.

Unfortunately, that was about as good as it got for Playa del Carmen. The road from the lunch place to the shoreline descended a slight hill, and I could see wonderful shades of blue in the sea ahead of me, but as I got nearer and arrived at the beach, I remembered the seaweed problem. The first hundred metres or so of water off the beach was a muddy brown colour, and while the scene didn't seem quite as bad as Tulum, it certainly wasn't pretty. As I turned to walk north along the beach, it got worse, with more of the seaweed and the smell catching the back of your throat, even if you didn't even breathe through your nose. Along the sand stood small gangs of masseurs, desperate for business but with no customers with whom to busy themselves which made for a rather sad scene. But this wasn't the bad bit for me. That came when I turned off the beach and arrived at the main pedestrian thoroughfare, 5th Avenue, which was block after block of tequila bar, rock bar, Italian restaurant, shopping mall, Starbucks, steakhouse – you name it, it was there. I hadn't done my homework and had booked myself into what was basically one giant resort town – it got worse after the bars, with warehouse-sized souvenir shops pumping out sombreros, maracas and other Mexican cliché keepsakes, and construction sites all over the place to jam in new condo developments. I know this kind of place is perfect for lots of holidaymakers, but it wasn't at all what I wanted and I was cross with myself for booking to stay here for three nights, and resolved to do something about it immediately rather than wallow in the error – and that was to plan a trip to nearby Isla Mujeres for the next two days.

I would leave most of my stuff at my place in Playa del Carmen, which it was too late to cancel in any case, and take a small bag to the island, where I had found a last-minute Airbnb option that I had immediately booked. I say the island was nearby, but it wasn't really, and I would need to get a bus to Cancun for an hour, then a taxi to the ferry terminal where I would get the catamaran to the island, which took about 25 minutes. So a bit of hassle, but it seemed vastly preferable to staying in Playa del Carmen.

I still had to wait until the next morning to do all of this though, so I took a walk back to town to find a few drinks and some food. I had a couple of drinks at a bar on 5th Avenue to kill a bit of time and watched the passing sights of an array of mariachi bands, each dressed in a different coloured uniform, presumably to stop them straying into the wrong one when they passed each other in full flight. After escaping the tourist drag, I hit a taco place that had been recommended to me, Don Sirloin, where funnily enough the signature dish was tacos served with beef sirloin, which was cooked on a giant spit not dissimilar to a doner kebab, a guilty pleasure of mine. These tacos were super tasty, and I wolfed down three of them and quickly ordered more, crossing my fingers there was to be no repeat of the outcome from the last time I wrote so effusively in praise of a taco stall visit. (There was no repeat – and I went back for more a few days later – sirloin genius). I also had a few beers with dinner and was a bit tipsy when I arrived home to debrief my day with Cassie and Cassie's Mum. I told them I hated the place in as polite a fashion as I could manage and they were actually in agreement that it was maybe a bit over touristy and 'American' so that conversation wasn't as awkward as it could have been. I told them my plan for the next day and that they shouldn't be concerned when I didn't return home, and then the cat I was playing with bit my hand, and I decided it was time for bed.

You might be wondering why you haven't heard any update on my dating escapades while I was in Mexico, and the short answer is that there weren't any. I would like to say I decided to leave it alone a bit after the Guatemala drama, but that would be a lie. I just wasn't in one place for long enough to get anything organised, and each time I looked, all of the preferred candidates were based in places too far away for a meeting to be practical. I was going to be running around quite a lot when I got to the US, so this was looking like being a lengthy break in proceedings on that front, which was a shame – but I had tonnes of cool stuff to see, and was confident I could still get myself in enough trouble on my own to still have some exciting tales to tell. But you will have to be the judge of that.

The next day I was back on another one of my favourite coaches for the quick hop up to Cancun – I was listening to music, but this coach had a big TV up the front, and the audio was loud enough that I could almost hear it over my music. The entertainment was some kind of soap opera episode that appeared to centre on a terminally ill boy, and the agony of his parents as they all went through his ordeal, with soft-focus slow-motion scenes of them pleading at an altar, looking at old photos and smashing up their living room in a rage. It all seemed a bit full-on for a coach ride, and we arrived at Cancun before the episode finished so I can't tell you what happened – and I wouldn't want to spoil it for you anyway. My one-hour coach ride cost 74 Pesos, and my eight-minute cab ride cost 100 Pesos, which didn't feel quite right, but the timing was perfect for me to walk straight onto the catamaran just before it left, so I wasn't complaining. I sat on the open-top deck for the ride where we were entertained by a very talented chap who sang, and played a miniature guitar, a recorder and the pan pipes – the setlist however I cannot praise, as it included (in succession) *'La Bamba', 'The Lion Sleeps Tonight'* and then *'Imagine'*. He seemed to do all right when the tip hat went round, but it was a fairly painful experience, and I made sure I sat indoors for the return journey. But let me stop my whingeing right there, for as soon as the catamaran arrived at the dock, I could see this was a place I was going to enjoy – yes, there were still some tacky souvenir shops and lots of other tourists about, but the small main town on the island had an energetic vibe to it, and the colour of the sea around the island, which we had seen flashes off from the ferry, was spectacular.

Isla Mujeres is a tiny island, only seven kilometres long with a width that varies from 650 metres down to not very much at all as you head south. Most of the action is in the main town, which is also where the best beach, Playa Norte, is found, but there are also enough sights around the island for people to venture further afield, and the mode of transport favoured by almost everyone for these outings are golf buggies. So I walked straight to a rental shop where I hired…a pushbike. It was filthy hot, but I felt like I hadn't done any decent exercise since I had been in Mexico, and the island looked fairly flat, so why not.

I rode down to the point at the south end of the island which has the claim to fame of being the most Easterly point in Mexico, but its more notable attraction was the colour of the sea off the coast, which was an amazing turquoise blue until a distinct line at the point of a change in depth out at sea where it turned dark blue, which continued until it met the light blue sky at the horizon, the three different blues combining to make a breath-taking view. There was also a sculpture park on the point, but it looked like it had seen better days, so I decided to save my money for something more worthwhile, like mojitos, and started the ride back north. A little way into the ride I passed a reggae bar called 'The Joint' (see what they did there?) which I had read reasonable reviews of, and which advertised all-day live music; as I rode by some guy was singing *'Hello'* by Lionel Richie, so suffice to say I can't tell you any more on what the place is like as I didn't stop. Back in the main town, it was time for me to check in to my Airbnb, this time hosted by a young chap called Edson, who had managed to cram five rooms with en-suites and a kitchen and social area into what looked like a tiny block. When I got in the room it was actually a bit of a Tardis, and given I was only there for one night it was perfect for what I needed – and jumping ahead, the breakfast next day was great – it even included a croissant, which I had not seen for a long time!

Once I had dumped my stuff there, it was finally time for the big reveal of Playa Norte, and it didn't disappoint. The beach was a couple of kilometres long and wide enough that it didn't feel crowded (even though it was, well, crowded), with beautifully soft, deep sand leading to a gentle incline into crystal clear warm waters, which you could wade out into for about 100 metres and still only be waist-deep. I went in for a swim, then walked to the end of the beach and back and then couldn't resist heading back out into the waters to just mong there a while. The only issue with being a solo beachgoer is that there is no one to look after your stuff, but I had overcome this issue by leaving it somewhere visible and then sitting in the sea-facing back to shore. This plan was working fine until a large-ish lady came across my line of sight and then crawled out of the sea in front of me on all fours, with her bikini pants hooked up her backside. This turned out to be deliberate, as it was the first of a number of 'provocative' poses she then worked through while her husband/boyfriend took photos – *'From Here to Eternity'* it most certainly was not.

The highlight of my day was, however, yet to come. You might recall back in Valladolid I introduced you to the concept of the marquesita, the waffle with the bizarre-sounding cheese and chocolate filling – well today was the day I got to eat one, and it was indescribably delicious, as Sara had warned me would be the case. I think there must be something in the combination of the saltiness of the cheese that brings together the chocolate and waffle to create snack food genius, but whatever the science behind it, it was awesome. As soon as I had finished it, I immediately walked to another stand at the other end of town to buy a second one, without the shame of revealing to the first guy that I was already addicted to them. A marvellous end to a marvellous day.

I was no more wowed by Playa del Carmen on my return, but my day was cheered when I saw that I had received another fun Airbnb review, this time from my new photographer friend, Albany, from Merida. Her review included the following:

'Alex is a really nice person! Very respectful, clean and full of good vibes and energy, always with a nice smile!'

Bless. But what was the story behind a second person praising me just for being clean? Do people routinely turn up to Airbnb accommodation looking like they slept in a dumpster the night before? Anyway, I was pleased to hear she had not picked up on the dark side of the force which lay hidden behind my smiling veneer, and I resolved to keep up my personal hygiene standards for the remainder of my adventures.

After a restful night's sleep, it was just about the end of my Central American adventure, with just the bus to the airport and my flight to LA to complete. At the bus station I was entertained by the American translations over the public address system, which followed the Spanish announcements that occurred whenever it was time for people to walk to the bus departure area, which went exactly like this:

"Your attention please, announces the departure with the schedule of ten hours forty minutes with the destiny of Puerto Morelos. For your attention and reverence, ADO (the bus company) thanks you."

Fifteen minutes later, my destiny of a bus to Cancun airport was upon me, and an hour later, I was checking in at the airport. Morning coffee was required, but I unwittingly walked straight to the area where you have to surrender all your liquids, which meant I had to sit on the floor in the departure hall until I had finished drinking it. I was immediately reminded of my only previous trip to Mexico when I went to Cabo on the Baja peninsula as part of my honeymoon. When we arrived at Cabo airport to leave, for some reason there was a bag check before you checked in your luggage for the hold, and they opened our main bags and picked out all the liquids one by one, shook their head and said, *"No pasa."* We tried to patiently explain (in English) that they were enforcing rules intended for hand luggage, but they weren't budging and just kept saying *"No pasa"* and putting the bottles to the side. My ex-wife wasn't having this and, given we were a bit early, rather than checking in, we went back outside to the car park and tried to get through as many of the liquids as possible. Forty minutes later, having drunk two beers and half a bottle of Dr Pepper and applied quite a lot of what I think was baby oil, we went back through the check-in process with a wry/tipsy grin and went on our way. Back in Cancun, I finished my drink, enjoyed my final Mariachi band in the duty-free area, ate an enormous burger for lunch as training for my next destination, and then it was onto the plane and off to LA.

And that was that for Central America. I had seen so many amazing sights over the last five weeks or so, it was difficult to come up with a neat way to summarise the experience, but the word I kept coming back to was epic. The beautiful Caribbean beaches of Panama and Costa Rica, the awesome force of the volcanoes in Guatemala, the mysterious ruins and latter-day Spanish colonial beauty in both Guatemala and Mexico and the vibrant colours in the towns and cities across the continent – like I said, epic. Sure, the lack of any decent Spanish had made life a bit difficult for me, not being to drink the tap water or put paper in the toilet was rather tedious, and I hadn't seen eye to eye with all the food I had eaten, but those were minor gripes in the grand scheme of things. I would be back.

Summary – Mexico

Kilometres travelled (air) – None
Kilometres travelled (land) – 1,150
Planned number of Cenote visits – Six
Actual number of Cenote visits – One

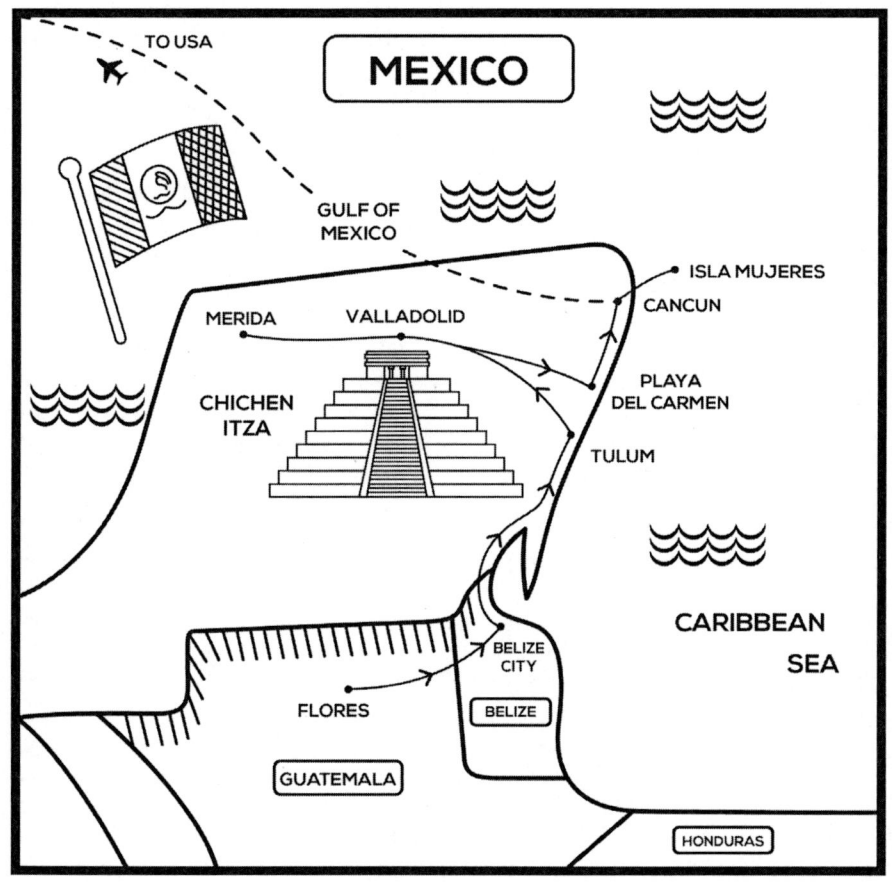

USA
Conquering Nature Whilst Bumbling on Bumble

And so, to the land of the free, and the home of the brave. The flight from Cancun had been largely uneventful other than serving as a reminder to me that you get pretty much nothing from a food perspective when you travel with American airlines (small second 'a' deliberate), even on reasonably long flights like the five hour one I had just taken. Two bags of nuts was the extent of it, so I was feeling relieved I had taken on the giant burger at Cancun airport, particularly as I had a three-hour drive ahead and didn't really want to be messing around trying to find food.

Step one of the USA itinerary was to exit the airport, an experience that had been time-consuming on prior visits to LA and collect a rental car. I was a bit apprehensive about today's plan, as my flight didn't arrive until after 6 pm (after a longish travel day already) and was worried that it could end up being a late night, but with upgraded customs technology, the usually painful US border clearance process was an absolute breeze, and I was soon on a bus to the rental car lot. I sidestepped the usual discussion about insurance options (which I generally don't understand anyway) as the guy let me have the cheapest option a lot more easily than they usually do, and the last decision was whether to get satnav. This decision was made very easy for me when he said it would cost USD 17 a day, which for a ten-day rental sounded frankly ludicrous, so I told him I would go without, and navigate instead with a compass and by reference to the position of the sun in the sky. And my iPhone.

I had swapped some messages with my host, Victoria, and had given her an estimated arrival time of 10:30 pm, but I actually arrived after 9:30 pm. Looking at my phone for the final details of the directions to her house I saw she had messaged me at 9:20 pm asking for an update, as her daughter had arrived home unexpectedly, and she was moving me to another room which wasn't ready yet. I replied, advising I was outside and would park up and come to say hello, and soon after she came out of the house in a bit of a panic about her domestic developments. I said I wasn't in a mad rush to go to bed and it wasn't a big deal, which didn't seem to settle her much, and she pointed at a chair in the front garden and asked if I was okay to wait there while she finished the room. It was a lovely warm evening, and there was a full sky of stars overhead, so this sounded fine to me, and I sat outside with the glass of water she brought me and caught up on my messages. Five minutes later, she texted me to say I could come in and use the bathroom if I needed to, which I thought was a bit odd when she could have just opened the door and said that. The situation got a bit weirder when half an hour later, I was still sitting outside having had no more updates, text or otherwise, and so at 10 pm, I decided to brave it and enter the house where mercifully the room was just about ready. I say it was ready, but the bathroom light didn't work, and the sink didn't really drain, but I was too tired to care by then, and Victoria had also said she would give me a refund for the night – so I had a very comfortable, free, night's sleep.

I was straight out the door the next morning at 7:30 am, dodging Victoria's Shih Tzu, which I had already established the night before hated me, and after a stop to get some water and cereal bars, I was at the national park visitor centre in the town of Joshua Tree one minute after opening time to get my park pass. I only had one day in the area, so I was in a hurry to see as much as I could and as quickly as possible. Entering the Western end of the park area (which is in the Mojave Desert), there were not many cars around, other than a few giant RV's, of which I would see many over the course of the next week. The scenery was quite unique, with strange boulders and rock formations scattered around the landscape and weird and wonderful trees and cactuses across the plains. When I had given my friend Louise, of 'Gandalf of backpackers' fame, the rundown on my US itinerary she had excitedly told me that Joshua Tree was a 'sick national park' and after a few minutes of driving around I was already inclined to agree.

So what is a Joshua Tree, I hear you ask? Well, to start with it is not actually a tree – it is a plant species belonging to the genus Yucca, but between you and me, they had big trunks and looked a lot like a tree. The branches go off the main trunk in seemingly random directions, and the combination of this weird structure and the clumps of bright green leaves at the end of each limb creates what appears to be a bit of a tree/cactus hybrid. The other thing that may have come to mind for you is the fact it is also the name of a U2 album – the band were apparently inspired by a photoshoot for the album which included a stay at the Harmony Motel in nearby 29 Palms, and other Joshua trees they saw in a tour around the desert landscapes in California. The tree on the back of the album sleeve is not actually in the park and is located over 200 miles away in a town called Darwin, and the picture on the front was taken in Death Valley, a story I might come back to later in my travels...

I was knocking off a few of the shorter loop walks while it was relatively cool, as I had read that you shouldn't attempt the more strenuous walks until later in the afternoon when the heat had come off a bit. So I had strolled around the 'Hidden Valley' loop and driven up to the 'Key's View', from where I could see miles and miles of the surrounding landscape, which was a bit like a moonscape, and I could even see where the San Andreas Fault ran through the valley. My thoughts from this reference turned not to the fairly average recent Dwayne Johnson disaster movie, but back many years to a fresh-faced Christopher Walken as Max Zorin in *'A View to a Kill'*, and his dastardly plan to flood the fault and the whole of Silicon Valley. This was one of the first films I remember seeing in the cinema and helped cement my lifelong obsession with James Bond films, though when I re-watch that one these days, I can't believe I didn't notice at the time how old Roger Moore looked – though he was still doing okay for a 57-year-old I guess!

Moving on from the lookout, I drove past the trailhead sign for the 'Ryan Mountain' walk, which was one of two 'strenuous' walks I had earmarked as wanting to do. I decided I just couldn't wait till the afternoon to do it – it didn't feel crazy hot, it was advertised as two to three hours return and, as it was still only 9:45 am, I figured I could cover the four and a half kilometre distance and 320 metres of elevation gain before it started getting too hot. I parked up, packed a decent amount of water and started my brisk walk up the hill, overtaking several groups on the trail. I should note at this point that I was viewing 'National Park Week' not just as an opportunity to see some amazing sights, but also as a chance for some serious fitness training, so I was generally going to be walking pretty hard on these trails. And so, it was on this one, as I powered up it without really taking a break and finding myself at the summit 28 minutes after leaving the car park. After a brief pause on the summit to catch my breath, take in the 360-degree views of the park and get a few photos (all of which came out a bit rubbish), I retraced my steps down the trail and got back to the car, an hour exactly after I had started – which was a useful reference point for the estimated times for the other walks on my hit list. In the restroom at the car park, I was intrigued to see what I will describe as a 'four-lane toilet roll dispenser', which had a padlock on the end to stop people, presumably from the nearby camping areas, helping themselves to the rolls. The designer of this security feature must have decided a budding toilet roll thief would not think of carrying out their crime by just pulling the sheets off the rolls in their entirety – or maybe even rolling it onto an empty cardboard core. If you hadn't noticed already, strange thoughts do sometimes appear to find their way into my head.

The brisk pace of my stroll meant there was still time for a couple of other stops before lunch, so I went and did a spot of giant boulder hopping around the aptly named 'Jumbo Rocks', and then drove down to the eastern side of the park (which is in the Colorado Desert) to see the 'Cholla Cactus Garden'. I walked around the garden, which was really more of a large square of dirt, behind a family and listened to the mother tell her children that the Cholla Cactus is interesting in that it has absolutely no useful application for us humans, and that the only value you can take from it is just the fact it is quite fun to look at. This sounded like quite a small positive, and on the negative side of the ledger, the spines are very painful if you get them under your skin and very difficult (and painful) to remove. I gave them a very wide berth and continued on my way, driving out of the park to the town of 29 Palms to find some lunch. It was at this point I was reminded of what I had read in Bill Bryson's books about small country towns in America, and how poorly suited they are for the English pursuit of 'having a bit of a look around'. The majority of the towns are basically just long strips of highway with a succession of well-spaced out restaurants, shops and gas stations, all of which have their own car park. So you can't park up, check out a few menus at different places and then pick your favourite – you must know in advance where you want to eat, which I didn't. The other problem is that all the places were chain restaurants and sounded fairly similar, in that they all served burgers and a few other dishes that were similar to burgers. For those familiar with the US, I am referring to places like Denny's, Carl's Jr, iHop, Applebee's, McDonald's and Jack in a Box – there are probably more. Anyway, after doing a few laps of town, racked with indecision, I decided the choice probably didn't matter that much and settled for Denny's, where I had what was a quite passable chicken and avocado salad but, as I ate, I reflected that three weeks of meal decisions in the US was going to be a challenge. Oh, and sorry, I made one other stop, to a 'drive-through ATM' – you seem to be able to do drive-through for almost anything in the States, so I thought I would tick off an ATM for novelty value.

Driving west up the highway out of 29 Palms, back towards the town of Joshua Tree, led me to my next 'strenuous walk' destination, the '49 Palms Oasis' trail. Following the success of the earlier walk and arrival of a cooling breeze, I was now ignoring the safety guidance and was going to be starting my walk at 2 pm. Two things gave me pause for thought on this plan, the first being a giant thermometer which showed it was currently 100 degrees, and the second being a photo of man, Paul Miller, who had gone for a walk on the trail in July 2018 (it was now September 2018) and had not been seen since. I read up on this later, and the story went that he was on holiday with his wife and left for what was meant to be a quick early morning walk, which his wife did not join him for as she was feeling unwell. When he didn't return later that morning, she raised the alarm, and the police found his car in the trailhead car park (where I was now), but no other trace of him or his belongings. This story was all the more surprising for me as it wasn't a very hard or long walk – it took me about one hour and twenty minutes to do the return walk, and the trail was clearly marked all the way from the car park to the oasis – one can only assume he took a wrong turn and got disoriented. The oasis itself was quite spectacular

– in the middle of miles and miles of grey rocky nothingness, there was a big grouping of palm trees that must have been a good 30 metres tall, with lots of green grass and plants around them. I clambered around some of the rocks up the hill behind them for a better view, but I was feeling a little nervous as I was the only walker out there and still thinking about the sign at the start, so I had a drink break and hurried back to the safety of my car.

Over dinner that evening, I did some more research on deaths in the park, given the scaremongering I had seen from various warning signs during the day. Recent related stories included one of a Dutch couple whose car had become stuck on a track and who had died in the heat attempting to walk for help and a near-death experience story of a lady from New Zealand, Clare Nelson. She had survived four days in the desert, before being rescued, after falling and breaking her pelvis having strayed off the Oasis Palms trail, but I found no reported deaths from hikes gone wrong. One story that took my eye was that of Joseph Orbeso and his girlfriend, Rachel Nguyen, who went missing after a walk in the desert and were not found until three months later, in a remote part of the desert, having apparently got lost on their walk. Shortly after the bodies were discovered, the father of Joseph revealed to the press, ahead of a police statement, that the couple had been found in an embrace, and that it was a testament to the kind of man Joseph was that he had held and comforted his girlfriend until the moment they perished. This imagery was rather soured a few days later when the police revealed the couple had died of gunshot wounds, with Joseph having shot Rachel before turning the gun on himself – not quite the romantic ending that had been described a few days prior. That said, the autopsy was inconclusive as to what had happened, and the family maintained their view that it was some kind of mercy killing after Rachel suffered a head injury. Muddying the waters further was the fact the couple had bought hallucinogenic drugs before their walk, and a mushroom was found at the scene, so to be honest who knows what on earth was going on.

***

The next day I was back in the car early, with 580-kilometre drive west to Arizona ahead of me. When planning the Grand Canyon part of the trip, I had been a bit horrified by the cost of accommodation in and around the park and had reached a compromise solution whereby I would stay the first night 80 kilometres away in the town of Flagstaff and then two nights at the entrance of the park in the expensive accommodation in Tusayan. After leaving 29 Palms, the boundary of the tourist area, there were literally zero other cars around, and I drove the gun-barrel straight roads through identical scenery for the next hour, with a bend in the road about every fifteen minutes the only stimulation. While this was quite dull, I do quite like the photos taken of the desolate scenes from the middle of the road and had been looking around for a suitable spot to stop, which I decided was near the top of a long uphill stretch and pulled off to the shoulder so I could take some shots. When I parked up, the car stopped quite sharply, and I realised the meaning of the signs I had been seeing for the last ten kilometres or so which read '*soft shoulder*' – there was no asphalt to the side, it was just sand. I took a couple of photos and got back in the car, put it in drive, but found I couldn't get any traction up the hill so put it in reverse instead and found to my horror that didn't work either. I gave it some more gas, jiggled the wheel around a bit and it moved back a little, but not much, and then stopped. And that was it. To my horror, I realised I had buried the car in the desert!

Now what? I couldn't get out myself, so decided I would need to flag someone down, who would hopefully have a tow rope to pull me out. After five minutes, a car turned up that I waved down, which didn't have a rope in it, but the driver said he was willing to try and help push me out. I said something like, "I hadn't realised how soft the shoulder was."

He said, "Yeah, that's why we have the signs," which was absolutely correct, but not that helpful to me at that moment. We had a go at pushing it out, but couldn't shift it, so tried wedging some things under the right front wheel for traction but that didn't work either. The series of attempts at trying to reverse just buried the front right wheel further, meaning the front left wheel, which did have some harder sand under it, became irrelevant as it was now almost airborne because of the car's angle. This clearly wasn't working, and eventually the guy suggested I would have to call for help – I said I would do that, but he was still loitering around and I didn't want to delay him any further so I thanked him and said he should go – which he did, shortly before I noticed I had no service on my phone. I waved down two more cars, neither of which had a rope, and ten minutes later a Winnebago appeared on the horizon – surely this would have some equipment to save me? But no, it was a young German couple in a rental van, and they had nothing helpful, but their giant vehicle parked up created more of a scene and a minute later two more cars came along, both of which I stopped. Still, no-one had any rope – where is a criminal when you need one? However, I realised that, including me, I now had four men at my disposal, and my thoughts turned from pull to push. I got the German guy (the smallest) to get in the car and hit the gas while the other three of us pushed from the front and, thank the Lord, we managed to shift it back onto the road. I thanked them all effusively, including an American guy who said 'no problem, it happens all the time', which I don't think I believed, and half an hour after beaching the car I was back on my way. Phew. Oh, and the photos I had taken at the start of this saga? They were shit.

I spent the next twenty minutes clutching the steering wheel as hard as possible to prevent any chance of the car veering off the road and was mighty relieved to turn off that road and onto one with a solid looking shoulder which the road sign told me was heading to Las Vegas, Searchlight and Needles. By now my spirits were back up, and the word 'Needles' reminded me of a story from a holiday that I had taken many years ago, in the early stages of my accounting career, with three work colleagues (and friends), Adam, Nick and Ed. We booked a very cheap week in one of the tackiest resort towns on the (largely) tacky Mediterranean island of Tenerife, a place called Playa de Las Americas. This is very much an 'England-on-sea' kind of place, attracting large groups of young English holidaymakers to basically reproduce their normal home life of speaking English and going to Irish bars, English restaurants and pubs and clubs, with the only difference to home being the sunshine, hot temperatures and the presence of a beach. We were of course 'above' this kind of holiday (ahem), and so we're going in an ironic kind of fashion, which also meant we had bought a set of 'boys on tour' matching t-shirts, with nicknames on the back, to go out 'on the town' in. Ed's T-shirt had the name 'Needle' on it, a derogatory way of addressing him, usually while playing PlayStation, referring to his (alleged) 'needle-dick'. For completeness, Adam and I had names which were more bizarre variants of this same derivation ('Noodle' and 'Poodle'), and Nick had a more routine surname related nickname ('Webbo'). The first night we wore these t-shirts with their 'cryptic' meanings, Adam was approached by a girl who had seen Ed's t-shirt and the following conversation ensued:

Girl – "Why does he have 'Needle' on his shirt?"
Adam – "Err, it's a bit of a long story."
Girl – "Is it because he has a needle dick?"
Adam – "Yes."

When I finally got to the town of Needles, I turned onto the I-40, which would take me the 370 kilometres west to Flagstaff, and almost immediately I drove over a massive bridge with the raging Colorado River far below. This triggered a memory for me, reminding me why the town name sounded familiar (apart from the above story). You may recall back in Panama I introduced you to the book *'Into the Wild'* and its unfortunate hero, Christopher McCandless. Well, one of the crazier parts of his journey was when he got hold of a kayak and decided he would paddle the Colorado River from California right down into Mexico – which he did. And where did he start this journey? Yep, right here in Needles. The river looked terrifying, and I'm not sure he had any previous canoeing experience, but then his whole journey didn't seem to involve too much common sense, so this sight didn't surprise me too much.

The river is on the border between California and Arizona, and a few miles up the freeway I saw a place name that conjured another popular culture reference for me, this time 'London Bridge'. In the 1993 film, *'Falling Down'*, Michael Douglas plays a former civil servant who has been made redundant and loses the plot over the course of an increasingly violent sequence of events in a day in Los Angeles, while being pursued by a soon-to-be-retired detective played by Robert Duvall. After retiring, Duvall's character is due to move out to Arizona with his wife, and there is a scene in the movie where he talks at length about the community they will live in, and the fact it has the original London Bridge in it. I hadn't previously read up on this backstory but driving past it was a prompt for me to do so, and it's quite a crazy story. In 1962, the original London Bridge (built in 1831) had been deemed not sound enough to support modern traffic loads and was sold, ahead of building a replacement bridge. The original bridge was bought by an American gentleman named Robert McCulloch as a tourist attraction for land he owned at Lake Havasu City, a retirement development on the shore of a large reservoir on the Colorado River. The bridge was disassembled, each stone was numbered, all of them were shipped across the Atlantic and the bridge was then reassembled in the new location. It all sounded like complete folly to me, but apparently, Mr McCulloch recouped his outlay of around USD 2.5million and made a heap of profit on top, so it was apparently not such a crazy plan after all!

As I drove along the I-40, the scenery finally started to change from the desert landscape I had seen since Yucca Valley, with the appearance of some green fields, trees and livestock, and a sequence of cuttings through, and passes over, small mountain ranges. This is an appropriate point in the driving section of my tour to introduce you to my driving speed formula, which calculates my cruising speed on any given road according to the following formula:

Speed = (A*1.1) – B + C; where
A = Speed limit.
B = Impact of traffic; and
C = Maycock adjustment.

The 'Maycock adjustment' can be influenced by a number of factors specific to that day's travel, such as urgent appointments/need for the toilet, as well as two other 'atmospheric variables', being the visibility of potential hiding places for police cars and the availability of 'blockers'. A blocker is any vehicle that is driving faster than me which I can accelerate to catch up with and follow, safe in the knowledge that if someone is going to get caught speeding, it should be the blocker and not me. On this day there was an ideal blocker available, a red pickup truck with Washington plates, which I had been pacing for about an hour as it travelled at around 85mph, sometimes a bit quicker on the downhill stretches. I had carelessly lost sight of it going up a hill and was daydreaming a bit when I suddenly saw a police patrol car sat on the central reservation. I was going at close to 90mph when I saw it and braked fairly sharply and pulled into the traffic in the inside lane in a 'nothing to see here, Officer' fashion. The car didn't move initially, but then to my horror, I saw it pull out and start driving up behind me in the outside lane, before mercifully carrying on past without pausing and putting its flashing lights on in the distance and then slowing. A few seconds later, I caught and passed the now stopped police car, just as the patrolman walked up to speak to the driver of the red pickup truck – blocker theory success!

In truth that was a bit of a lucky escape, and I drove at a more respectful speed for the remainder of my journey, passing through a landscape that was now dominated by pine trees and the distinctive shape of a volcano cone as I arrived at Flagstaff, which I later learnt was a dormant volcano called Sunset Crater. Flagstaff itself was a quaint little town, with a neat historical area centred on the rail track that passed through the centre of town alongside 'Historic Route 66'. This area comprised a number of motels still sporting their 1950's era signage and a newer generation of breweries, bars and coffee roasters bringing it up to date with their more contemporary feel. I had a satisfying lunch at a cafe recommended by my next host, Suzanne, before driving a few kilometres north of the historical centre to my lodgings, which was a small house in a quiet wooded suburban street where Suzanne's daughter, who worked at the nearby observatory, lived. I walked straight through the living room to drop my bags in my room and freshen up, and it was only when I had come back out of my room and sat down in the living room of the empty house that I noticed the decor.

Against one of the corners of the room stood a cardboard cut-out of Chewbacca and as I looked around, I saw there was a Darth Vader in another corner, a stormtrooper leaning on another wall, and that the remainder of the wall space was covered in framed sci-fi movie prints and other memorabilia. There was also a cardboard Millennium Falcon hanging from the ceiling by the front door; and a small cardboard R2-D2. I had been planning to sit there and do some writing for the afternoon, but as I sat there in silence, being stared at by the cardboard cast in the room, I felt strangely uncomfortable; and had to go out. Returning, later on, I went to my room, and didn't come out again until it was time to leave in the morning – just in case there were to be any late-night cult activities.

***

The drive from Flagstaff to Grand Canyon National Park the next day took a bit over an hour, and I got to watch the sunrise along the way as I was on my usual routine of trying to beat the crowds. I drove through the park entrance at about 7:10 am and was immediately greeted by the sight of a small herd of elk grazing in the early morning light on the side of the road which was quite a surprise given the volume of traffic that must pass that point each day. A few kilometres later, I arrived at the reasonably empty first car park (of about ten) and organised my walking gear and bag. I had two full days of walking available to me here, and my strategy was to spend the first day walking around the top of the canyon, mainly on the 'Rim Trail' plus any visitor centre or other stuff there was to see. This would warm my legs up for day two, when I would walk down into, and then back up, the canyon on one of the two trails available to do this (South Kaibab Trail and the Bright Angel Trail), an activity described in the guidebook as 'moderately strenuous'.

The Rim Trail was twenty kilometres long in total, and my car was parked three kilometres from the eastern end, so I set off in a westerly direction with the intention of carrying on till the end and getting the bus back to the start. Even at this early hour there were a lot of people around, and it was clearly going to be heaving later, so I was glad I was covering this section now. This is one of the parts of my journey that it is impossible to do justice in words because the scene over my right shoulder as I walked along was just out of this world. Around every corner, there was a new 'overlook' or 'look-down' towards the valley floor, where the Colorado River lay, out of sight, almost one vertical mile below, or a view across the mighty canyon to the North Rim, about fifteen kilometres away. The rock formations on the canyon walls and the various outcrops and stacks were different in every view, as were the colours that ranged through the whole spectrum of reds, oranges, browns and greys. Not only was it almost impossible to describe, but it was also proving very hard to photograph as I took and immediately deleted photo after photo, not happy they were coming anywhere near accurately depicting the wonderful scene in front of me. So in summary, what I think I am saying is you really need to go and see this one with your own eyes – it's mesmerising.

What I can describe for you is the experience of walking the Rim Trail. I walked the length of the trail until the far western end at Hermit's Rest which took me about four hours, stopping to gaze in amazement from the countless different viewpoints. The shuttle bus stops at each of the more remarkable lookouts, which meant that those spots either had tonnes of people or no one, depending how well you timed your arrival relative to the bus arrivals. Once away from those points, there were hardly any people who could be bothered to actually walk between them, so it was really quite peaceful on most of the trail. There was also a lot more wildlife to be seen away from those crowds, though in truth that didn't get too much more inspiring than squirrels and lizards. My walk had taken me far enough that I actually had to get two different buses to cover the whole journey back to the start, and the bus drivers both liked to give a bit of a running commentary on the way, so I learnt and forgot lots of interesting facts about the park. One thing I did remember was that most of the staff also live in the park, in accommodation built especially to house them, and that it is the only national park with its own school (for the children of the staff). Back at the start I found myself some lunch and gave the visitor centre short shrift, as there didn't seem much to see, before catching a bus over to the South Kaibab trailhead. I had decided I would make the Bright Angel Trail the next day but I had read a lot of comments in the park materials about how hard and time consuming these trails were and decided that given my legs were feeling good, I would go and try a section of South Kaibab to give me some guidance for how long the walk the next day should take.

The guidebooks were all quite definitive that you should not try to do a day walk from the rim down to the Colorado River and back up again. While I was still tempted to try that, I had decided that the following day I would do a return walk to Plateau Point on the Bright Angel Trail, a total change in altitude of around 900 metres, which the trail map said would take between nine and twelve hours. On the South Kaibab Trail, there were suggested turnaround points at Ooh-Aah Point (150m) and Cedar Ridge (350m) so I decided to walk down to the latter, which was advertised as taking between two and four hours. I set off at about 2:15 pm, so it was pretty hot but, unsurprisingly the continuous downhill was quite easy-going, and I arrived at Cedar Ridge after only walking for about half an hour. Still feeling good, I decided I would carry on down further to the next turnaround point, Skeleton Pass, which was about 600m total descent from the top, and I arrived there after about one hour and five minutes. The pass runs out across a land bridge into the middle of the canyon, and the views back up to the South

Rim, and all the way around to the North Rim were quite spectacular. Walking back up was not such a pleasant experience. I knew it was going to be a bit of a challenge, particularly given I already had about 25 kilometres in my legs for the day, but about five minutes in I started getting stomach cramps and was really starting to feel the impact of the sun beating down from above. My brain doesn't have a 'stop and rest for a bit' setting, always wanting to get stuff over and done with, so I pushed on regardless, but after about half an hour I was starting to feel a bit nauseous and regretting not having turned around on the descent sooner. Luckily the cramps started to relent, and I was back to a straight challenge of weary legs versus the hill, dragging myself back up the final steep switchbacks to the trailhead after an exhausting two hour 25-minute round trip; which was still pretty good in comparison to the advertised four to six hours for that walk. My legs were pretty much shot, but my competitive spirit was telling me I had to do the last leg of the Rim Trail from here (the eastern start point) back to my car, so I could say I had walked it in its entirety. Which I did, with more than a little staggering around, before getting in the car and driving back to my nearby hotel (a hotel!), where I slept rather well!

But wait. That was the warm-up walk, remember? So I was back at the Bright Angel Trailhead the next morning at 6:10 am (in the dark) to get my 'big walk' done before the heat of the middle of the day arrived. Unbelievably, my legs were feeling quite fresh despite the punishment they had taken the day before, and I was still harbouring ambitions to change my plan and go right down to the river and back. Ten minutes into the walk I passed a group of young people walking back up the hill with a stereo blaring out *'Staying Alive'* and this further lifted my spirits as I almost jogged down the track. Unfortunately, I wasn't paying quite enough attention and, after about three kilometres, I misjudged a rock and rolled over on my left ankle, wrenching the ligaments on the top of my foot. As the lucky folk who have played football with me over the years know, I have dreadfully designed ankles and feet, and I take myself out of action for prolonged periods of time from this kind of mishap on an all too regular basis. I stopped and sat on a rock and wiggled it around a bit, trying to decide how badly I had rolled it and whether I could continue; given I was only three kilometres in, that meant I had another six kilometres down to Plateau Point, and then nine back up, so fifteen in total. But I really wanted to do the walk and didn't know if I would ever be back here again. Dilemma.

I walked on a bit, and it seemed okay, apart from the occasional step where I put it down wrong and winced at the sharp pain of pulling on the tender ligaments. I took some Nurofen and carried onto the five-kilometre turnaround point and sat and considered my options again. It was 50:50 in my mind, but I decided to carry on, perhaps foolishly given what the guidebooks tell you to do in those circumstances. As it turned out, I think it was the right decision for as I descended further, it started to bother me less, probably because of the drugs, and the trail started to level off which took the pressure off the problem area. I soon arrived at the next landmark, Indian Campground, where the trail to Plateau Point forked off – I definitely wasn't going to the bottom with an injury, so that addressed that decision, and an easy half an hour walk later, with the first experience of direct sunlight for the day, I was at Plateau Point, having seen no other walkers since the Campground.

Plateau Point was incredible. It was now 8:30 am, and back up the hill, at the top on the Canyon, I could picture the thousands of people who would now be arriving and milling around the trails up there like swarms of ants. Meanwhile, down here, I was standing on a rocky outcrop, with not another soul in sight, and from where looking back I could see the cliffs under the South Rim winding their way along their jagged route, follow the panorama around to the North Rim in front me, and then look 600 metres below to see and hear the mighty Colorado River crashing its way along the valley floor. I sat and drank in the scene for a while, stood and looked around, then sat down again, not wanting this completely private wonderment to end. I ate some fruit and a cereal bar, wondered why I had bothered to carry lunch to a point I was going to reach this early hour and decided it was time to start the slog back uphill.

The walk back up was, predictably, quite hard, particularly given the sun had now arrived on the trail, but it did feel like it was less steep than the South Kaibab Trail, so I was glad I had tested myself there first. I should have stopped for a while and eaten my sandwich but as usual, I was in a hurry to just get the walk done, the result being my body didn't have enough fuel for the final stages, and I was coming very close to completely cramping up in both my calf muscles, walking more and more like a robot. I did make it through, arriving back at the start for a quite glorious sit-down and a sandwich about five hours and fifteen minutes after I had begun. One relationship that had soured over the course of the walk was the one with my watch, which was telling me I had walked down the equivalent of 345 flights of stairs but, to return to the same point, had only walked up 74 flights – I wasn't impressed.

***

The next stop on my itinerary was something of a bonus one, as I had decided the drive from Grand Canyon to Yosemite was longer than I wanted to be doing in one hit and needed an interim stop along the way. The obvious candidate was Las Vegas, but I really wasn't inspired to go there, and, looking for other options, saw that Death Valley was nearby. I didn't know much about Death Valley other than the fact (from my childhood Guinness Book of Records knowledge) that it held the accolade of the hottest ever recorded temperature on earth, 56.7 °C on July 10 1913, but the fact it had a national park meant it qualified for inclusion in this section of my trip. Even as an interim stop, it was still going to be a seven-hour drive to get there, retracing my drive to head back towards LA, before turning off at a town called Kingman to head north towards Las Vegas. Shortly after the Kingman turn, I started seeing signs for an attraction called Grand Canyon West, with helicopters flying overhead from Vegas in that direction. This solved a mystery for me from my Grand Canyon visit as to why I hadn't seen the oval glass walkway that goes out over the canyon which I had seen in travel photos previously. It was because it was in this separate area, which I assume is targeted at the day-trippers from Las Vegas – not to worry, I felt I had seen the canyon from enough different aspects to have fully lived the experience without needing to go there too. The scenery for this part of the drive was the classic US Western desert kind of scene, yellow and brown shades of dusty floors, the odd squat shrub of some description and a cactus or two (or what I now knew to be Joshua Trees). It was real autopilot kind of driving, and I was only jolted back to full concentration when driving on a rumble strip or at the start of a hill, where the car slowed down. Arriving at the Nevada border at Lake Mead, the scenery started to get interesting again with the return of the dramatic canyons and the impressive sight of the Hoover Dam, where I stopped to stretch my legs for a few minutes and think about Superman…

Skirting past Las Vegas along the six-lane freeways with endless strip malls, condo developments and housing estates going further and further into the desert, I passed over a hill, and the scenery changed once more, this time to what looked like an area that was at some point in time a giant inland lake or sea. The view remained unchanged for about the next 40 kilometres before I arrived at the other side of this vast flat at the town of Pahrump, where I would be staying that night. However, I was to continue on for another hour to spend the afternoon in Death Valley, before doubling back in the evening. Arriving at the visitor centre in the town of Furnace Creek (all the towns had 'hot' names...) I picked up some lunch and maps and whatnot before quickly leaving again, passing the local petrol station which was selling petrol for $5.10 a gallon. I had filled up outside Las Vegas for $2.90 a gallon, so this was a clear case of exploiting desperate people whose only other option was probably to expire in their car. I headed to the southern end of the park first to Badwater, whose claim to fame was being North America's lowest point, at 86 metres below sea level.

The tourist attraction there was a path leading out to a salt flat in the middle of the valley, and the car park was full, with a steady stream of walkers doing the return walk. As soon as I opened the door, I was blasted with the hottest wind I have ever experienced, and as I walked further out towards the salt flat, it intensified to the point I had to concentrate on not being blown over. I was very glad I had brought my water bottle as with the intensity of the heat and wind, my mouth and throat dried out every couple of minutes and actually made me feel a bit nauseous. On my official heat scale, this was up at 'Captain Insano' levels. When I arrived at the main part of the flat, it was quite a cool sight, with the bright white salt fanning out in all directions. I had seen photos from friends who had visited the Uyuni salt flats in Bolivia which looked similar to this scene, and those photos used the lack of perspective from the fully white background to create scenes where one person looked like they were tiny enough to stand in someone else's hand and that kind of thing. Well, I didn't have any friends with me to do that – so I sat down and took some pictures of my feet instead. As you do. I didn't stay long before starting the fifteen-minute return walk, and by the time I got to the car the water in my bottle was at about bath water temperature – I could see why people didn't survive long when they found themselves out in these conditions.

A few miles back up the road was the 'Artist's Palette', named so on account of the many different colours that made up the rock formations in the area. I wasn't that impressed with the sight initially, but carried on around the single lane, 'Artist's Drive' which got more and more narrow, weaving between rock formations, and then the colours just went nuts. There were dark orange sections with dull green patches next to them like you see on rusting iron, and then there were pinks, purples, greys and browns, a different scene around every twist and turn. The road served absolutely no purpose other than being a tourist loop, and I assume it was blasted out specifically for this reason. Only in America would they make an effort to create a nine-mile road to nowhere like this, but I was glad they had, as it was quite beautiful.

The next stop was a more 'standard' lookout, Zabriskie Point, and while this was less colourful, it did take in some quite unworldly rock formations, with large sections of rocks that looked like a jagged set of waves. I didn't realise at the time, but when I came to write about the Joshua Tree, I discovered that the view from this point was actually the front cover of the U2 Joshua Tree album sleeve, so older readers might be able to picture the scene exactly. This wasn't my favourite view, however, as my final stop on the road back home took me to Dante's View, a mountain lookout 1,669 metres above the valley, from where I could look down at the swarm of ants, which was actually people walking on the salt flat where I had been earlier. The valley floor went on for miles and miles to both the north and south, so the view from up top was immense, and thankfully it wasn't so bloody hot up there!

From there it was back across the plains to Pahrump, a town that didn't seem to have much going for it other than being the gateway to Death Valley, but it was functional if nothing else. Given the climate, I was surprised to see the number one tourist attraction was actually the Pahrump winery which I was amused to see advertised itself as offering 'desert wine', which I assumed was not a typo.

My host in Pahrump was a lovely lady called 'Kc', and she was absolutely one of my favourite characters in the story so far. Kc had signed off one of her messages to me as 'Kc and Tater', and when I arrived I found out that Tater was actually her Chihuahua, who she instructed to 'Say hello to him!' which he did by running up a tiny flight of stairs to his sofa, standing on his hind legs and waving his front paws at me – bless! Kc lived on her own (apart from Tater) and had two spare rooms which she rented out on Airbnb. I could see that she clearly took a lot of pride in her role as host as she gave me the intro walk around, showing me all the helpful local info and maps she had put on the hallway walls, the world map where she had pins for the home location of all her guests, and the carefully organised guest towel system in the bathroom. The chat, when I could get a word in edgeways, turned briefly to the weather, and she told me that a few months prior a couple of her guests had been in the Valley at a town called Stovepipe (!) Wells when the temperature had been 132 degrees Fahrenheit (56 degrees Celsius), and they had fried some eggs on the road for comic photo purposes – now that really is hot! She then talked me through how breakfast worked. Kc premade and froze batches of blueberry waffles and each night placed them out, so they were ready to go in the toaster oven in the morning, along with detailed instructions on heat and time settings to warm them to perfection, before the guests were to enjoy them at the breakfast table, which was laid with fine china crockery and silverware. This was my new gold standard for an Airbnb property, and I had found it in the strangest of places, on a dusty street on the edge of a desert town with houses that looked not dissimilar to large trailers. Kc then excitedly talked me through the origins of all the native Indian art in my room, including the 'rain sticks' placed as ornaments, before recommending a Thai restaurant for dinner whilst looking at her watch in a slightly worried looking fashion, and saying, "You might just about get in if you go now." (6:15 pm)

I was quite keen for an early dinner, and an early night, so I headed back out and found the restaurant – which had four people eating in it. I had a red curry, which was surprisingly authentic given the random setting, with authentic Thai flavours coming through and a serious kick to it. It was also massive, and about fifteen minutes into ploughing through it the waitress came over and said, 'How y'all doin' there? You ready for a box?' presumably as no one ever finished it. Well, I did, and it was superb.

Back at the house, I sat on the outdoor furniture and caught a beautiful sunset over the trailer homes, and Kc came hurrying out to show me an app for stargazing a previous guest had downloaded for her. By pointing the device at the night sky, it showed all the stars and planets up there that may or may not have been visible to the eye and joining them up to show the famous constellations. Kc was in awe of this thing:

Kc – "Look over there – that one there's a planet, now which one is it?"
Me – "I think that's Jupiter."
Kc – "Darn, I can't get the name to come up, what is it…"
Me – "It's Jupiter."
Kc – "Ah, there you go, its Jupiter!"

It was quite a fun app, and we looked around a bit more while she showed me which one was 'the major', which one was 'the minor', and the stars that made up Sagittarius – my sci-fi loving, observatory working housemates back in Flagstaff would have loved it. After she went back inside, I sat and wrote for a while before realising, it was pitch black, and I went inside to bring a close to what had been a long day. In the room I saw a note on the wall I hadn't seen earlier with some more house instructions, which included the comment 'Please don't ask me if you can do your laundry', which made me quite glad I hadn't remembered to ask the one question I had on my mind when I arrived. And how was the note signed off?

"Kc and Tater Doggins."

Fantastic.

***

The next morning, I had my final really long drive of this leg of the trip, taking me seven hours north to Yosemite, and I was out the door in the dark, thinking it would be quite cool to be driving through Death Valley for sunrise. This turned out to be a flawed plan as I was down in a depression surrounded by mountains which meant it wasn't till about an hour after sunrise that I could actually see the sun, so there weren't any pretty sunrise colours, it just got light. The other, more unfortunate, development at this point of the journey was the realisation I had left my best pair of sunglasses in my room back in Pahrump. Kc emailed me that evening to confirm I had indeed done that, and I asked her to find them a good home – in truth, I like to think Kc kept them and gets them out for Tater to wear for comedy photo shoots, but that could be wishful thinking on my part.

It took about ninety minutes to cross the valley, and I was on edge as, 1) the 'Soft Shoulder' signs had returned, and 2) I was a little bit low on petrol, but I safely made it through, joining Highway 395 near the town of Lone Pine, where I got some petrol and made what was now a regular Starbucks stop. Buying a coffee was the third most important feature of these stops, with the main reasons being to use the bathroom and to check in on their free Wi-Fi. Later in the trip, this practice would evolve to just casually loitering outside Starbucks to use the Wi-Fi to check in on anything important – anything to avoid paying Telstra a $10 daily roaming fee. Highway 395 ran south to north along the eastern side of the Sierra Nevada, and Kc had told me to go this way, saying the drive was second in beauty in the State only to the Pacific Highway, and it was a spectacular sight indeed. The first town of interest was Lone Pine, which is a town that has been used as a filming location for many westerns over the years, sitting at the base of Mount Whitney, which at 4,421 metres is the highest peak in the lower 48 States. As I drove north through a number of other small country towns, the mountain range continued over my left shoulder, with farmland and grazing animals on the plains which stretched out to a smaller range of hills on the horizon to my right. This scene continued for a couple of hours, with the next tourist landmark being Mammoth Mountain, the popular ski resort which was now of course in hiking, biking and other summer activity mode.

Driving along, I was feeling a bit melancholy at this point, as the Starbucks check-in had included a few divorce and house sale-related emails, which I had managed to not think about for a while, but which I knew I would eventually need to divert some attention to. A little further on, I changed the radio dial, and it landed on a station called 'KIBS – The Greatest Country in the World!' which was knocking out high tempo country songs, in a style which I think you would call 'honky-tonk', and in the space of about five minutes my mood was completely changed. There I was, driving through this amazing scenery, with Mammoth Mountain right in front of me and the radio turned up to a deafening level, tapping my fingers on the wheel and having a bit of a full-on car boogie – it was awesome – who knew country and western music had such magical restorative powers.

Turning off the freeway not long after Mammoth, I was on the 120 'Tioga Pass' that climbed to an altitude of 3,030 metres at the eastern entrance to Yosemite. To give a sense of the scale of the park, it was a further ninety minutes' drive from the entrance to the main tourist centre, Yosemite Village, which sat at the bottom of the valley at an altitude of about 1,200 metres. A large proportion of the traffic that was winding its way around the park roads was accounted for by two vehicle types, the now ubiquitous giant RV's and secondly a load of convertible Ford Mustangs. On holiday to Hawaii many years before, we had arrived at Maui after an overnight flight from Sydney and a connecting flight from Oahu, and we had decided to divide and conquer, my ex-wife waiting for the luggage while I went and collected our 'economy' hatchback rental car. When my ex-wife came out with the bags she was surprised to see me waiting for her in a Mustang with the roof down – the rental guy had pounced on the bleary-eyed foreigner and landed a major upsell. This turned out to be a regrettable decision when I found the island speed limit was only 55 mph and the clutch weighed a tonne – and my ex-wife managed to get sunburnt on the one-hour drive from the airport to the hotel at nine in the morning. I have stuck to the economy car rentals since.

The drive through the upper parts of the park was spectacular, with the hulking granite towers peering out from between an endless forest of pine trees and the occasional mountain lake further enhancing the scene, and the sun overhead sparkling on the dark blue waters. The scene was rather sullied however by being stuck behind a slow-moving RV with nowhere easy to pass, but after fifteen minutes I seized a chance to get past and then had twenty kilometres of clear driving, stopping only to allow a deer and her two young fawns cross the road in front of me, which was quite magical and which also reminded me of one of my favourite 'dad jokes':

Q – "What do you call a deer with no eyes?"
A – "No idea."
Q – "What do you call a deer with no eyes and no legs?"
A – "Still no idea."

About five kilometres before the village is the enormous soaring rock face of 'El Capitan'. I parked up at the side of the road, got out, and adopted the same open-mouthed look of disbelief sported by the other people at the roadside, while trying to take some photos to capture the scene – which was impossible as the cliff filled the whole photo, allowing no context to the viewer. El Capitan rises 900 metres from base to summit on its tallest face, and as I gazed up, I made a mental note to check how this compared to similar epic granite monoliths I had seen on my travels, namely the Tre Cime di Lavaredo in the Italian Dolomites, and Cerro Torre in Patagonia in Southern Argentina. The answer was that Tre Cime has a 'prominence' of 568m, but the peak of Cerro Torre is over 1,200 metres above the glacier below, so this was one contest in which the US was going to have to settle for silver.

I was staying at a place called 'Housekeeping Camp' which had sounded like basic cabin accommodation when I booked it, but when I arrived, I found it was more basic than I had pictured, as it was just a concrete bunker with three walls and a canvas curtain for the front wall, housing a double bed, a bunk bed and a wire rack for storage, with a picnic table out the front. The beds just had mattresses on them, but you could hire sheets to go on these, on which you were advised to put your sleeping bag or duvet on top. Regrettably, I had neither of these items. Still, it didn't feel that cold, so I wasn't too concerned and decided I would work out a plan later on how to stay warm using the stuff I had at my disposal. When I checked in, I had to sign a statement that I understood the terms and conditions of camping, one of which intrigued me greatly, relating to the storage of food. Each 'room' came with a 'bear-proof' storage locker, and there were very clear instructions (with lots of capital letters) that you were not allowed to store any food, drink (including unopened, sealed bottles) or toiletries with any kind of scent in your car, and must instead put all of these in the lockers where the bears could not get to them. If they caught you contravening this regulation, you were likely to be expelled from the park, so it seemed to be quite a serious business. In my head, I couldn't help but try and think through the crime they were trying to prevent against with these safety measures – let me walk you through it…

A bear – let's call him Ben – arrives in the campground in the dead of night and, passing by my car, smells an unopened bottle of Gatorade in the boot. After a busy day of bear business, Ben realises he is a bit dehydrated and could do with a boost to his electrolyte levels, so decides he is going to steal it. To get into the car, he has to tiptoe into my camp (somehow knowing which one is mine) and grab my car key – all of this without waking me – before returning to the car. This is where it gets really tricky, as he then has to use his massive paws to somehow select the tiny button on the key fob to open the boot (and press it twice) before he finally gets hold of the drink. I had found this task challenging, so I just couldn't picture Ben having the dexterity to pull it off. Also, let's not forget Ben is a bear – when you think of famous bears, historical figures like Yogi, Paddington and Baloo are the names that spring to mind, and I think you'd agree that those guys would be collectively best described as 'hapless' – and they probably got famous because they were more talented than their peers, so what chance has an average bear-like Ben got? And…He has to do all of the above in the dark! I just couldn't see how he would get the job done.

In anticipation of the walking ahead, I tried for an early night, remembered how noisy campsites were and then had a not quite so early, but not late-night instead. I had gone to sleep wearing many layers of clothes but woke around midnight cold enough to realise I had underestimated the conditions and had to walk out to the car, checking for bears, to get the rest of my jumpers and jackets, whose warmth saw me through the rest of the night. While I was lying there, the thought crossed my mind that I was basically sleeping rough here – and it was costing me a positively mind-boggling $160 a night to do so!

The walk I had chosen for the next day, which I began in darkness at about 6 am, was called the 'Mist Trail' on account of the fact it went up into the rocks alongside two waterfalls, the Vernal Falls and then the Nevada Falls. September was just about the driest time of year for the falls, so I wasn't expecting much mist along the way, but I had my fingers crossed for spectacular scenery, nonetheless. The route I was taking also formed the first half of one of Yosemite's most famous walks, the trail to the top of 'Half-Dome', which, alongside El Capitan, is the most recognisable landmark in the park. The Half Dome Trail is a 'very strenuous' trail, and for once I believed this description, as the walk was a 26-kilometre round trip with an elevation gain of 1,600 metres from the valley to the summit. I had read up on this walk a bit too late in my planning, as you needed a permit to do it and the limited numbers available meant I couldn't get one. The permit system was introduced to limit numbers of the trail, and this was mainly due to a bottleneck at the final section, where walkers climb up a very steep section on the granite face with the use of metal cables attached to the mountain. This is not a walk for the faint-hearted, with 20 deaths on Half Dome alone, and that number climbing to over 60 if you include the trail leading up to Half Dome. The latest of these was as recent as May 2018 when a 29-year-old man, Asish Penugonda fell off the cables to his death, the eighth time this had happened. But I wasn't going to be walking that section so I would be fine, right? Well, I then read that Yosemite averages twelve to fifteen traumatic deaths a year, most from drowning, and that statistically, the most dangerous trail was…the Mist Trail! I suspect most of the issues occurred when the rivers and falls were considerably more ferocious than they looked today, so I was confident I would not end the day as the latest Yosemite statistic. (Postscript – a few weeks later I read about an Israeli teenager, Tomer

Frankfurter, who had fallen to his death taking a selfie at the top of Nevada Falls on September 7, eight days before my walk).

The walk itself was the latest instalment in me completing a walk in a time that bore no relation to the suggested time, and I overtook a lot of early starting groups on the way up. The majority of these groups were female, and as I came up to the third of these groups and thought about what banter I could come up with for the slightly awkward overtaking section, knowing the Americans love an English accent, I decided to put on my best Hugh Grant accent and go with,

"Excuse me, is it okay if I pass? It seems to be Ladies Day up here today and I feel like something of an intruder!"

They loved it, I was told I was a very welcome intruder and when I got to the next group I repeated the routine to similar results – a bit sad maybe, but you have to entertain yourself as a solo walker somehow. When I got to the top of Nevada Falls, it was still very early, and I realised I would have to add some extra distance to the walk or I would be back at my camp with most of the day left to kill. So I walked further along the route that would lead to Half Dome, figuring I would turn around when I got to the point where you needed a permit. On this section, I passed a small group with a guide, who I heard explaining that if they needed the toilet later in the walk, they should urinate directly on the granite rocks, as the deer liked to lick it off. This sounded bizarre and when I tried to 'fact check' online later there were conflicting stories on whether deer like urine or actually dislike it – from this research, I did however very much enjoy the following information found on a permaculture chat forum, from a gentleman called Bob Dobbs, and wondered how it was he had come to discover it:

'I do know for a fact that human shit repels deer quite effectively. As well as hunting/butchering in an area. Both keep my garden deer-free.'

This section of the walk was a bit flat and dull, and it dawned on me that it would be quite depressing if I got right to the end and had to turn around at the final face of Half Dome without being allowed to climb it, so after twenty minutes I doubled back to return to Nevada Falls. This diversion meant that I ended up meeting all of the groups I had overtaken on the climb, who clearly all had permits for Half Dome and I had a succession of comments like 'What, did you run up and down it already?' (Ladies Day Group Two) and I meekly had to say I didn't have a permit and had to go and make my fun elsewhere. Back at the falls, I continued on to the John Muir trail, which was an alternate route back to my starting point and which had hardly any people on it. While taking photos at the top of the falls, I could hear a man, who had just arrived from the other direction, warn a couple of lady hikers that there was a bobcat on the trail up ahead and they should take care. I had no idea what a bobcat was, but I saw the ladies arm themselves with some small stones before carrying on, so I figured that must be what you do and did the same. They were walking quite slowly, and I soon overtook them, joking as I passed that I would let the bobcat take me first, and one of them said, "Oh, you have stones too!" which I failed to confess was not an original thought of mine.

A way further down the path, just after I had discarded my stones, I came across another lady who told me excitedly about the bobcat she had just seen and the great photos she had taken, it didn't sound violent, so I didn't restock my armoury and carried on expectantly. Well I never saw it, so I can't tell you what it was like – I saw loads of squirrels, but you probably know what they look like, so I won't go into detail. I should, however, tell you about the views, which had all of a sudden, become amazing. The trail led away from the rock walls I had walked up earlier and I now looked back across the ravine, where the water was rushing over the top of the walls, and a giant granite rock face to their left rose up towards the patchwork of blue skies and high clouds. Framing this view were pine trees and other vegetation on the surrounding hills, which were just starting to reveal their autumnal colours – spectacular.

A little way further on, I passed a small group of people on horseback taking a break from their ascent and continuing on a bit further I came across the steaming piles of horse shit they had just deposited which prompted a thought. Why is it that people have to clean up after dogs, but horses, which are basically (much larger) pets as well, get away with it? Dogs have to suffer the indignity of walking around with poo bags attached to their collars, dog owners get the even greater indignity of filling up these bags, but horses just stroll around shitting where they like, and neither they nor their owners seem to have any remorse imposing their foul smell on others – this is an inconsistency that the authorities surely need to look into? While I am on poo stories (again – these seem to come up a lot in my writing – I might need to read up on what Freud would make of that), I was reminded of a story I had read about another occasional character in my book, Jon Krakauer. He had been climbing the highest mountain in the States, Mount McKinley with a friend, and found himself in desperate need of a number two during the walk. Climbers on this walk are required to put their waste into a 'McKinley Clean Mountain Can' and dispose it away from the trail, but Jon had not brought one and was caught using a 'natural toilet' instead. What amused me about this story was how they were caught – climbers at base camp were using spotting scopes and watched him – who does that? And what are the odds of it happening in their direct line of sight? I also enjoyed the related quote on the incident from head climbing ranger John Leonard, as reported in the *'Alaska Dispatch'*:

"They were taking a (poop). I don't have much tolerance for people (pooping) on the mountain."

When I joined back up with the Mist Trail just below Vernal Falls, I found myself walking against literally hundreds of people – it was Saturday 10 am which I imagine is serious rush hour, and I was very glad (as always) for my early start. At the bottom, I caught a shuttle bus back to one of the villages where, surprisingly, there was a Starbucks. I read later it had opened in March of this year, and only after surviving a petition with more than 25,000 signatures, raging against what those people saw as a first step in the commercialisation of the park. Time will tell whether they were right. After lunch, I went to the visitor info centre to get some walk recommendations for the next day. The man suggested I should head up to the Glacier Point area of the park where there were two trails I could combine into a more substantial loop walk and the point itself had the best views of Half Dome. He said the best time of day to go was sunset, which prompted me to change my plans. My legs were still feeling fine, and as I didn't have plans for the afternoon, I decided to do all of my walking today and take the next day as a rest day to do some writing and travel to my next destination.

Glacier Point was about a forty-minute drive from the village, and at an elevation of 2,220 metres gave me views back down to the valley where I was staying. The first part of the walk took me to a look down called Taft Point which I have to say was quite terrifying, or as my notes from the walk say, 'scary as f***'. I am generally good with heights but standing at the top of the outcrop with just a small railing to guard the edge of the sheer 300-metre drop to the valley below was a bit much. I would say I didn't linger there long, but the time I stood there was so insignificant it would not even qualify as a 'linger', and I retreated from the edge to a safer distance to take in the impressive scene. (Another postscript – six weeks later, on October 26, a couple fell to their death from Taft Point in unexplained circumstances, though most likely while taking a photograph).

Taft Point and my second target, Sentinel Dome, had relatively accessible trails which were therefore quite busy, but as soon as I ventured on to the longer trail linking the two points along the cliff path, I was back to walking with hardly another soul in sight. The walk along the cliff had a number of additional look downs into the valley far below which I cautiously passed, following the path as it wound away from the cliff edge and up through some woodland to Sentinel Dome. This afforded 360-degree views of the whole park, including Half Dome and El Capitan – and was understandably quite popular. A quick update here on my watch, which I had made friends with again as it was rating my efforts highly in a category which it called 'Intensity Minutes'. I was meant to do 150 of these a week, either 'moderate' ones or 'vigorous', the distinction between the categories being my heart rate level while I was exercising. My national park exertions meant I had been hammering the vigorous minutes, but I've been unable to bring myself to tell you about these yet due to my aversion to the word 'vigorous' which I find is used most typically to describe activities of a more sordid nature…

I wrapped up the day with some time at the Glacier Point lookout, having spent half an hour waiting to get into the car park due to a very poorly designed and non-patrolled parking system, but the view was definitely worth the wait, and I amused myself watching the succession of comedy photos that people were taking of themselves. A group of English tourists had brought along paper hats from 'In And Out Burger' for their group shot which I enjoyed and which also served as a reminder that I needed to find one to visit, as, in my opinion, they make the best burger in the States. I also saw a number of people doing jumping photos and this reminded me of a related tale from my time in Peru. The most recent death at Machu Picchu had been caused by a tourist doing one of those jumping shots on a hill towards the back of the city and he had quite literally jumped off the mountain while doing so – and killed himself. What an absolutely nonsensical way to throw away your life – I can only assume his family made up some other story when they had the awful experience of having to explain how their son had died so young. With that slightly sobering thought and feeling a bit cold I decided I wasn't going to make it to sunset, so drove back to the camp and another night of sleeping rough – but I was so tired this time it really wasn't much of a drama.

***

A few days later, I back on the road, cruising up the freeway on my way to Napa. On this freeway, the outside lane was reserved for 'HOVs' or 'High Occupancy Vehicles' and this concept had been bothering me ever since I had first seen the lanes on my way out of Los Angeles the week before. 'High Occupancy' for these purposes was defined as there being two or more people in the vehicle – if we ignore two-seater cars (as they would be a tiny minority) and consider 'regular' vehicles, two people in a car really didn't sound very high to me, representing 40% occupancy in a saloon car, and 29% in one of those small people carriers. I don't think there are too many exams where a score between 29% and 40% would be classified as high, so this acronym just didn't sit well with me – don't get me wrong, I think it's a great idea, but it needs a better name to avoid aggravating pedants like me – why can't it just be the '2+ lane'?

So evidently, given this was where my thoughts were, the scenery on the drive wasn't really holding my attention. I should maybe explain at this point why I was going to Napa in the first place, given it's not a place well known for backpacking or hiking. Since living in Australia, I had discovered the concept of going to wine growing regions, exploring the many cellar doors for the day and eating dinner in a smart restaurant before sleeping it off and repeating the next day. This combined the excellent pastime of drinking wine 'til merry and enjoying beautiful scenery while doing so, and culminated with the arrival back home with an extraordinary amount of wine in the boot of the car that you hadn't really planned on buying – what's not to like about that? Nothing, in my opinion, and so the initial trips to wine regions near Sydney had expanded to visits to the wine-growing areas around Australia and then trips further afield to places including New Zealand, Argentina, Chile, France and Italy – which I think qualifies wine drinking as a bona fide hobby for me. So while I was on a bit of a different holiday this time around, I didn't think it would be right to visit California without stopping off at their most famous wine regions – to quote my guilty pleasure film *'A Good Year'* again, as Christie Roberts says while talking to the local French winemaker, 'Back in Napa, we're known to gargle and spit on occasion.'

Except I am not a gargle and spit wine taster, meaning my tour around the area could only include a wine tasting or two given I was travelling solo and driving. With this in mind, my first stop was the visitor centre to get some recommendations on the best things to see in the valley, both to make the most of my precious tastings, and also to get some eye-catching photos. After getting said briefing and lining the passenger seat with maps and brochures I was back on the road, heading north, from where I would work my way back to Napa and have dinner in the town – Napa has the most Michelin stars per capita of any wine region in the world, so I was confident of a good feed.

The winery I selected for my tasting on the advice of the visitor centre guy, was a place called Sterling, another grand affair, perched on top of a hill with views over the valley and its own scenic cable car from the car park below to the winery. This is not the kind of winery I would usually visit, preferring the less showy boutique winemakers, but given it apparently combined a wine tasting with some good photo opportunities I decided to give it a go. When I got out of the cable car and started the mandatory tasting tour, I quickly regretted this decision.

The tour was 'self-guided', and a glass was provided at the first tasting which I then carried as the walk continued around the winery, taking in the main points of interest (grape crushers, fermentation room, barrel room etc.) before ending up on a sunny terrace overlooking the valley where visitors could buy a glass or two more and a cheese plate. I like to learn a bit about the wine when I visit wineries, so at the first stop, after a young guy had poured me a glass of their Sauvignon Blanc, I asked him if that was the predominant white grape in the valley, to which he said:

"Yeah, we make this wine with a grape called Sauvignon Blanc, and that's why we call the wine Sauvignon Blanc."

He really said that. My spirits sank a bit, well a lot, and I cringed at the fact I had paid $35 for this 'educational' tour before moving on to the next tasting point, which was a Pinot Noir. The lady there fared a bit better, dealing well with my question about where they were up to with the harvest, and I thought that maybe the first guy was a one-off, but sadly the next two stations were also manned by guys who I would politely describe as being less than knowledgeable. If my Dad had been with me, I am pretty sure he would have used the word 'drongoes' to describe them, and he would have been spot on in doing so. In fairness, the view from the terrace at the end was superb, but this did not come close to making up for the disappointment of the tour, so I finished up my wine (which totalled four of the most miserly pours you are likely to see), chided myself for having made the ill-judged decision to visit in the first place and got back in the car to find somewhere else to cheer me up.

I found this reasonably quickly, as it happened, as the towns in the valley were quite lovely, first of all, St Helena with its smart streets filled with galleries, wine tasting rooms, chocolate shops, bakeries and the like, and then Yountville, where I parked up for a walk around. This town was the polar opposite of the soulless country towns I grumbled about back in the Joshua Tree area, with manicured lawns, well-tended plants, bushes and colourful flower beds and hanging baskets lining the streets, where there were quaint arts and craft shops, more wine tasting rooms and cafes and restaurants, including French Laundry, one of the most highly regarded in California. I stopped in at a bakery called Bouchon and had a sensational blueberry muffin to fuel the remainder of my walk around town, before leaving with the smile having returned to my face.

Now ten days into my US visit, I found myself reflecting on the nuances and idiosyncrasies of this country that were exercising my mind, including key unanswered questions like:

- Why is the letter 'h' in the word 'herb' invisible to all Americans?
- Why do wait staff put the bill for the meal on your table while you are still eating – are they worried there will be an awkward moment in the end when I realise it wasn't free?
- Why do price tags never actually reflect what you have to pay? Everyone has to pay the tax so why can't they just add that on too? (It's a big frustration for weirdoes like me who like to pay with the correct change).

Putting these thoughts to one side, I headed back to town, where I set off on foot for a tour, with my main destination being the Oxbow Public Market across the river, a collection of stalls and restaurants I had read was the 'foodie go-to place' in town. And so it was – housed in a high ceilinged warehouse building, it held an air of excitement about it, with a good late afternoon crowd of people milling around the upmarket grocers, butchers, delicatessens and cheese and wine stalls while others drank at the wine bars or ate an early dinner at the relaxed open plan restaurants, which included an oyster bar and a fancy looking taco place. This was very much my kind of place and was an excellent final stop to cement my final verdict on Napa and surrounds as a thoroughly agreeable place to spend a day or two.

Returning to American Canyon, where I was staying, I was rudely jolted back into thrifty traveller mode when I walked through the front door of the night's Airbnb house and straight into a bit of a bomb site. To the left of the door was the tidy but simple living room I had seen in the photo on the website, but out of that shot, the living room was then divided into two by a big pile of packing boxes and cheap bookshelves, and there was a mattress on the floor – it looked like a homeless sleeping area located within a home, which I thought was an interesting concept. As I had done at the sci-fi theme house in Flagstaff, I quickly found my room and didn't come out again, especially after hearing further arrivals at midnight and then 1:30 am – who knows how many people the guy had jammed into his house, but it sounded like several. The bed also creaked terribly when I made even the slightest movement, so I didn't sleep very well and rushed out the door early in the morning for the short drive to my second wine region, the neighbouring Sonoma Valley.

***

Sonoma had a different feel to Napa, less polished and manicured and with more of a rustic feel, with wide tree-lined roads, a large grassy main square and old wooden historical buildings scattered around the place. A lady called Sue at the visitor centre was able to fill in the gaps for me on the story behind these buildings, many of which saw their origins back to the founding of the San Francisco de Solano mission in 1823, the final of the missions established in California, running in a northerly direction from the first one in San Diego in 1769. She also armed me with my day's leaflet, map and brochure ammunition – I was determined to have a better experience on the wine-tasting front today and got some good sounding recommendations for tasting rooms and headed out of town and into the vines.

After a few roadside photo stops, I arrived at Imagery winery, one of Sue's tips and a certified biodynamic winery. In winemaking, on the fanciness scale (invented by me), you go from regular to 'organic', where you don't use pesticides or other artificial ingredients, and then up to 'biodynamic', which I define as organic plus additional black magic and voodoo. I won't try and explain it in detail, but it involves following the moon cycle (not the 'wind cycle' as the lady in this tasting room suggested), picking and harvesting by hand and doing weird things like burying a cows horn filled with manure amongst the vines. Really. Go read about it.

The 'wind cycle' lady who was doing my tasting asked where I was from and when I said I was from Australia, her eyes lit up, and she went straight to telling me about her friend in Johannesburg who was in the winemaking business there. I let this comment pass as I was quite enjoying their wines and she was full of joy for her day so far, so I listened as she told me a bit about her experience of the massive fire they had suffered in Sonoma in October the previous year. The fire had come right up to the cellar door where fortunately they had stopped it from doing any further damage. The consensus view from other discussions I had on this topic, was that the actions of the wineries in trying to put out the fire had most likely saved all of the towns in the area, so the wineries and their owners were held in high regard by the local community. The impact that the fire had on the vines was yet to be discovered, as the previous year's harvest had been completed before the fire came through and the grapes were just being picked now for this year. The early signs were that the grapes seemed to be okay, which I am sure was a massive relief given the local economy's reliance on the industry.

At $15, my tasting here was much better value to the previous day's experience, and this got even better when the lady gave me a voucher for a free tasting at their sister winery Benziger, which I had already read was the poster child for biodynamic winemaking in the area and celebrated for the quality of their wines. So my decision on where to go next became very straightforward, and about fifteen minutes later I was at the bar in the Benziger tasting room, hoping for great things for what might be my last wine of the day. And it didn't disappoint – I went straight into the reds and had a decent Pinot Noir from the nearby Russian River area, an excellent Bordeaux blend and three more decent reds. I had made friends with a lovely Canadian lady called Tonya who was doing the tasting, and once she realised I knew a bit about wine and had a bit of chat, she pulled out a number of additional wines to try beyond the ones I had paid for – if I had paid for them in the first place – if you know what I mean. This chat with Tonya also rewarded me with some recommendations for lunch and for food stalls to visit at the Sunday evening Farmer's Market in Sonoma (which Sue had told me I had to visit), so it was a very productive tasting all around. I bought a bottle of red and then went down the hill to eat lunch and sober up before driving anywhere else. I had an awesome turkey sandwich for lunch – why is it that only the Americans eat turkey all year round? In the UK and Australia, I see it once a year for Christmas Day, eat it every day in various guises for about a week after and then don't see it again until the following Christmas. Weird.

Back in Sonoma I parked up at about 4 pm and decided that given I was going to the markets and wouldn't be driving home for a while, it would be okay to have another tasting, so I went to a tasting room that Tonya had recommended for its excellent pinot noirs. I forgot to ask the price before starting and cringed a little when I found it was $30, but the wine was pretty good, and the pours were very generous. So much so that I was feeling a little bit tipsy when I left, something which was confirmed when I crossed a road looking the wrong way and was almost run over by an alarmed looking lady driving a car full of kids. This was a clear sign that I shouldn't be driving anywhere for a while, so I found a bench in the park and did some writing in the evening sun while I waited for the markets to start. This was a popular event, with the park packed with people with picnic furniture and big spreads of food, and a load of food stalls and food trucks to feed the hungry masses while they enjoyed the live music as the sun started to set in the distance. The coverage of global cuisine from the food offerings was impressive and included paella, meatball sandwiches, corn dogs (I'm not brave enough to eat one of these), tacos, oysters, doner kebabs, yakitori skewers, tri-tip steak rolls and many kinds of fried potatoes (of course). There was a really warm atmosphere to the event, which Tonya had told me attracted the majority of the local community. I was still full of wine and not super hungry so didn't end up eating, and after what seemed a long enough period of time to get back below the limit, I made the drive back to my doss house and hid in my room again.

***

Sneaking out the next morning, I saw there was actually a guy sleeping on the mattress in the living room, who I think I recognised (from the Airbnb photo) as the house owner. He appeared to have taken his money-making scheme so far as not even keeping a bedroom for himself, which seemed a bit extreme, but each to their own I guess. I went to the nearby Starbucks for coffee and to hang out for a bit until the morning rush hour had passed and then set off for the ninety-minute drive to San Francisco, where I would return the hire car before finding the Airbnb which would be home for the next three nights. I had planned my route so I would drive over the Golden Gate Bridge and while it was a bit of a cloudy morning, I still found myself looking up above as I drove across, picturing Max Zorin's airship above the famous red steel structure and James Bond sending him to his watery grave. I didn't realise at the time, but this was the first event in a series of recurring moments where I found myself recognising places from films I had watched, a sequence that continued when I turned onto the first hill in the city and found myself looking at the street thinking that it looked exactly like where Nick Curran, Michael Douglas's character in *'Basic Instinct'*, lived. I will warn you now, not all of the films that I will reference in the coming weeks are Academy Award-worthy material.

Dropping the car off, the odometer told me (it didn't speak, I read it) that I had covered 3,600 kilometres in the last ten days, which I was quite pleased with given how much it had cost me to do a one-way rental, and I caught an Uber over to the Haight-Ashbury suburb where I was staying. I was too early to check-in so just left my bags in the entrance hall and set off on a walk through the Golden Gate Park which, conveniently, was located just a couple of blocks from my house.

This park was massive, stretching approximately five kilometres from the entrance out to the coast on the westerly end, and is larger than its famous equivalent in New York, Central Park. Every day in California seemed to be a blue-sky day, and this one was no exception, so it was a very pleasant stroll as I passed wide grassy meadows, a large pond with several families of geese, lots of picnickers and recreational areas including a disc/Frisbee golf course and a 'real' golf course. Walking through the park I was struck by the fact that everyone was avoiding eye contact as I passed them, and there were none of the greetings that I would always get when taking a walk in the country, as I had been doing for the last week. Why is that? I mean, the people that you pass on those walks in the country are probably mostly people on holiday who live in the city, yet when you pass these same people in this different scenario, different rules apply. Which is both interesting, and also probably a bit of a shame.

At the end of the park, there was a wide sandy beach and a very uninviting angry looking sea which was reinforced by signs which read 'Beware of rip currents – people have died here!' Given the park name I was expecting to be able to see the bridge and was surprised to find I couldn't, so I started off up the hill to walk around the headland until I could. Since arriving in the middle of San Francisco, I had been hit by the unmistakable smell of urine that seemed to be present wherever you went, an early indicator of the impact of the homeless problems in the city which I would see much of during my stay, and even here that smell lingered by the seawall. It didn't seem a great area at all in truth, as I had just read the sign which cautioned against leaving valuables in your car when I walked past a man talking to a policeman scribbling in his notebook, as the man said, 'Yes, there was an iPad, a MacBook Pro…' – clearly he hadn't taken heed of the sign. At the top of the hill, I arrived at Land's End Park, which wound its way further round the coast, finally revealing the first distant views of the bridge. I carried on along the coastal path for a few kilometres, eventually arriving at some signs of civilisation, with houses along a grand looking street called El Camino del Mar, which are probably better described as palaces, overlooking the bridge and no doubt commanding eye-watering prices. From here, the path dropped down to the beach, and I continued along as far as I could, by which point I wasn't too far from being underneath the bridge.

At this point the walk got a little bit strange as the mix of people on the beach was roughly 50% tourists like me looking for the best photo vantage point, and 50% naked men. In front of the city's most celebrated sight this felt a little bit strange, but the city is also famed for its liberal outlook on life, and the two groups of people seemed to be just going about their respective business quite happily, so why not? After taking photos of the bridge from many angles I set off to return home, but I hadn't really planned this bit of the walk, and I got a bit lost in an area called The Presidio. I had not brought a drink with me and had been walking for a few hours at this point, so getting lost in a woodland area at this point was less than ideal, but I was soon saved as I arrived at a golf course which had a food and drink hut where I rehydrated in preparation for the remaining hour or so walk home.

I was amused to see a sign that warned 'Beware of errant golf balls', as if the guilty party in the unfortunate event of the ball hitting you in the face was the naughty ball and not the person who had hit the wayward shot. I survived unscathed from the errant balls, and eventually arrived back at the grid of city streets and found my way back across to the park to my house, where I could now check-in.

The room I had here for the next two nights was 'TINY' – think Harry Potter's broom cupboard, put a Jimi Hendrix picture on the wall and you have it. The Hendrix relevance wasn't immediately obvious, but I later learned that he used to live in a flat on the corner of Haight and Ashbury, one block from here, and also played gigs in the area, as did other luminaries of the time including Bob Dylan and Janis Joplin, so I had stumbled into what appeared to be a celebrated area from a cultural perspective.

One feature the accommodation had going for it was the speed of the Wi-Fi, which was an important consideration at this point in time as I had some homework to do on the dating apps to try and engineer a date during the three-night window I had here. San Francisco is a massive city, and this meant that there were absolutely tonnes of people on the app that I had to work through, trying to choose a large enough population of women I liked the look of to have one or two who would be willing to go on a date with someone who clearly wasn't in town long, and who therefore presented zero long term potential. I didn't get to the end of the list on either of the apps, but I literally spent hours working through it, until eventually, I decided I could swipe no more and called it a night, hoping for some positive outcomes the next morning.

Thankfully, after all that effort, there appeared to be some progress, as the next morning I had seven matches on Bumble, so I now just had to wait for them to message me, something the woman has to do first on that app. While they all thought of something funny to write, I spent the morning on a walking tour, heading east from my house and walking for an hour or so to the downtown area where I wandered around the main points of interest that the books and blogs told me I had to visit. The first of these was 'The Painted Ladies', a block of classic San Francisco (clapboard) houses which are meant to be the finest example of that style of building in the city and which can be viewed from an elevated park across the road. I had seen some quite cool photos of these buildings from my friends' travels, but the light must not have been right today, as I really wasn't that impressed and didn't actually take any photos. Continuing east, I came across multiple pockets of homelessness, with people sleeping on the street, on benches, in tents and even in abandoned cars – it wasn't a great sight as you can imagine. It seems no one has an answer for this endemic social issue and the thought that crossed my mind as I walked past was, what happens when we get to what seems to be the inevitable outcome of a cashless society? I'm sure these people don't make loads from begging, but it's probably enough to make a difference for some of them, and what happens to them when we transition to this cashless economy?

A while later I arrived at Civic Square, and immediately recognised the City Hall Building from, you guessed it, *'A View to a Kill'*. For those of you who haven't seen this film as many times as me, this is the location where James Bond rescues Stacey Sutton, played by Tanya Roberts, from the burning building before going on a car chase around town driving a fire truck. For me, these scenes are ruined by Tanya making some of the most annoying screams ever heard on the big screen (while dangling over a burning lift shaft), but it cheers me slightly to know this performance took her no further than 'straight to video' movies and reasonably rapid film world anonymity. I'm not a complete meanie though, so hopefully, she is still doing well for herself in whatever new vocation she found.

Back on my walk, I had found myself in another fairly grubby area, and the homeless issue was actually making me a bit uncomfortable. It was not the homelessness per se that was the problem for me, it was the percentage of these poor souls who were clearly also mentally disturbed. Reading up on this topic, I learnt that the majority of the blame for this issue is levelled at President Reagan, who, shortly after entering office embarked on a policy of 'deinstitutionalisation'. In more simple words this meant he closed down a load of mental hospitals, releasing a whole population of mentally ill people back into the community with no plans in place for their treatment or rehabilitation. As many of these people had no-one looking out for their welfare and nowhere to go, they ended up homeless. I read an extract of a book on this subject, by a gentleman called E. Fuller Torrey, called *'American Psychosis: How the Federal Government Destroyed the Mental Illness Treatment System'* and this referenced two studies which had been carried out on patients discharged from mental hospitals. The studies found that 27% of the 187 patients discharged from Metropolitan State Hospital in Massachusetts, and 36% of the 132 patients discharged from Columbus State Hospital in Ohio had become homeless – dreadful statistics. The extract also referenced other statistics, including alarming increases in police call-outs in New York City to deal with 'emotionally disturbed persons' through the 80s, and painted a bleak picture of the problem that had been created and the apparent lack of any action from government to do anything about it. I would experience this issue again first-hand in Portland and also in Seattle (though to a lesser extent), as well as seeing a number of organised fundraising events in support of the cause, but for the time being, it doesn't seem anyone has the answer.

My feeling of unease meant I diverted to the main shopping area for some solace, which was a shame as it meant I didn't make it to the Mission area, which I later discovered was one of the most vibrant parts of town and somewhere I should not have missed. Next time. My diversion took me into some of the more well-trodden tourist areas, starting at the Ferry Building in the Embarcadero district, which had a load of smart food shops including cheese from Neal's Yard Dairy in Covent Garden, which I, therefore, couldn't fail to love, and ending up at Fisherman's Wharf, which looked to be the most touristy area in San Francisco, if not the world. Suffice to say I didn't like the area and didn't linger long, though I did take away a couple of positives, being the view across the bay to Alcatraz and the sea lions who hang out at Pier 39, making those ludicrous noises that only they can. Back on my movie references, I celebrated the fact I could still see Alcatraz, something that would not have been possible were it not for the efforts of Stanley Goodspeed and John Mason (aka Nicholas Cage and Sean Connery in *'The Rock'*) to disarm deadly VX gas rockets back in 1996. My eye was also taken by the distinctive structure of the Trans America Pyramid building, the second tallest on the skyline, but more famous to me as the structure recently disarmed (again) by a nuclear warhead, which Ethan Hunt and crew bounce off in *'Mission Impossible IV: Ghost Protocol'* before landing safely in the bay. I did warn you they weren't going to be Oscar contenders...

After briskly ticking off these tourist hotspots, I walked up my first giant San Francisco hill to the suburb of Pacific Heights, where I had the novelty of a lunch meeting with a human being who I actually already knew. Gus was from my team at work in Sydney but had been on secondment to San Francisco for the last year or so. He was loving life in San Francisco, particularly the consistent climate and taking advantage of the abundance of outdoor activities nearby, whether it be on foot or bicycle. He wasn't loving the latter quite so much at this point in time, as he had just had a big spill and fractured his scapula so was sporting a sling for his troubles, but we had a good catch up before he brushed me off to get on with the more important things in his day (rude!) and I walked back across town to return to my house.

Back to my dating app homework. Only one of the seven matches from the morning had sent a message, Audra, who seemed quite fun and with whom I swapped several messages on travel-related matters, as she was planning a year out and was basically hitting me up for advice. However, she surprised me by saying she was up for going out the next day if I was interested, an offer I swiftly jumped on, and we agreed to meet at 4:30 pm the next day after school – before you judge me, she was a teacher, not a student.

***

The next day was bike day, and I had rented one from a place down the road so I could take a ride over the bridge, down to the popular bay side suburb of Sausalito and then onwards around a few more bays and maybe a loop up into the hills if I was feeling energetic. There weren't too many people on the trails at that time of day, so I made fast work to Sausalito and carried on round the bays on some very well maintained and signposted cycleways, away from any traffic. As I followed the trail around the various inlets, the scenery became more rural and more spectacular, and as I rounded one bend, I had a deer running along the road to my left while a seaplane took off from the bay to my right – not a sight I see on every bike ride. The only downside was the cloud cover, which was obscuring the view back across to the bridge and over the bay to the city – the silver lining here though was that I had an excuse not to continue my ride up into the hills, knowing the views wouldn't be worth the effort. About two hours in, I arrived at the bay side village of Tiburon, where I stopped for a refuel before continuing around the bay on 'Paradise Drive'. While this did have some good bay views, it wasn't as spectacular as the name had led me to believe, and after twenty minutes I looped back round to the trail I had arrived on and retraced my tracks to Sausalito.

The usual way to visit Sausalito is to either ride your bike there and then ferry back to Fisherman's Wharf, or just take a return ferry. Being so accessible, it was absolutely rammed with tourists – and I had to pay $3 to park my bicycle – outrageous! The village itself was very pretty, with lots of quaint boutiques, cafes and restaurants to satisfy the tourist crowd. I grabbed a sandwich there before heading off back up the hill to the bridge, which was apparently beyond the abilities of most people. Even on a reasonably shit bike it really wasn't that hard, so if you make that trip and are considering the easy option I encourage you to go against your instincts and ride back up the hill – just imagine the sense of accomplishment you will have! Without wanting to spoil the sermon, it was absolutely freezing when I got up to the bridge, which was now shrouded in cloud, and I was in a hurry to get home. Blocking my passage to do so were thousands of bike riding tourists who had now arrived at the scene. Gus had warned me the day before about this, and I hadn't taken him seriously, but now I was confronted with a procession of people on bikes in quite heavy traffic, riding along while videoing the event (or themselves) and not looking where they were going – absolutely absurd. Shortly after, I passed a speedometer on the bridge that told me I was going at fifteen mph, without any commentary as to whether this was a good or bad score, and I was relieved to finally get to the end, where I turned off and recreated my previous walking route through The Presidio to get me back to the bike shop and then home to prepare for my date. We had some debate later in the evening as to whether we were really on a date, or just on a 'meet-up' (Audra's expression) given I was leaving town the next day, but she referred to it as a date more than once, so I'm going to stick with describing it as so.

When we had agreed to meet up, Audra had suggested I should come and meet her at North Beach, the suburb where her school was, at the early kick-off time of 4:30 pm. She would give me a walking tour of this historical suburb and neighbouring Chinatown, where we would then go and eat the best soup dumplings, which she confusingly referred to as being 'solid'. When I asked her later how a soup dumpling could be solid, she laughed at me and explained that the word solid is a Californian slang term for something that is really good – a little bit embarrassing for me. Audra was about the same age as me and had grown up in a country town to the east of San Francisco before going to college on the East Coast ('same place as Hillary Clinton!'), working in New York for a while and then Los Angeles for a number of years, before returning closer to home to live in San Francisco, where she had been for about the last eight years. Audra taught middle school English, and her school mainly serviced the children of the newer immigrants to the area, mainly from South East Asia and North Africa, and she positively beamed as she spoke about how much she loved her job and her students. I quickly established that Audra was quite a 'force', brimming with infectious energy and talking fifteen to the dozen as she pointed out the local sights and explained the history, while also continuing separate discussions with me at the same time on 'get to know you kind of stuff'. I could instantly tell I was going to enjoy her company and she seemed to get my sense of humour, so I was already looking forward to the rest of our date, sorry, meet-up. The shops, bars and restaurants in North Beach were seemingly stuffed with stories of historical intrigue, and Audra showed me places that had been owned and frequented by Joe DiMaggio, including during his relationship with Marilyn Monroe, before walking past a famous bookshop (City Lights Booksellers) and bars that had been popular with Jack Kerouac, Allen Ginsberg and the 'beatniks' in the 1950s and 1960s – it was fascinating stuff, and I was feeling very lucky to have a personal tour guide for the experience.

After a quick circuit of Chinatown and a look in some of the stores that sell those horrifically smelling dried fish and sea cucumbers that the Chinese pay inordinate amounts of money for, we ended up in a bar called Vesuvio which had opened in 1948 and was apparently one of Kerouac's absolute faves. Audra taught me a few more things about San Francisco, including the introduction to the Ronald Reagan related homeless content which I casually passed off as my own material a few pages back, and also explaining to me why all the street names in San Francisco were also scratched into the cement by the kerb at the end of each road. I had been puzzled by this phenomenon since I had arrived, so this was a well-received piece of trivia. The reason dated back to the Great Fire of 1906, when the smoke from the fire obscured street signs, and people had become completely disoriented with no idea where they were and unable to find a route to safety. The town planners decided this must never happen again and hence the ground level signage had been added.

Over several glasses of wine, I was able to partially reciprocate Audra's tour guide role sharing my travel experiences which may or may not serve to assist her in planning for some upcoming travel of her own. Audra had recently successfully applied to a sabbatical scheme at work which meant she could take fourteen months off to go and do whatever she liked, while still receiving 60% of her pay – which sounded a great scheme to me – and from reading my dating profile guessed that I might be a good person to bounce ideas off. I had also updated my profile to reference the fact that I was writing a book, which I thought maybe a useful 'lure' and she was very interested in talking about that, so it was pleasing to see that strategy had paid off! Audra had already decided that as I was leaving for Portland the next day, there was zero potential for a relationship. Therefore, she was completely relaxed about telling me anything, knowing it wouldn't come back to bite her later, and as a result, the conversation ended up going in all sorts of bizarre, but hugely entertaining directions. I promised I would not commit some of the more 'exotic' content to paper so as not to reveal the identities of other parties involved, so I will keep those for rainy day storytelling to a more select audience. The time raced by and soon we had a logistical issue to deal with, in that Audra needed to move her car to somewhere it could be left overnight before she could have any more to drink, so we headed off to attend to this before finding somewhere to eat nearby. That wasn't quite how it played out though, as Audra decided the best place to relocate her car was to her apartment, about a 25-minute drive away, though she insisted it was 'kind of on your way home'. She was also keen for me to see how people lived in San Francisco, so seeing her apartment was effectively part of my 'tour', and I was fine with that.

We had some more wine and chat, with Audra telling an interesting story about her experience with 9/11 which occurred while she was living in New York. In the aftermath of the plane strikes that day, she said that like many other people, she was out wandering the streets in a state of bewilderment as to what was happening and what they should do. At which time she came across a couple of guys dragging suitcases around who told her they were from Poland and due to fly home that day but didn't know if that was still going to happen and they did not have any money left to do anything else. She told them she didn't think they would be flying anywhere that day, gave them her contact details and wished them the best before heading back to her apartment to work out what she should do next. Audra described she and her housemate had a feeling that the country was under attack and that they should go into survivalist mode, which for them meant going to buy canned food – which they did. However, a concerned relative had called Audra and said it would be better for them to escape the city and go and stay with them in the safety of the countryside for a while. As they packed and got ready to leave there was a knock on the door, shortly after which, her housemate came into Audra's room with a confused look on her face saying that two random foreign men were asking for her – the Polish guys! Audra had told them if they were stuck they could come and stay with her and they had arrived to take her up on the offer – which she honoured, leaving them to sleep in her bed, with canned food on which to survive, while she and her housemate left the city. I thought it was a great story as it brought out the feelings of fear and uncertainty that the people of the city must have all been feeling, while also shining a light on the power of human kindness to help others during that dreadful time.

At this point, while Audra got changed, I was doing my best to read where we were at on the meet-up vs date scale. It was nearly 10 pm when we headed out for what was now a fairly late dinner, to Audra's neighbourhood Italian, in a suburb called Bernal Heights. We shared some pizza and pasta before realising we were the only remaining diners, and they were cleaning up around us and it was probably time to move on. Audra then took me to a nearby bar called Wild Side West (opened in 1962), which had some historical fame in that both Janis Joplin and Bob Dylan had frequented it back in the day. Audra said it was alleged that Janis Joplin had sex on the pool table in the bar, but I couldn't find any support via Google for this claim, but who knows, maybe she did! The bar had a great patio that sadly was not open, but while Audra was establishing this fact and popping to the ladies, I was left in charge of buying some more drinks. There were maybe 20 people in the bar, all women as it was a popular lesbian hangout these days and as I waited to order, an old lady at the bar was having a conversation across me, so I thought it would be polite to say hello. The lady asked me where I was from and we exchanged pleasantries before the conversation quickly veered into a whole lot of weirdness, the starting point being when she took her teeth out – the whole top set. Over the course of the next minute or so she replaced and removed the teeth two or three more times, as Audra, and I flashed slightly baffled looks at each other, but the stuff she was saying was even worse and went something like this:

Teeth lady – "Ah, your name is Alex. I had a nephew called Alex, but he passed."
Me – "Oh, I'm sorry to hear that."
Teeth lady – "Yes, he got into trouble because they found out he was a molester. And then he disappeared. They never found the body."

After a brief stunned silence, I grabbed our drinks with a parting, 'Well, we had better leave you to it, nice to meet you', and headed for a table in the corner. Incredible.

A while later, finishing our drinks (and after some more content I would blush too much to contemplate repeating), Audra asked what I wanted to do next, and the options were either to drink more or for me to go home. I was hoping for a third option, but it wasn't suggested, and given it was midnight and I had to be up to get to the airport, I begrudgingly went for option two to avoid any Guatemala-esque late night disasters.

***

Even with the surprisingly sensible decision to stop drinking at that point, I was a bit dusty the next morning, but managed to get myself packed up and into an Uber to go to the airport – the driver asked where I was off to and we had the following exchange:

Me – 'I'm going to Portland.'

Him – 'Wow, how long is the flight time?'

Me – 'Err, about an hour, I think?'

Pause...

Him – 'Oh, Portland! I thought you said Poland.'

Which I thought was a bizarre coincidence given the 9/11 story from the night before.

On the plane ride, I was back into the Lonely Planet to compile the must-do list for a couple of days in Portland. A lot of the content was beer or beer-related, as I learnt that there are over 70 microbreweries in the Portland metro area alone, more than any other city on earth. I also read that one of the shopping malls in town housed the ice rink where Tonya Harding had learned to skate. I had recently watched the excellent *'I, Tonya'*, so the ludicrous true-life tale of the plot to incapacitate her rival, Nancy Kerrigan, ahead of the 1994 Winter Olympics was fresh in my mind and I made a mental note to take a look if I happened to be in that area.

I was staying in the north-west of town in a leafy area called the Alphabet District, in a room of a house hosted by a chap called Ben, who was a tour guide. He was out when I arrived, but I was just dropping my bags anyway as I wanted to walk into town to catch the Saturday markets before they finished at 4:30 pm. The walk from the Alphabet District and into the Pearl District, was very pleasant, housing a number of cool looking bars, restaurants and shops in converted warehouse buildings, a large pub in a repurposed power station, and 'Powell's City of Books', a bookstore which covered a whole city block and housed over a million books in its four floors. As I neared the centre of town, I was presented with the now-familiar scenes of homelessness and mental illness I had seen in San Francisco and was relieved when I made it to the into the throng of tourists who were in attendance at the Saturday markets. The market was a mix of art, crafts and food stalls and an early indicator of just how cosmopolitan the Portland food scene is. The food stalls included offerings from Turkey, China, Argentina, Italy, Nepal, Lebanon, Thailand, Mexico, Poland and North Africa – quite an array! Whilst other stalls had a mix of clothes, jewellery, pictures and the like, plus a few genuine oddities with my favourite two being a stall where you could buy a wide range of headwear all of which looked like you had a knife or some other sharp implement stuck through your skull, and another stall where a man took a photo of you and made a gnome based on your likeness called, 'Getting To Gnome You' – someone give that man a prize!

I continued on to a square on SW Alder St that was filled with food trucks, something of a common sight around town and taking the international food coverage to the next level. In addition to the countries represented at the markets, this square included offerings from Egypt, Vietnam, Persia, Iraq, Korea, Hawaii, Germany and, last but not least, Scotland, whose stall included its nation's most celebrated contribution to world cuisine. No, not haggis, I'm talking about the deep-fried Mars Bar. I should confess after that sledge, that I did share one of these with my fellow hikers on my Nepal trip earlier in the year and it was really rather good – though not so much for one's cholesterol levels I suspect.

Stopping off at the bookstore on my way back, I marvelled at the vast selection and in particular the travel writing section, and I decided I would like to return one day to find my book – there was a shelf note recommending one of Bill Bryson's books so I could see the staff here had excellent taste. By now I was starving so made my way to one of the brewery restaurants in the centre, Deschutes Brewery, to try some of their beer and what had been voted by some publication as 'the best crab roll in Oregon'. The beer selection was quite overwhelming, and I thought I could have done with the company of my old University housemate, Steve, as he was a massive beer fan and even organised a large annual event called the Bristol Beer Week as part of this hobby. Except Steve couldn't be with me, as he had a pathological fear of flying and didn't get on planes anymore. The last time I had flown with him was almost twenty years earlier when we had persuaded him to take a flight to Geneva for a ski trip. He got through this (short) flight by drinking about half a litre of vodka (which he had disguised by adding Robinson's 'Summer Fruits' cordial to it) whilst repeating 'We're going to die!' at regular intervals inflight, at a volume loud enough for much of the cabin to hear, while sweating profusely. On arrival, he did not look in a good way, and I was mighty glad I hadn't been sat next to him and was actually able to pretend I wasn't with him. Sorry, I am off on a bit of a tangent again – anyway I didn't have the skills of the other drinkers with orders like, 'Can I have an IPA of your choice please, more floral, less hoppy' as an example, so I asked for the one that had 'lager' in the name. And it was fine.

***

Next morning I woke to find I had some action on the dating app front, a sarcastic sounding message from a lady called Angela saying, "You are on a wonderful adventure around the world, and you came to Portland, Oregon!" This was a good start, and after a bit of back and forth she also asked the 'What is your book about?' question and I could see there was potential. I had plans for the day which I wanted to get on with and feeling a bit more confident about this dating app malarkey, I quickly cut to the chase and asked her if she wanted to meet up before I left. Angela was also planning some travel, so I had that angle again, and sure enough, she said she wanted to meet, which we agreed we would do the following evening. This was definitely just going to be a 'meet-up' as I would be driving to Salem that night, a town an hour south of Portland, but I was keen to have dinner with someone again, so this was fine with me. Having organised this, I set off for the centre of town, to walk 60 blocks to the east to an elevated park in a suburb called Mt Tabor which apparently offered stunning views back down to the city. As I walked through town and the various suburbs, it was easy to identify the 'in' venues as they all had big groups of people waiting patiently outside for a table to free up. By now, I had learnt of two things Portland residents love – eating brunch and standing in lines. I also saw several more indicators of Portland's hipster status, including multiple breweries, a ping pong bar, 'kombucha taprooms', more food truck parades and what appeared to be the next level of shared bike system, battery-powered shared scooters. Too cool for school…

As I neared Mt Tabor, the scene got leafier and I positively beamed at the sight of horse chestnut trees, replete with a full armoury of conkers, which is something I had not seen for many years, and the leaves on the trees became more colourful, a dramatic mix of greens, yellows, oranges, crimson and brown that positively screamed 'Fall'. The park itself was very scenic, with a network of paths winding through the woodland to the summit, where tall maple and oak trees provided a shaded area from where to take in the city views and shafts of light glistened through the canopy lighting up the colourful foliage below. Against this backdrop, the park was filled with families walking, joggers and the odd cyclist, giving the place a lovely feel for spending a crisp autumnal Sunday morning. Working my way through the park from north to south, I came out on a different road to walk back to town, which would take me through the suburb of Richmond, where a number of the recommended restaurants in the Lonely Planet were to be found. I chose a Thai restaurant called Pok Pok for lunch and arrived early enough to avoid the lines that are apparently always endured. I had a wonderful Asian style half roast chicken with sticky rice, a spicy papaya salad and a couple of dipping sauces – and a Singha beer as a reward for the walk completed and to come. Very good food, very cool place.

My feet were grumbling at me again after walking back across town to get home, so I had a bit of a lazy afternoon, before heading out for an early evening outing recommended by the waitress in Pok Pok. This was a September-only event that was very popular with the locals and involved going and sitting in a park and watching a load of small birds called 'Vaux's swifts' fly around the chimney of a school for an hour or so on dusk before they all piled in to roost there. I'm not exaggerating when I say 'a load' – they had a website where they recorded counts each night (who knows how) and the most recent two days were both over 12,000 birds. This scene attracted as many as 2,000 people each night, bringing picnics and drinks, neither of which I had the foresight to bring. It was quite an impressive scene as the swarm of birds got denser, but eventually, hunger and the cold got the better of me, and I made a dash to a nearby brewery, Breakside, for what turned out to be an insanely good burger for dinner. And more 'lager'. As I ate, I reflected on the bird display and my hopes that the swarm would culminate in a memorable conclusion by assuming a unified, recognisable form, like maybe a face, or one giant swift, or like something out of *'The Mummy'*. I acknowledged that maybe my hopes were a bit high, and I was asking too much from the little guys and gals; next time, I would manage my expectations more appropriately.

After an epic ten hours of sleep, I bode farewell to Ben and walked across town to collect the car that would be facilitating a three-day tour around some of the nearby Oregon countryside and coastal scenery. My first stop was to be a walk on Mt Hood, the dormant volcano that loomed large on the local skyline, just an hour or so drive out of town. The freeway driving on the edge of town quickly turned into a scenic drive, with trees absolutely everywhere, a mix of deciduous trees in their colourful fall outfits, mighty evergreens and also what looked like a number of large tree farms. I passed by the town of Boring, which boasted both a boring winery and a boring brewery before a brief petrol station stop to get some walking provisions. On leaving this petrol station, my attention was drawn to a sign at the exit advertising the fact they had been voted 'cleanest restroom in town' – who comes up with these ideas?

Shortly after, the view of Mt Hood was looming large through the tall pine trees which now lined both sides of the road. Passing through the winter sports village of Government Camp, I turned onto a road which wound its way up the side of the mountain to the giant hotel at the base of many of the ski lifts, called Timberline Lodge where the trail I had chosen to walk would begin. I was due at my meet-up at 4:30 pm and wanting to take the scenic drive through the Columbia River Gorge back to Portland, I was just walking a relatively short section of the Pacific Crest Trail for a couple of miles to a lookout called Paradise Park. The view up to Mt Hood was not that exciting, a large grey mass of rock with some patches of snow covering towards the top, but the view in the other direction was awesome. It was a completely clear day, and I could see right across to the peak of Mt Jefferson, with the dense forests of pine trees forming different shades of indigo and dark blue in the foreground. The path itself alternated between rock and gravel sections and woodland, and each time you came out of the woodland sections, you got a different flash of autumnal colour from the trees ahead until the final vista which looked down over the Zigzag Canyon and across to Mt Jefferson.

Some of the names of these places were sounding vaguely familiar, and later in the day, I remembered a few weeks earlier reading on BBC News, about an animal attack, which was being reported as the first confirmed case of a walker being killed by a cougar, or mountain lion, to use the more dramatic name. The attack was on a lady called Diane Bober, right here in Mt Hood National Park near the Zigzag Ranger Station. Today's outing was an unplanned addition to my itinerary, so this hadn't really registered at the time, but I was intrigued that I found myself walking in almost exactly the same area. It had been reported they had found and killed the cougar they thought was the culprit (how?) so I was unlikely to have been stalked by the deadly predator on today's casual stroll, but it was good to be reminded there were more animals than just squirrels out here in the wilderness, which was about the only animal life I ever saw!

Back in the car, there seemed to be massive mountains whichever way you drove in this area, and for this section, I had Mt Adams in Washington State ahead of me before joining the freeway. This is, without doubt, the most scenic freeway/motorway/autostrada/autoroute I have ever driven on, with the road following the route of the river at the base of the deeply cut gorge, with high canyon walls to the left of the road and the river to the right. The river was wide enough to look more like a lake, and the sun was glistening on the blue water which, for a lot of the time, was just a stone's throw away from the passenger window, and I could see a number of birds-of-prey circling above. The top of the canyon walls was lined with thousands of pine trees, their outline on the blue-sky background like tiny teeth on a fine comb, and the scene further enhanced by waterfalls tumbling from the top, including the most spectacular Multnomah Falls – and this drive went on for sixty kilometres! It was amazing, the only shame being that I didn't have time to cross over and drive back along the road running along the other side of the river.

After gorging on that scene (sorry…) for an hour or so, I arrived at the outskirts of Portland and continued on to the small satellite town of Tualatin, which was where Angela lived and where we had agreed to meet for dinner given it was also on my route south to Salem. I had timed my day's excursion well, reaching the restaurant at 4:20 pm and got a table outside by the ornamental lake, which I think qualified as the prettiest spot in town. Angela arrived shortly after, saying the front of house lady had said to her, "Are you meeting the gentleman with the darling accent?" – and yes, she was.

Angela worked for a local academic institution in a government policy guidance role that I didn't completely follow, but I didn't have long to dwell on this before the conversation turned to children, I asked if she had any and she surprised me by saying that she had four, aged between fifteen and 22. As I did the mental arithmetic on how this was possible (she was about my age), I also wondered why I hadn't noticed this on her profile, all while trying to also pay attention to what she was saying. The answer to the first was that she had got married very young, and the answer to the second was that she hadn't actually written anything on her profile, but I had decided to take a flyer as she looked quite attractive and had lots of photos of outdoorsy activity stuff and giant dogs, which were apparently Great Dane Mastiffs. The four-child revelation was more of a surprise than an issue for me, as we were just there for dinner anyway and she was very good company and had plenty of good chat, which we got into over a few glasses of local pinot noir.

After her early start to married life and child production, things had gone a bit south for Angela, and she had divorced at 32, and with her children moved from Montana, where they were living at the time, to Oregon where she had been born and raised. She shared with me about the culture shock of having to get back into the singles scene at that stage in life and spoke of a two-year period where she and a friend had gone pretty hard going out and drinking and hitting bars and clubs until all hours every weekend. At the end of this story, I forget the exact expression she used, but it was along the lines of

'I went a bit crazy for a while there', and she then paused for thought for a minute, and I was readying myself for a statement of remorse when she instead came out with,

"I had a 'LOT' of fun."

Legend. The discussion on this topic then moved seamlessly to strip clubs in Portland (not raised by me), and Angela told me that Portland has the highest number of strip clubs per capita in the USA. I checked this claim later and found a study that had been conducted proving this, though apparently the definition of a strip club is a very subjective process so this could be open to debate, regardless it is a point of fact that they do have a lot. I think this came up as Angela was trying to come up with interesting local info for my book, which she was very intrigued about, and she then came out with something quite bizarre that it would be unthinkable for me not to share with you. Tualatin is a small town and seemed to be famous for not much, but one event that does attract wider attention in the region is the annual 'West Coast Giant Pumpkin Regatta', first held in 2004. Each year, people come to witness the sight, at the lake where I now sat, of people in fancy dress paddling hollowed out 1,000lb pumpkins in a series of 'wacky races' – have you ever heard of anything so ridiculous yet so awesome at the same time? The race takes place in October, so I was too early to catch it, but I had a look at some photos on Google Images, which I recommend you also do, as there are some impressive vessels and fancy-dress outfits on there. And that was about it – the dinner was excellent, and I had enjoyed Angela's company for the evening, but it was time for me to continue my journey. After saying our goodbyes, I made the short drive south to my Airbnb in Salem, where I was making the briefest of stays before continuing on the next day for a look around the Willamette Valley, the local wine region.

***

Angela had warned me Salem was a bit sketchy which had put me a bit on edge and when I came out of the house the next morning I cursed under my breath as I saw someone had left some rubbish on my car roof. However, when I got to the car, I realised it was actually something I had accidentally left there while getting my bags out the car the night before, a homemade peanut butter cup wrapped in napkins that Angela had given me the night before. So apologies to Salem for that slight, and apologies to Angela, but it was nicely chilled from its overnight adventure and made a fantastic accompaniment to my morning coffee, so it didn't go to waste. On the way out of Salem, I passed the Oregon State Capitol where Angela had said that with Oregon being such a liberal state you were legally allowed to walk into this building to do things like lodge a protest (about whatever) while carrying your gun, as there were no scanners on the way in. My already limited interest in visiting this place was reduced to nil now that I knew there could be gun-toting protesters wandering the halls, and I headed straight out of town, passing through a scene of corn and other crop fields and atmospheric farm buildings on my way to the town of Dundee.

Unfortunately, the wineries didn't open until 11 am and I was there somewhat earlier, so I took advantage of the morning light to capture photos of the vines, drank more coffee and caught up on some writing before heading to Stoller Vineyards, another recommendation from Angela. They had a beautiful tasting room which overlooked the lawns to the vines, with a separate view out behind the tasting table to Mt Hood in the distance. I went through my usual process of making friends with the guy in charge of the wine and settled in for a long list of pinots and other reds. This area sits at the same latitude as Burgundy and is famed for the quality of their chardonnays and pinot noirs, and that was why I was here, having bought and enjoyed pinots in Sydney from this exact area, and the wines here lived up to my expectations, making for a very satisfying start to the day. The guy behind the bar also armed me with some tips for my upcoming time over on the Oregon coast and I was on my way shortly after, passing through more vineyards and hazelnut and walnut farms on the valley floor, before reaching wooded scenery and winding roads as I approached the coast.

At the coast, I joined the 101, which runs the length of the Pacific Coast, before turning at the town of Pacific City onto the 'Three Capes Drive', which hugged the spectacular coast from Cape Kiwanda at the southerly end, up to the clifftop viewpoint at Cape Lookout and then further north to Cape Meares at the northerly end of the peninsula. At Cape Kiwanda the scene was one of giant sand dunes and a wide beach with the imposing sight of the 100m high sea stack just off the coast, Haystack Rock, which Wikipedia claims is the fourth highest sea stack in the world – I didn't go hunting to find out the top three as frankly, I wasn't that interested. Heading north, the coast road rose to Cape Lookout, where I had read there was an excellent walk to be done, but my legs were in need of a rest, so I decided today was going to be a driving day, and I took the lazy option of a few pictures from the roadside lookout. As I looked north at the cliffs lined with pine trees behind the windswept beaches, I couldn't help thinking the scene looked familiar and realised that the memory it was evoking was of the final scene in *'Point Break'*, where Patrick Swayze's character 'Bodhi' paddles out into a monstrous wave to commit 'suicide by surf' in the 'hundred-year storm' at Bell's Beach in Australia. Except they didn't film it in Australia, which you can tell by the awful Australian accents and the fact the beach in the film looks nothing like the real one, and I thought I recalled reading they used a beach in Oregon. I later confirmed this was the case, though I was a bit premature, as the beach they filmed at was Indian Beach in the Ecola State Park, north of Cannons Beach, half an hour further north.

Cannons Beach was the most popular beachside town in the area, with a spectacular wide sandy beach and a collection of stacks and needles offshore (which confusingly included another 'Haystack Rock'). It was a very polished looking town with lots of expensive looking galleries, boutiques and tourist shops and a number of cafes and restaurants. If this had been in England, I guarantee it would have been right up there in the 'Tidy Towns' awards as it was absolutely immaculate. I had planned to spend a bit of time here, but I was quite tired from all the running around of the last couple of weeks and ready for a chill-out, so I just had some fish and chips and then got back in the car for the last half an hour of my journey to Astoria, a town at the far north of the Oregon coast, where the Columbia River meets the sea.

I couldn't find any Airbnb's here, so was staying at a '50s themed place called the Atomic Motel which had a giant retro cinema film board style sign outside that boasted, 'We're fun!' The place was decked out in a sky blue and pink paint job, and with cardboard cut-outs of Frank Sinatra and Dean Martin and a super happy lady in reception, I could see no reason not to believe the claim on the sign. There was also a map of the top sights in town, which the lady excitedly talked me through, but I hardly heard a word she said as my eye had instantly been taken by three words written on the map – '*Goonies House Viewpoint*' – I was staying in the town where they filmed The Goonies! I had been enjoying my passing references to film locations I had recognised over the last week or so, but this was moving things to a whole new level. I dismissed my concerns over fatigue and sore feet and dumped my bags and set off immediately on my pilgrimage to the house, which was about a 45-minute walk on the other side of town.

As I walked along the road that tracked along the waterfront, I remembered I had read a few years ago that the owners of the Goonies House had experienced issues with the number of film fans turning up to see the place, leaving rubbish behind and getting a bit carried away doing 'truffle shuffles' on the front lawn, and consequently it had been closed to visitors. Hence the need for a viewpoint, and when I arrived, this scaled-back experience was worsened by the fact the current owner had hung tarpaulin over the roof and first floor to ruin any potential photos. I ignored the instructions on the map and went up the street for a closer look, only to find a shitty sign warning against sightseers and saying, 'the police would be called', so I continued, consoling myself with a photo of the school from *'Kindergarten Cop'* which was located just around the corner. Disappointing. I walked back across town, and that was about it for the day, with the exception of finding my favourite 'like' on Bumble, a large grey-haired, middle-aged woman whose profile told me she worked as a cashier at Walmart and had eight children – that was one meet up I decided I could definitely live without.

I thought the town reminded me not so much of The Goonies, but more of another favourite film of mine of a similar vintage, *'Short Circuit'*, and I looked up the location on IMDB. Sure enough, it was filmed here and even better, Stephanie's (Ally Sheedy) house was two blocks up the hill from my motel – this I had to see, and five minutes later I was standing outside the house, which looked to be sitting vacant. This was a special life moment for me, standing right next to the yard where 'Johnny 5' had disassembled Daryl's Trans Am and outside the house where Johnny and Stephanie had danced to *'More Than a Woman'* by the Bee Gees. I had booked to stay here as it seemed to make geographic sense but realising the town was a veritable hotbed of film production, I decided I had to learn more and would pay a visit to the town's film museum which was housed in the old county jailhouse building, where the main bad guy, Jake (Robert Davi, also the villain 'Sanchez' in *'License to Kill'*) breaks out of at the start of The Goonies.

And so, on Day 66 of my trip, I made my first visit to a museum. This was the smallest museum you are ever likely to visit, comprising the jail cells, three rooms and a gift shop. I think it was targeted more at budding filmmakers, with some fancy technology that allowed you to make your own movie scene which you could then also edit yourself. I wasn't interested in that as I was just here for the trivia, and there was plenty of that to be had, as I learnt that tonnes of films are made in Oregon, giving it the reputation as the unofficial Hollywood of the north. Older films of note included *'Stand By Me'*, *'The River Wild'*, *'Free Willy'* and *'The Shining'* – this was of particular interest to me as the property used for the deserted hotel was Timberline Lodge, where I had been just a few days earlier. More recent films included *'Gone'*, *'The Ring 2'* and *'Twilight'*, which, while theoretically based in Forks, Washington actually used a number of locations in Oregon including Portland, Indian Beach ('Bells Beach') and Multnomah Falls where, again, I had just been. My stay in Astoria and this visit to the film museum seemed to knit together my film location sightseeing over the last few weeks in a rather neat way, meaning the $6 entry fee for the fifteen minutes it took to exhaust the content didn't feel quite so egregious.

***

I made the trip back to Portland the next day but didn't make it over to the Lloyd Centre of Tonya Harding fame in the end, realising I would only be going there on the off chance that Alison Janney was at the rink, in character as Tonya's mother, and using the 'c-word', the odds of which seemed fairly remote. At Union Station later in the day, I sat in the waiting room for a while to soak up the ambience. I don't know if all major US city train stations are identically styled, but this one had the classic marbled floors and walls and long oak bench seats that you see in the movies and had a lovely feel to it. I had booked the train, which took three and a half hours as I thought it would be a good way to see some more scenery. However I think I must have forgotten this plan as soon as I boarded the train, as I spent nearly the whole trip reading and writing, and therefore can't describe the scenery for you other than saying, "I saw Mt Adams at the start," various bodies of water and then Mt Rainier just before we arrived in Seattle. Sorry. At the other end, I got an Uber to my Airbnb, which turned out to be in a completely random area about fifteen kilometres out of town. My rationale in booking to stay here was now unclear, but it wasn't too far from the airport, which could have been the reason, and I was paying less than $40 a night, which is the more likely reason. I was staying with a friendly lady called Linda parent to an attention-seeking cat called Romeo who came to keep me company, and the bed was super comfortable, so it looked like it would do the job and I got an early night ahead of my final full day in the States, exploring Seattle.

My cheapskate Seattle experience continued the next morning when I walked up the road to find the bus stop where I joined the morning commuters for the 50-minute ride downtown. This trip was meant to cost $2.75, which sounded an absolute bargain, and it got even better when I got on, as the machine wouldn't take my dollar bill and the driver got impatient and just waved me on for free. The area I was staying in was predominantly populated by Asian immigrants, so there were lots of Asian shops around as we drove around the suburbs, including the delightfully named 'Hung Long Asian Market'. In the first of a number of planning fails for the day, I had ventured out for the day without the last $100 of cash I had, and also forgot my sunglasses which set the tone for a day that never threatened to become one of my favourites of the trip.

The bus had filled to capacity, and we passed through the residential area emerging at the freeway to the city on to a bridge giving a view of the vast port area with a load of giant cranes and thousands of shipping containers and the city skyline. I was immediately struck by how much smaller than expected the famous Space Needle was on the skyline, as it was dwarfed by nearby buildings and not commanding the cityscape in the same way the Sydney Tower or the Sky City Tower in Auckland do. To be fair it was built in 1962, a whole 56 years ago, so when I considered it again in the context that it was built in the year that The Beatles released their first single, I was able to afford it some more respect. I arrived at my first planned stop of the day, the Columbia Building, the tallest building in town, almost exactly one hour before it was due to open at 10 am, so I decided I would return later and instead head to the number one attraction in town, the Pikes Place Market. This market was housed in a complex of old buildings which overlooked the waterfront and had been in operation since 1907, making it the oldest continuously operated farmers market in the US. It still traded heavily on this heritage with lots of old painted wooden units for the stalls, retro neon signs all around, and old-fashioned stores selling vintage prints, posters and books down in the maze of lower levels. The top floor was all about food, with several large fish stalls run by burly looking gents putting on a noisy show for the crowds, and several rows of food stands and antiquated looking restaurants contributing to the vibrant atmosphere of the place – it was great fun.

I had planned to walk to the bottom of the 'Pike Street Hill Climb' and then walk along the waterfront a couple of kilometres to the Olympic Sculpture Park but, and I am going to sound like a bit of a snowflake here, I was having big problems with my right foot. I think I had got a bit of dirt or something by the nail of my big toe as it had swollen up and was rubbing on my shoemaking me a bit queasy, so at the bottom of the steps, I had to abandon that plan and return to the retail area to try and remedy the issue. I had a very frustrating hour or so where I failed to find either a shoe shop where I could buy some thongs or a chemist and was very close to having a tantrum when I realised not having eaten was probably not helping and that I should stop for an early lunch, take a break to clear my head and calm the f*** down. The decision on a venue for lunch was made very straightforward when I found myself in a shopping mall that had a branch of Din Tai Fung, a dumpling restaurant of which I am a massive fan, having made multiple visits to the Sydney branch. I rushed in to make my usual order of 'soupy dumplings' and 'porky beans', and while they, unfortunately, didn't have the porky beans on the menu, the dumplings were as good as always, and I also had a beer to help the calming process.

This plan worked a treat, and after I had eaten and wrapped up my angry toe in lamb's wool found at a chemist, I was back on track, taking a walk to the base of the Space Needle before visiting the Sculpture Park. I wasn't that enthralled by the sculptures, but the park had an expansive view over the bay, and it was another blue-sky day, so the overall experience was agreeable. I am perhaps a bit spoilt living in Sydney, but even with the improvement in my mood, I couldn't help feeling a bit disappointed at Seattle, which had been built up for me as a truly beautiful city. Maybe it was because I was a bit grumpy, but it didn't live up to the hype for me on that day, and from a purely visual perspective, I thought I preferred both Sydney and Vancouver, where I would be visiting in a couple of weeks' time.

The night before I had written a list of things to see, which I now checked and saw it only had two items on it, and I had done both. I had also already eaten lunch, and it was only 12 pm – like I said earlier, I had really failed on the planning front today. I decided I would head back to the Columbia Building to visit its 75th-floor observatory of the city and pass some time by doing what some Australians charmingly refer to as, 'sinking some piss', which ended up being an inspired idea. The building was at the southern end of the city offering great 360-degree views; north across the whole city and then working around to the west to the bay and the Olympic Mountains, to the south to the giant sports grounds and commercial areas and then Mount Rainier in the distance to the east. Taking in the various cleverly engineered bridges that linked the landmasses, and the ferries zipping around the bay, it was an impressive sight. The sight of the mountains to the west was the most informative for me, as I realised that Seattle was not actually on the coast, as I had always assumed it was. More impressive than the views, however, was the fact that they had beer on special for $3 (plus tax – of course) so I got myself a seat with a view and settled in for several of those. While sitting there, I found myself tuning in to the following exchange across the room between an American man, and a couple from Eastern Europe who were chatting away in their mother tongue in a table by the window.

American – "Hey, sounds like you guys aren't from here, where are you from?"
Lady – "You should see if you can guess!"
American – "Okay, give me a clue."
Lady – "It's a country next to Ukraine."
American – "Err…Scotland!"
Lady (pissing herself) – "No! It starts with an 'M'."
American – "Morocco! No? Mumbai? No? I give up."
Lady – "It's Moldova."
American – "Ah okay…I've never heard of that, but you guys have yourself a great time!"

Bless him for giving it a go. I had a few more beers, went back into the city and had a wonderfully fragrant pho for dinner at the bizarrely early hour of 5 pm before catching a bus home to put an end to an ill-conceived day out – sorry Seattle, we didn't quite bond, but it wasn't you, it was me…

And with that whistle-stop tour of Seattle, my stay in the US was over. The initial apprehension I had felt on the plane into LA was long forgotten, replaced by fond memories of the succession of spectacular national parks I had almost literally ran around, brief but positive introductions to the cities of San Francisco, Portland and Seattle, scenic (and tasty) diversions around the wine regions and local brewery scenes and unexpected amounts of movie trivia. And even a couple of meetups. The only downside was that even doing stuff on the cheap, I had spent the same amount of money in three weeks here as I had spent in six weeks in Panama, Costa Rica, Guatemala and Mexico combined, but that should probably not be a surprise given I was now firmly back in the developed world. And just one thing had eluded me in my time here – a conversation with a person who had anything nice to say about President Trump…

USA – Summary

Kilometres travelled (air) – 4,280 (Inc. Cancún to LAX)
Kilometres travelled (land) – 3,900
Kilometres walked – 330
Cereal bars eaten – 30
Number of Starbucks visited for Wi-Fi (and occasionally coffee) – 22
Number of days (of 21) where I saw any rain – zero.

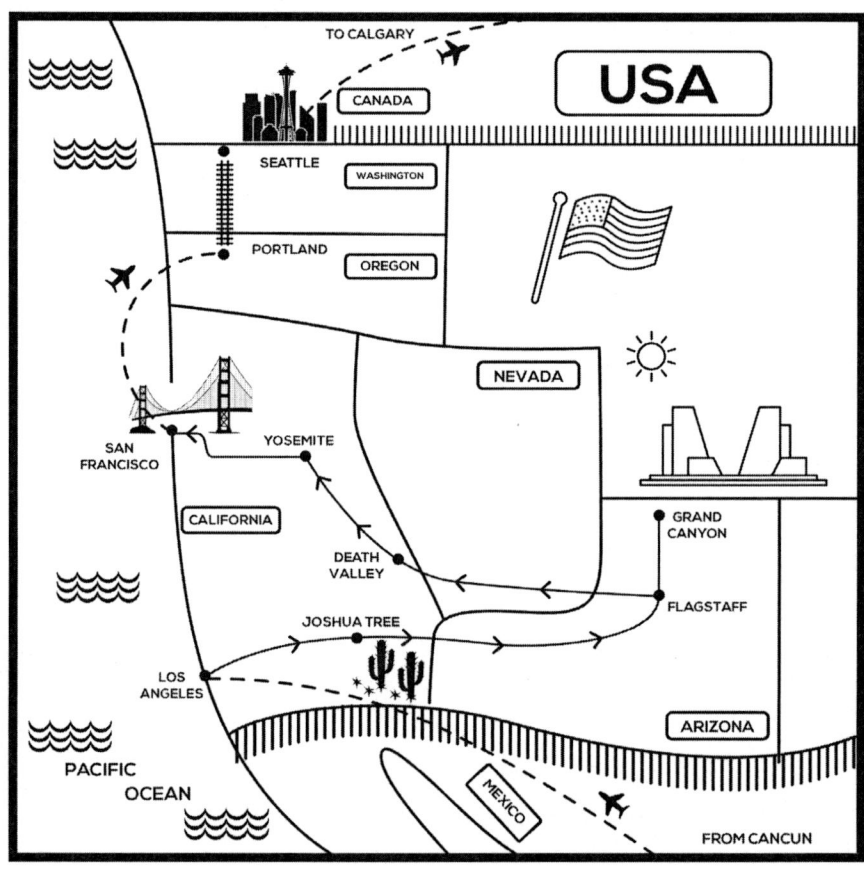

Canada
Winter Comes Early
to the Rockies

My first business upon arriving at Calgary airport at about 6 pm, was to collect the hire car that was going to be my main mode of transport for my travels. I had initially been planning to spend all my time in British Columbia, but Ben and Bec from my Peru tour had told me about their trip where they flew into Calgary and then made their way through various stops in the Rockies to finish up in Vancouver, so I had shamelessly copied their itinerary instead.

Finding Airbnb options to match my itinerary through the mountains had been somewhat challenging, so I had reverted to booking.com options, but I had managed to book Airbnb's in both Vancouver and Calgary, so this was where I drove to first. My host was a chap called Curtis, and his page boasted that he had 'the most reviewed Airbnb in Calgary'. Checking in on Bumble I saw I had a like from a lady called Misty and deciding a name like that would be guaranteed page-turning book content, I quickly liked her back in the hope of organising something on my second night there. Sadly, she never messaged me, so we'll never know whether, in reality, she would have been as intriguing as her name suggested.

The next morning, I had a proper look around Curtis's place and decided this was the new gold standard of Airbnb properties I had seen to date (sorry Kc and Tater, you are still second though). Curtis lived in the basement (with his cat, Henry) so the ground floor was basically for the sole use of the people staying in the three bedrooms advertised on Airbnb. There were detailed instructions on how everything worked, the rooms were all clean and tidy, the bed comfortable, the shower satisfactory, and there was a free laundry area, with detergent, softener and a giant brand-new washer and dryer – what else would you need? It cost about $35 a night, was near the airport and just a ten-minute drive from the city, so I could see why he had the most Airbnb reviews in town, and I added to this list with another glowing write up when I left the next day.

The scenery on the drive west to Banff the following morning looked a bit bleak, to begin with anyway, and the arrival of daylight coincided with the start of the now-familiar mountain scenery of dark pine trees with yellow leaves in the foreground and light snowfall. A few years before I had been to Grindelwald in Switzerland in late summer and the landscape had still been quite green, with rolling meadows and wildflowers, like a scene out of the Sound of Music, and this was the mental picture I had when planning this part of the trip. The view through the windscreen as I approached Banff was unfortunately somewhat different, and my slight sense of disappointment was amplified when I got to the visitor centre. Running the lady through the list of epic walks I wanted to do, I was crushed to find nearly all of them would not be possible given current conditions and forecast snowfalls – I would not be escaping from the Nazis through the mountains after all it seemed.

The lady did manage to come up with a couple of consolation prize suggestions for me, and I went back to the car, donning as many jackets as possible and my hat and gloves, before setting off across town on a walk along the river to a place called 'The Hoodoos' via 'Surprise Point'. When I later referenced this place in response to a query on a photo I had posted on Facebook, Dom, a smart-arse from my work, replied with, "What was the surprise – frostbite?" This actually wasn't far off the mark, as it was minus six degrees and you couldn't take your hands out of your gloves for long without losing functionality. I also realised that amid the disappointment at the visitor centre, I had forgotten to ask about bears so I was looking around nervously each time I heard a noise in the woods and thinking I should have maybe read up on how to be 'bear-safe' before starting. The walk was more atmospheric than scenic, as the cloud and snow rather dulled the colours of the river and trees, but there were some captivating vistas along the way, including a view of the giant gothic-looking Fairmont Banff Springs Hotel on a cliff across the river. There was no one else around and the only sound along the way, other than non-bear noises, was made by my feet crunching through the snow and brought a sense of tranquillity and solitude. The cold was not that enjoyable though, and I didn't stop for long at the Hoodoos, taking the shorter route along the road back to town so I could warm up with a coffee and put even more clothes on for the afternoon's walk. The vast majority of the other tourists in Banff were from Asia, something I had been told to expect by our friend back in Pahrump. When Kc had been proudly showing me her world map, she had pointed at the grouping of pins in Asia and said, 'we get all the Orientals a bit later in the year', and as predicted, here they were – though mostly contained to places near where the tour buses could stop.

I was soon back on the road, heading 30 kilometres north of Banff to my afternoon walk destination of Johnston Canyon, where the lady in tourist information had suggested I would still get some good views even with all the cloud and snow around. The drive, which basically paralleled the highway, was serious fairy-tale kind of stuff, passing through windy tree-lined roads which presented a black and white scene in the dark snowy conditions until rounding a corner, the splatter of yellow deciduous trees broke the monochrome. It was like one of those greyscale photos where they have added in one colour 'post-production', as there were literally no other colours to be seen other than black, white or yellow. Amazing.

The snow was getting more insistent as I arrived in the parking lot, so I quickly layered up in the cold, covering every available inch of skin, and found my way to the start of the walk. The trail led me along a man-made path through a canyon that ran directly alongside the river and past two sets of waterfalls which could be seen as I climbed the reasonably gentle incline. I had been warned this was one of the more popular walks in the area, and it was indeed heaving, meaning I had to pass a load of people on what was without question, as result of all the ice the most slippery path I have ever walked. It was very tricky going, and I decided not to stop and look at the falls along the way, figuring I could see them on the way down when, hopefully, there would be less people around. At the top of the three-kilometre waterfall walk, there was a connecting trail which continued up the hill a further four kilometres, to a place called the 'Ink Pots', which was where I wanted to get to. By now, the path had gone from having a bit of snow on it to a completely snow-covered trail, feeling more like a ski trail than a hike as it continued uphill on a number of switchbacks. Indeed, just before I arrived at the Ink Pots, I passed a sign that read 'End of Nordic Ski Trail', but my hiking shoes were just about equal to the challenge – apart from being drenched from the snow.

Arriving at the Ink Pots was like stepping out of the wardrobe in Narnia into a completely different world, with the view opening to reveal a large alpine meadow area, surrounded by mountains and snow-covered pine trees, with the strange Ink Pot ponds and the snow now positively dumping down from the still, windless, skies. The Ink Pots are a group of seven spring-fed ponds, which on a blue-sky day are crystal clear and jade green, but which today were a murky dark grey. The source of the warm water that feeds the ponds is apparently unknown, but it could be seen bubbling up through the loose soil at the bottom of the pond to give the appearance of a witch's cauldron in today's black and white scene. This was another one of those moments where I had to take a minute to just stop and turn around 360 degrees and immerse myself in the pure beauty of the scene – it was a total Winter Wonderland – on October 3.

Crunching my way back through the snow to the falls below, I was pleased to see quite a few groups of hikers braving the conditions towards the rich rewards I had just seen. On my way down, I approached a group of ladies a bit too quietly and just as I was about to say 'Excuse me' so I could pass, the lady at the back turned her head towards me, not realising I was almost right next to her and attempted a Premier League style nose clearance. Luckily she failed, and it quickly turned into her instead pissing herself in embarrassed laughter as I hurried past saying, "Well that was quite a greeting!" The number of people on the path meant a lot of pleasantries were required and I was alternating between my English identity greeting of 'Hello', and my Australian alter-ego greeting of 'How's it going?' I could easily identify the nationality of the respondents to the latter greeting as apart from the accent, the English people immediately revealed their flag by thinking I was actually after an answer, offering up a polite 'Fine thanks' or 'A bit cold'. The correct Australian response is to answer the question with the same question, 'How's it going?' and then continue on without breaking stride, neither of us any the wiser as to the other's welfare – which is quite all right, because we didn't care anyway. After a few more of these exchanges, I was back at the falls, stopping to take in the serious amounts of water thundering down the hill, and made it back to the car without any ice-skating related injuries. A gentleman I saw near the bottom was evidently not so lucky, having taken a nasty spill on the death trap ice path and sporting a large patch of blood through the knee of his jeans for his efforts – don't say you weren't warned if you ever find yourself there in similar conditions.

***

I was staying about 25 kilometres east of Banff, in Canmore at a place called Rundle Cabins, located just off the highway but three kilometres away from the town centre and any shops or restaurants, so I popped into town to eat before returning for the evening. It was still snowing, with more forecast overnight, so I cranked up the impressive heating system in my simple cabin, settled down with a glass of red wine from the bottle I had been carrying since Sonoma, and went online to read up on bear safety. I was feeling a bit bad about those mean things I said about bears when I was back in Yosemite, so I thought I should check what the chances might be of them getting their own back on me. According to Wikipedia, there had been seven fatal bear attacks in Alberta since 1990, and just two in the area where I was staying: Rick Cross, a hunter, in September 2014, and Isabelle Dubé, a jogger, in June 2005. Isabelle was out running with two friends when they came across a 90 kg grizzly bear on a golf course in Canmore. While her two friends backed away and ran for help, Isabelle decided instead to climb a tree, and while her friends were gone, the bear pulled her down from the tree and killed her. A ranger killed the bear soon after and found it was the same bear that had been relocated from Canmore to Banff a week earlier, following regular sightings at the golf course. Unfortunately, it had found its way back, and the tracker which had been placed on it was not accurate enough to alert the authorities as to its location in time for them to take action.

Having scared myself a bit with this research, I went on to read about what you are meant to do if you meet a bear, as I didn't even know if you were meant to run away or not. The guidance outlined that if you see a bear from a distance, you should back away slowly, avoiding eye contact and leave the area, as the bear is usually not interested in a confrontation with you. However, this situation changes if you find yourself inadvertently coming between a bear and its cub, as the bear will instinctively assume you are a threat and will act to defend its young. The advice on this website got a bit more worrying from here as it then recommended if the bear got up close, you should, first of all, deploy your bear spray, which is capsicum based, to scare it away. If that doesn't stop it, and it comes into contact, you need to assess the style of attack by the bear. If it appears to be attacking in a defensive manner, the guidance says you should play dead, but if the attack becomes aggressive and the bear starts eating you(!), then you should fight back, concentrating your attack on its face, eyes and nose. Right. Attacks that get to that point are relatively rare, and the first line of defence is not meeting a bear at all, and it suggested you could improve your chances by singing while you walked, playing music, or walking with a 'bear bell' on your bag – all measures to alert the bear of your arrival so as not to surprise it and to give it a chance to go elsewhere. I didn't have a bear bell, but this information gave me licence to walk with my iPhone playing music over the speaker as opposed to using headphones, which I did on all walks thereafter when there weren't other people around.

After a slightly restless night digesting bear information, I woke up to find midwinter had suddenly arrived. About six inches of snow covered the doorstep, the path to the car, the road, and burying the car, with snow still coming down. I had heard on the radio the previous day that up to 20 cm of snow was expected overnight, but my common sense deficiency had struck again, and I failed to have the foresight to buy provisions in the event I wasn't able to go out in the car – and I certainly wasn't walking three kilometres in the snow. So all I had was three cereal bars (of course), some filter coffee provided by the cabins and the rest of the bottle of red. Hmmm. After drinking a whole pot of coffee and eating the cereal bars it was obvious that amount of food was not going to sustain me and I would have to venture out, I could see some traffic on the freeway, so it was clearly possible, and with a further 30cm of snow forecast, this had to happen sooner rather than later. I rugged up and after twenty minutes of clearing snow from the car with a kitchen spatula, the best (only) tool available, and warming the car with a running engine, I set off cautiously for Canmore. The word that comes to mind to describe the drive is 'terrifying' as the road was covered in snow and ice and even though I was driving very slowly, on several occasions I applied the brake pedal to find either nothing happened or there was a crunching noise, and the car started skidding. Passing by several cars in the ditch and driving behind cars that people had not even bothered to clear the snow off the back windscreen, I made it to Safeway, where I bought some supplies before taking several deep breaths and saying a quick prayer for the return journey, which I somehow managed to navigate without incident. On the radio, I learnt there had been 40cm of snow in some parts of Calgary, the highest ever for a day in October, and there had been 251 vehicle collisions in the fifteen-hour period since the heavy snow began. There was also a report that the Trans-Canada Highway was closed in both directions just east of Canmore as two jack-knifed lorries had blocked the road – I read a news report later in the day which said people were still stuck there nine hours later, so I was glad I hadn't tried to venture too far!

I amused myself in the afternoon by digging the car out of a fresh four-inch layer of snow, watching the mouse I was sharing the cabin with having a bit of a run-around, and then turning my attention to some holiday admin, more specifically sending shitty complaint emails. I alluded earlier on that I am not a fan of car rental firms and today was the day my anger boiled over, so I'm afraid you are going to have to sit through a bit of a rant. The overriding issue I have with these companies is that they have the most opaque pricing structures of any business I can think of, meaning you just have no idea how much it will end up costing you. The headline rate per day is of complete irrelevance, as it excludes a number of items for which you also need to pay, with the chief offender in this regard being the insurance. I find car rental insurance options to be a complete mystery, with each different company having their own set of indecipherable three-letter acronyms for products they insist you would be foolish not to purchase. Let's consider the two companies I had booked cars with on this trip:

- CDW – Collision Damage Waiver.
- LDW – Loss Damage Waiver.
- PAE – Personal Accident and Effects.
- PAI – Personal Accident Insurance.
- PEC – Personal Effects Coverage.
- SLI – Supplemental Liability Insurance.
- TLI – Third-party Liability Insurance.
- LIS – Liability Insurance Supplement.
- ESP – Emergency Sickness Plan.
- Roadside Assistance.
- Premium Emergency Roadside Assistance.
- FPA – Fuel Purchase Option.

When you are at the counter, you usually get a garbled summary of what each one means, and other than sticking with my stock request of 'What's the bare minimum I am allowed to have?' I have no idea what I need and/or what might already be covered by the insurance the online aggregator made me buy, my travel insurance, or my credit card insurance – it's all just too hard. But it's not just the insurance that drives me nuts, it's the experience as a whole, and the endless number of ways they try and stiff you for more money. My 20 years' worth of renting cars is best characterised through the following example conversation at a car rental desk, which is fictional, but which I think you will recognise as being largely grounded in fact.

Me (M) – "Hello, hopefully, I have a reservation with you."

Him/her (H) – "Credit card and driver's license, please…Ah yes, Mr Maycock, you have an economy car booked for seven days. I see you have booked the basic cover insurance option – would you like to upgrade that to our full cover package? It's only another $29 a day."

M – "No thanks, I'm only paying $30 a day for the car, so that sounds a bit extreme."

H – "Err, Okay, Sir. You realise that the basic package gives you very limited coverage?"

M – "Yes, I do, thanks."

H – "And you have an excess of $500 for any incidents – do you understand what that means?"

M – "Yes, if I put a dent or scratch on the car, you will charge me for the costs of repairing it up to $500."

H – "No, we will charge you for the estimated repair costs."

M – "Isn't that the same as what I said?"

H – "No, you assumed we would fix the damage. We probably won't bother; we will just mark the damage on the checkout report for the next person who hires it and keep the money we charged you to repair it."

M – "Ah okay, that sounds like a bit of a scam."

H – "Oh, it gets better – if we don't mark it on the damage report, and the next person doesn't notice it when they collect it, we might be able to charge them for the non-repair as well!"

M – "Well anyway, I'll stay with basic cover thanks, worst case it will cost me $500."

H – "Actually, maybe not – windscreen damage isn't included so if you break that it will probably cost you more."

M – "Windscreen damage isn't covered? But that's quite a likely event, and one I probably have no control over if a passing car flicks up some stones. That doesn't sound right – isn't that the point of getting insurance?"

H – "Yes, but we can't avoid having to fix windscreens if they are cracked and they are expensive, and we aren't a charity, so it's just tough luck I'm afraid."

M – "I think we should move on from insurance – what's next?"

H – "Do you need to rent a satnav unit?"

M – "We don't need to cover that in this skit, I wrote about it earlier on in the book."

H – "Skit? Book? What?"

M – "Never mind, what else?"

H – "Okay, what about fuel. The car is full now – Would you like to take the option where we fill it up for you when you return it for a price that is slightly more than it will cost you at a petrol station?"

M – "Sounds like it makes more sense for me to fill it up myself. What happens if I don't get around to doing that?"

H – "We will fill it up and charge you three times the amount you would pay at the petrol station to compensate us for the inconvenience."

M – "But you just offered to fill it up for me – where is the inconvenience for you – you clearly have access to cheap petrol at the drop-off point?"

H – "Oh it's no inconvenience really – but this means we can get a load of extra money off people who haven't been able to find a petrol station near the depot, or who didn't have time as they were running late for a flight."

I could go on, but you probably get the gist of it. The main reason this was front of mind for me was because of some charges bestowed on me by Budget car rental, from whom I had rented the car for the LA to San Francisco leg. When I dropped the car off in San Francisco, the guy at the check-in desk gave me a receipt that, at first glance, appeared to say there were no outstanding charges. However, when I looked at it again later, I saw the reason there was nothing more to charge was that on the line above he had already charged me USD 250, with no breakdown of the constituent amounts. Reconciling my check out receipt, I could see that USD 125 of this was for insurance and breakdown protection which I had agreed to, but that still left me with USD 125 unexplained, so I emailed Budget for an explanation, who replied advising it was a fuel service charge as I had returned it with less fuel in it than when I started. This was clearly incorrect as I had stopped and filled it just before coming over the Golden Gate Bridge and I was also annoyed this was not mentioned when I dropped it off, as I could have stepped back to the car to show them the full fuel gauge. I wrote back to explain this, to which their reply was that they would only consider a refund if I provided a credit card statement or receipt showing I had filled it up. As I had paid in cash, I had neither, which I explained in a follow-up reply, politely suggesting they could check the starting fuel level for the next rental, which would prove my point. But no, they weren't interested in doing that – no receipt, no refund, and I was left with the cost of filling a whole tank of petrol at USD 9.90 a gallon – even the cowboys in the middle of the desert didn't have the nerve to charge even half of that amount! While I was tempted to persevere with my complaint against this nonsense, I was also still wasting time on emails and online chats trying to get my $1,200 back from Jetstar for the phantom flight (six weeks on), and I didn't want to waste any more of my trip getting cross with people, so I let it go. Sorry, I did warn you I was going to have a bit of a rant – but in summary, car rental companies, grrrrr!

***

The next morning I woke with a bit of a red wine head and went through my now well-practised spatula snow clearing procedure for the latest four inches of snow, before trying to reverse out and finding for the second time this holiday, that I had got a car stuck. This time I didn't need to solicit any additional manpower and only had to dig for a while longer to get the car out and I was on my way. It had stopped snowing, but the roads were still not great, so I drove down the freeway behind the safety of a snowplough for a good half an hour before I worked up the courage to overtake it and drive a bit faster. The update on the radio was that the road to the east was STILL closed and some people had spent all night in their cars, with others having been taken by police to 'warming stations' in Canmore in the early hours of the morning – madness. It was much better news for me, as I was more than a little excited this morning, as a) the blue skies had returned so I could actually see the mountains which had been hidden to this point and b) I was on my way to Lake Louise, where I was hoping to see one of the best views of my entire trip. Lake Louise is a tiny town with a few shops and a petrol station, and nearly everyone goes straight to the lake itself, which is about five kilometres out of town and dominated by the giant 'Chateau Lake Louise' Fairmont Hotel which sits at the head of the lake. I arrived a bit after nine and there was already a small army of Asian tourists milling around the lakeside walk at the front of the hotel, rugged up in their winter best to deal with the temperature of minus six degrees, which was feeling seriously chilly in the still morning air. I got some photos before heading straight for the most celebrated walk at the lake, the three kilometres Lake Agnes trail through the trees to the side of Lake Louise to the tea house on the lake, which apparently had epic views.

The trail was completely covered in snow, but it was well packed and fine for walking up in hiking shoes, and after about an hour of a decent uphill slog offering views back across the valley I arrived at the teahouse. It did have good views but not, as I was expecting, of Lake Louise, but instead of Lake Agnes, the mountain lake on which it sat – I guess the clue was in the name of the walk. The viewpoint I was chasing looked directly down on Lake Louise, so I knew I must have to walk further to find it, so I skipped past the tea house and followed a trail that was heading to something called 'The Big Beehive'. There were no walkers on this trail, which was basically just a couple of sets of footprints making a small ridge path in the deep snow and it was fairly easy-going until it got to the end of the lake, at which point it turned uphill passing along a surprisingly steep set of switchbacks through the snow, which was now getting deeper. I was quite out of breath by the top of this section and starting to feel a bit nervous about being the only person there, so I was actually relieved arriving at the lookout to find three other people who had also been crazy enough to walk through the snow.

After a quick chat, I turned my attention to the view, and it was absolutely mesmerising. The lake is famous for its vivid turquoise colour, coming from the glacial meltwaters that feed it, but today was amplified further by the clear blue skies overhead lighting it up. With all the snowfall in the previous days, I was worried I wasn't going to get to see this view, but now I realised the snow had actually been a blessing. The branches on the trees which framed my view down to the lake, were groaning under the weight of a couple of inches of snow and the white dusting in front of the chateau lifting an already amazing view into the stratosphere – I actually felt a bit emotional taking it all in. Epic.

I took a different path back down the other side of the hill, which was even less trodden and buried under a good foot of fresh snow. I basically jogged down, falling over a few times on the way into the softest of snow cushioned landings, and generally behaving (and feeling) like I was about eight years old – it was lots of fun. This path joined up with another which ran along the side of the lake and delivered some of the views I had expected on the other trail and led me to a junction of trails at a place called Mirror Lake. Back on the main path, I was going against the flow of traffic, with lots of hassled looking people trudging their way up, a Japanese man stopped me at one point and said, "Excuse me, this is the halfway point yes, how much further?" I didn't have the heart to tell him he was nowhere near halfway but told him he still had an hour to go which he seemed fine with. However, his wife behind him pulled a face of horror at my reply, which suggested to me they would probably not end up getting to see the beautiful mountain reflections of the lake which I had witnessed a few hours earlier. At the bottom, I stopped into the chateau in the hope of a coffee fix, but it was an absolute zoo, so I abandoned that plan and instead hit the road to cover the three-hour drive west to Revelstoke in British Columbia.

The roads were still a bit dicey, and along the way I saw an articulated lorry that had rolled over a safety barrier and a car and trailer jack-knifed upside down in a ditch, prompting me to keep to a fairly sedate pace. The border between Alberta and British Columbia passed by without fanfare, with the only indicator that it happened being a number of signs saying if I had a boat I had to stop and get it washed to prevent the spread of invasive mussels. I had never heard of such a thing, but they are apparently all kinds of bad for the ecosystems in the rivers and lakes and both British Columbia and Alberta are on a mission to stop the issue worsening further. I was boat-less, and thus just an interested observer so continued, through the picturesque mountainous scenery before dropping into the valley floor for some epic fall colours in the appropriately named town of Golden and arriving in Revelstoke an hour or so later.

I checked in at my motel where it became evident I was the only guest who wasn't driving a pickup truck or wearing a high-vis vest (or both), but the room ticked all my usual boxes, so this wasn't a problem. Realising I had left something in the car, I left my door ajar and went to retrieve it, returning to find a random man on my bed – except it wasn't my bed, as I had absentmindedly walked into the room next door which coincidentally also had its door ajar, so I quickly apologised and hastily retreated to the correct room. This event was made more ridiculous by the fact it was the second time it had happened to me in the last six months; when I was in Kathmandu, I had returned to my hotel room which I opened using a key, to find an Indian gentleman taking the liberty of eating a bag of crisps on my bed – again, it was actually his bed, and I had turned the wrong way at the top of the stairs and walked into the wrong room. The reason for the lock and key access being identical between the two rooms was a mystery I decided I couldn't be bothered to ask reception to explain.

***

Revelstoke had found its way onto my itinerary more as an interim stopping place between Banff and Whistler than anything else, but from my walk around the previous evening and the next morning, it seemed a pleasant enough little town. The main attraction of the place for me was the 'Meadows in the Sky Parkway', a 26 kilometres road just on the edge of town which took you through the Mount Revelstoke National Park from an elevation of 470 metres on the highway up to 1,835 metres at Balsam Lake, just short of the summit of the mountain, meaning I could have a day off walking up hills, and let the car take the strain for once. So after an excellent eggs Benedict at a lovely little place called the Main Street Café, I drove to the entrance of the National Park, but when I went to pay the entry fee, the lady said the road wasn't open all the way up, and I could only go as far as someplace along the road the name of which I didn't really pay attention to. I said that was fine and I would just take a walk from the closed section, but I had only been driving for about five minutes when I got to the chain across the road which marked the start of the section that was closed, which was basically nearly all of it – so the mountain drive wasn't happening after all.

My hiking shoes were still soaked from walking through the snow at Lake Louise, and as I had thought I was going to be mostly driving, I had put my canvas trainers on, which were clearly not sensible footwear for walking in light snow cover. Feeling I needed to get something for the $10 fee I just paid, I decided to walk up the path through the woods and up the hill as far as I could – which wasn't far before I was slipping around. I was also embarrassed when I encountered other hikers, knowing I was now 'that guy' with the inappropriate footwear, who I would shake my head at if I saw them on the trail, so I soon called a halt to proceedings, walking back to the car along the road switchbacks. There were some quite good views to the mountains across the valley and down into the town, but I was also struck by how much tree debris there was on the roads. I found a ranger at the bottom and asked whether the road was closed because of snow cover or bear activity and she said it was actually due to the tree damage arising from the recent unseasonably heavy snowfall, snow which continued to slightly sabotage my plans.

I now needed another way to spend the day so dropped into the visitor centre for a couple of alternative walk suggestions and, after a quick stop to get my hiking shoes, which had now just about dried out, I set off to find the trail to Begbie Falls, at which point the day went from bad to worse. Firstly, a pickup truck overtook me and kicked up a stone onto my windscreen, making a crunching noise I immediately knew was going to be expensive. It was only a small chip, but I knew from experience it was probably too large to get away with. Feck it. Distracted by this, I missed the turn-off to the trail and added 20 kilometres to a journey that should have only been 16 kilometres in total. Feck it. Then when I got my bag out for the walk, I realised I didn't have my wallet. Feck it. While I didn't need it for the walk, I was slightly panicked as to where I may have left it, so I decided to go back to the motel to check for it and was relieved to find it was there – panic over. I did go back and do the walk, but it was a bit boring, to be honest, so I won't bother to describe it and will instead end my Revelstoke write-up by sharing its nature-related claim to fame with you, which is that it is located in the world's only inland temperate rainforest – just in case that ever comes up in pub trivia.

The next day I had 510 kilometres to cover to get to Whistler, which Google Maps told me would take a bit over six hours. The first leg of the drive was to a town called Sicamous, which claimed to be the houseboat capital of Canada, but I was more interested in the road itself as I had read an article in the local Revelstoke paper that had described the circumstances of the construction of this section of road. In 1942 after the Japanese bombing of Pearl Harbour, Japanese Canadians were declared a national security threat and labelled as 'enemy aliens' despite the majority being Canadian by birth. Over 22,000 Canadians of Japanese descent were forced out of their homes on the West Coast of BC and made to sell their belongings. 1,700 Japanese Canadian men were then separated from their families and taken to road internment camps, where they were forced to build many of Canada's highways, including the road I was now on. Those who refused to be separated, or who refused to work, were arrested and sent to Prisoner of War camps in Ontario. One of the more disturbing points in the article was the fact that these internment camps continued to exist until April 1949, four years after the war had ended. This was a chapter of Canadian history that they were not particularly proud of, with an official apology issued by the Prime Minister in 1988 and compensation packages paid to those affected, and the article referred to new memorials that were being opened on the roads to commemorate the efforts of the interned Japanese Canadians – interesting stuff.

The drive continued past Sicamous to a larger town called Salmon Arm, tracing alongside a number of rivers and lakes, which I couldn't quite see through the morning cloud and fog, before reaching the large town of Kamloops. Ben had described this town to me as 'a bit of a shithole', and I had no inclination to stop and even less so as the scenery had changed to uninspiring bleak moorland. Turning back onto the mountain roads after a town called Cache Creek, the landscape improved markedly as the road carved its way through the mountains, alongside beautiful rivers and snow-covered pines.

After arriving in Whistler, I took a walk around the confusing labyrinth of odd-shaped streets that make up the town centre, and I was suddenly struck by the fact that nearly three months into my trip, this was the first place I had actually been to before. I had previously holidayed there with my ex-wife and walking past some of the shops and restaurants we had been to together, felt a rather empty experience on my own. I suddenly felt quite sad to be there, and I was immediately regretting my decision to stay here for five nights. This regret was compounded by the amount of snow and the clouds hanging over the mountains, which looked like they would scupper the alpine walks I had thought I would be doing, something the visitor centre folks soon confirmed. There was better news in that there were still some good walks I could do lower in the valley, but all round I was feeling quite disappointed which was not helped by the fact there were no walking maps left, presumably because it was too late in the season to make it worth printing any more. I took a photo of the one laminated copy they had and went for another look around town, which was still quite busy with families milling around the shops and loads of mud-splattered people of all ages on mountain bikes, which seemed to be the thing to do here at this time of year.

I didn't need any motivation to get up and out the next day as the weather forecast was for a sunny day before the rain arrived for the following two, so I was desperate to get some good views in while the sun was shining, and had decided I would do the walk to Garibaldi Lake, about 20 kilometres down the valley from Whistler. The day got off to a sub-optimal start though as I reversed out of my space in the underground car park, apparently with plenty of clearance to the car parked on the other side, when I felt a jolt. Surprised I had hit it, I got out to confirm it was just a bumper nudge and saw to my horror there was a large bike rack attached to the car I had hit which I hadn't seen, and it had put a number of chips on my bumper. If there was any chance of me getting away with the windscreen chip, they definitely wouldn't miss this one, so I mentally wrote off my $500 excess and tried to put it out of my mind given I couldn't now undo my gaffe.

Feck it. I drove the 20 kilometres thinking about nothing other than what I had just done, but was finally jolted out of it when I arrived at the trail-head car park at 9 am to find there were already about 50 cars there – where had they all come from?

The endpoint of the walk promised stunning views of the lake and the mountains behind it, but the walk description was also quite honest in its assessment of the trail you had to walk up to get there – eight kilometres of walking up switchbacks in a forest to climb an elevation of 800 metres, with nothing at all of interest to see along the way. After fifteen minutes of walking, I decided the summary was spot on and the gradient was also reasonably taxing, so the sign that told me I had only covered one kilometre of the eight was a little bit depressing. I needed something else to think about so turned my focus to keeping count of the number of people I could overtake on the way up, this kept me amused for about an hour until something awful happened – someone overtook me! Out of the corner of my eye, I could see a figure dressed in black a couple of switchbacks behind, and even as I sped up a bit, I kept seeing glances of him closing in. I was for some reason reminded of the film *'The Princess Bride'* and the scene where the outlaws abducted Buttercup and are being pursued by the Dread Pirate Roberts, and whatever crazy terrain they go over they simply can't shake him off. This was now the case as he pursued me relentlessly up the hill until, with my heart rate the wrong side of 170, I eventually had to admit defeat and let him pass. He also rubbed it in as he passed, saying, 'You've got a great pace going there,' before sweeping by at his vastly superior pace and disappearing into the distance. Inconceivable!

After six kilometres I turned off the main path taking a suggested detour to see some alpine meadows, which turned out to be a bit of waste of extra effort as they were covered in snow but nonetheless enjoyed the view from there of 'Black Tusk' mountain. My initial disappointment at the walk was quickly forgotten when I arrived at Garibaldi Lake as this was, as promised, well worth the long slog up the hill. Like Lake Louise a few days earlier, glacial waters fed this lake so it also had the picture-postcard turquoise colours and was surrounded by pine trees on the lower slopes, and mountains behind which were covered in deep snow. The cloudless skies overhead meant that whichever way you looked across the waters, the scene behind the lake reflected vividly in the perfectly still water in the foreground, making for some eye-catching photos. My haste up the hill meant there were not yet many people at the lake, so it was a peaceful, serene setting for me to enjoy my predictable apple, banana and cereal bar 'celebratory meal' for making it here. I took the more well-trodden path for the return trip to the start of the switchbacks and regretted not having come up this way, as there were several more lakes and stunning views down into the valley far below. Reaching the dull section, I was in a hurry to get it over and done with as there were now tonnes of people coming the other way, meaning I had a one-hour descent of this six-kilometre section that sounded like this:

"Hello. Hello…Hi. Hi. Hello. Hello. Hey. Hi…Hello. Hello. Hello. Hi. Hi."

For a whole hour. Never mind, the lake at the top was still worth it. On the way back to Whistler I stopped in an area called 'Function Junction' which was a collection of commercial, light industrial and retail units which were hidden in the woods I think because they didn't pass the beauty test for being near the main town. I had read there was an innovative bakery and some good coffee shops there, and indeed there were, and I feasted on an amazing bacon and egg brioche creation from the bakery ('Pure Bread') and a pumpkin spice latte, the latter serving as a prompt that it was Canadian Thanksgiving Weekend. I had to read up on what this holiday was commemorating as I knew the American version related to their Pilgrim Fathers celebrating their first harvest on US soil (in 1621) and I was pretty sure they hadn't also been to Canada. The origins of the Canadian version actually predated the US, with the first recorded instance taking place in 1578 when an English explorer called Martin Frobisher celebrated the harvest in Newfoundland. So it seems the Canadians thought of it first, and also celebrate it first, with their Thanksgiving falling on the second Monday in October, whereas the American celebration is not until the fourth Thursday in November. Consider yourself fully briefed on pumpkin pie related festivities.

Back in Whistler, not content with the car mishap from the morning, I managed to lock myself out of my apartment. Access was via a six-digit code on the keypad, which I had instantly committed to memory, rather than taking the option that was available of changing it to a number that was memorable to me. I had successfully entered the code about six times already without giving it much thought until now when I walked out to the car to get the phone charging cable I had left there and returned to find the code I had in my head, 974742, was not correct. I composed myself to clear my thoughts and tried some close variants, but none of them worked. The details had been sent to me by email so I could access them if I did forget, on either my iPhone or my iPad – both of which I had left in the room, along with my wallet. Feck it. The condo development had no onsite admin facilities, and I found a sign advising to contact my rental agency directly with any issues, of course, these details were located on my phone and in the information folder in the room – not helpful. The situation I found myself in was an excellent reminder of why you should pay more attention to this kind of stuff when travelling solo, a lesson that might help me on another day, but not today. I didn't want to add to the Pacific North West homeless population for the night, so some initiative was required to overcome the bind I found myself in, which came to me in the form of a walk to the library, where I assumed I would be able to access a computer paying with the $2 of change in my pocket if required, and check my email and get the code. The computer was actually free, and while I couldn't find the email in the Internet version of my email account, I was able to Google the rental agency and phone them up to get the code, which for completeness, was 974724 – I was close…crisis averted, and hopefully my last idiocy related mishap for a while – or at least a few days.

***

My final full day in Whistler brought with it a more promising weather forecast, and I was up early to drive about 60 kilometres north of Whistler to do a walk at a place called Joffre Lakes, which I had seen described as 'British Columbia's Lake Louise' and thus needed to investigate. As I walked across town at 7:30 am to the free car park where I had left the car (cheapskate), there was hardly anyone else around apart from a couple of council workers sweeping up by the Olympic Rings on the Olympic Plaza at the south end of the town and…'A BEAR!'

Finally, I had seen an animal larger than a squirrel, a decent-sized brown bear wandering around an area, he/she really shouldn't have been in. I started to walk towards it to take a picture before remembering that was not one of the recommended steps in my bear safety training. So I backed away hiding behind the cleaners, who then walked towards it banging their cleaning equipment to encourage it to go elsewhere which it quickly did, leaving just enough time for me to get a blurry video of the event. A super exciting start to the day. Arriving at the trailhead for the walk my spirits sank a little to see the weather wasn't really as good as I had expected with a load of cloud overhead which would probably spoil my turquoise lake photos, and it was also pretty cold, but this was my last day here, so I was going to be doing it regardless! There are three of the eponymous lakes, the lower one a short walk from the car park, the middle one an hour and a half and 300 metres elevation higher, and the upper one a further twenty minutes or so further on. I skipped the first one which I would visit at the end and headed up the path which had a number of signs along it warning of icy patches before the middle lake, and they weren't joking, making for slow progress to avoid falling over. The middle lake still made for a few good photos despite the grey skies and snowy backdrop, including a fallen tree that disappeared into the deeps from the shore, which I had seen referred to online as 'the Instagram tree' as this was where everyone went and carefully balanced for that epic shot of the lake. I was on my own of course and unable to persuade the squirrels away from their nut gathering business to take the shot for me, so you will just have to take my word for the fact I was there – though if something isn't posted on Instagram, did it really happen at all?

The trail to the upper lake was rather more sketchy as the snow had melted and made the path a bit of a mess of mud, puddles and tree roots, so again slow going. I wasn't too bothered as I was hoping if I took long enough the weather would improve for better photos on the way down, but this wasn't looking very likely when I arrived at the upper lake and was hit by the icy wind blowing off the Matier Glacier that overlooked the far end of the lake. I got the woolly hat and gloves on and carried on past the lake lookout for another half an hour on an increasingly treacherous path, that eventually turned into a boulder hopping exercise before the trail ended at the campsite at the foot of the glacier. About ninety minutes earlier on the trail, I had passed the occupants of the only other car in the car park, and there were no campers here, so the place felt desolate and just a little bit eerie. Parts of the final section of the trail had twisted ankle written all over them, and I couldn't help but think of the film *'127 Hours'*, the true story of Aron Ralston, played in the movie by James Franco, who got his hand stuck in a rock crevice after taking a fall while walking alone on a remote trail in Utah and ended up cutting off his own arm to avoid perishing there. I had left my Swiss Army knife in the boot of the car, so this wasn't going to be an option for me if a similar fate befell me, so after eating my breakfast, I briskly (but carefully) made my back around the lake where there might by now be some other people, which indeed there were. I paused on the trail for a proper look at the spectacular waterfalls cascading down between the top two lakes and over about fifteen different stepped levels, before finally conceding defeat that the better weather was not going to arrive and making my way to the bottom. That said, I think this would be the first walk I would return to when I am next in the area, as between the glacier, the mountains, the lakes and the falls it really did have it all.

For my last meal in Whistler, I returned to a place I had eaten a few days earlier called Bar Oso, purely on account of the charcuterie board they served, which I had decided was the best example I had seen of this kind of meal anywhere in the world. It included a selection of meats, cheeses and homemade terrines, pates and chutneys, everything on it was delicious and the board was the size of a picnic blanket, so it was winning on all fronts. To top it off they also had great wine, so my seat at the bar here had quickly become one of my favourite spots in Whistler. It took an hour for me to eat everything off the board, during which time a lady sat next down next to me ordering the same meal, and I could immediately tell she was keen for a chat. Her name was Rachel, and she was from San Francisco but had a holiday place here, she was and in her late 50s at a guess and had recently retired from a tech-related marketing job in Silicon Valley. After speaking about her work for a bit, I commented it sounded like she did 'search engine optimisation', which I knew a little about having looked at the potential acquisition of a business in that space for one of my Australian clients many years before. Her slightly surprising response was, "Yes, I basically invented search engine optimisation back in 1996," which seemed a bold claim, but I let it pass making a mental note to investigate further when I got home. Later I realised I didn't know her surname, so I was only able to Google 'Rachel search engine optimisation', but to my surprise, the first five results related to her, and I could see she went by an internet-related nickname and she did indeed appear to be a prominent figure in the industry. Fascinating. I paused for thought here; however, as if you are in that line of work, you probably know a thing or two about making yourself look impressive if someone Google's you. Anyway, back at dinner, I was still trying to work out whether she was friendly or a bit flirty when the following exchange took place:

R – "Do you like oysters?"
Me – "Oysters? Err, yes?"
R – "Would you like to go get some? My treat."
Me – "Err, where do you go for oysters in Whistler?"
R – "The restaurant next door."

On the spot, I couldn't think of a reason why I wouldn't let someone buy me some oysters, even though it felt a bit weird and given it was just next door I said yes, shuffling out the door in a slightly embarrassed fashion as the barmaid, who I had been talking to, asked me where I was off to next. So we went next door and had a glass of wine at the bar and chatted a bit more while watching the Yankees vs Red Sox playoff series decider which was on the TV. When that had finished, Rachel drained her wine, stood up and said, "Right, I have to go and find my car, nice chatting to you, enjoy the rest of the trip." And left. With no mention of the oysters we were supposedly there for. A bit weird had quickly progressed to a lot weird. It was the most abrupt departure from a 'meet up' since Christian Bale's Patrick Bateman 'Had to return some videotapes…' in the film adaptation of *'American Psycho'*. I finished my wine and then felt compelled to go back next door for a final glass of wine there to prove it was an innocent trip for oysters, but my barmaid had left for the night, so I wasn't able to 'clear my name' – which I do right now instead. When I later relayed this tale to my friend Jane, her immediate reply was, "Did the lady have teeth?" The San Francisco episode was clearly going to continue to haunt me.

***

The next morning it was time to move on to Vancouver, and I had been doing some research in the Lonely Planet and also on the Airbnb tour adverts, and it seemed there were some quite unusual things on offer amongst the latter, including:

- Catfe, a cafe where you get to enjoy your coffee or tea in a separate room where there are cats for you to hold and play with.
- Sea glass hunting on Bowen Island.
- 'Forest bathing', guided meditation in the woods; and
- 'Nude spiritual hike to Wreck Beach'.

I say again – 'Nude spiritual hike to Wreck Beach'. This was the clear standout activity, and while I certainly wasn't going to be doing it, I thought it would be a crying shame if I didn't bring this to your attention and give you a bit more colour on what is involved, so I read some more about it and extracted a few more salient points for you below:

'The trail is clothing optional, so feel free to do it naked – there is nothing quite like walking nude in a forest…For the evening tour, we will stay until sunset, when howling like a coyote is encouraged.'

The route from Whistler to Vancouver follows the 'Sea to Sky Highway', one of the most scenic drives in Canada. The better weather I had been waiting for had finally arrived on the day of my departure, and the blue sky showed off the drive at its best, winding its way down from the snow-capped peaks and passing the towering rock faces on the outskirts of the town of Squamish before arriving at the coastline. The road tracked right down into Vancouver, which is entered over the Lion Gate Bridge, a green version of its larger San Francisco equivalent. I returned the car, which was now 2,100 kilometres more experienced but slightly battle-scarred and waited nervously as the guy disappeared off to 'do a quick walk round'. On his return, it was good news-bad news as the windscreen chip was apparently big enough to warrant attention (surprise, surprise) but he hadn't noticed the bike rack damage. The windscreen repair was going to cost me $240, which was a bit painful, but I was mentally prepared for worse, so I paid the man and celebrated the end of hire cars for the trip. I was back into an Airbnb here, and my latest host, Jackee, was in her mid-thirties, originally from Kenya but had lived in Canada since arriving as a student sixteen years previously. Jackee was very friendly and chatty, and after some discussion about my travels and writing, she gave me some tips for things to do the next day, one of which involved a body scrub and massage at a Middle Eastern spa. I didn't tell her at the time, but I immediately pictured myself back in the men's changing room massage place in Guatemala and knew I wouldn't be risking a repeat of that, so I smiled politely and said I would definitely try and fit in a visit there.

On my first walk around town, I had immediately been struck by the number of drug-addled looking people sitting around, including a couple who I saw quite openly preparing whatever they were about to stick in their arm in broad daylight. I was straight onto Google for a 'please explain' on this topic and found there was a long history of drug problems in the city and the current day policing of the situation, had resulted in it being deliberately concentrated in the Downtown Eastside District in which I had been walking. I decided 10 am the following morning was a safe enough time for a reconnaissance of the area and headed for Hastings Street, the most infamous street for the issue.

It was a very confronting experience with about three blocks worth of harrowing sights; men and women with skeletal, drawn looking faces, many of them looking confused or deranged, either sitting next to, carrying or wheeling around their possessions in bin bags, while many of them fiddled around with their drug paraphernalia and whatever it was they had in their pieces of foil. I had asked Jackee about the issue the night before, and she had told me that while it wasn't a pleasant sight, they were harmless, but I wasn't convinced judging by what I saw here. The strangest bit was that about two or three blocks further on you were into the gleaming CBD area and wouldn't have been able to tell there was any problem at all in the city. Over the next few days I walked around a few more streets in the area as there were some good bars tucked away amongst it, and I saw the drop-in centres and other facilities to help these poor souls, including legal injection centres, but from reading a few recent articles online, it doesn't sound like they are on top of the issue just yet. I couldn't help thinking how lucky I am to live in Sydney, a comparable harbour city, which has one of the most non-threatening city centre areas you could find in a city of that size. I do need to provide some context; this is a fairly small area I am describing, and as you will read in the remainder of my Vancouver reflections, the rest of the city is really quite beautiful and hugely walkable – but I do think it's important to acknowledge nonetheless.

On the ferry, or 'sea bus', over to North Vancouver, I sat with my back to the direction of travel, so I could get a good look at the city, and I was quickly reminded why I had liked it so much the last time I was here on a brief work visit four years earlier.

This side of the city had largely risen up in the last thirty years or so, meaning it has only a handful of the 1950's concrete buildings that I have grumbled about in other cities, with the skyline largely comprised of modern glass and steel constructions, which today were glinting in the morning sunshine. As we moved across the bay, I could also see the trees and green spaces of the extensive Stanley Park to the west of downtown, and then towards the northwest, I could see the lower slopes of the mountains towards Squamish and beyond and to the direct north of the city, Grouse Mountain, making a spectacular backdrop for the city. While this view was part of the reason for taking the sea bus, I was also here to visit the North Vancouver Public Market, a small collection of shops and restaurants by the dock, many of which have traded there for more than 30 years. There was a good spread of stalls, but it wasn't very big and didn't really capture my attention, so I was quickly out the door and on the hunt for a walk to explore this side of the city. I could see the Lion Gate Bridge in the distance to the west, and while I didn't really know how far away it was, I thought it would probably be a nice walk to make my way over there and cross the bridge into Stanley Park, where I could join the famous sea-wall walk that would take me back to the waterfront area where I had caught the ferry. Which was quite a long-winded way of avoiding paying the $4.20 return sea bus fare. A little way outside of the market area I found there was an official path for what I wanted to do, 'The Spirit Trail' so I joined that and headed west, chuckling at a sign by the road that read 'I just sold my homing pigeon on eBay…again!'

Arriving at Stanley Park, I was quickly marvelling at what a fantastic resource it is for the residents of the city. It was a beautiful sunny day, so the path was well populated with walkers, cyclists and rollerbladers but it's a wide path with separation between foot power and pedal power, so it didn't feel crowded, and the views as it winds its way back to the city are superb – you would have no idea you were right in the middle of a massive city. The final couple of kilometres started to feel busier, as I entered tourist bus, scenic tram territory and the like, but there were lots of fancy-looking yachts in the marina to distract me from the other tourists and my sore legs before I finally reached my intended endpoint, the Cactus Club Cafe in the Canada Place area – just in time for Happy Hour. Result.

Happy Hour had not been part of the plan for the day, but it ended up being an extended stay and the rest of the day ended up quite beery, as I also visited one of the best-regarded brewery bars, Alibi Rooms, all in the name of researching the local beer industry of course. This bar had no less than 55 beers on tap, so I decided to be a bit braver than usual and try something weird and wonderful sounding – no, I didn't really, I had three pints of the one with 'lager' in the name again. A brief interlude at this point on drink sizes as I didn't get round to telling you while in the US, of my learning of the fact that a pint in the US is different to a pint in England or Australia, where a pint is more precisely defined as an 'imperial pint'. A US pint is 16 fluid ounces, or 454 ml, whereas an imperial pint is 20 fluid ounces or 568ml – why can't a pint just be a pint? To confuse matters further, the 'pints' of lager the lady was serving in Alibi Rooms were 14 fluid ounces, and the Canadians seem to use the words 'sleeve' and 'pint' interchangeably with no consistency on what size of drink that meant. This topic would be hard to follow even sober, but on this day I had no chance, and after a quick detour to a taco place for dinner, I decided I had probably had enough to drink and made a move back to Jackee's place.

Jackee was having her post-work evening wind down, and we ended up having quite a lengthy chat, as she was intrigued by my travels and writing and wanted to learn more about them, and I was interested in hearing about her business. Jackee had previously worked in the corporate world but had decided a few years earlier that she would be better suited to doing something more entrepreneurial and had done just that, setting up a business that imported fair trade leather products from Kenya, which she then sold through a store in Vancouver and also through her website. Two years on from opening, all was going well, and as she spoke about the journey so far, I could really feel the pride for what she had achieved having basically taking a gamble to walk away from a 'steady job' to do something she felt genuinely passionate about. It was quite inspiring, and I agreed that I would factor a visit to her store into my walking tour for the next day to get a better feel for what she was selling.

***

The next morning it was time for a spot of culture in the form of a visit to the Bill Reid Gallery, recommended by Rachel (of oysters fame) so that I could get an understanding of the art of the Haida, the local indigenous people, which she told me I would see everywhere. I didn't have a feel for how big the gallery was so I took my time to have a look around the various pictures and sculptures in the first room and the display in the mezzanine floor above, which was fortunate, as those two rooms represented the entirety of the gallery. Rachel had shown me a picture of a three-metre-high wood carving entitled 'Raven and the First Men' which was one of Reid's most celebrated pieces and depicted the Haida version of human creation, with a raven cracking open a giant clamshell to find a number of small human beings inside, the first Haida. I was expecting to find this in the gallery but could only see a small onyx reproduction and soon learnt the original was actually housed in the BC Museum of Anthropology, wherever that was. Fail. Never mind, there was also a number of excellent screen prints in the traditional style of black and red ink on white backgrounds, most of them depicting line drawings of animals important to the Haida, including the raven and the salmon. A collection of Reid's work was included on the back of the Canadian $20 bill in 2004, and it's certainly worth a Google Images search if, like me, you have never heard of him before.

With the gallery having taken up rather less time than anticipated, my next stop was at Jackee's shop, which was in the shopping mall underneath a large complex of office buildings in the downtown area, known collectively as the Bentall's Centre. The shop was much bigger than I expected with a double width shop front and a completely open facade displaying a wide range of leather goods, travel bags, homewares, scarves and various other pieces for home and travel. Jackee gave me a brief tour around the product range, which is made in Kenya and Zimbabwe, talking me through the evolution of the design of each of the bags, wallets and purses. Her comments were at a level of detail like, 'I wanted a travel wallet that stored money, cards and passports, but which also had a section to fit boarding passes without having to fold them,' revealing that the design of every product had been carefully thought through. I was quite jealous of the outlet for her creativity that she had built, as she basically had her own leather goods 'train set' to play with here. The briefcases and bags were all embossed with her 'Kasandy' logo as well as one of three animal motifs (lion, elephant or giraffe) as a reminder of their African heritage. Given this was effectively a one-man-band start-up, it was impressive how polished it all looked, and if I hadn't been luggage space-constrained, I would certainly have picked one up. Watch out for the name and website as I'm confident by the time you read this, Jackee will have advanced her plans for expanding into a second physical store and broadening the online presence.

From downtown, I set off in the direction of English Bay, a bayside suburb on the south side of the main peninsula, passing along the eclectic selection of Asian eateries on Robson and Denman streets. It was a bit of a grey day for the beach at English Bay, with its slightly surreal sea views of ten giant tankers waiting at anchor for their turn in port, but on the promenade, I found a fascinating bronze sculpture of fourteen men, about three metres in height, entitled 'A-maze-ing Laughter'. The men are images of the artist himself 'in a state of hysterical laughter', and behind the group scene is an inscription, which reads:

'May this sculpture inspire laughter, playfulness and joy in all who experience it.'

What a beautiful sentiment and I for one certainly felt all three as I carried along my way with a smile, not even letting the ghastly concrete towers that lined the shore on that side of town get me down. A little way further along the waterfront I arrived at the Granville Public Market, one of the city's most popular attractions and I was excited to find this place lived up to my lofty food market expectations. Inside the large area of connected buildings, there was a wide range of greengrocers, butchers, small food stalls, fishmongers and bakeries – the Canadians seem to love a good cake and here they were spoilt for choice on that front. It was a bit hectic to linger long, so I continued my walk along the waterfront to the Olympic Village area where a number of apartment blocks had been built to house the athletes in the 2010 games, and the area seemed to have now matured into a busy community, centred on a number of brewery pubs.

One of these, Craft, was housed in a giant timber structure that begged a look inside and having a bit of a thirst on from all the walking I was powerless to resist. The main hall was raised above a giant keg room in the basement below, which fed the incredible array of beer taps at the bar with over 100 beers on tap – one hundred! I had my mandatory lager and for once did actually try something more exotic (a kolsch) before completing my planned loop walk so I could catch up on a bit of writing in the afternoon. My time in North America had really seemed to have reawakened my taste for beer as I was back on the hunt later that evening, stopping at another brewery bar en route to dinner, finding drink size options here of 16 oz. or 24 oz. I wasn't exaggerating when I said there is no consistency to drink sizes in Canada. On the way I passed a sign outside a restaurant that had me literally laughing out loud – vegetarians look away now, as it read:

'There's plenty of room for all God's creatures – right next to the mashed potato.'

My walk to dinner took me past the Convention Centre, where I was entertained by the sight of loads of people in what looked like sci-fi character fancy dress. Intrigued, I followed them in to see what was on and found it was an event called the 'Fan Expo', with lots of actors, writers and other celebrities apparently in attendance. Over dinner, I checked the event website to see who the top names were, and the three best I could come up with were as follows:

- Jason Momoa, who played 'Khal Drogo' in Game of Thrones.
- Lou Ferrigno, the original Incredible Hulk.
- Kristy Swanson, who played Buffy the Vampire Slayer.

Hang on, I hear you say, Sarah Michelle Gellar played Buffy the Vampire Slayer! And yes, you are right that she did in the series, but there was also a film version in 1992 that preceded the series, which was where Ms Swanson found fame a mere 26 years ago, which made me feel they were scraping the barrel a bit for 'stars'. And these were the best three remember. Returning home at a decent hour I had the novel experience after three months on the road with no television, of having a quiet evening in watching Netflix with Jackee who, the next morning went above and beyond by giving me a lift to the train station for my trip to the airport the next morning. Straight to the top of the class of Airbnb hosts!

And that was my action-packed couple of weeks in Canada. The wintry weather had been rather different to what I had been expecting but this hadn't proved a dampener at all, instead just painting the epic scenery with a slightly different palette. The landscape in Canada is simply breath-taking, and I had barely scratched the surface in what I had managed to cover in the two weeks I had available to tear around the place, which I think means I will have to, begrudgingly, commit to returning. And next time, I will be jangling with bear bells and have bear spray at the ready.

Summary – Canada

Kilometres travelled (air) – 730
Kilometres travelled (land) – 1,050
Number of bears seen – One
Number of unseen 'bears' heard in the undergrowth – Many
Number of car snow clearances with a kitchen spatula – Three

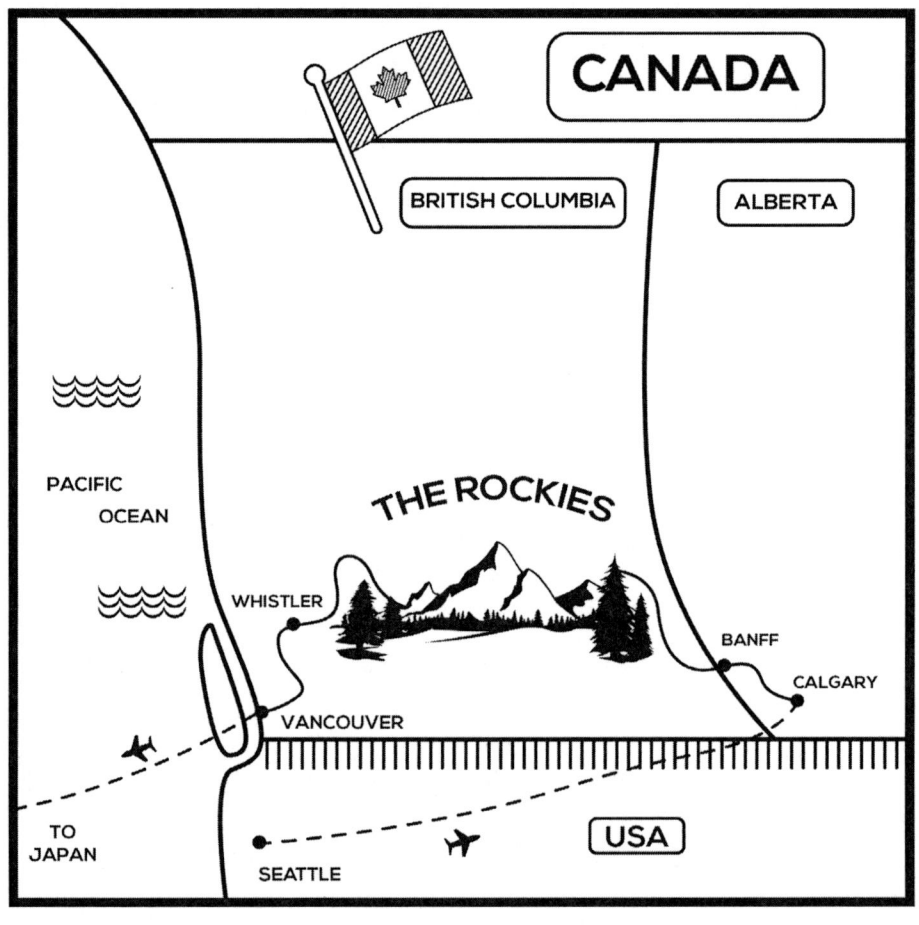

Japan
Romance (at Last) in the Land of the Rising Sun

Flying from Canada to Japan involves crossing the International Date Line, something I had done a handful of times before but still really confuses me as to which day I was on, which day I am now on, whether I lost a day, and if so, where did it go? I was on a 1:25 pm flight which was estimated to take about ten hours arriving into Tokyo at 3:30 pm. Leaving during the daytime and arriving during the daytime would mean it wouldn't ever be dark, making it easier for me to enact my plan of staying awake the entirety of the flight and on arrival powering through to stay awake and not sleep until their bedtime. This plan was going fine until about four hours into the flight when the cabin became dark, and everyone started to go to sleep. This time zone darkness anomaly was really bothering me until I finally realised the plane had fancy windows that did not require the use of a window shade, but instead the window somehow artificially controlled the cabin light – that's just too clever for my tiny brain to comprehend. Now at this point, I might give you a potted summary of my planned itinerary for the country I am about to visit, but when I looked at what I had booked, it looked like such a silly schedule that you might just question my sanity if I recounted it. So I won't, and you can just learn about it as we go along and pass judgment at the end. And if you do have feedback at that point, please direct it to the Lonely Planet, as I just copied their suggested itinerary for two weeks in Japan.

    The flight was running a bit late so I didn't land until 4 pm (12 am Vancouver) and it took an absolute age to get through immigration, customs and baggage reclaim, and then a twenty-minute queue to get a ticket for the Narita Express to Tokyo. You may recall many moons ago I told you I was getting a Japan Rail pass for this part of the trip, which would allow me to ride free on all JR trains, most of the bullet trains and the Narita Express. I mentioned this because of the complicated logistics which meant I had to organise for it to be sent to my friend Jane, who was also holidaying here now, to bring to Tokyo and give to me when we met – at the wrong end of the airport train. Never mind, forty minutes later and forty dollars lighter I was on the train at which time I remembered if you get the non-express Express, it can take an almost incongruous ninety minutes to get to the centre of Tokyo – even more, ridiculous than getting to London from 'London' Stansted Airport. All of this whingeing led to me arriving at my Airbnb in the Shinjuku area with just enough time for a quick wash and change before heading straight out for a short walk through the neon lined streets to a bar in the same area, where I was due to meet Jane, and her friend Bec. We had agreed to meet at 7:30 pm, which on their time zone apparently actually translated to 8:30 pm, as that's when they got there.

    I will stop grumbling now, as what followed was a hugely entertaining, perhaps slightly sleep deprivation influenced night out in Golden Gai. This area is a small block of laneways in Shinjuku, which is populated by about a hundred of the smallest bars you have ever seen, each seating no more than ten and some of them as few as five, so it's basically just a barman and a few groups of friends – and many drinks. We started at one called 'Soirée' for a few warm-up drinks before deciding it would be prudent to soak up some of the alcohol with some food. We found a place nearby for some dumplings, where we had a giggle at a guy in there who was struggling to control his other half, who was hammered and absolutely all over the shop. With the benefit of hindsight, I regret laughing at her misfortune and feel karma may have been activated at this point. Why do I say this? I say this because returning to the laneway bars after dinner and between two venues the names of which I couldn't tell you, we drank until 4 am. There were shots, there were sing-alongs, there were new friends, Jane's passport photo got stuck up behind the bar with '*Call me*' written on it, and there were mystery green drinks – in short, it got messy. I should also report that my phone was requisitioned at one point so that Bec and Jane could 'help me with my Bumble', though this seemed to involve rather a lot of no-look swiping if I'm honest and I didn't think to check their credentials in advance for being able to assist me in this regard. At 4 am the place finally shut, the girls got a cab back to Shiodome where they were staying, and I set off for the short 900-metre walk back to my place in Shinjuku – in completely the wrong direction. I'm not sure where I went, but I got to my place at 5 am (1 pm Vancouver), with a distance of five kilometres step activity showing on my watch when I looked the next day. Welcome to Tokyo, Arex-san.

***

The place I was staying for my two nights in Tokyo was described as a guesthouse, but it was essentially just five very small rooms on the second floor of a building which housed a restaurant run by the guesthouse owners. The street was packed with restaurants, all of which seemed to be open to all hours, so at any time walking around (apart from at 5 am) there was a great energy to the place. My room was just large enough to house a tatami mat with a double futon mattress on it and an area alongside where I parked my bags. The only place where there was enough room to stand was by the doorway, where there was a mirror mounted on the wall at a height which allowed me to see my whole body from the sternum down. I assume I was meant to go to the bathroom to check out anything higher up than that, including, for example, my face. The 'bed' was comfortable enough though and my alcohol-fuelled coma kept me asleep until about 11:30 am. When I woke, it took a few moments to work out where I was and to process with mild horror and some laughter, the memories of the previous night's antics. One of these memories was triggered by a number of alerts on my phone, showing I had quite a few matches on both Tinder and Bumble and some introductory messages had arrived, all of them from really quite unattractive ladies – thanks to Jane and Bec's swipe activity.

We had loosely agreed I would head over to Shiodome to meet them the next day for some undefined sightseeing. So after loading up on Panadol, I got the metro in that direction arriving around 12:30 pm, just in time to receive a message from Jane saying they would be in no condition to receive visitors until at least 2:30 pm and that we would then go to visit a place whose name I can't remember. By excellent fortune, it turned out there was a Din Tai Fung in Shiodome, so I went and found some soupy dumplings with which to bring myself back to life (still no sign of porky beans though sadly) and went for a walk around the shopping district Ginza for a while, before heading back to Shiodome for the 2:30 pm meet time. Except we weren't going sightseeing any more as the only way Bec could be roused from her slumber was with the promise of the best burger in Tokyo, so we were going to do that instead. The cab to Jane's claimed 'best burger' place took a very long time, a journey length which was not well received by one of the more green looking passengers in the car, but fortunately we made it without anyone having to use the sick bag that was provided in the back pocket of the front seat.

Given I had already eaten, I was just an observer to proceedings, and I stuck to the tried and tested hangover cure of full-fat coke and more beer while watching the fairly sorry sight of the girls nursing their burgers. Bec got delivered a double burger by mistake which they didn't seem to want to take back, so she just took out one of the patties placing it on a side plate, which I then had to cover up with another side plate as the look of it was making us all feel ill. Before she had started to eat it, the correct burger arrived, and the waiter motioned that he would take the other one back – cue embarrassed looks around the table, before I had to lift the side plate to reveal we had already commenced surgery on the patient. Luckily, the Japanese are way too polite to express displeasure, and the offending items were quickly and discreetly cleared away. After finally finishing this torture of a meal, the girls took a taxi home to go back to bed, and I went to find a train.

The one positive from this outing was that Jane had remembered to bring the exchange voucher for my JR pass having forgotten the night before, which although annoying at the time, actually turned out to be hugely fortuitous given how the evening had played out and the 99.5% chance I would not have got the thing home. At Shinjuku station, I found I couldn't exchange the voucher for the pass without my passport, which meant a twenty-minute diversion to collect it before I finally got my JR pass or 'golden ticket' as I had decided to christen it. This pass was another example of the low-tech anomalies lurking in the hi-tech Japanese world, as it was just a piece of card stuck on another piece of card, with no electronic functionality. Whenever taking a train, I couldn't go through the normal gates but had to take a side gate where it was physically inspected. And if I lost it at any point, that was it – it couldn't be replaced. So backward, and another item I needed to worry about losing.

Having to return to Shinjuku to do this actually wasn't too much of a disaster, as I had already decided I wanted to have dinner at 'Omoide Yokocho', a small area near the station which housed a few alleys filled with yakitori restaurants, the first of a long list of food types or cooking styles I wanted to try in Japan. I arrived shortly after seven, so darkness had fallen and the alleys and the autumn coloured leaves on the small trees within, were lit by the red and yellow lanterns outside the restaurants, and the night air was filled with the smoke and smells coming from the wooden skewers cooking over hot coals – it was very atmospheric. The venues weren't much bigger than the bars from the night before, seating on average about eight people around a U-shaped bar, with the chef cooking on a hot plate in the middle. I skipped past the ones advertising weird options like horse and whale and settled on a place playing a light jazz soundtrack and which had one free seat at the bar, where people seemed to be eating 'normal' food. That said, when I got the menu, I could see there was still a bit of weirdness on offer, with dishes including cartilage, skin, hard liver and salt-cured fish guts up for grabs. I passed on those and ordered chicken in various forms and some liver which was all cooked to perfection, and of course, washed down with a few Japanese beers.

Walking back to the guesthouse I was questioning whether I had rather wasted my time in Tokyo, given I hadn't made it to any 'sights' and was already leaving for Kyoto in the morning, but I quickly dismissed those thoughts. In my mind, what I had done, taking several walks in the captivating energy of the neon streets of Shinjuku, and eating and drinking in character-filled bars and restaurants had given me a much richer experience than I would have got from a trip up the Skytree, or walk around the Imperial Palace. I was here for a taste of Tokyo life, and I felt like I had got exactly that over the course of a slightly crazy 24 hours. I also had one more day back here at the end of my two weeks, maybe I would see some sights then, or maybe not.

***

The next morning my brain's time zone confusion meant I was awake at 5 am so I decided to make an early start on the trip to Kyoto and made my way to Shinagawa station to catch the bullet train. At the station, I had time for a coffee stop, opting for a regular latte over the 'kiwi and avocado frozen latte' that was also on offer while continuing to clear out my dating apps. Fortunately, the law of large numbers meant I ended up with messages from three girls that I liked the look of, but I now had the problem that I was moving to a new city 450 kilometres away, which was a bit of a commute for a date. The gods were smiling on me, however, as one of the messages was from Belinda (Bel), an Australian currently in Tokyo on business and as we chatted more I learnt that she was taking a week of holiday at the end of her business trip, and would be visiting Kyoto and Koyasan, both of which I was due to stay in. The timings of our stays in each place didn't quite coincide, but they were close enough to make meeting up at some point a possibility, so we agreed to keep in touch to see if we could make it happen. The banter on the messaging was excellent from the start, and I could tell she had a very similar sense of humour to me, so this was feeling quite promising if the logistics worked.

The two and a half hour train journey went by in a flash, and on arrival to Kyoto I got my phone out to open the PDF file my Airbnb host had sent me to guide me from the train to the house, including photos of each stage of the walk and large colourful arrows which had been added to the photos to show me where to go. The guest house in Shinjuku had sent me a similar photo-assisted walk plan and had also gone a step further, sending a link to a YouTube video of someone doing the walk holding a camera – the Japanese are just so thoughtful! I had agreed I would be at the house at around 11:30 am to drop off my bags and I met my host, Wakiko, to do so. Wakiko was effectively an onsite caretaker living in a downstairs room, so she was always around for anything the guests in the five rooms needed, and she seemed very friendly. I use the word 'seemed' as she had practically no English and communicated by talking into Google Translate on the iPad she always had in her hand, then showing me the written translation on the screen and looking to me for some form of visual confirmation that I understood. Even at this brief first exchange, I could see my time conversing with Wakiko was going to bring me much enjoyment and this did indeed turn out to be the case over the course of my three-night stay – but more on that later, let's go and see some stuff first.

Over lunch I pulled out the Kyoto travel planning map which Wakiko had given me and tried to decipher what had to be the most complicated map I had ever seen, folding out to the size of a flipchart to reveal a multicoloured labyrinth of train, subway and bus routes. The map also gave me my first inkling of just how many temples and shrines there are in Kyoto, with what looked like hundreds of the reverse swastika symbols which signify a Buddhist temple. I had been a bit alarmed when I first saw these symbols on temples in Nepal earlier in the year until someone explained to me what the symbol meant and pointed out the Buddhists had used that symbol for rather a long time before the Nazis bastardised it. The number of temples in Kyoto was an illustration of the rich history of the place, which had served as the capital of Japan for over a thousand years! from the year 794 through to 1869 (when the imperial court was moved to Tokyo), and also meant I had a rather long list of places to visit in my three days here.

The first stop on that list was Nijo Castle, a short train ride from Kyoto station and a place where several hundred other people had also decided to visit at that time, so I joined the procession making its way through the castle grounds and the buildings that you were allowed to look inside. The castle was built in 1603 on the orders of Tokugawa Ieyasu, who was the first Shogun of the Tokugawa Shogunate, which ruled Japan from 1603 to 1867. You might be wondering at this point, like me, what a Shogun is, so let's take a brief Japanese history interlude. Rule by the Imperial Court was formalised in the 4th century, but when the first samurai government was established in Kamakura many years later in 1185, the actual political rule was taken over by the samurai, with the Emperor maintaining his position as the head of state. The head of the Kamakura samurai government was granted the title of Seii-Taishogun, later abbreviated to just Shogun. The Shogun was a very ancient court appointment dating back to the 8th century a role roughly equivalent to a commander-in-chief, and Nijo-jo Castle was the symbol of Tokugawa shogunal authority in the Imperial Capital. The building the public are allowed to walk through had a succession of rooms with painted murals on the walls and hardly any furniture in them. After seeing a couple of them you had the general idea, but the 'nightingale floors', named for the squeaking noise they made as you walked over the dark wooden floorboards made for a reasonably interesting walk. I was feeling a bit jet-lagged and not really in the mood for the tourist conga-line around the grounds, and I walked around the remainder of the route briskly, taking no photos on account of the cloudy conditions and then made my way back to the train station.

Taking a short train ride to the edge of the city my next port of call was the small town of Arashiyama, The number of tourists at Nijo turned out to be a mere appetiser to the scene that greeted me here, it was a very popular place due to a number of excellent temple and garden complexes and the location alongside a very pretty river made, to use the relevant contemporary adjective, the place highly 'Instaworthy'. This also meant the local vendors had dreamed up a host of ideas to relieve the tourists of some yen, with rows of green tea ice cream shops, a cat and owl café, a cat souvenir shop, hand-pulled rickshaw rides and even kimono hire by the hour. It was a bit of a circus, to be honest, but cutting through all this noise, the place still had a lovely village feel about it, and the gardens that I chose to visit at Tenriyu were absolutely immaculate, with their ornamental trees, tiny streams, perfectly pruned plants and meticulously raked gravel beds.

As usual, my main takeaway from the place had nothing to do with the actual attraction itself, as here I was fascinated by the toilets. Yes, the toilets. To walk around the building, you first had to take off your shoes, but upon entering the toilet, there were pairs of wooden sandals located in the doorway of each stall and a pair at the foot of every single one of the twelve urinals in the room. There was no one else in there which made for a fascinating scene (well, for me anyway), the cluster of sandals waiting patiently for someone to come and stand in them and go about their business. On the more conventional tourist trail, there was a huge bamboo forest in the far corner of the gardens which was meant to be one of the must-see sights in the city, so I walked over to check it out, took one look at the human mass of people waiting to get in there and turned around to go back to the station – how exciting can bamboo get anyway?

I decided I had reached my fill of temples, castles and the like for the day but I still had some gas in the tank for more sightseeing, so I made my way to the Nishiki Market, a long covered arcade in the middle of the city which held an array of food shops and stalls and other tourist gift shops. The arcade went on for about six city blocks and was covered by a red, yellow and green stained-glass roof high above, which threw an interesting light down over the hordes of shoppers and vendors below. After a brief walk around the stalls, I could already tell this was going to be one of my favourite places in the city. The food selection was vast and scattered with unusual looking items of all shapes and sizes, and I could only identify with any confidence, about half of the items for sale. From the stuff I could recognise, there were pickled cabbages and giant cucumbers, dried baby sardines, smoked eels, all sorts of fish, baby octopuses stuffed with a quail egg, Japanese pancakes, fish cakes, tempura and probably most bizarrely, sparrow on a stick. Funnily enough, I didn't feel the urge to try that and just tried a yuzu juice (a local citrus fruit), but it was a fascinating place, and I did a couple of circuits before moving on to grab an early dinner. This was my first experience of 'okonomiyaki', a Japanese pancake made with egg, shredded cabbage and other vegetables mixed together with pork, squid, and other seafood with a sauce on the top which tasted a bit like a barbecue sauce. It was cooked in the kitchen and then served in front of me on the teppan (hot iron plate) built into the table, with a spatula for me to cut bits off while the rest of it stayed warm. It was a really interesting mix of textures and flavours, and I had read that there were different styles of the dish in different cities, so this was definitely a meal I would be having again.

Wakiko was waiting for me at my Airbnb to deliver a detailed briefing, and this was where I discovered an aspect of Japanese life which I would quickly come to love in my time there – their love for instructional signs and more specifically, bizarre English translations of instructional signs. Wakiko took me through a whole book of laminated A4 pages of house rules, written in a giant font so there was only two or three per page, including critical rules like 'Please do not leave big trash' and 'You cannot leave the veranda'. Wakiko also showed me where the tea and coffee could be found and gave me the good news that I was allowed one slice of bread per day for breakfast. I don't eat much in the morning, and that sounded like way more food than I would be able to manage, but it was good to know it was available if required. I was then shown to my room which was another futon mattress on a tatami floor job and I found to my delight that there was a folder with more rules for me to learn – the font was a bit smaller and as there were many rules listed, I won't repeat them all, but these were the last five on the list:

- Do not make a loud voice or any other noises that will cause you any troubles with the neighbourhood.
- Please do not smoke outside the prescribed places. Smoking on the veranda and indoors is prohibited.
- Please do not look inside the neighbouring residence.
- Smoking is not allowed in the facility and all around. If you smoke, please go to a nearby convenience store and smoking.
- Please do not look inside the neighbouring residence.

So it didn't sound like there was actually a 'prescribed place' for smoking and my mind was immediately racing with theories on what might be going on at the neighbouring residence. It seemed highly unlikely I would last three nights here without feeling the urge to sneak a peek.

***

I still wasn't making any progress with my jet lag and was awake again at 5 am the following morning but unable to make an early start to my day because of another house rule – no showers before 7 am. I waited impatiently for this hour to arrive while working out places I wanted to visit for the day, the first of which was the Nishi Hongwanji temple, which was just a five-minute walk from the main station but almost completely deserted when I arrived. The temple comprised two large wooden halls, the Goeido (Founders Hall), which was built in 1636 and the Amidado (Hall of Amida Buddha), built in 1760, with a number of other smaller buildings set around a gravel courtyard entered through a pair of imposing wooden gates. Standing in front of the Goeido and looking across the courtyard there was a really interesting view, with the Hiunkaku tea pavilion in the south-east corner in the foreground, and the Kyoto Tower, built in 1964, rising up above it in the distance. For some reason, these contrasting period buildings had me muttering to myself, 'the old gods and the new', perhaps getting subconsciously impatient for the final season of Game of Thrones to come around.

I had spent some time the previous evening with the crazy multicoloured travel map of the city and the slightly clearer reality version provided by Google Maps and had decided that the place was nowhere near as complicated to get around as I had initially thought and in fact, looked fairly walkable. This was indeed the case as I continued the walk that had already taken me from home, past the station and to the temple, and which now took me across town to the main shopping area to where I had taken the underground train the previous day. I continued past the market to Pontocho and across the Kamo which is the main river and into the Gion district, an area most famous for the Geishas who live and work there. It was too early in the day for them to be out and about, however, so I walked on to the nearby Yasaka Shrine, a collection of shrines which were painted in a vivid shade of orange that I would later hear referred to as 'vermillion'. I had read this word many times in the descriptions of Kyoto's sights in the Lonely Planet without actually having any clue what it meant, so it was good to find out it meant something as simple as orange.

Yasaka shrine led into a landscaped garden called Maruyama Park which was under fairly major renovation, rather spoiling the tranquillity, but before long I arrived at another temple complex, the Chion-in. It was difficult to miss this one owing to the giant main gate, the Sanmon, which was built in 1619 and is the largest surviving structure of its kind in Japan. I walked through the gate and up the flight of stairs behind it and looked back to the gate to see a school group of about 100 children, who couldn't have been older than four or five, all dressed in bright yellow jumpers, come swarming through, providing an interesting contrast both to the towering size of the structure and also the dark colour of its wood. Continuing around the complex, I found it had another claim to fame in the form of the largest bell in Japan which, depending which source you believe, requires between 17 and 25 men to sound it. The walk that I had been on for the last hour, which wasn't following any predetermined route, turned out to be a really good example of walks in Kyoto in general. It was just one giant treasure hunt, with parks, temples and shrines around every corner, over a thousand years of history crammed into the stories of its buildings and, today, the sun was shining to show it all at its finest.

In the afternoon, I was back on the train to Fushimi Inari-Taisha, Kyoto's most popular tourist site. This shrine sits at the bottom of Mount Inari and has a number of walking routes, combining to make about four kilometres of trails, which are almost entirely covered by avenues of three-metre-high wooden gates, known as *'torii gates'* all painted in vermillion orange. The main path has around ten thousand of these gates, and the visual spectacle they provide as they wind their way up the mountain is truly unique. At the lower reaches of the paths, there were literally hundreds of tourists swarming around but working my way further up the 210-metre elevation of the climb and marvelling at the torii wondering if they would ever end, the crowds started to thin out, and there was a bit more peace and quiet in which to take in the scene. There were also views back over Kyoto, but it was not a very inspiring skyline, and the real magic was not looking away from the shrine, but looking at it, through it, up it and down it depending on where on the path you were standing. There were a number of turnoffs on the way up the mountain, each with their own smaller shrine and offering areas, with thousands of tiny replicas of the orange torii gates scattered around to complement their 'big brothers' in the structure itself. It was truly breath-taking, and I even managed to get a few pictures near the top with no other people in them – no mean feat at that place, unless you have done what the book tells you to do and turned up around opening or closing time.

After escaping the crowds at Mt Inari, I headed back to the Pontocho area where I had arranged to meet Jane and Bec, who were day-tripping from Tokyo, for some drinks. They had been to some of the more famous temples that I didn't think I would find time to visit, so it was great to be able to check out their photos as a consolation prize. At one of the temples, they had been lured into buying some professional-looking photos from an enterprising local salesman and had some awesome, deliberately comically posed, 'couple photos' at some of the scenic spots around the temple. I was also amused to see that Bec was 'marking up' some of the photos of Jane with crude hand-drawn additions of the type usually found on the walls of gentlemen's toilets – good to know that there are 'grown-up' ladies, as well as men (and schoolboys), who find that to be an entertaining pursuit. After drinks, I took the girls on a walk through the market, mainly because I wanted to get my daily local market fix, but they were also quite taken by the place and ate some random-looking fish cakes on a stick, before returning to the station to get the bullet train back to Tokyo. I headed back to the Airbnb, and as soon as I was through the door, Wakiko confronted me, saying, 'You take a shower now.' I think it might have been a question, but it sounded more like an order, and I was too scared not to comply if that was the case, so I hurried to collect my wash bag so I could do what I was told, before retiring for the night after what had ended up being quite a big day of walking.

***

The following morning, I was off on a brief diversion out of Kyoto for a visit to Nara. Nara was Japan's first permanent capital from the year 710 to 794 and thus had a rich history, with lots of interesting sounding temples and shrines all crammed into a reasonably small area and mostly within what sounded like a giant deer park. It didn't take long after walking through town from the station to find my first deer, which of course I wasted a number of minutes trying to photograph without considering that given there were more than 1,200 in the park, this probably wasn't going to be the only opportunity of the day. My walking route for the morning took me first to the Daibutsuden, the town's most celebrated temple. This was famous for two reasons, first of all for having the largest wooden structure in the world and secondly for the enormous Buddha that it houses and which accounts for its size. I read up on the first of those claims, and it seems that it was true until 1998, when the return to popularity of building with timber saw it surpassed by several modern buildings, including the Nipro Hachiko baseball stadium in Odate in northern Japan. It doesn't seem anyone is in a hurry to update this fact on the promotional materials and I guess we could still call it the largest old wooden structure in the world.

Regardless, it was a mighty impressive building, set at the end of a large courtyard with manicured lawns in front of it and on either side of the wide path of the entrance. As I arrived, there were a couple of men further perfecting the setting by using a strimmer to trim the hedge that ran alongside the lawn, one man to operate the strimmer and one man to walk alongside with a plastic shield to stop the hedge trimmings from falling back onto the path which had been immaculately swept earlier in the morning – the Japanese certainly know how to make gardens look nice. The only slight blot on the perfect landscape was a sea of schoolchildren who had made an early start too, moving through the grounds and into the temple in noisy swarms, chatting away to each other and playing on their phones without paying much attention to the sights they were here to be marched past. The Daibutsu, or Great Buddha, was made with 437 tonnes of bronze and a further 130kg of gold providing a gleaming finish and seated in his 'den', he was an imposing sight up close, rising to a height of sixteen metres and covering a large area of the floor space in the building as a result of its giant dimensions. The Buddha was flanked either side by another two large statues, and the temple included a number of other wooden carved sculptures, as well as some scale models of how it had looked before it had burned down and been rebuilt in 1708 when it was scaled down to two-thirds of the original size – and it was already enormous!

The Daibutsuden was an incredible sight, and I already felt the train trip had been worthwhile, but as I continued my walking route, I found that Nara, like Kyoto, was also a treasure trove of fascinating temples and shrines but in Nara, the sights were conveniently concentrated into quite a small area making for an epic walk, particularly with were the friendly deer roaming the town as constant companions. Another highlight for me later in the walk was the Kasuga Taisha Shrine. The shrine buildings here were reasonably similar to ones I had seen before, but the point of difference were the paths to the shrine, which passed through woodland and were lined on either side with what seemed to be hundreds of stone lanterns. The lanterns sat on stone plinths of various heights most of which were about two metres high and the stone was weathered and covered with moss, reminding me of the gravestones and statues you might see in an old English graveyard and also of the free-standing bird baths seen in English country gardens. I say it looked like there were hundreds of them, but when I checked the guide, it claimed they numbered approximately two thousand. Whatever the exact number it made for a charming scene and my only regret was that I wouldn't see what it looked like in the dark when all the lanterns were lit.

My early arrival meant I was able to get around all of the places I wanted to see in time to arrive back at the start for another excellent okonomiyaki lunch, before catching the train back to Kyoto. I had to stop at a shopping mall on the walk back to the Airbnb, conceding defeat that my trainers were now almost completely disintegrated, and were probably not good for my feet and ankles, therefore needing to be replaced. A creature of habit, I managed to buy a replacement pair that were nearly identical but, on the walk home, I realised my strategic error of bringing the shoebox home and thus finding myself stuck with some 'big trash', which of course I was not allowed to leave behind. This reminded me of the other rules I was meant to be abiding by and feeling a bit mischievous as I waited for my phone to charge, I sneaked a look at the neighbouring property. Unsurprisingly there was nothing interesting there for me to report back to you, but it just felt like something I had to do.

My afternoon comprised a lengthy walk around the nearby streets to find somewhere to dispose of my shoebox and a visit to the last place I had on my to-do list, the Toji Temple, which boasted the highest pagoda in Japan, a five-storied structure measuring 55 metres. I had been a little disappointed to find that several of the temples I had seen so far (and others I would see later in the trip) were modern reconstructions rather than the original building, so I was excited to find that this one had significant historical pedigree, having been built in 1644, a mind-boggling 474 years earlier. The similar structure I had seen earlier in Nara was in the middle of a bland gravel park and didn't make for appealing photos, but this one was a cracker, set beside an ornamental pond with trees in front whose leaves were just starting to turn, so this turned out to be an excellent final stop on my Kyoto sightseeing tour.

***

It was time to say farewell to Kyoto the following morning as I was moving on to stay in Osaka for the next few nights. I had a crack at shuffling out the door quietly at 7 am but got caught by Wakiko, and as she got the iPad out, I knew we weren't quite finished here. Five minutes later I was on my way, having inherited a new Facebook friend, had my picture taken grinning inanely at the front door, and agreeing that we would definitely stay in touch – I wasn't sure quite how we would manage that, or to what end, but it made a beaming Wakiko very happy, and that made it a jolly start for my day too. I got to the station and managed to wedge myself into a commuter train to Osaka, which gave me flashbacks of my old Clapham Junction to Waterloo run, and I already had my answer to the Wakiko communication question. A number of comments from Wakiko had already appeared on the Kyoto photos I had posted on Facebook, each one of them a sticker or animation of some sort, conveying her approval in the universal language of cartoon and further enhancing her cult status in my eyes.

I was hosted in Osaka by an absolute sweetheart of a lady called Yoko, who had enough English to be able to explain how everything worked in the house, while repeatedly apologising for being in a bit of a hurry as she had to prepare for a cooking class she was giving shortly. The house was lovely, a large family home with so much spare space that there were four guest rooms on the top floor, as well as a guest lounge that opened out onto a roof terrace with superb views of the city, and it was looking like I had really lucked out with this place. I was due to stay here two nights, giving me most of today (Friday) and all of Saturday to explore Osaka, but this original plan had been complicated by developments in my dating planning, which I will bring you up to speed on now.

You may recall that on the journey to Kyoto, I was trying to coordinate my travel plans with Bel so that we could organise a date, and this time I really do mean date and not a meet-up. On our original schedules, the only overlap was looking like half a day in Koyasan, when she would be arriving, and I would be leaving. For want of a better word, this sounded like a shit plan, so once I had realised that Osaka and Kyoto were quite close, I offered up another option whereby I could make a day trip on the Saturday from Osaka back to Kyoto, where Bel was due to arrive on Friday night. It turned out this would work well, as Bel had booked a 'privately curated' six-hour tour around Kyoto for that day, so we decided I would just crash that. She had shared the itinerary with me, and it didn't look like there would be much double up on stuff I had already seen, so we locked it in. This did have one obvious downside; however, in that my second day exploring Osaka no longer existed, meaning if I wanted to see the sights, I needed to hit them all in one day instead.

This actually didn't seem to be too much of an issue as Osaka was more of a modern bustling city than its historical sight laden neighbour, so I had a fairly short list of things to see, which started with a trip to the Osaka-jo castle in the middle of town. The castle looked quite imposing from afar, set on a hill in the middle of a fortified complex surrounded by high stone walls and a wide moat. It was built in what I was learning was a fairly typical Japanese castle style with white walls, a number of triangular gables with gold decorative elements on each level leading up to pea green roofs. The building was a pyramid shape, with a square base rising through progressively smaller floors to a temple-like structure on the roof. For me, the word 'castle' evokes images of dark, menacing-looking structures from medieval times, and I would probably describe the Japanese versions as being more like a palace than a castle, but I wasn't in charge of naming them, so I was just going to have to live with it.

The castle was undeniably a captivating sight, but there were two things that bothered me about it. The first was that it was a twentieth-century concrete reproduction of the original sixteenth-century structure, so for me, it wasn't a 'real castle', and the second thing was that the whole complex was teeming with more groups of school children, who had apparently followed me here from Nara the day before. Osaka was also suffering a bit from the fact I had seen a load of amazing historical sights over the last few days and was quite close to reaching the limit of interest for such things, so I decided I should instead go and check out the shopping and entertainment area, which I thought might have a better chance of capturing my interest. I got the train over to the main shopping area which had a covered arcade which sounded like the one in Kyoto, so I was hoping for a similar experience but again was a little disappointed as the Osaka version didn't have a food market area, rather just a load of high street shops. This arcade took me down to the Dotonbori area, which is probably the most photographed area of Osaka on account of the giant neon signs that line the riverside area that passes through it. There were already a load of tourists there getting their selfies in front of the signs, including the most famous one, which was a picture of a giant running man advertising a company called Glico, which has been on that site for 80 years, but deciding this would be better by night, I moved on and would return later for dinner.

The only other attraction on my shortlist of things I wanted to visit in Osaka was the Umeda Sky Building, one of the tallest buildings in the city and the location of the best observation deck. The ride to get to the deck was high on entertainment value, starting in a glass elevator taken up to the 35th floor, from where you then took an 'escalator in the sky', from one of two tower structures, up onto a bridge on the 39th floor which joined the two towers and giving the building its distinctive arch structure. From the observation deck, there were views of the whole of the Osaka Bay area, comprising Osaka, and the neighbouring cities of Kobe and Sakai. These cities are also effectively joined up with Kyoto to form one giant urban area known as Keihanshin, which has a population of getting on for 20 million people. This sounded like a mind-boggling number until I read on to find that the Greater Tokyo urban area houses an even more incredible 38 million people, or one and a half Australia's. I took in the views with a beer which I had bought from the observatory café's '50 Bottled Beers of The World' display. I felt obliged to have a Japanese beer and went for a Suntory, but I was amused to see that Australia was represented in the selection by Fosters, and the UK standard-bearer was Bass. I think it's fair to say that neither of those would be regarded as their respective country's finest ales.

Taking the subway back into Osaka at rush hour was an absolutely electric experience, as I was swept along the pedestrian tunnels by the mass of people making their evening commute, sometimes finding I was holding my breath with the concentration of trying to carve my route through the crowds. Now I think back to the experience, it was a bit like trying to cross the road and the river in the game of 'Frogger'. The atmosphere back at Dotonbori was buzzing and after a few swift beers at happy hour in an Irish Pub (yes, a cop-out, sorry), I was on the hunt for a dinner venue.

I picked out a nearby restaurant with a menu that looked sufficiently expensive for me to try some local delicacies, without fear of quality or hygiene issues and sat down at my table in the middle of what was pretty much a full restaurant – another good sign. I picked a set menu option with pictures of reasonably regular looking food and things started off quite well, with some fresh-tasting sashimi and a few pieces of tempura vegetables, but things quickly went downhill from there. For the next course I was presented with a big bowl of Asian greens and vegetables, some pieces of tofu the size of a Rubik's Cube, lots of pieces of fish on the bone and a large pot of water on a camping stove, which they turned on and then left me to it, with no instructions on timing, or the order, of what I assumed was a self-cooking exercise. None of the waitresses seemed to have any English, but after a few minutes of trying to get their attention, I managed to get my mimed instructions, which were essentially, wait for the water to boil and then chuck it all in – which I did.

I had no idea how long it needed, so I over-cooked everything to be on the safe side and then cautiously nibbled the fish pieces to get the tiny bits of meat off before spitting out the other bits. The vegetables and greens were quite tasty, but it was the tofu that was my downfall. Attempting to transfer a piece from the hot pot to my plate, my chopstick skills failed me, and I dropped a whole piece, opening my legs quickly enough to dodge the falling food bomb which instead absolutely disintegrated on hitting the floor, leaving an unsightly mess under the table between my legs. Looking around to see how to salvage the situation, I found to my horror there were no napkins for me to pick it up with and my trauma worsened when a lady appeared at the table with more bowls of food, crouching down to do some 'at table cheffing' to convert my hot pot into 'rice porridge'. I closed my legs tight and moved my body to shield the tofu disaster below from her line of sight, smiling politely through the process. Her table chef effort was made more challenging by the fact there were glass noodles swimming around in the broth, as I had neglected to cook them using the sieve provided which would have allowed me to get them out again once they were cooked – fail. When the awkwardness was finally over, the porridge she had produced was very tasty, and after eating that and waiting to see if yet more food arrived (which it didn't) I had to abandon my station to go to the toilet. You can probably guess the sight which greeted me on my return – yes, a lady on all fours under the table with a selection of cloths and cleaning products, up to her elbows in tofu fallout. So embarrassing.

***

The following morning, I started my day by taking a shower at 5:50 am (illegal under house rules again, so don't tell Yoko), wondering to myself if this was a new record for the earliest shower taken in preparation for a first date. The 'curated tour' was due to start at 10 am, so Bel had suggested that we should meet at 9:30 am, which I had countered by telling her my compulsive habit of arriving early would mean I would probably be there by 8:30 am, which she seemed okay with. I was, however, underplaying how early I would arrive and got to Kyoto at 7:30 am, heading to Starbucks to sneak in some writing time before I headed over to meet Bel at her hotel. The lady who was serving my coffee was smiling at me, even more than the ever-cheery Japanese normally do and she soon plucked up the courage to excitedly deploy some English to say, 'You were here yesterday!' Yes, embarrassingly I had also been the first customer in here the day before on my way to Osaka, and this was another sign that the Starbucks habit was getting out of control.

I can't remember what I was writing, but I got a bit carried away and looking at my watch, realised I was going to be late to being early. I rushed out to get the metro, found the hotel name on Google Maps and walked there briskly, letting Bel know after I had arrived that I was in reception and she could come and meet me. It was only then that I checked back on the hotel name she had sent me and realised I had only typed the first three words into Google Maps and the hotel lobby I was sitting in now had a different fourth word – dreadful start! Luckily the two (sister) hotels were not too far apart, and I recovered the situation with another brisk walk to the correct hotel, where Bel was waiting for me.

Having seen Bel's photos and exchanging a multitude of messages to learn a bit more about her (about the same age as me, five-foot-three, athletic), I had a reasonably good idea of what Bel was going to look like, and I wasn't disappointed by our first meeting in the real world, where I got a proper look at her striking facial features, sultry blue eyes and dramatic looking long blonde hair. The fact we had already swapped a tonne of messages and knew a fair bit about each other before actually meeting was just the first slightly out of order aspect of a crazy first date, with the second following immediately thereafter where I found myself in her hotel room, five minutes after meeting, so that I could drop off my bag. This would have been four and a half minutes later, but we had been intercepted on the walk to the lift by a panicked hotel employee chasing Bel to ask who I was and reminding her that only guests were allowed in the hotel rooms – a strange start to the day indeed.

We headed out for coffee and agreed it would be a good idea if we got our story straight before we met the tour guide, as to what we would tell him about our relationship, but we got straight into talking about other things and it was only when we met our guide, Luke, an hour or so later and he started asking questions about what 'we' had been up to on our stay in Japan, that we realised we had not devised our cover story. Bel kept quiet and left me to answer the questions, which I did in a suitably vague fashion so as to not give away the fact that we had actually only just met. Luke was in his late twenties and was dual-nationality, having grown up initially in Japan before getting his education in the UK and then returning to Kyoto, where he now worked as a tour-guide, coincidentally spending most of his time working for Intrepid Travel.

This initial, slightly awkward conversation with Luke took place on a tram from the city to Arashiyama, and by fortunate coincidence, our first stop was at the bamboo forest, which I had been too impatient to visit a few days earlier. This made for some quite good photos, despite some damage from the three major typhoons that had hit earlier in the year, but it was already quite busy, so Luke took us on a walk to a quieter part of the town where he showed us a street which had been carefully preserved to remain in the same form as hundreds of years before. It was quite an interesting walk around, but the pace of the tour was already feeling a bit slow to us both, and I was wondering just how much, or how little, we were going to end up seeing if he kept up this ponderous rate of progress all day.

The walking route took us next to one of the beautiful gardens on the edge of town, in the grounds of a mansion owned by a gentleman who was apparently a massive silent movie star back in the day, and it had some great viewpoints along the way. At one of these, Luke said 'Ah, let me take a photo of you both for you' and gestured for Bel to hand over her phone. We did our best to fast forward through a first date photoshoot and pose naturally for a couple's photo that didn't betray the relative infancy of our relationship. The route around the gardens was indicated by a number of small arrow signs by the path, but early on in the route, another comedy translation sign caught my eye, this one advising:

'Before look around. You should go over there', with an arrow pointing to the right.

We dutifully did what we were told and went over there, before continuing around the rest of the garden and then having a cup of traditional green tea in a teahouse within the grounds. We walked back to the station and took the tram back to the city where we waited a while to get a connecting train over to Gion, where we were meant to be having lunch. However, Luke's dawdling meant we had arrived here at peak lunching time, and we couldn't get in at the scheduled place, so we had to carry on walking while he searched around for another lunch place worthy of our custom. Given neither of us had eaten any breakfast, and it was now getting on for 2 pm, we were both mighty relieved when he finally picked a place, and we quickly scanned the menu for something to eat, skipping over the bizarre instruction on the menu of 'One person one order, please. (An infant removes it.)' and ordering and devouring a very tasty bowl of udon noodles.

After lunch, he took us to see a nearby weird shrine, where ladies crawled through a small hole in a statue, apparently in the name of securing good fortune. I think Luke was hoping this was an activity that Bel would want to take part in, along with the rest of the tourists queuing up to do so and I was relieved to see she looked as disinterested with the place as I was. Luke got the hint, and we carried on to a nearby temple, Kennin-ji, that had a very impressive giant picture of two dragons on the ceiling of the main room, which became less impressive when I established it only dated back as far as 2002. One of my main takeaways from this place was again a comedy translation sign, a phenomenon that Bel and I were quickly bonding over, which was a good initial indicator of a similar shared sense of humour. This one was to remind people how to conduct themselves in the temple, and read:

'Attention – A person with a cameraman can't enter. Because the person who doesn't protect manners increased.'

Love the signs. After we had finished up at Kennin-ji it was nearly 4 pm already, which was the scheduled end of tour time and as I had predicted, we really hadn't seen very many sights in a city that I knew from first-hand experience, was absolutely jam-packed with them. Still, the main aim of the day was to go on a date with Bel and see if we had some chemistry and it felt like we had both confirmed this over the course of the day and I certainly wasn't feeling like I wanted to go and get my train back to Osaka any time soon.

At the end of the tour, we walked over to a find a bar in Pontocho for some drinks and to continue the meet and greet part of the date, eight hours after we had started it. The bar we found was, of course, tiny, with seating for about ten people in total and no-one in there apart from the two people manning the bar, but there was a table for two in a window seat overlooking the river, they served beer, and they were playing 80's and 90's rock music – what else do you need on a date? Bel was originally from Tasmania, and while her current role in risk management working for an Australian corporate didn't sound that promising for book stories, her previous profession very much did – a police officer. This meant I heard dramatic sounding stories, including one of a high-speed car-chase of 'fugitives', and other stories involving words like 'surveillance', 'cadaver' and 'undercover operatives' which were just a little bit more exciting than my work stories.

Actually, let me give you a bit more detail on the car-chase story as that one was great; the story went that in the very early hours of the morning whilst on patrol with a more senior officer who was driving, they tried to stop a suspicious-looking car, but the driver accelerated away, showing clear intent to evade interception, as I guess the police might have described the unfolding scenario. The senior officer was driving while smoking a 'durry', which he did not remove from his mouth as the pursuit continued and with his left hand on the steering wheel, he then proceeded to lean out the driver's window and try and shoot out the tyres of the fugitives' vehicle with his pistol in the other hand. Perhaps unsurprisingly, this plan failed, and after pursuing the car for a distance of around ninety kilometres, he misjudged a manoeuvre and ended up rolling the police car, leaving it on its roof in a ditch, though fortunately neither of them was seriously harmed. I mean, really, WTF! Bel told another story of when a different fellow officer had accidentally shot her in the arm – it was beginning to sound like real-life Keystone Cops! She even had a famous person story to throw in the mix, recalling as a fresh-faced 18-year-old new recruit to the force, being deployed to a large bush property to search for a missing person, who was later located, unfortunately deceased. However, during this, a relative of the deceased person had asked her out on a date, highly unusual and somewhat inappropriate given the nature of the scene she was attending. Obviously, she said no, but it later came to light that the guy was actually Martin Bryant, who would later carry out the Port Arthur massacre killing 35 people and injuring 23 others, an event which shaped the gun control rules now in place in Australia. I'm not sure what my equivalent celebrity encounter story to that would be – I think sitting next to Alf from Home and Away on a flight from Sydney to London might be the best I have.

Over the course of the afternoon, the bar had filled up with other people and now had a humming vibe, but it was time for us to move on as dinnertime was calling. We found a restaurant nearby which was set up in the typical Japanese horse-shoe shape around the cooking area and took our seats next to a middle-aged Japanese couple, who nodded at us excitedly as we sat down. After enjoying some excellent sashimi and chatting away for a while more, Bel was glancing over her shoulder and appeared a little distracted. She turned around and seemed to be in conversation with the couple seated next to her, which I left her to do for a bit while I ate some more of the food that arrived. After a few minutes, it became apparent the Japanese couple were excited about being sat next to a western couple and were keen to have a bit of a chat, which, after a very brief English language exchange moved onto Wakiko's technique, with the guy using Google Translate on his iPhone. In the part of the conversation I had missed, the gentleman had apparently made a comment about me being her husband which Bel had not corrected – this was a surprising development in our relationship and yet another out of order aspect of our first date, but apparently it was easier for them to understand and to not have to try and translate. Anyway, the guy was leaning forward so he could see me and was smiling, laughing and pointing at me, he then started typing into the iPhone signalling he wanted to tell me something, which he then showed me on the screen. And what did it say?

'Cool and handsome.'

Seriously – that is what he wrote! I can say with absolute certainty that this is the first time this has happened to me on a date, and I wouldn't be surprised if it's the first time it's happened to anyone. I can't remember what the guy's name was, but let's just call him 'Hiro'.

After dinner we walked back through the market, which was now unfortunately closed, looking for a place to have a few more drinks, which we found at a brewery bar. It was about 10 pm by now, and we had not yet broached the topic of how the evening was going to end, I was meant to be returning to Osaka, and it wasn't going to be too much longer until it was last train time. I can't recall exactly how I did it, but I somehow managed to take the conversation in a direction where Bel was the one who asked me if I wanted to stay over, an offer I was, of course, happy to accept. This time when we returned to the hotel and greeted the front desk staff, they didn't seem so bothered about me not being a guest there – perhaps it's only frowned upon to have a 'gentleman caller' in the morning.

***

The following morning I was straight into dealing with the consequences of falling into 'dirty stop out' mode, as the unexpectedly 22-hour long first date meant that I now needed to play some catch-up logistics, getting a train back to Osaka where I would likely be making a walk of shame past Yoko to get to my room. I would then need to quickly pack, before heading back to the station to then get the four trains, a cable car and a bus to get to my next destination of Koyasan. Got all of that? Good. Oh, and I have one other update of relevance, the previous day's date had gone off sufficiently well for us to agree to meet up again, this time in Koyasan on the day after next.

The journey got off to a good start, and I managed after the fourth time of trying, to catch the 'special rapid' service between Osaka and Kyoto, using the time to pick out a few photos from the Kyoto 'curated tour' for my now daily update on Instagram/Facebook. On this topic, while I was in Canada, I had received the following heavily sarcastic message via a university friend WhatsApp group, from my friend Tall, revealing that not everyone was enjoying my relentless Facebook photo updates of the great outdoors:

'Maygay. Am really enjoying the trees and lakes photo extravaganza. When are you moving on to birds?'

This had given me pause to moderate the number of photos I had been taking of trees, which was a shame as they were quite spectacular in Japan, and eventually, I decided to disregard the feedback, posting a number of photos of Kyoto under the headline, 'A few more tree photos especially for the person who told me they were sick of me posting tree photos.' The photos had been on Facebook for approximately ten minutes before I got the following comment from my friend Joe:

'It's not just that person who is sick of the tree photos.'

Thanks, guys.

There was further good news to follow the rapid train, as I managed to sneak into the house and up to my room without alerting anyone to my movements, emerging an hour later, washed and changed, to say my farewells, Yoko completely oblivious to the nefarious night-time escapades of the 'friendly and polite' gentleman she later described me as in her Airbnb review. This run of good form continued through the day as the succession of well-timed train connections whisked me out of the urban landscape and down south towards the countryside and mountains where Koyasan was located. The town of Koyasan was established around the ninth century by a solitary monk named Kukai, who had travelled to China and learnt about 'esoteric Buddhism', astronomy, geology and civil engineering, before returning to Japan, where he then apparently got busy sharing his skills and stories around the country and established a base for the Shingon sect of Japanese Buddhism in Koyasan in 819. The original monastery grew into a town with a university for religious studies, 120 sub-temples, and Kukai's mausoleum at Okunoin, which is surrounded by the largest graveyard in the country and which is regarded as one of the holiest sites in the whole of Japan. Many of these sub-temples offer lodgings for 'pilgrims', but for 'pilgrim' you can probably read 'tourist', as a stay in a temple here, along with the experience of the elaborate vegetarian meals served there, seemed to be the main drawcard of the town. These temple stays are also pretty expensive and not quite in keeping with my current travel style, so I had managed to find an Airbnb at a simple-looking guesthouse in the town instead, at what I estimated was about a quarter of the price of the temples, so this felt like an excellent outcome, assuming the place I had booked turned out to be satisfactory.

On arrival, this did seem to be the case, as the location was right in the middle of town and my host here, Takashi, was very friendly, spoke pretty good English, and took the time to give me a comprehensive list of 'lecommendations' as to how I should spend my time here. My room was quite big, but in typical Japanese style didn't really have anything in it apart from a table and the bed, which Takashi would prepare for me later on, including firing up an electric blanket contraption which apparently went under the mattress. Intriguing. There were two other guestrooms, but I didn't hear anyone else while I was there, which was surprising given the thickness of the 'walls' could best be described as 'paper-thin' – given they were actually all sliding screens made of paper. I found some udon for lunch at a nearby place and then set off for a look around the town, which Luke, our guide in Kyoto, had described a bit unkindly as 'the Disneyland of Buddhism'. You might recall back in Mexico I had visited a place that someone had described as the 'Mayan Disneyland', so this was the second Disney visit of the trip, though this place, disappointingly, didn't seem to have a log flume ride either. I kept my tour of the sights to a reasonably superficial walk around, on account of there not being loads to see and the fact that I would be basically covering the same ground for 'Date #2' the next day.

I met Bel off the bus, and after dropping our bags at the front desk of the impressive looking temple, we set off on what I will describe as a 'privately curated' tour of my own, taking in the sights of Koyasan in a vastly more efficient if a marginally less informative version of Luke's tour of Kyoto. The highlights of Koyasan are found in two main areas of the town (or 'sanctuaries'), and we started at the western end of town at the Danjo Garan Complex, the first place where Kukai established a temple in Koyasan. This complex comprised a large red and white entrance building, called the Chu-mon Gate (which failed my historical integrity test having been rebuilt in 2015), Kon-do Hall, the main hall of the temple complex, and the Konpon Daito Pagoda, a vermillion coloured 48-metre high building, which was probably the most eye-catching of the complex. We took a look inside this building to see the giant statue of someone called Taizokai Danichi Nyorai and four statues of Kongokai next to him, and pretty much had the place to ourselves as there didn't seem to many tourists around for some reason, a welcome change from the Japanese temple experience which I had by now become accustomed to.

We then took a walk to the western entrance to the town, the 25-metre high Dai-mon Gate, which I was pleased to read did pass my authenticity test, dating back to 1705 and after finding for the second day in a row, that it was too large to fit in a decent photo, we walked back into town to find some lunch. With the addition of some very attractive company for today's lunch, the meal lasted a significantly longer amount of time than the previous day's effort, and it was getting on for the middle of the afternoon by the time we got round to making the walk to the eastern end of town to check out the other sanctuary, the Okunoin. This complex included the KoboDaishi Gobyo Mausoleum, which was built in memory of Kukai after his death, and the Sando, a two-kilometre path, which led from the Ichinohashi Bridge on the edge of town up to the Mausoleum. This path was lined with several 100-year-old cedar trees, and more than 200,000 tombs for people of all classes had been built amongst the woods surrounding the path, making it the largest cemetery in Japan, and once I had got lost in the dark of the previous night's walk. There was a fascinating range of tombs and statues scattered throughout the cemetery which I had looked around the day before, and which we now explored together in the vastly preferable lighting conditions until we arrived at the Mausoleum itself.

The Mausoleum had a large veranda surrounding it and in the eaves of the roof hung literally thousands of lanterns, of about 50cm in height, organised in rows across the length of the roof and then about four or five rows deep, each of them individually numbered for some purpose that wasn't immediately apparent, other than maybe helping to identify which bulb needed replacing. After walking across the veranda and into the building, the main room had loads more of the lanterns hanging inside with a long wooden barrier across the room to protect the various altars and other religious artefacts, which the monks inside were tending to. When we entered, one of the monks was doing the hoovering of the deep red plush carpets in front of the altars, which made for a slightly surreal sight, and there were a couple of other monks sitting at desks selling what looked like some scrolls of calligraphy and, more interestingly, some small necklaces which the sign in front of the stall said were:

'Traditional amulet to ward off calamities'

This sounded like a fantastic item to have on your person should you find yourself in a situation where calamity threatened, but for some reason, I didn't buy one on the way through, though I did curse not having done so on the walk back to town later. After passing through the main room, we walked down into the basement of the building which was filled with racks of thousands of identical 10cm high statues of one of the Buddha's. I know there were thousands of them as they, like the lanterns, were individually numbered, and I followed the numerical sequence of the racks around the room until I found the number 50,000 at the end. I didn't get round to reading up on why you might need that many statues of Buddha in your basement, but it did make for a really interesting visual spectacle – which sadly you were not allowed to photograph. The Mausoleum was a fascinating place, even second time around and seemed a fitting way to bring my privately curated tour to a close and we walked back through the cemetery and town to our temple, timing our arrival perfectly for the check-in time to our room.

Our room was basically a larger version of the room I had slept in the night before, with tatami mat floors, futon bedding and a few low tables, so there wasn't really anything comfortable to sit on during the brief wait until dinner, and we amused ourselves instead by searching for comedy translations in the room information. This time, however, it wasn't the dodgy English that took my eye, but rather the subject matter of one of the terms and conditions, which related to condolence money. This referred to legislation, so I assume it's a Japan-wide concept, but the essence of the relevant clauses was that if one of us died in the night, the temple would send condolence money to our next of kin, to a value of 'up to 100,000 Yen per deceased guest' (c. 1,200 AUD), which I thought was a very thoughtful concept. Like any good contract, there were, of course, a number of carve-out provisions, in this case including exemptions in the case of:

4 – 'Diseases caused by the radioactivity, explosiveness, other harmful qualities or other accidents arising from such qualities of nuclear fuel materials (including used fuel materials; this meaning applying hereinafter) or materials contaminated by any such nuclear fuel materials (including nuclear fission products).'

Wow. They really wanted to make sure there was no ambiguity on any deaths that might have been attributable to nuclear materials! But wait there was more...

5 – 'Diseases caused by nuclear radiation or nuclear contamination other than those stated in '4' above.'

And both of these clauses ranked ahead in importance to 'bacterial food poisoning', which came in at number 6 – bizarre! And let's not get into why they would be allowed to carve out liability for that one, which they would be far more likely to actually be responsible for.

I was also amused to see you only got the money if you provided a death certificate, where you might expect that upon them finding a lifeless corpse in their lodgings and handing it over to the mortuary this would be evidence enough, but best not to dwell any further on the topic as I'm sure you are waiting impatiently to read about tofu and vegetables, so let's get to that.

The dinner was served in our room by our young, enthusiastic if slightly awkward hostess, Kuma, who had just about enough English to explain what the dishes were and not a lot else beyond that. I took a picture of the meal to help me describe it after the fact, but as I look at the photo now, it doesn't help much, as there were so many mystery items set out across seven (7) miniature tables spread over the floor. I can identify the Japanese tea, the small pots of miso soup, some tofu cubes and several of the beautifully carved miniature vegetables, including carrot, taro and potato but after that my descriptions can be no more precise than words like 'purple cube' and 'mystery pickle'. One of the more curious dishes was some kind of tofu and mixed vegetable creation, which sat in a milky looking liquid in a small bowl over a small burner which Kuma lit, instructing us to wait until the flame had gone out before eating the dish itself. As she did this, Bel leaned over for a look and said, 'What is it?' Kuma, who had been concentrating on lighting the burner, looked a little bit confused and after a brief pause, held up the match she had just blown out in front of Bel, looked at the match and said – 'Err, this is wood?'

After we politely explained that we understood how fire was made, she described what was in the food, but I registered none of the information, as I was still chuckling about her unintended comic genius. If the chef was in the room and asked me at the end of the meal what I thought of the food, I would have said something like 'Oh, its beautifully presented – and really interesting flavours and textures,' which would translate as 'I don't like it much', but I was starving so I still managed to eat all of it, before going to sleep dreaming of double bacon cheeseburgers.

The temple stay experience most certainly does not include a lazy lie-in, with a check out time of 9 am, and breakfast, that you must take between 7 am and 8 am, that comprised of more mystery veg, more tofu creations and a couple of dishes which I am 90% sure was baby food. Just two meals into the experience we were already a bit over this and didn't eat much, heading out for a walk to find something more palatable. Our morning prayers were answered in the form of a guest house we found down a back street, which advertised coffee and croissants, and had another excellent sign outside, this time on the umbrella stand:

'Prepare for Rain – Raindrop is a drop of water with the size of more than 0.5mm in diameter and comes down from the sky.'

I had always wondered where that wet stuff came from – now I knew.

The place was run by a quintessentially excitable and cheery Japanese husband and wife, who were super proud of their croissants which, when we queried, the lady said she 'half-made herself'. I'm pretty sure that means I have also 'half-made' every croissant I have bought and taken home to heat in the oven, but these ones were flaky and delicious and came with a jar of chocolate spread and we were ravenous, so this was no time to be nit-picking. That second breakfast also marked the end of our second date, which had just outlasted the first one to hit 23 hours, when I got on the bus to start my journey to Hiroshima, and Bel set off for a hike for the rest of the day to try and take her mind off the second evening of vegetables and tofu ahead of her. I had thoroughly enjoyed Bel's company again, and the connection we had established seemed ridiculously strong given our relationship was only two dates old – though the 8,000 odd WhatsApp messages outside of the time together had probably helped that. It was pretty obvious to me that the WhatsApp deluge was unlikely to dissipate anytime soon, and I would definitely be organising date number three on my return to Sydney, so this felt like an appropriately happy ending to my trip's internet dating adventures. And yes, that choice of words is completely intentional.

***

My route for the day involved retracing my steps to Osaka, where I would catch a bullet train to Hiroshima and take a short tram to my lodgings which while badged as an

Airbnb, was actually a capsule hotel, a novelty accommodation experience I had been looking forward to. I had worked through the scheduled timings of the various forms of transport to Osaka and having identified the departure time of the bullet train I was aiming for and arriving with about fifteen minutes to spare, I had time to inhale a burger from McDonald's on the way to the ticket office to reserve a seat. At the ticket office, I found I had done a shoddy planning job as I realised I could not use my rail pass on the bullet train I had planned and the next one I could take did not leave until an hour later. With some time to kill I wandered out of the ticket office in the other direction and came across another McDonald's store, which I strode into confidently and ordered a whole meal as if the burger ten minutes earlier had never happened. This was quite an intense vegetarian recoil I was experiencing, but it seemed the only course of action which would successfully restore my body's factory settings. This health food extravaganza was followed up with a latte and clutching this, I was walking up the steps to the bullet train platform when disaster struck. My main bag was on my back, and the smaller one slung over one shoulder creating what I believe lorry drivers call an 'uneven load', when one small stumble up the steps sent me toppling over. My instincts prevented me from letting go of my coffee or the rail pass in my other hand, which would have broken my fall, and instead, I landed heavily on my elbow and knee. It was quite painful, and I briefly looked like a tortoise flailing around on its back before I could upright myself and continue on my way, still drinking the largely un-spilt coffee. In the context of my trip, this was quite clearly a calamitous event, and I kicked myself for not having purchased the amulet in Koyasan that, without doubt, would have spared me the limp I was now sporting.

A few hours later after another rapid train journey further west and a tram ride, I arrived at my hotel which was, as had been claimed, right next to the tram stop and with the help of another of the PDF files with photos and arrows, I successfully completed the one-minute walk. At check-in I was given two keys, one for a locker and one for a lock to secure my luggage with and was directed to the 'pod room' on the fourth floor. Looking firstly in the locker, I found towels and wash stuff along with some very fetching looking blue and gold 'sleepwear' (pyjamas) – this was getting more exciting by the minute. The pod room turned out to be a mix of accommodation, with one side taken up by small bedsits like rooms which had a bed, a desk, a kettle and a curtain for a door and the other side where I was going to be sleeping in, had a bank of the pods two high and five across. My pod was 'downstairs' so crouching down, I commando crawled in to find I had a super comfy mattress, a bank of plugs with an alarm clock and on the side of the pod, even a TV mounted on an angle bracket, with a pull-down blind as my door. This was basically just a really flash bunk bed and I was excited to try it out, but unfortunately, it was only 6 pm and a bit early to get into my sleepwear just yet, so I went for a look around the rest of the floor, finding an outdoor terrace and a number of brand-new looking showers and toilets. These were the first toilets I had seen which also had English translations on the buttons, and I amused myself briefly by trying out the 'privacy' button, which played a tinny sound effect of a toilet flushing for the benefit of people who didn't like others to hear the sound of their "kids being dropped off at the pool". I had briefly read up on the concept of capsule hotels on Wikipedia, and I thought their summary of how they had come to exist was rather fun:

'They provide an alternative for those [businessmen] who may be too drunk to return home safely, or too embarrassed to face their spouses.'

Who hasn't found themselves in that predicament?

The next day was always going to be relatively sombre as the majority of the tourist sights in the city are, as you would imagine, related to the dreadful event that befell the city back in 1945. My first stop was the Peace Memorial Park. The park is located at the northern end of an island, formed by two waterways that flow through the middle of the city and sits opposite one of the most recognisable buildings in the city, the Atomic Bomb Dome building. When the bomb detonated over the city at 8:15 am on August 6 1945, nearly 92 per cent of the 76,000 buildings in the city were destroyed and this building, despite being located almost directly under the explosion, was one of the few which avoided destruction and the decision was made to preserve the building as a reminder of the tragic event. In the park itself, there are a number of other monuments, the first one I arrived at was the Bell of Peace, where I read the following inscription:

'We dedicate this bell as a symbol of Hiroshima Aspiration: Let all nuclear arms and wars be gone, and the nations live in true peace! May it ring to all corners of the earth to meet the ear of every man, for in it throb and palpitations the hearts of its peace-loving donors. So may you, too, friends, step forward, and toll this bell for peace!'

A short walk from here was the Children's Peace Monument, a concrete statue with the figure of a child standing on the top, holding a wire crane above her head. The child is Sadako Sasaki, one of the children of Hiroshima who contracted leukaemia as a result of radiation poisoning from the explosion. Despite her illness, Sadako had a vision that she would make a thousand 'orizuru' (origami paper cranes), which Japanese tradition said would mean you would be granted one wish, and Sadako's wish was for a world without nuclear weapons. Sadly, she passed away before reaching her goal, but her classmates completed the task for her, with the story inspiring many others across the globe, schoolchildren from around the world still send colourful paper cranes to Hiroshima in her memory, where they are displayed in the Perspex cases that form a semicircle behind the statue. This was really thought-provoking stuff and after taking a look at the nearby Peace Clock and the Flame of Peace, I decided it would be helpful to have some more context for the memorials I was viewing and so headed in to the Memorial Hall, which was just opening as I arrived. This opened in 2002 and is centred on The Hall of Remembrance, a circular chamber in the basement which is accessed by following a descending path from the ground floor in a counter clockwise direction, intended to convey a walk back in time to that moment. Just before the entrance to the Hall was the following inscription:

'We hereby mourn those who perished in the atomic bombing. At the same time, we recall with great sorrow the many lives sacrificed to mistaken national policy. To ensure that no such tragedies are ever repeated, we pledge to convey the truth of these events throughout Japan and around the world, to pass it on to future generations, and to build, as soon as possible, a peaceful world free from nuclear weapons.'

Standing in the centre of the Hall, you are surrounded by a 360-degree panoramic recreation of a black and white photograph taken by US forces from the proximity of the hypocentre shortly after the explosion. The wall surface is made up of 140,000 tiles, representing the estimated number of people who died in the initial explosion and subsequently in the period up until December 1945. I was the sole person in the hall, the only sound was the air-conditioning unit and the gentle trickling noise from the water feature in the centre of the room, which made for quite a moving experience. I next went for a walk around the Hiroshima Peace Memorial Museum, which had a load of information about the bombing and the aftermath, including some quite confronting content with harrowing photos of burns victims and torn and bloody clothes. There were a number of groups of fairly young school children passing around these horrific exhibits, which I found a little bit surprising, but then reflected it was probably a necessary evil of the country's intent, seen in the inscriptions at the various monuments, to make sure the dreadful events are acknowledged and learnt from. From my reading on Japan's military history, I had learnt that the bomb and the second one in Nagasaki a few days later, had effectively changed their stance on war overnight. Moving from a country that had historically looked to expand their reach overseas in an often highly aggressive (and controversial) manner, to one that wanted no part in any conflicts going forward and whose people seemed genuinely remorseful, which must have been a huge change for the generations of people who had experienced both the before and after.

A sombre morning indeed and I decided I had probably learned enough and should move on to see what the modern, reborn city of Hiroshima had to offer. Well, that's not strictly true, as the first place I went after that was the city castle. For obvious reasons this was again a modern reconstruction and had a similar look to the one in Osaka, but for some reason, it captured my interest more than Osaka, and I walked up the tower to check out the city views (not exciting), and the displays of historical information within (surprisingly, more exciting). Here I learnt about how the Shogunate system, which I spoke about back in Kyoto, broke down over the course of the nineteenth century, prompted mostly it seemed by other countries turning up on Japan's shores and trying to persuade them that they should be playing more nicely from a world trade perspective. The US started this process in 1853, when a fleet led by a chap called Commodore Matthew Perry (not the one from Friends) invaded and the changes that followed resulted in the breakdown of the feudal clan system and the abolishment of the Shogunate in 1867, marking the end of the age of samurai.

This busy morning of nineteenth and twentieth-century history lessons had given me quite a hunger, and my next stop was at a place called Tonpopo, a tiny little husband and wife run restaurant, celebrated for their okonomiyaki. Before you start complaining about me eating the same meal again and again, this one was different, all right? The okonomiyaki in Hiroshima was made in a different style to the ones found in Kyoto and Osaka, and the main differences seemed to be that they also had noodles in them and were twice the size. I had read that the portion sizes were a bit excessive and that you should share one serve between two but, a) I was 'Billy no-mates', and b) my holiday appetite was still immense, so I got one for myself and put it away with no issues. Unlike the English Gap-year students next to me, who were struggling through theirs while complaining about how spicy they were, and mopping sweat off their brows with paper napkins. Absolute national disgrace! The food here was superb and the best okonomiyaki of the trip by a distance, it was so good, I'm actually drooling a little bit as I write about it now. I had a quiet afternoon after this, riding around a bit more on the trams and eating – again. But I'm not writing a food book, so I won't bore you with the details of how delicious the oysters I had at a riverside restaurant, lit by fairy lights, were. In summary, Hiroshima was getting a big tick from me.

I do have one other update for you at this stage on matters unconnected to my tour of Hiroshima, and this is on the topic of my lengthy ongoing correspondence with Jetstar on the mystery $1,200 transaction on my credit card. After a frankly ludicrous nine-week period of investigation, Jetstar had finally concluded their enquiries and had sent me an email that said:

'Hi Alex, thank you for contacting Jetstar. I'm sorry to hear that you're concerned that your credit card was used to pay for a booking that you didn't authorise. Due to privacy restrictions, I'm not able to give any information about this booking to anyone other than the listed passenger or contact. We will be happy to cooperate with any investigation by your financial institution or by the police, and I would encourage you to contact them as soon as possible about your concerns. Thank you for following this up with us.'

So as I had suspected, it was a fraudulent transaction, but even though it was on my card, they weren't allowed to tell me what it was, which seemed a bit bizarre. I did manage to find out through the bank's investigation what the transaction was, and apparently, I paid for a lady called Alicia Maycock and two friends to fly from Darwin to Melbourne – an amazing coincidence that she had that name.

***

Back in Hiroshima, after my highly satisfying stay in the capsule hotel, it was time to move on and today's travel was just a short hop via a tram, train and ferry combination to Miyajima, an island slightly to the south of Hiroshima. The tram ride was straightforward, and I quickly got a connecting train, only to find that after three stops, we stopped for what felt like an age. I was listening to music and was away in my own world so just waited patiently until we finally got going again – in the opposite direction. For people in possession of fully functioning brains, there were clues that this was about to happen. When the train had stopped, everyone apart from me had got off, and a whole load of new people had got on and flipped the reversible chairs around to face in the other direction. While I had registered that this was an interesting but not wholly unusual turn of events, my brain had not joined the obvious dots, and I had just stood by the door, listening to my music. Now, nearly 100 days into my trip, there was still no sign of any 'travel common-sense' brain development, which sadly meant that was probably never going to happen. My saving grace, as always, was that I was travelling way earlier than I needed to be, meaning I had time to get off and catch the correct train back in the other direction and then ferry across to the island to still arrive before 9 am, well in advance of the droves of tourists who would follow later.

I hadn't walked far from the ferry when I discovered Miyajima was another deer place, with a small posse of them wandering around the path that ran along the coast to the Itsukushima floating shrine and the Ohotorii Gate, a 16-metre high vermillion shrine gate that sat in the sea just off the coast. Miyajima is a popular destination for hikers as there are a number of trails that wind up the hills behind the town to the top of Mt Misen, the highest peak on the island and that was, of course, my main destination for the day. Mt Misen is viewed as a sacred site, as it was here that Kukai, the monk I introduced you to back in Koyasan, underwent 'ascetic practice' for one hundred days on the mountain. The fire he lit here, known as the Eternal Fire, is said to have been burning for 1,200 years and was used to light the Flame of Peace in the Hiroshima Peace Memorial Park, so it seemed Kukai was proving quite a useful character in joining together the strands of my journey through Japan.

In addition to the walking trails, there is also a 'cheat's route' up the mountain in the form of a 'ropeway', which is basically a cable car leading to a point not too far from the summit. I had read a couple of blogs about the Mt Misen walk, by people who presented themselves as serious walkers who had completed the hike but then said they had taken the ropeway up and just done the walk down, justifying this by saying they did it 'to save time'. Yeah, right. On the same topic, the Mt Misen hike website includes the following guidance:

'We recommend a short course with a single ticket of ropeway for a busy or lazy person.'

They're not scared to call it how it is! This was probably just another slight fail of direct literal translation, but it wasn't the only sign here that managed to provide translation humour, as I walked up the lower parts of the trail, I saw the following sign:

'8 min. walk to ropeway station (6, if run a little!)'

I, of course, was not going to the ropeway station and instead took the Momijdani Course up the hill, which was a steep trail through the trees alongside a stream with nothing much to see along the way. That was academic however when I got to the observatory at the summit, which had awesome views along the coast towards Hiroshima in the distance and then out to sea, where there were a number of densely wooded islands. I couldn't see the floating shrine gate from this lookout but as I headed back down one of the other climbing routes, the Daishoin Temple Course, the distant orange blob of the gate came back into view, getting larger as I neared the aforementioned temple. The temple is named after Kukai, using his posthumous name of Kobo Daishi and covers a large area rising up the side of the hill with a number of halls and other buildings. My temple fatigue was still strong, so I didn't have much of a look around the buildings, but I was excited to see the temple had a large set of prayer wheels, the Mani Wheel, a number of forest green coloured wheels embossed with golden Japanese text which ran up the middle of a flight of stairs to one of the halls. I had been fascinated by the prayer wheels I had seen in each of the villages I had passed through while walking the Annapurna Circuit in Nepal earlier in the year, but this was the first one I had seen in Japan, which could also mean I just hadn't been looking very hard for them.

This temple was, unfortunately, the point where I found myself back amongst the large crowds of tourists, who had rolled in on the later ferries while I had been up the hill, so I made a quick break to find lunch and take a bit of a breather. I had picked up a Mt Misen walking guide map at the observatory at the summit, which I now had some time to read with my lunch. This map folded out to A2 size and was packed with info on the walking routes, the main shrines around the island and a section on the mountain itself, titled *'Misen's Seven Wonders'*. I was slightly cursing that I hadn't read this before the walk and looked to see what I had missed, and found two of them, or 29% of the 'Wonders', described on the map as so:

- Ryuto-no-sugi (Sea-fire Japan cedar) – The cedar is dead, and only the stump can be seen now.
- Shigure-zakura (Showered cherry blossoms) – Can't see the tree now because it has been dead.

So I didn't miss much.

***

After leaving Miyajima the next day, the suggested Lonely Planet itinerary had me making the long journey east towards Tokyo, with a diversion at the end to visit the Hakone area, famed for its onsens and views of Mt Fuji. This was probably the day in the schedule I had been most sceptical about, as it meant I had to travel about 750 kilometres on a variety of boats, trains and buses to get to Hakone, where I then didn't seem to have that much time to do anything given I was due in Tokyo the following day. I justified the effort required in my head, with a mental image of me sitting in an onsen with dramatic views of Mt Fuji in the distance and it was this picture that served as my motivation as I embarked on the journey.

After the ferry to get off the island, I was back into commuter mode, joining the hoards on their way to work in the city. I felt a slight pang of guilt that I wasn't going to work too but that passed when I reminded myself I was already at work, in my capacity as a travel writer and that I wasn't even getting paid to do this job. I arrived in Hiroshima a bit earlier than planned which turned out to be a blessing, as the online bullet train timetable, which I had already been suspicious of, had again proved to be a work of fiction. The train I was aiming for did not exist, but fortunately, there was a Hikari train leaving shortly, so I reserved a seat and hopped on. After about two and a half hours, this brought me into Osaka, for the seventh time of the trip, where I then took another bullet train for a further two hours to a place called Atami. This was quite a lot of time to kill, and I wasn't in the mood for writing, so I spent the time reading the Lonely Planet to learn a bit more about Japan's history. I won't bore you with all the interesting information I learnt and then immediately forgot again, other than to educate you of two completely unconnected facts, that Japan has ten per cent of the world's active volcanoes, and that the premise for the movie monster Godzilla was that he/she/it was created in the aftermath of the atomic bombings in Japan in World War Two. So now you know.

At Atami, I had to get off and wait for twenty minutes for one of the slower services that would stop at Odawara, the station from where I could get a bus up to Hakone. While I stood on the platform, a number of the fast services thundered through on their way back to Tokyo, and I found myself reflecting that they are quite an amazing sight in full flight and from a practical perspective, a great enabler for travel around this fascinating country. After completing the final (seven-minute) bullet train leg, I found the bus I needed and wedged myself in with a load of other tourists, for what was quite an uncomfortable hour and a quarter ride up into the greenery of the nearby hills. When I had booked the guesthouse I was staying in, the only room left had been an 'emergency room' behind reception, and I was quite intrigued to find out what this meant and then strangely disappointed when I arrived to find that a regular room had become available, unfortunately, I will never know what emergency features I missed out on. The guesthouse was fairly simple, but it did boast both indoor and outdoor onsens, which were the main reason for me being here and I found that both were private and available to book for a half an hour slot. I had thought that getting your junk out in public at an onsen, was one of those things that just had to be done on a visit to Japan, so I was (strangely) a little bit disappointed that I wasn't going to be able to say I had ticked that box – but not that disappointed if I'm really honest about it.

It was 3 pm once I had finished the tour of the guesthouse and given it got dark at five, I thought I should get out and see the local sights, which the man at the guesthouse had circled on the map for me. To my disappointment I quickly found there wasn't very much to see, he had told me to go to a 'beautiful field' which I had to walk up a busy road with no pavement to get to, and which really wasn't very exciting when I got there. The wooded hills that surrounded the village gave an amphitheatre-like feel to the place, particularly with the trees starting to turn to their autumnal red but it was a grey and dreary afternoon and the experience as a whole was feeling quite uninspiring. This initial assessment got worse when I walked back to the centre of the village to find all of the buildings looked to have been built in the 50s and 60s of the ugliest materials available and there didn't seem to be much going on. I walked to the sights marked on the tourist map, a shrine and a temple, to find they were almost right next to each other but that some bright spark had built a five-storey dark grey tiled apartment building in the middle of them, ruining the aspect of both. By now, I had resigned myself to the fact that this stop in the itinerary had, as I suspected, been an error. This felt like the kind of place where you went and stayed in an all-inclusive spa hotel and then got in your car to drive up to the mountains on a clear day to take in the views of the lake and Mt Fuji. I had no spa hotel, no car, very little time here and shit weather, so this was clearly going to be a fail, and I turned my thoughts instead to things I might do in Tokyo the following day. However, as was often the case during my time in Japan, there was something lurking around the corner to cheer a bad mood and this time it was my dinner venue, a restaurant just around the corner from my hotel.

Going back to my earlier observation of all-inclusive spa resorts, the restaurant was completely empty, so not for the first time on my trip it was just me and the background music and again, not for the first time this trip, the background music was *'The Sound of Silence'* – this time, music box style! This immediately lifted my spirits, which were further boosted when the owner asked me where I was from, and disappeared into the kitchen, before soon returning and proudly placing a small Australian flag on my table. I ordered the house special of a 'tamago donburi', which was a grilled pork fillet with spicy sauce on rice and amused myself listening to the music box selection, which progressed through *'Wind Beneath My Wings'* and *'The Sound of Music'*. The music was complemented by the two gents in the kitchen making cooking noises and regular shouts of 'Hai! Hai! Hai!' which entertained me every time I heard it. After a thoroughly enjoyable feed, I asked to pay the bill, and after doing so, the guy asked me to wait a minute and reappeared with two boxes of gifts of which I was allowed to choose one item from each. The first box was full of origami cranes like the ones I had seen in Hiroshima, and the second one was filled with homemade bookmarks. I chose one with a geisha on it who looked like she was made of old sugar sachet wrappers and chopstick packets, thanked the guy warmly and left with a huge smile on my face – you just have to love the Japanese.

Having made my way back to Tokyo the following day and checked into my next capsule hotel, my thoughts had quickly turned to food. My first stop was at a restaurant called Harajuku Gyoza-ro, which as you could probably guess, was a dumpling place with about 25 seats around the cooking area where they made up the dumplings and then steamed or fried them. There was a very short menu, as this was another example of the Japanese style of just doing one dish but doing it bloody well and after eating a couple of serves of the delicate pork gyoza, an impromptu idea came to mind. Why not turn my final lunch in Japan into something of a 'lunch safari', and go for three courses at three different restaurants around the city? I had more recommendations for places to go to eat in Tokyo than I would have time to visit and this seemed a cunning way to sneak in a few more, so from Harajuku I walked down to Shibuya where I caught the train north to Shinjuku, where Bel had recommended a place called Ichiran Ramen that served, you guessed it, excellent ramen.

The restaurant drew a big crowd, and I had to join a queue on the street when I arrived, but this moved quickly along the street, then down into the basement where I was then sent to get a lift to the sixth floor. It was here I started to realise how complicated the ramen ordering and eating process was, as I then had to place an order on a vending machine that I previously described in Kyoto and Miyajima, before joining another queue, this time to wait for a table to become available. While I was waiting in the queue I was then given another clipboard to fill in a form with further details on the ramen, asking questions like how rich I wanted the stock to be, how much garlic, what kind of onion, did I want sliced pork, how spicy, and what noodle texture I wanted. No two ramens are the same; it seems! When I got to the end of the bench, it was finally my turn for a table, and I got ushered into a room which had a horseshoe of maybe 25 one-person booths which faced small serving hatches on the inside. I likened it to a prison visitation room but bizarrely the hatch that allowed you to see through to where the food was being served from, did not allow you to see the face of the person you were interacting with, you could only see their lower midriff and legs as you had the conversation to confirm the final details of your order – so bizarre. After the food arrived, the unseen guy on the other side then fiercely pulled down a bamboo screen so you couldn't see anything apart from your food and the wooden booth you were seated in. So in summary, the experience was super weird, but the ramen was absolutely to die for, and if I had been in Tokyo for any longer I would have been straight back there for lunch the next day too.

After thoroughly enjoying that novel experience, I got back on the train and went to Shiodome from where I walked over to the fish market area for my dessert stop. This was a recommendation from my Peru trip friends, Ben and Bec, to a place called Celi Sweets, which sold cream puffs. I am not much of a dessert fan, but these sounded quite interesting, and I wasn't disappointed when it arrived. I would probably describe it as a giant profiterole, though with firmer pastry that had a bit of an almond taste to it, with a filling that tasted like a mix of cream and vanilla ice cream. Delicious and a great way to finish.

With my food safari complete and declared by me, as an unbridled success, it was time to head back to the hotel to check-in and get ready for my evening outing. In the lift on the way up to reception, my eye was taken by a bizarre-looking sign on which all the writing was in Japanese, but there were four pictograms in the middle, with red lines through them to indicate you shouldn't be doing what the stick people were doing. They also had this sign in reception where I got a better look but was no nearer to working out exactly what was going on in the sequence of events depicted. Let me describe the four pictures for you:

1. Person on all fours with an outstretched arm holding wine bottle.
2. Two people, person on left kicking person on right in groin area – wavy line around impact area to convey force of kick.
3. Two people, person on the right on knees with arms up (maybe begging for mercy?), the person on the left standing over with arm in the air, apparently poised to strike the person on the right.
4. Two people, person on the right on their backside on floor, legs akimbo, person on the left in the air, holding a wine bottle in the right hand, about to land on the other person. Three drops of liquid (blood?) to the right of the head of the person on the floor.

I assume the message here was 'No drunken fights. Please'. If that was the case, I'm glad they decided to go with the pictures and not just write that, as the sign was hilarious and it still makes me smile every time I go back for another look at the photo of it on my phone.

This capsule hotel was a larger scale operation than the one in Hiroshima, with separate floors for men and women and on my floor, this time all of the accommodation was the same, with 24 pods in the main room and again, modern and sparkling clean communal washroom facilities. After getting settled in, I was back out for my final evening in Tokyo, first of all catching the train over to Shibuya to get a look at the famous crossing there at rush hour. You may have seen photos or videos of the sea of people crossing the road in all directions in front of the neon-lit skyscrapers every time the traffic lights stop all the traffic to allow them to do so, but it was an invigorating experience to be part of the crowd, many of whom I suspect were just crossing back and forth for the fun of it like myself. I had picked a perfect day for it, as it was Halloween weekend, so there was an array of bizarre fancy dress on display in the crowd, including a guy wearing a through the head meat cleaver hat I told you about way back in Portland. When the lights changed, and the people on the crossing were replaced again with traffic, I saw the cars included a procession of people in fancy dress attire driving go-karts in the style of Super Mario Kart, a sight I had read about previously and had hoped to see in practice.

From Shibuya, I walked across the city, stopping along the way for a few happy hour beers, before arriving in the Roppongi area for the 'gala dinner' I had planned for the evening. Jane had messaged me earlier in the week to say they had been for a fantastic meal at a restaurant called Atelier XEX and that I must go there too. When I had looked it up, I saw the full name of the place was actually 'Atelier XEX Morimoto', and it was another restaurant run by the Morimoto chap I told you about while I was back in Napa, which had immediately sealed the booking for me. I had also sent Bel here for a meal on her final night in town which she had positively raved about, and she had sent me details of the teppanyaki chef who had looked after her, who she said I should also ask for. The twist to this was that pre-empting my visit, she had decided it would be humorous to continue the 'wife' role-play from the Kyoto night out and told him I would be visiting a few days later, meaning I had to navigate a number of questions from him about why I was travelling on a different schedule to my wife. The food was absolutely divine, and I had an entertaining chat with a Mexican couple who arrived for a late dinner, completely hammered, after having been at a Kygo concert. Exquisite food, engaging company and an excellent way to cap off what had been a fascinating and often hilarious trip around Japan.

Summary – Japan

Kilometres travelled (air) – 7,500
Kilometres travelled (land) – 2,300
Kilometres walked – 270
Okonomiyaki's eaten – Four
Number of comedy signs photographed – 22

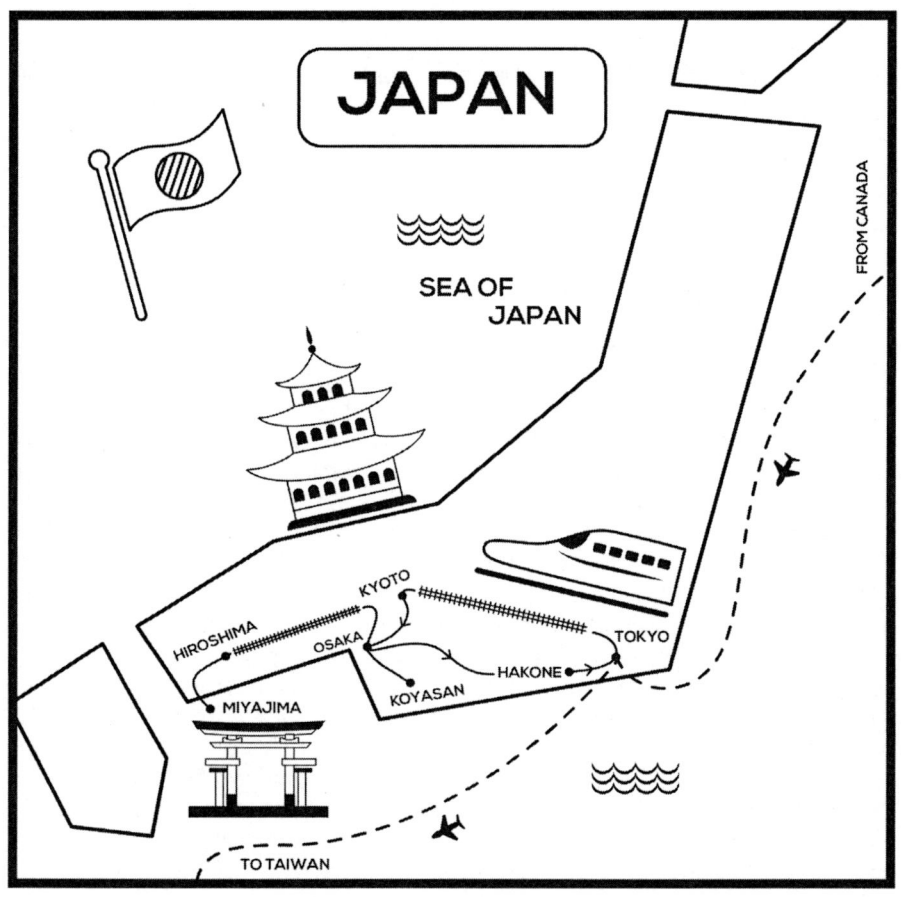

Taiwan
The People's Republic of Stinky Tofu

And so to the next stop, the 'bonus' destination of Taiwan, where I was going to be spending three nights in the capital city of Taipei as a result of finding cheap flights via here which would link my travel between Japan and Vietnam. My background reading on the plane had taught me that Taiwan, or the Republic of China if you are feeling controversial, has a population of 24 million people jammed into only 36,000 square kilometres, leads Asia alongside Hong Kong when it comes to gender equality, is regarded as having the best coffee in Asia and is the birthplace of instant noodles and bubble tea. More on the final point later, but that's a sufficiently random country snapshot to get you started.

The thirty-minute train ride to the city was my first taste of what transpired to be a really excellent 'Mass Rapid Transit' (MRT) system, which made getting around the city an absolute breeze and for a total cost of about $30 over three days. Actually, the low cost of Taipei, in general, became a recurrent theme of my stay, as I would find out that it was really quite hard to spend any money here! The ride from the airport initially passed over some dense forest on highly elevated tracks, before arriving into the high-rise urban environment I had expected, with a number of colourful temple buildings scattered amongst drab concrete tower blocks. I had booked a hotel located right outside the main city station, so after a very easy check-in, I headed straight out to find my first night market, keen to fit in as much as possible into my brief stay. The night markets included some general goods stalls but were predominantly about the food and are one of Taiwan's most famous attractions. I made a beeline to Ningxia Night Market as that was the most central and was easily walkable from my hotel, as long as I didn't get run over by one of the thousands of scooters swarming around in the rush hour traffic.

The market was made up of a corridor of food stalls in the middle of the street, some with a seating area on the outside of the main corridor which wasn't really wide enough for the positively mental amount of visitors, and you basically just got pushed along by the crowd unless you took a step to the side to get a proper look at a stall or to buy some food. I had arrived with expectations of the weird and wonderful but was starving and thought I should eat something 'regular' to start with, which came in the form of a big carton of Angus beef cubes, cooked to order with a blow torch that looked fierce enough to power a hot air balloon. My expectations were more than met by a selection which included unidentifiable meat skewers, pork feet and knuckles, giant grilled mushrooms, grilled squid, sweet potato balls, dumplings, okonomiyaki, 'pork rib stewed in Chinese medicine', 'dongshan duck head', fried octopus balls and a bucket of frog eggs! I decided to go for some stewed pork in a steamed bun (just okay) and a mountain pig sausage (better), before sitting down for my main dish of the evening, 'stinky tofu and duck blood curd'. Yes, I really did eat that. Stinky tofu is one of Taiwan's most famous/infamous dishes, so I felt duty-bound to try it for research purposes. The smell is indeed pretty rank, and I didn't enjoy the taste that much either, but the spicy broth it came in was really tasty and I can say with certainty this will be the first and only time in my life I will utter the words 'I preferred the duck blood curd'. The evening's culinary journey could not have been in more stark contrast to the fine dining precision at Morimoto in Tokyo the night before, the atmosphere at the market was electric and let's just say it was an education to see just how much of an animal it's possible to eat.

The next day I woke to find, to my relief, that there appeared to be no ill effects from the alien foodstuffs I had subjected my body to and I was out the door early to get straight into the sightseeing. I armed myself with a day pass for the MRT and headed straight to the end of the 'red line', which took me one-stop past Taipei 101, the tallest building in the city at 508 metres and previous holder of the crown for the tallest building in the world until it was usurped by the Burj Khalifa in Dubai. I was planning on going up the tower but had read the best views of the tower itself were to be had by climbing the stone staircase of nearby Elephant Mountain, so that was to be my first stop. 7:30 am on a Monday morning was apparently prime time for ladies to exercise in the park as I walked past two tai chi classes, a step class, what looked like a line dancing class and one lady who wasn't a fan of group discipline, choosing instead to dance around on her own to the music in her head, throwing a few moves with a slightly maniacal look on her face – each to their own. A bit further on I found where all the men were, with several games of three-on-three taking place on a bank of basketball courts, including some impressively old looking gents still rolling back the years.

My gentle morning stroll got serious once I arrived at the stairs, which I hurried up for a bit of a heart starter, an activity that many other people kitted out in their exercise gear were clearly there for. There was even an open-air gym area at an area near the top where a handful of people were working out on weight benches and doing crunches and the like. Reaching the top lookout area, the pace of activities was rather more sedate, with four ladies working their way through a very organised looking picnic breakfast, including a camping stove they had brought with them to make the tea. Oh, and there was a view up there too, of the imposing emerald green building shaped to resemble a giant Chinese pagoda or bamboo towering over the skyline with just a couple of other buildings anywhere near its height, and the greenery in the foreground a reminder of just how close the mountains were to the sprawling city below.

I walked back down the hill and covered the short walk to the tower itself at a perfect time to grab a coffee before the lifts fired up for business. The first claim to fame for the building is that it has the fastest lift in the world, covering the 500-metre ascent in just 37 seconds, with a top speed of 1,010 metres a minute, or 61 kilometres an hour to use a more recognisable measure, and it was fitted out with a fancy pressure release system that stopped your head from exploding during the ascent, or something like that. As I walked around the observatory on the 89th floor, I was trying to compare back to my experience of the Burj in Dubai, but it wasn't really a like-for-like comparison, as I had skipped the tourist observatory there in favour of the bar in the Armani Hotel, which is at a similar height and my main memory from there was being amazed that they allowed people to smoke in there – not helpful in comparing the tourist facilities.

From a stand-alone perspective I thought it was a good set up, with lots of interesting information on the surrounding sights and the construction of the building, including the 'wind damper', an engineering aspect they were so proud of that they had made it into the building's cartoon mascot. On the 88th floor, you could walk around the damper, which is a giant yellow ball suspended by eight massive cables and acts to counterbalance the movements of the tower and provide stability. The damper weighs 660 metric tonnes, which I quickly converted as being equivalent to 1.5 Giant Buddha's from Nara and with this serving as a hugely useful statistic for me for future use, I decided I had accumulated enough useless information about the tower and made my way back down again.

Taking the MRT red line, I rode its entire length to the final stop to the north, a town named Tamsui, after the mouth of the river at which it sat. The river is flanked by mountains and was the main entry point for historic seafarers arriving in Taipei (and modern ones as well I guess), making it a strategically important site. Recognising this, the Spanish established Fort San Domingo here, which is one of the oldest surviving historical sites in Taiwan, and this was where I walked to first. After the Spanish, the fort had been occupied by the Dutch and then the Chinese before being handed over to the British at the end of the Second Opium War, which opened up Taiwan for trade. I found the fort pretty boring to be honest, with voluminous amounts of detail on the reasons for the layout of the buildings that I couldn't see would interest anyone, though to be fair the main building, which had served as the British consulate from 1863 to 1972 was a bit more interesting. This had been preserved with the furniture and decor as it had been in the middle of the 20th century and there were some informative exhibits in the rooms on the history of the consulate and the men who had served as consul. It seemed to me that a key prerequisite for securing this role was to have an impressively upper-class sounding name, as four consecutive holders of the post in the early 1900s had been:

- William Scrope Ayrton.
- Henry Alfred Constant Bonar.
- Raymond de Burgh Money Layard.
- Frank William Walter Playfair.

And it's only now, as I write up my notes, that I see the second gentleman on that list also managed to combine double entendre with his aristocratic name – wonderful. The building had a wraparound veranda which afforded views of the gardens in front and the river down the hill below, and there were signs on every bit of the low wall warning you not to sit on it – I didn't need to be told this twice when I read the remainder of the sign and learnt the minimum penalty for violating this rule was $25,000! I would love to know if anyone has ever been made to pay that fine.

By now I was happy I had got my money's worth for the $4 entry fee and walked back along the river to the town centre and uphill to one of the town's temples, the Tamsui Qingshui Temple. Being free to walk around anywhere in the temple, means you can get a really good look at the artefacts which present a really colourful scene, with ornate carvings on the ceiling finished in gold, red globe lanterns hanging throughout the room, and a number of banks of bright red, floor to ceiling high, cylindrical cabinets. These held hundreds of mini statues of deities in 30cm bright yellow cubes, reminding me in concept of the thousands of mini Buddha's I had seen back in Koyasan. Outside the building, the roof was covered with colourful dragon sculptures which gave the structure a vivid outline against the bright blue sky above. While the temples in Japan had been impressive, the level of intricacy in the detail of the decor took this one straight into contention for a place on my newly invented 'Top Five Temples' list.

After a short train ride back towards the city, I found myself searching for a bus to go to the Yangmingshan National Park, up in the hills above the city for a hike. The Lonely Planet helpfully told me that the bus fare would be 15NT (75 cents) and when the bus arrived, I found to pay you either swiped a travel pass or dropped your cash into the farebox. This was just a Perspex box behind the driver's head which he couldn't see, so presumably, he just listened for the sound of two coins, and as I paid my fare, I thought to myself that surely you could just put in any two coins. Anyway, half an hour later we arrived at the Yangmingshan Bus Terminal, and I followed the signs to the information centre, which was one kilometre further uphill to get a map and info on the trails.

When I got there it seemed a bit quiet, and the door was shut, which seemed odd until I read a sign saying it was closed on the final Monday of each month – no prizes for guessing what today was. Unperturbed, I decided I would go for a walk anyway as I could see some trail signs and map boards around, so I headed further uphill to join a trail that went towards somewhere called Mt Qixing. I was soon onto a never-ending flight of stone steps, and as I walked up, I realised I still hadn't eaten anything, apart from a small croissant in Tamsui and I only had about 100ml of water on me, neither of which were really appropriate preparation for a hike up a mountain. I decided I would just carry on for the time being and turn around if I felt tired or had finished my water. The summit of Mt Qixing was 2.4 kilometres from the start of the trail, but I had no idea how much vertical ascent was involved in getting there, so it was basically a complete mystery walk.

The gradual incline of the stone steps continued for the first 1.4 kilometres, at which point there was a turning for the final kilometre. I was feeling pretty good and hadn't needed any water yet and given it was only one kilometre further I decided to carry on. Shortly after that junction, I found the answer to the amount of vertical question was lots, as the depth of the stone steps and their gradient suddenly increased significantly and wound up the hillside like a giant narrow rockery. When I read up on the trail in the evening, I found this section of the walk had an incline of nineteen degrees which is, quite frankly, ridiculous. I have described many fairly tough walks on my journey so far but don't think I have used the word 'brutal' yet, and I am glad it has been reserved for this one, as that's exactly the right word for it. My hopeless watch decided to stop counting floors climbed once it reached 172 for the day, which, by coincidence, was also my heart rate at that stage in proceedings. The trail info revealed the walk had a total elevation gain of about 600 metres from the visitor centre up to the main peak at 1,120 metres and it was a cracking view from the top when I finally made it. It was blowing an absolute gale up there, but you got a wonderful view of Taipei way down below and pretty much the whole of Northern Taiwan around to the coast in the east. Making my way back down I was amazed to see a local couple climbing the steepest section with their Jack Russell, for whom every step was at least twice his height – he was having one serious 'leg day' with that workout.

When I got off the bus at the start of the walk, there was a dreadful eggy smell in the air, and on the bus journey back down, I could see the reason for this. The fumaroles on the side of the hills were clearly visible and shooting out plumes of the sulfurous gases which were also responsible for producing the hot springs that the bathers were enjoying in Beitou down below. It was about 5 pm now, so when I got back to the MRT, I decided to make a stop at another night market, this time at Shilin. While I was a bit early and not all of the stalls were open, I could see that this one, which was largely housed in a covered arcade, was more of a general goods market with some funfair style games for the kids, which wasn't really what I was after, so after piling down some minced fish balls and deep-fried sweet potato balls (late lunch), I got back on the train and carried on to another one which I had on my list, the Raohe Street Night Market. This one was much more food-focused and was absolutely buzzing, so I had a good look around to see whether it had any different weirdness on offer to what I had seen at Ningxia the night before. It was mostly the same offering, but I thought there was a bit more 'regular' looking food here for the tourists, though that said, I did see some funky looking dishes involving honeycomb tripe, tendons and intestines. I really went nuts here and just ordered a freshly squeezed orange juice, partly because I was stuffed with sweet potato and batter and partly because I didn't want to spoil my main dinner, for which I was planning a visit to the very first branch of my favourite dumpling joint, Din Tai Fung, branches of which you may recall I had already visited earlier in the trip in Seattle and Tokyo.

Din Tai Fung opened in Taipei in 1972 as a restaurant specialising in xiaolongbao 'soupy dumplings' for me and had managed to develop something of a cult status over the years, with The New York Times including it in a 1993 article 'Top Notch Tables', which featured ten restaurants around the world that inspired a pilgrimage. My elation at finding 'porky beans' on the menu was short-lived when I found out they had sold out, but I consoled myself with some fried rice and ten morsels of soupy dumpling perfection, washed down with a Taiwanese beer. All this while having a chuckle at the name badge of my waitress, which read 'Trainee' and then her English name – 'So Young', more like So Funny, and after settling up there it was back to the hotel for me for a well-deserved rest after what had ended up being something of a massive day out.

***

My room in the hotel was in the much sought after location of right next to the lift-well, so I was woken up early the next morning by a succession of high-volume foreign language discussions, which seemed a reasonable prompt for me to get out and about and see some more. It had taken me the first day to get my head around the currency conversion, so it was only now that I realised I was paying $7.50 for my morning coffee (up from about $5 in Japan), but given my ongoing struggles with spending money I decided I was okay with this. Someone who was not okay with this was the security man on the MRT, who approached me and told me in broken English that eating and drinking was banned on the MRT. Looking around, I saw there were signs everywhere to alert me to this and of the associated $1,250 fine, so I smiled apologetically and carried my drink for the remainder of the journey. Today my first destination was the final stop on the brown line, Taipei Zoo, from where I was going to catch a gondola up into the mountains at Maokong, an area famous for its tea plantations and tea houses where I would learn a bit about the ancient art of tea. Unfortunately, the crazy wind I had experienced up the mountain the previous day was still blowing, and the gondola wasn't running, so I had to switch to Plan B and take a minibus up the hill instead.

It was standing room only for a lot of my fellow tourists on the way up, presumably as a result of the non-operating gondola and after about half an hour of winding roads, I saw we were at the top gondola station and got out. I didn't have any maps or information on the local area but had read in the Lonely Planet that if I walked for thirty minutes from the top of the gondola in a poorly explained unspecific direction and looked out for the Chinese symbols of its name, I would find a tea house in a picturesque setting. I walked along the road for about ten minutes before deciding this was feeling like a futile mission and instead turned off down a nature trail that appeared to be heading down the mountain and thus appeared directionally sensible to get back to the city. The trail was a combination of stone steps and wooden boardwalks and was well maintained, but there wasn't much to see, and I soon found myself at junctions where there was either no signage at all, or they were all in Chinese, so it didn't take long for me to have no idea where I was or where I wanted to go. I decided I just needed to get back to the road to find a bus, hopefully to the temple in the area that was apparently a local highlight or, failing that, back to Taipei and I kept walking until I found the road half an hour later.

On the road, I found a bus stop, but with its Chinese signage I still couldn't work out where I was, so I admitted defeat in my attempts at not turning on the roaming on my phone and fired it up to consult Google Maps, finding to my amazement that I was less than one hundred metres down the road from the tea house I wanted to get to in the first place. Having made the short walk up the road, I found this was a 24-hour teahouse, for reasons that were not immediately obvious, and I wandered in to find out what the authentic Taiwan teahouse experience involved. To find the answer to this I would have to have a pot of tea, paying firstly $3.50 for hot water, which was basically a cover charge, and then buy a small tin of tea leaves from the lengthy selection on the menu and brew it up myself using a tray of tea making apparatus that I was provided. I asked the waiter to recommend which tea to buy, which cost me $14 for a 40g sachet and tin but which I could take the remainder home with me afterwards. This would have made sense if I had any of the kits I needed to make it with at home, but I decided I would just write it off as the cost of the experience itself and hey, it was a way of spending some money. Now, this might sound quite dull, but I am going to repeat for you the instructions I was provided along with the tray of apparatus to make a cup of tea, as it was somewhat more involved than my idea of making tea, which involves putting a tea bag in a cup and adding hot water. It went like this:

- Place the teapot on the tea boat first and then open the lid of the teapot.
- Pour hot water into the teapot. It is a step for warming the teapot.
- Pour the hot water from the teapot into the pitcher.
- Pour the water from tea pitcher into a cup for warming the cup.
- Pour the water from tea pitcher into tea bowl.
- Put appropriate amount of tea leaves into the teapot.
- Pour hot water into the teapot.
- If tea leaves are stuck in the mouth of the teapot, please move the leaves back into the teapot by using the specific tea stick.
- When the tea is ready, slowly pour into tea pitcher.
- Please hold the teapot vertically and pour all tea into tea pitcher.
- Pour the tea into the smelling cup.
- After the smell, pour tea into the teacup.
- After several infusions (while tea becomes insipid), use a tea clip and remove tea leaves.

I mean seriously, what? Even with these seemingly fool proof instructions, I had issues making my tea, as I didn't know what an 'appropriate amount' of tea leaves was and I also didn't know how to judge how long it would take until 'tea is ready', and so my first effort was basically just slightly scented hot water. The tea I had been recommended, a local infusion called 'Wensan-pouchon' tea, was described as being somewhere between green tea and oolong tea and on my second attempt, which produced a result that looked like a healthy urine sample, I felt like I could actually taste something that resembled tea. For me, with the benefit of my extensive tea knowledge, I thought it was much closer to the oolong end of the scale, though.

While the science of this operation was potentially rather wasted on me, the setting was wonderful, a picturesque terraced garden amongst the steep, heavily vegetated slopes that surrounded the area and I left the tea house with about 28g of tea in a tin feeling satisfied that I had adequately dipped my toes in the tea making experience. I did still want to go and see the local temple so waited outside for the bus service (that ran every fifteen minutes) for twenty-five minutes and got on it feeling more than a little bit 'hangry', given it was now midday and I had again failed to eat anything. As the bus got nearer the temple I realised I was going to have to do a decent walk from the nearest bus stop to get there and frankly with my food deprivation I couldn't be bothered, so remained seated when we stopped there and returned to the zoo MRT station to find some lunch. Oh, but there was one more event to report – I tested my 'any two coins will do' theory on this bus journey, and it was a success, saving me a whole 4NT (20 cents) of the advertised fare, which I chalked up as a massive win until I reported this event to Bel, who replied, "So the system relies on honesty then?" immediately making me feel bad. 'Shame! Shame! Shame!'

Back on the MRT, I was on another local food mission, this time hunting down the best 'Gua Bao' in town, which was described as a slow-braised pork hamburger with pickled mustard and ground peanuts in a steamed bun. I had to ride three of the MRT lines to get to the restaurant, 'Lan Jia', which I had read produced the finest rendition of these in the city, but the magic of the rail network had me there in no time. There wasn't much on the menu apart from these steamed buns, and I had to choose between five variants of how fatty I wanted the pork to be. I started with 'half fat, half lean' before conceding that I was delaying the inevitable and ordering the full-fat version, which was of course, way better. That said, they were both delicious, with the only downside was that my lunch lasted all of about seven minutes before I was back on the MRT trying to work out my next move. This ended up being a completely out of character visit to the National Palace Museum, as I had seen most of the other things on my to-do list and felt ready to bow to the peer pressure of the 'you must visit the Chinese museum' recommendations I had received from friends who had been here previously. I had to take yet another bus to the museum, but I didn't have the correct change for the 15NT fare and instead tried to give the driver a 50NT coin. He told me it was only 15NT, and I nodded saying I knew, but I didn't have the change and again tried to give him the coin. This proposal made him look like he was about to have heart failure and he instead waved me onto the bus for free with a smile, so there was no karma here from my earlier bus fare payment crime.

I had read that the museum had become overly busy since it had been opened up to Chinese tour groups a few years before, but I wasn't prepared for what this was actually going to feel like. I have never seen so many people in a museum, with packs of 30–40 audio guide wearing people rushing around the rooms, blocking the view of the exhibits and filling all available corridors and stairwells, with the din from their constant chatter reverberating around the low ceilings so that you couldn't hear yourself think. To compound this less than ideal experience, I had started off in some seriously dull rooms and was really not feeling *'The Magic of Kneading Clay'* nor inspired by *'Agarwood and the Culture of Incense'*. In this second room, a Chinese lady was walking around the room and methodically photographing every single porcelain cup, bowl and incense burner that was on display – the holiday photo slide show back at her house must have been an absolute blast. When I got past the pottery and found the painting and calligraphy rooms, I finally found some slightly more engaging and interesting exhibits, most of which I could actually get a decent look at between crowd surges. The museum holds one of the largest collection of Chinese imperial artefacts and artworks anywhere in the world, and I was impressed by the age of some of the exhibits and the mint condition they were still in, including a fifteen-metre long scroll painting of a mountain and river landscape which was dated around 1200, and a gilt bronze Buddha that they had apparently determined was made in 477, which was just slightly mind-boggling. There was, what looked like a fascinating timeline on the history of world cultures in the orientation room on the ground floor but, again, a large group blocked my view, and it was at this point that I decided it was time to abort the mission, heading instead for some afternoon tea at the cafe by the entrance.

This was my opportunity to discover some of Taiwan's more recent history, in the form of the 1980's invention of bubble tea, ordering a drink described as an 'iced bubble latte'. Bubble tea, or pearl milk tea, or boba tea, is a cold tea drink whose main distinguishing feature is the inclusion of sticky tapioca balls at the bottom, which you suck up with the help of an extra-large straw that the drink comes with. The balls don't taste of anything specific, rather just sweet sticky goodness along with the flavour of whatever liquid they are in and I was rating my first taste of this slightly odd-sounding concoction as a success. When Audra was taking me on my walking tour through Chinatown in San Francisco, she had pointed out a shop and said, "And this is a really popular place for people to buy boba tea," and I had nodded knowingly, despite having no idea what she was talking about, well now I did.

While I couldn't see it through the clouds, I knew that the sun was close to setting on my whistle-stop tour of the sights of Taipei and that could only mean one thing – it was time to visit another night market. Today's pick was the Linjiang Night Market (also known as Tonghua), and on the train, on the way there I found a blog which had a helpful summary of the author's favourite stalls to visit, including one that ticked the box on my 'weird food to try' list, something called a pork blood cake, so I made a beeline for this stall for my 'starter'. This was a sticky rice cake that was soaked in the pork blood, rolled in crushed peanuts and coriander leaves and came on a lolly stick, resembling something akin to a ghoulish Magnum. It had quite a nice flavour to it, if slightly rich, but the texture was a little bit weird, and while I put in a brave effort, I couldn't quite finish it all and binned the remainder, looking for something else to take the taste away and take my mind off it. I found this in the form of some 'duck eggs made of cake', which when the description was un-jumbled, translated into six small airy sponge cakes made in a press that embossed the word 'Love' on them – which as it turned out, I did. The rest of the food selection was quite similar to the other markets but as this one was a bit lower down the tourist 'must visit' lists, it had a more relaxed vibe and made for a leisurely evening stroll amongst the stalls of 'chicken ass'.

Arriving back at the hotel after another big day of walking around, I checked my watch and worked out I had managed about 60 kilometres of foot-powered travel in a little over two days. When I continued further on this topic, I found I had now walked over 1600 kilometres since I left home (or a thousand miles in old money as that sounds more poetic) and was beginning to wonder whether a better name for the book might just be *'Alex Takes a Big Walk'* – I would pick that up for a look in a bookshop. This also got me wondering how big a walk that actually was and I went and looked up another book I had enjoyed, *'Walking the Himalayas'* by the English action man and writer Levison Wood, to see how far that walk had taken him. The answer was he had walked 1,700 kilometres over a six-month period, so in terms of kilometres per month, I wasn't too far behind him. He clearly would have been up, and down a few more hills on the route, he was on, but I decided this was offset by the fact he did not have to contend with the challenges of internet dating along his way, so on balance, I thought we could call it a draw – particularly given his job title was 'explorer' and mine was 'accountant'. I would also hazard a guess that he had probably spent a lower proportion of his kilometres either getting lost or recovering from being lost, giving him a better 'walking productivity' outcome but, again, his profession gave him a clear advantage in this regard.

The next morning brought another coffee-less ride on the MRT, this time back to the airport to conclude my tour of Taipei, a bonus stop on the itinerary that I decided had really been worth the gamble with the electric atmosphere of its night markets, temples hiding around every second corner, its slick public transport system and the easily accessible natural beauty in the surrounding hills. Plus, the fact I had only managed to spend a couple of hundred dollars on seeing it all. Given the success of the MRT, I was not surprised to find the process to get through the airport was similarly efficient, and before long I was at the departure gates, taking in a few final Taiwan sights including the intriguingly named 'Kung Fu Massage' centre, and an aircraft at one of the gates which was painted in full 'Hello Kitty' livery – know your target market! I was flying with another random budget airline, an outfit called VietJet Air, and a quick Google search on them revealed one of their more interesting claims to fame was that on some 'special flights', the stewardesses did the service while wearing bikinis. I boarded the flight with eager anticipation, curious to see whether this would turn out to be a special day for me or not...

Summary – Taiwan

Kilometres travelled (air) – 1,180
Kilometres travelled (land) – 220
Kilometres walked – 60
Number of night markets visited – Four
Number of incorrect bus fares paid – Four

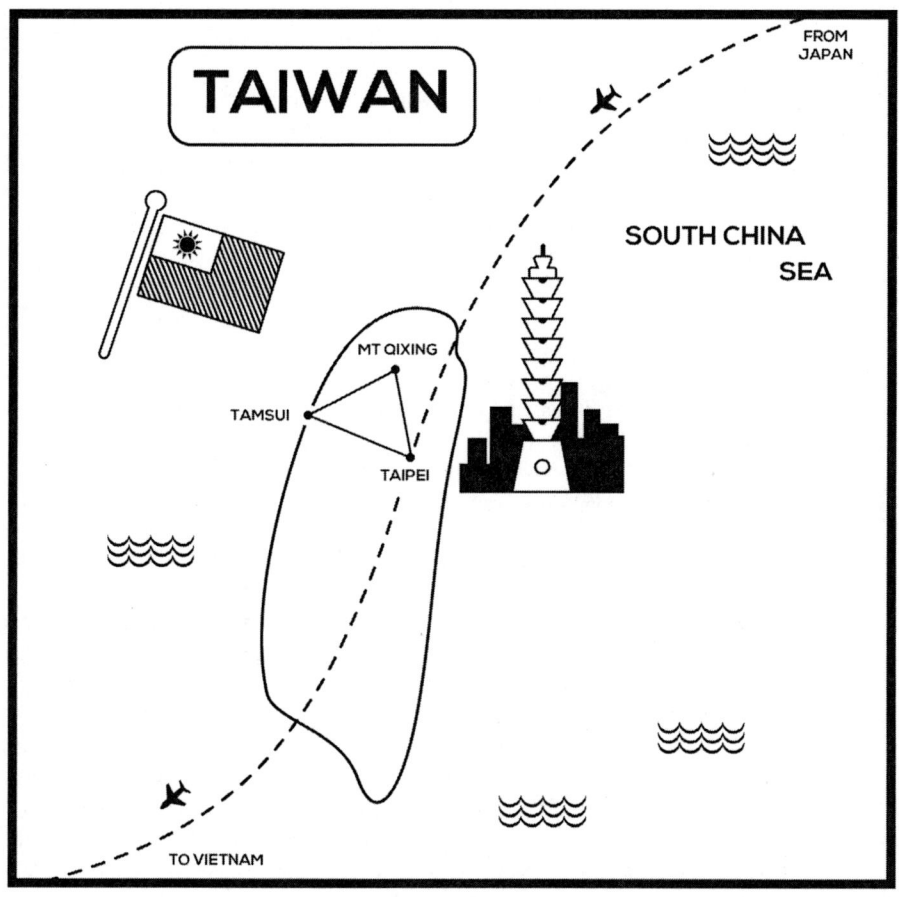

Vietnam
Planes, Trains and Scooter Tours

So, unfortunately, it wasn't a special day, though the regular uniform they had on was still quite fun, a red blouse with Burberry check shorts and a Burberry check hat. I was due to fly with them again to get from Ho Chi Minh to Singapore as part of my journey home, so there was still hope for a bikini sighting then, and all was not yet lost. For the final stop of my world tour, I was going to be finishing in the same way I had started, on a group tour run by my friends at Intrepid Travel. I had booked this tour while I was in Costa Rica as I wasn't sure how easy it would be to get around Vietnam as a solo traveller and I also thought it might be nice to have someone else to take care of the logistics for me at the end of my trip. I was feeling quite tired from all of the running around I had done in Japan and Taiwan over the last few weeks, so as I passed through customs and immigration to find a cab to the city, this was feeling like an excellent decision. I had booked the 'Vietnam Express – Southbound' tour, which started here in Hanoi, from where we would take a trip to Halong Bay, returning to Hanoi to catch an overnight train south to the city of Hue where we would be staying for two nights. From Hue, we would take a bus ride to the nearby ancient city of Hoi An where we would also stay for two nights, before catching a plane down to Ho Chi Minh City for a look around the city and to take a day-trip to the Mekong Delta river system and from Ho Chi Minh City, believe it or not, I would finally be calling time on my trip, completing my circumnavigation by returning to Australia via Singapore.

As the taxi approached the city centre, I was immediately struck by the increase in traffic volume from the swarm of scooters buzzing around, constantly tooting on their horns. I made the mistake of looking up and watching some of the manoeuvres my taxi driver was making to carve his way through the traffic, quickly regretted my decision as I watched him almost ram the car in front out of the way and decided I would keep my head down until we got to the hotel, hopefully still in one piece. After checking into the hotel, I headed off out into the city for an initial look around, as I wasn't due to meet the rest of my tour group until later and given we didn't have much time in Hanoi I figured I had better make a start on the sightseeing. I had made it about fifteen metres from the hotel front door before I realised that my assessment of there being lots of scooters in Taipei was well off the mark. If I were to score the relative 'volume' of scooter traffic and noise between the two cities out of ten, Taipei would probably scrape to a five or a six, whereas Hanoi was clearly an eleven. It was nuts. The pavements on the side roads were not very well maintained and often blocked by parked scooters, so on some of the streets, you had to walk along the road itself, with scooters buzzing along next to you and driving straight at you from the other direction before making a last-minute adjustment to return to the correct side of the road. I had got a map from the hotel and had a vague plan of where I wanted to go, which required me to get across what seemed to be a fairly major road junction. I waited patiently for a break in the traffic as there were no traffic lights to help me cross, and waited, and waited and waited – and there was never any break. Looking around to see how the crossing was possible, I saw some locals just stride out confidently into the road with a bank of scooters maybe ten across heading straight for them and then some magical ballet took place whereby the pedestrian didn't break his stride, and none of the scooters slowed down, slightly adjusting their course to sway outside of his crossing route so that everyone got to where they wanted to go.

Except me, as that looked to be well beyond my level of Hanoi road crossing expertise given my fifteen minutes of experience of the place, so I gave up, worked out a slight detour that didn't involve crossing that road and went that way instead. It turned out it wasn't a slight detour though, as my navigational skills had failed me again and when I finally worked out where I was on the map ten minutes later, I found I was heading in a completely different direction to my planned route to the Old Town area. I wasn't going to head back for another go at that crossing though and decided that if I didn't have a firm destination in the first place, I couldn't really be classed as being lost and carried on to spend the remaining two hours of my available time wherever the road I was on ending up taking me. That road ended up taking me to an area with lots of roads with signs saying I couldn't walk down them and large buildings that looked like they were either government or military offices, guarded by soldiers with machine guns. The slightly menacing feel that this military presence brought to the place was compounded by the sight of a number of giant red and yellow hammer and sickle flags, familiar to me as the old flag used by the Soviet Union and which Hollywood movies of the 1980s had conditioned me to see as being the 'bad guys' flag'. I hadn't seen that flag, which was being flown here as the party symbol for The Communist Party of Vietnam, in a very long time and it was interesting to see that it still evoked that initial reaction in me and it took a few days of seeing it around the place, alongside Vietnam's national flag of the same colours, before I got used to it again.

It soon became evident that all the military presence and flags were due to the fact that I was walking around the large complex of government buildings that surround Ba Dinh Square, which is where the Ho Chi Minh Mausoleum is found, housing his embalmed body. Ho Chi Minh was a Communist revolutionary leader and a key figure in the foundation of the Democratic Republic of Vietnam (North Vietnam) back in 1945, which he served as both Prime Minister and President of. The Mausoleum was guarded by soldiers in very fancy looking white uniforms, and there were lots of signs around telling me not to take photos, not to chew gum, not to cross the red line and not to look at them a bit funny, so I was treading carefully so as not to end up in prison within my first hour in the city. I couldn't go in the building in any case, as it was closed for maintenance – not the building, the body. I learnt that each year the body is sent back to Russia in October and November for a two-month routine that involves washing and re-embalming the body as well as doing maintenance on his facial features. For two months! The website I was reading said that the result of this process was a 'near-immaculate, albeit a little plastic-looking preservation of Vietnam's revered leader' so if this is something you want to see, make sure you don't visit at the same time of year that I did.

After finally finding my way out of the military-controlled area, I arrived at the Hanoi Botanical Gardens where things were a lot less serious, with people walking their dogs, jogging around the lakes and a number of games of badminton taking place on the numerous courts around the grounds. My eye was immediately taken by a couple of these games where I saw that the gents playing were not holding badminton rackets and were instead using their feet to propel what looked like a rubber shuttlecock. It was a bit like people doing 'keepy-ups' with a hacky sack (do they exist anymore?), but they were playing a game of men's doubles, juggling it between them before sending it over the net to their opponents. The skill level involved in keeping the small rubber projectile in the air was very impressive and just as I started videoing the scene one of the guys even put in a scissor-kick to send one back over the net, evoking memories of Ralph Macchio's final winning kick in *'The Karate Kid'* – a hugely up to date cultural reference for you.

Walking back across town, my confidence had grown with the road crossings, and I was striding out into the traffic and letting them find their route around me. It felt a bit like the 'hold-your-breath' walks I had been making amongst the human traffic on the Osaka metro system, but with slightly higher stakes here if you got it wrong, which, fortunately, for today at least, I didn't, making it back to the hotel in one piece to meet my tour group for the kick-off meeting. Our tour-leader was a Hanoi local called Hung, who was in his late twenties and who you could tell right from the outset, was brimming with excitement about the tour we were about to embark on and his role in making sure it was a success. He gave us the brief run-through of the itinerary and then we had the obligatory round-the-table group introductions on who we all were, so why don't I give you a quick heads up on the group now as well. There were eleven of us in total, with Australia represented by Rob, a paramedic from Victoria in his late twenties, Shane and Alison, a middle-aged couple from country South Australia, Peter, a solo traveller from Victoria in his fifties and Jackie, a bar manager from Mackay in Queensland, who I would also guess was in her fifties. The complement of 'youngsters' was completed by Shell, who was from the UK where she worked in HR but who was currently on a career break to do some travel, Ines and Tania, a pair of friends from Portugal, and a lady called Rie from San Diego, who we didn't hear much out of over the course of the trip, so this is probably the last you will hear of her. And finally, we had Charles, who was in his fifties and worked in aviation. Charles was a bit of a free spirit at heart and was on his annual solo-holiday away from his wife and children where he 'just threw on the backpack and went for a bit of an explore' – well, why not! As we would find out along the way from their exploits, our group had some interesting characters.

After the meet-and-greet, we headed out to a restaurant for dinner, and the first drinks order of the meal was my first insight into some of the slightly unusual behaviours in the group. Rather than the usual order of beer or wine as you might expect, we had Charles ordering two beers for himself at a time, Shane ordering a tequila and lemonade with Jackie topping that with a Midori and lemonade. Midori? Really? Once we got past the novelty drinks ordering and into the food, we were into the first instalment of what I had been hoping would be an awesome week or so of food and this restaurant delivered to my expectations, with some beautifully flavoured pork spring rolls followed by a pork belly stew with coconut rice – washed down with 'many' Hanoi beers.

Over the course of the meal, we got to know each other a bit, and it was clear from the start that Jackie was probably the strongest character of the group and a sure bet to provide some entertainment along the way. She made no secret of the fact that she was a big fan of holidaying in Bali, where it sounded like she had taken the majority, if not all, of her previous overseas holidays and where her typical holiday comprised sitting by the pool or on the beach, drinking Midori and lemonades, and buying souvenirs. These Bali holidays were her point of reference for every topic that came up over the course of our trip, e.g. 'If we were in Bali, this would cost x', 'The way they do this in Bali is y', 'The food is much better in Bali' – I could go on, but this did provide a source of entertainment for some of us, with the secret game of 'Bali Bingo', which broadly meant you had to take a drink every time she made a reference. Jackie had booked this Vietnam tour on a bit of a whim for reasons which were unclear, both to her and the rest of us and right from the intro briefing she was questioning herself as to why she had booked it, given it involved a decent amount of walking, a pursuit which held no interest for her. In the briefing, Hung had said we would get a taxi to the restaurant and then afterwards take the short, fifteen-minute walk back through the Old Town to the hotel so as to take in a bit of the city atmosphere. And Jackie's reaction to this.

"Fifteen minutes' walk? No chance! I'll get a taxi and see you'se back at the hotel. I'm lazy!"

So Jackie missed out on the walk through the town which turned out to be a lot of fun as the streets were packed with people out for the Halloween festivities. I dropped my guard with one of the street vendors for a moment and ended up buying a massive bag of sugary doughnuts for about $5, which I thought the rest of the group would help me with but which they did not. I felt duty-bound to eat about ten of them myself, and I was already sensing that my week in Vietnam might be having a rather different food to exercise ratio than the majority of my travels to date. I was quite taken with the vibe of Hanoi as we walked the streets at 10 pm, with loads of groups of people sitting on little plastic stools around simple street camping stoves, and the sweet smell of meats cooking in sugary sauces filling the air. At this hour there weren't so many scooters around, and some of the more touristy streets were pedestrian-only which made it a bit easier to get around and having Hung to lead the way, meant that I was able this time to get across the major junction which had proved to be beyond me earlier in the day. Back at the hotel, I was mighty relieved to find that my roommate for the night, Peter, did not provide a repeat for me of the snoring misery provided by Robin in Nepal.

***

The bus journey to Halong Bay the next day was the first opportunity for Hung to show his stuff and he was straight into it, clutching the microphone that projected his commentary around the bus at an inappropriately loud volume, which no-one quite had the courage to point out and waxing lyrical about the passing sights. It didn't take long for us to discover that Hung loved to chat and he also didn't worry too much about straying away from the topic that he had started on, going off on all sorts of random tangents, which were as entertaining as they were useless, from a tourist education perspective.

To be fair, he did start with some useful facts as we drove out of the city and saw the absolute car park of a traffic jam going in the other direction, as the masses tried to get to their places of work. Hanoi is a city of about nine million people and incredibly, for me anyway, has over five million scooters, with very few people owning cars. The absence of cars was for two reasons, firstly they would take absolutely hours to get anywhere through the gridlock of traffic and secondly because they are prohibitively expensive. While not a great example of a family car, as a point of reference Hung told us that a 'RollRoy' in Vietnam would set you back the equivalent of two million USD, a multiple of what the same car would cost in the States. In the absence of family cars, people instead got around on 'family bikes', meaning you had the regular sight of four or even five people on one scooter, with the most popular configuration being dad driving, a small child standing behind him, then mum, and then another child hanging on to mum at the back. Practical to avoid traffic congestion and a much more environmentally friendly alternative than a car, but decidedly rather more dangerous.

After half an hour we finally left the Hanoi city limits and moved into the countryside, passing through the occasional small town but mostly driving through farmland, where people in the classical Vietnamese conical hats were tending to their vegetable crops. The rice harvest had already taken place, so the rice fields were quiet, but you could see the vast scale of the production, nonetheless. Vietnam is second only to Thailand, in volume of rice exported and while we didn't see any plantations on this journey, Hung also told us that Vietnam is second in the world for the export of coffee beans, with Brazil, the leader for that product. After a mid-journey stop at a ceramics factory, we were back on the road, and Hung was back into his monologue, covering topics such as how his grandparents had lived back under the stricter Communist rule, having to use food coupons and being provided with an annual ration of fabric with which to make clothes for their family, before moving on to the healthcare system. It sounded like this system was basically self-funded with little government assistance, so if people got ill and couldn't fund their treatment, more often than not that was the end for them. Hung spoke of an aunt who had contracted breast cancer and had to sell her property and all of her belongings to raise the fifty thousand dollars she needed for treatment but she sadly still passed away during the early stages of the treatment.

It was clearly a system which he saw as being inadequate in comparison to the health systems in other countries, which he had learnt about from the guests on his tours. He also spoke of issues in the country from the sale of counterfeit medicine, which then led him on to a common theme that came up a worrying amount in his talks about the country, corruption. I did some reading on the counterfeit medicine issue and found some information on a paper released by a researcher called Tun Anh Nguyen, which found that 'informal payments' to doctors, or 'bribes' to you and I, accounted for as much as 40 per cent of the price of drugs in Vietnam. And the stories about what they were actually using to make the drugs were even more worrying. In summary, it was a reminder for me of how lucky we are to have a health system in Australia that first of all people can afford and more importantly that they can trust.

Hung's stories on corruption moved on to education, an area which I wasn't expecting, and he told stories of how pupils whose parents gave gifts and/or donations to teachers got magically better grades than those who did not. He actually shared a specific story from his own experience, where he had seen his grade in a class increase from a score of 6.5 to 7.7 and not because he had put in higher quality work, but because his parents had given the teacher a ceramic tea-pot set. Simply gobsmacking to hear that kind of behaviour taking place in the context of the education environment and involving children.

Now I told you a few pages ago that Hung had a habit of going off on tangents and you might be thinking that all of the content I just shared sounds quite relevant as an introduction to the country. Well in the course of the introduction we also learnt that his girlfriend takes about one hour to organise her clothes, hair and make-up before she is ready to go out and if they are going to the cinema he phones her up with a one-hour warning of his arrival, so he doesn't have to wait through that process. I'm still not sure how that managed to come up, but it did, and I was already warming to Hung quite a lot, particularly the way he was now referring to Jackie as 'Miss Zackie' and how he started every one of his speeches to us with a beaming smile and an enthusiastic, 'Okay, lady and gentlemen!'

With nearly four hours on the clock, we finally got our first look at Halong Bay, turning onto a bridge which led to a man-made island housing a mass of docks and marinas, from where the armada of junks and other tourist boats headed out each morning. Looking across from the marina, you could see the silhouettes of the limestone island formations out on the bay, and there was a steady stream of boats both heading out for the day and also returning from the previous day's overnight cruises. Halong Bay is made up of around 1,969 separate islets, the majority of which are made of limestone and are believed to have been formed over a period of as many as 500 million years. The name Ha Long means 'descending dragon', with local legend saying that the gods sent a family of dragons to protect the Vietnamese from invaders and these dragons rained down jewels and jade, which then formed the vast network of islands and acted as a protective barrier against would-be invaders.

When it was time for our departure, we were pleased to find we had a whole boat, the *'Bien Ngoc 06'* to ourselves, with the cabins distributed around the lower two decks, a large bar and dining area on the middle deck and a roof deck along the length of the boat for us to catch some rays and take in the view. In terms of describing the view, I'd like to say it was unique, but the forest-covered limestone rock formations which were scattered through the bay reminded me of somewhere else where I hadn't actually been, and that was the seas near Phuket in Thailand. The reason I know what it looks like is because that's where they filmed the scenes for Scaramanga's ocean hideaway in *'The Man with the Golden Gun'* – I'm never far away from a James Bond reference. Today was a perfect day for our boat ride, as the water was absolutely millpond flat and the sun was beating down from the cloudless skies, giving the same kind of contrast between the aquamarine waters and blue sky that I had seen at Isla Mujeres in Mexico and again at the glacial lakes in Canada. A few days later I was talking to some people who were about to do the Halong Bay boat tour, and I told them how calm it was, and they would sleep like babies, when one of them told a story of some friends of theirs who had been on the same trip the year before and their boat had capsized in rough waters. This sounded ridiculous given what I had seen, but when I looked it up, I found there were indeed incidences of boats capsizing, mainly because of the fact the junks were not designed to sail on rough seas. Indeed in 2011, one of the boats had sunk very quickly, and twelve people had lost their lives, so I was glad I had not read up about this until after I had completed the trip myself.

Back in the present, we had an excellent lunch as we cruised out amongst the islands, or karsts, as I understand they are more accurately described. We were closely followed by a small flotilla of similar-looking craft, and after a few hours of cruising we arrived at our first stop of the day, the 'Surprise Grotto', a large cave system on one of the larger islands, called Bo Hon Island. The French discovered this cave system in the early 1900s, and the main chamber was huge, about 500 metres from front to back and rising up to a height of about 30 metres. Each of the chambers was covered with stalactites and stalagmites of all shapes and sizes, and they had done quite a good job with the additional lighting they had put in the cave to add to the drama of the scene. Around the walkway, there were a number of rock formations which apparently resembled various animals including a horse, a mammoth, an elephant and even King Kong, but these claims got more and more sketchy as Hung pointed them out and the general reaction from the group evolved as we walked around from 'Oh yes, I think I can see that' to 'Sorry, Hung, but what are you talking about?' Even without sighting these phantom animals in the walls, it was quite an arresting sight which not even the droves of noisy Chinese tour groups could spoil.

Our arrival had supposedly been timed to avoid these groups, but the plan didn't appear to have worked, for as we pulled up to the next stop, Titov Island, there didn't appear to be any spare space along the jetty for us to park our boat. This didn't seem to be a concern for our Captain, who now appeared to be skippering the *'Phuc Yu'*, ramming his way into a non-existent space and breaking a bit of wood off the bow of the boat that was, quite fairly, already moored there, much to the obvious disgust of that boat's crew. We pretended we hadn't seen that take place and walked onto the island which had two reasons to justify a stop; first of all a steep trail up to the top of the island for a view over the rest of the bay and secondly a man-made beach where we could cool off with a quick dip after the walk. The view from the top was awesome, not just for the panoramic view of the islands but also for the aspect it provided of all the junks moored in the bay below for their overnight stay, of which I counted 40, some of them rafted together like they were having a 'tailgate party' in the middle of the sea. All of the boat traffic wasn't great news for the water quality and while the temperature was fine for a relaxing soak, you would have to be a relatively bold person to put your head under the water. About eight of our group braved the waters, and we realised we were actually a bit of a novelty as we floated around and looked back to the beach, where every single Asian visitor remained, most of them in completely inappropriate attire for the beach.

However, to our surprise a few minutes later, a middle-aged Chinese gentleman came strolling out through the shallows and dived into the water, putting in a few front crawl strokes as our group gave him a big cheer. The man, who Charles immediately christened as 'Turner' loved this, stopping his swim to stand up and raising his arms aloft to us in celebration, before going back to swimming and looking at us as if he wanted one of us to race him – which we didn't. Turner was great fun and was probably the reason we stayed out in the water as long as we did, but when we decided it was time to return to the beach there was a slightly unhappy ending, with both Charles and Shane getting stung by jellyfish, which we could now see were present in large numbers. The last time I got stung by jellyfish, was while diving off North Bondi and the reaction I had ended up with someone calling me an ambulance, so I was more than relieved not to be subjected to that aspect of the afternoon's aquatic activities.

After treatment of their stings, our captain once again rammed the boat back into a position on the jetty where we could get back on, and it was sundowner time, which meant the start of our assault on the junk's supply of canned beers. I had two or three before dinner and was feeling a little bit merry, but I was a bit confused by Charles's behaviour. He had only had a couple of beers too but was coming out with some quite bizarre conversation, including a suggestion that at the start of dinner we should all share in the boiled egg that he had brought with him from breakfast at the hotel this morning. I wrote this off at the time as him just being a bit eccentric and we went along with his plan, watching on as one of the staff, who was understandably a bit bemused, carefully cut the boiled egg into eleven pieces for us to share; but we might come back to Charles again later in the story.

The following day began with our captain driving us back to the marina, the wheelhouse was filled with smoke as he chain-smoked pretty much the whole trip back, and then us getting back on the bus for the four-hour return journey to the same hotel in Hanoi from where we started. Hung was back in good form on the microphone, first of all telling us some of the legends of Halong Bay and the surrounding area, before moving seamlessly into more of his entertaining tangents, which this morning included telling us about some people in Vietnam who still use a firm slap on a woman's backside as their way of showing their love. He then moved on to his observations regarding the differences between wedding receptions in the north and south of the country, with the main one of note being that you were more likely to see a transsexual wedding singer in the south, which was information we absolutely could not have done without.

***

Intrepid has a sister company called Urban Adventures who run shorter tours, usually in the cities and today they were running an evening street food tour which sounded great, so I signed up to do that along with the Rob and the two Portuguese girls. This wasn't due to start until 5:30 pm, so Rob, Shell and I took a walk around the Old Town for a few hours first, finding a hidden roof-top coffee shop called 'Café Pho Co' overlooking the lake and which one of Rob's friends had told him he had to visit to have one of the 'egg coffees' that Hanoi was famous for. This sounded a bit weird but had to be tried, and it was basically a latte but with frothed egg replacing the frothed milk. We had a bit of a fail as we made the mistake of not mixing it at the start, meaning we had half a cup of frothy egg and were left with half a cup of super-strong coffee to finish, which wasn't the best experience, but you could see that the drink had potential – if drunk correctly.

Stopping back at the hotel, we ran into Shane and Alison who had been on at outing of their own. I introduced these two as being from country South Australia and I should probably extend that description by saying they were very much at the 'Strayan' end of Australians, with Shane's main hobbies comprising watching the footie, watching the V8's and drinking with his mates. It felt like the cultural tour of Vietnam was probably Alison's idea but, unlike Jackie, Shane didn't mind getting stuck in and trying some of the 'foreign food' and generally having a go at embracing a different culture. That wasn't the case today though as, in a city famed for the quality of its coffee, they had gone to find a coffee at, in their opinion, the most reliable place in town – McDonald's. Shane had also put away a burger while he was there – 'Well you've got to eat, haven't you!' I shouldn't scoff as I had made a number of cop-outs fast-food visits in the course of my travels, including one to KFC in Jaco in Costa Rica that I just didn't have the courage to admit to back in chapter four and which I confess to you now in a show of solidarity for Shane, though his McDonald's on day three in Vietnam did feel like a relatively early fail in comparison.

Hung dropped us off at the start of the food tour by the market, where we joined up with a group of six Australian ladies from another Intrepid Tour and met our guide, whose actual name was 'Uoc', but who unsurprisingly preferred to go by his alternative name of 'Lucky'. Lucky was another Hanoi local, and well, there's no other way of describing it, he was massively camp, and this made him massively entertaining. He delivered his introductory speeches for each dish we tried in dramatic fashion, with long pauses, extravagant hand gestures, pointed looks around the group and flicks of his hair punctuating his sentences, it was almost theatrical. And that's before I even get to describing the way he martialled our walk around town and across the busy road junctions, there he was at the front of the group, quickly scanning back down the road to make sure he had his whole flock near to his wing, before thrusting his arm straight up in the sky and walking forward in an upright fashion, shouting over his shoulder,

"With me! 'TOGETHER!' Like sticky rice!"

He was straight into the upper echelons of my favourite holiday characters list for sure. Oh, and sorry, we were on a food tour weren't we, I had better tell you about the food as well, which, as Lucky might have put it, 'was beyond divine!' We opened up with a 'Banh Mi', which is a small baguette filled with pate, sliced pork, coriander, cucumber and pickled carrots and daikon. The stall we were at was apparently one of the most celebrated in the city, having been operated by the couple who ran it for over twenty years and selling out every day. The magic ingredient, which raised theirs above your average Banh mi, was their 'Happy sauce', the contents of which was a closely guarded secret. I had already eaten two Banh mi at this stage of the trip (which I didn't tell you about) and this one was streets ahead, with a perfectly crispy baguette and the winning sauce with just a hint of chilli making the difference for me.

The next stop was a bit weirder with Lucky getting us to line up on the street while he disappeared off to an unseen stall and came back with some deep-fried patties of some description which he was reluctant to explain until we ate them. The reason for his reluctance became apparent when he admitted the meat in them was a seasonal product, the 'nereididae sandworm'. I wasn't too bothered by this given the weird stuff I had been eating in Taiwan and gave it a go, but the taste wasn't particularly memorable, so I probably won't go out of my way to find the worms to make it at home. The following stop was much more palatable, fresh rice paper rolls with a filling of pork, mushroom and fried onions, accompanied with a fish dipping sauce and some insanely hot chillies that I added sparingly, so as to add the zing without taking the roof of my mouth out of commission for the rest of the tour.

Lucky then took us on a short walk across town which included a walk along some train tracks which had houses, cafés and restaurants right on the tracks, with no fence or barrier to separate the trains that came through every half an hour or so. He said there were some very cheap Airbnb's available in the shed-like buildings along this strip which were advertised as having a 'railway view', and I was quite glad at that point to be staying in a hotel and not still ticking off Airbnb novelty options. Back on the tour, our next stop was for a bowl of 'Bun Cha', a bowl of rice noodles served in a broth with pork balls and fresh herbs and beansprouts, a slightly different variant of the Vietnamese soup with which I was more familiar, the pho. The Bun Cha had achieved local fame on account of an episode of the (recently departed) celebrity chef Anthony Bourdain's show, 'No Reservations', where he dined on the dish in a nearby restaurant with Barack Obama, much to the surprise of the other diners and the interested crowd that gathered to see this most unusual sight for a restaurant serving $3 noodles.

With the savoury selection completed, it was time for dessert, which in Vietnam seemed to almost always be some version of fruit salad, and that is what we sat down to here. Fruit salad has been one of my least favourite desserts right back to my earliest childhood memories of tinned peaches, pears and apricots, so I wasn't very excited about this part of the tour. However, I was pleasantly surprised to find I did enjoy and finish this one, though this was probably on account of the condensed milk and coconut cream they had poured over it rather than a new-found joy for the fruit itself. After dessert, our final stop was for coffee and would you believe, in a city the size of Hanoi, the final stop was in the same place we had gone to that afternoon, and the reason for our visit was to try the egg coffee. Given I was now a veteran of that drinking experience, I managed to mix it properly this time around, and the properly blended finished product was really quite excellent and a highly satisfying way to finish a top-notch food tour. The final word does, however, have to go to our budding amateur dramatic tour-guide Lucky, who had some cautionary words about the dangers of ordering this slightly unusual drink elsewhere on our travels:

"You might go to other places in Vietnam, outside of Hanoi, where people will tell you that they know how to make the egg coffee – [dramatic pause] – 'THEY DO NOT!'"

And with that, well-fed and watered and richly entertained by Lucky's one-man show, we walked back to the hotel via a convenience store to load up on some munchies for the train journey, and after meeting up with the rest of the group, it was back onto the bus for the short ride to the train station and our overnight rail adventure.

***

The overnight train was going to take us from Hanoi to the city of Hue, the capital of Vietnam from 1802 to 1945, a journey of around 650 kilometres which would take us thirteen hours. As a comparison, the fastest service from Hiroshima to Tokyo covered that journey of around 810 kilometres in four hours and four minutes, so this train clearly wasn't built for speed, and it wasn't really built for comfort either as it was a bit of a boneshaker. The saner people would have opted for the seventy-five-minute flight between the cities, but our itinerary had us on this mode of transport instead for 'the experience', and an experience it certainly was. Our group were spread across three of the first-class cabins, which translated into a room with four bunk beds in it, just enough room to walk between them and a small fold-down table by the window. The lower-class options had six beds in them with the addition of a middle bunk jammed in on each side and if that was a bit claustrophobic for you, there were also cabins with (slightly) reclining chairs as an alternative option. There was a dining car right at the end, but this looked a bit shabby and was serving some strange looking food, so after an initial walk of the train it was evident that we would be spending much of the marathon journey in our cabin. To supplement the dining car catering options, there was a lady pushing a food and drinks trolley through the carriages, but upon finding her feature offering was a duck embryo, we decided to give that a miss, feeling rather grateful that we had bought some beers and snacks at the convenience store back in town. Our carriage had a further three cabins, and early on in the journey, we could already hear the worrying sound of excitable children – but more on them later on.

The train left Hanoi at about 10 pm, and after having a few beers and eating the biscuits and crisps we had bought for a bit of a midnight feast, the lights went out and the cabin, which comprised me, Rob, Peter and Hung, managed to get some sleep through the small hours of the night. I was on a top bunk and Hung had a lucky escape when I kicked my iPad off the end of the bed and it fell perilously close to his face, but he didn't stir from his light snoring and was none the wiser about his close shave and apart from that the night passed by without incident. It's fair to say the sleep quality wasn't the best and my watch monitor didn't actually detect me having any sleep at all, though I'm pretty sure I did. People started to stir a bit after 6 am which was disappointing news given we still had five hours left of the journey and there wasn't much to do, as the position of my bunk in relation to the window meant I couldn't really see the passing scenery. I had a 7 am Chunky Kit Kat, the breakfast of champions, but that didn't fill me up, and I decided to brave one of the cup noodles that the catering trolley had delivered for our breakfast.

This turned out to be a big mistake as when I walked out of the cabin to find the hot water tap, I walked straight into the three children from the cabin down the hall who were playing and making an increasing amount of noise and who took an immediate interest in me. Realising I was now out in the open with these wild animals, I tried to change course and head for a hot water tap in the next carriage, but I could sense them following me and, sure enough, when I looked over my shoulder, there they were, grinning expectantly at me. I walked back to the cabin and sat on the lower bunk to eat my food, but the kids were not to be shaken off and started running up and down the carriage, ending up back at me each time, where they laughed hysterically before running off again. I closed the door and latched it from the inside, and after they tried and failed to open it, they still stood outside staring at me through the gap between the sliding door and the wall and starting a slightly hysterical chant of:

'Teacher! Teacher! [Pause for running around] Teacher! TEACHER! TEACHER! TEACHER!'

The kids' parents were in their own cabin, presumably pretending they couldn't hear this din, which carried on until Hung took charge, walking into the corridor and telling the kids in Vietnamese if they didn't stop that he would tell their parents they were being naughty. This worked for about five minutes before the 'TEACHER! TEACHER!' chant started up again, but luckily they lost interest once I jumped up to hide on my top bunk and they couldn't see me anymore. Who knows what that was about, but I can only assume they must have had a cool and handsome teacher at their school, who I reminded them of?

When we arrived in Hue, which was noticeably hotter and stickier than Hanoi had been, it was about 11 am and I was feeling decidedly average and not hugely excited about the day ahead. After checking in to the hotel, we headed to a local restaurant where I had an absolutely delightful chicken, lemongrass and chilli dish, but not even this improved my mood. While I was having lunch, simultaneously back home in Sydney, the auction was taking place for the sale of my house, meaning I was paying no attention to the group and had my head buried in my phone for the text updates on progress. While only one bidder was registered, the process dragged on a long time as they had made an unacceptable bid which had basically ended the auction before it had begun. However, an hour later they changed their mind and made a much better bid which was acceptable, but by this time the agency had pretty much packed up the auction. This meant the real estate agent then had to chase the buyer back to their house and everyone had to return to complete the sale under auction conditions. It sounded like a bit of a palaver, and I was glad I wasn't experiencing it first-hand but this distraction, combined with my tired head and the heat of the place, meant that after lunch during our guided walk around the city, I really didn't pay very much attention and so can't tell you much about Hue. The city is centred on a large citadel which was built in the 19th century and is surrounded by a moat and imposing stone walls, and within the citadel, there are a number of palaces and shrines that make up the Imperial City, spread over a vast area that I imagine you could probably spend the best part of a day exploring. Many of the original buildings were destroyed in the Battle of Hue in the Vietnam War, and so large parts of the old city are just ruins, but there are a number of gates still standing, where the fading colours give you a feel for what the place would have once looked like and, even in my slightly jaded mood, I still found the overall experience of the walking tour an intriguing one.

I met some of the gang later in the hotel bar, which had a great vantage point of the city from its 11th-floor terrace, for a drink later on and I had just made my order and sat down when the sounds of a musak version of *'Sound of Silence'* filled the air – that song was seriously following me everywhere! When we got in the lift to head out for dinner, my attention was taken by a selection of TripAdvisor reviews that the hotel had proudly blown up to A3 size, laminated, and stuck on the wall of the lift. These caught my eye because the reviews they had picked, presumably the best ones they could find, didn't really say much about the hotel itself and instead covered some quite weird material. Let me share my favourite one with you:

'Nice hotel in a great location. The best thing was the wonderful staff. So polite and helpful. Especially 'Thang' who befriended our group and looked after us. I'm a bit overweight, and Thang christened me…'Happy Buddha!' That was my nickname for the rest of my wonderful trip.'

So the key takeaway of this author's review was that one of the staff had basically called him a fat bastard and the hotel had also decided this was something to be celebrated and promoted. Bizarre.

I headed out for dinner with Shell and Rob, and I decided that four days into our trip we were well overdue a pho, which we found at a nearby restaurant full of locals piling into the famous broth, which I deduced was a satisfactory indicator of the quality of the food. This hunch proved correct as the pho was excellent and only cost about $3 and it was a great place for a relaxed dinner and some beers, over which to learn a bit more about each other. Rob worked as a paramedic in a small town on the coast of Victoria called Lakes Entrance, which sounded like quite a sleepy town with Rob saying that a lot of the calls he had to attend could be classed as 'nanna down' calls, which I thought was a great expression. I had told Rob about my book and my dating app education along the way, a topic he seemed quite experienced on, bemoaning the fact there were only about four ladies on Bumble in Lakes Entrance and that he had already been out with all of them. He was also keeping tabs on his apps while he was travelling, so I asked him to keep me posted on any good tales coming out along the way. Shortly after this discussion, we were surprised to see Charles walk up to our table to join us, surprised because we hadn't actually told him where we were.

Charles was clearly very merry and had a similar demeanour to his slightly eccentric behaviour in Halong Bay, and it was only now that I looked at him, sipping the bottle of Sprite he had taken with him on his walk, that I realised what was going on. It wasn't Sprite that he was drinking, it was gin and tonic and it was clear to me now that Charles really was taking advantage of his solo trips to the fullest, combining his sightseeing with getting pissed – well why not! Charles was in very entertaining form, so we took him with us on our walk into town to find a bar for some more beers, which we found in the centre of an area where the streets had been closed off for pedestrians and a band playing live music had drawn a large crowd, with the surrounding bars all packed.

We were still a bit peckish and the food that the locals were eating looked very appealing, but after getting hold of the menu, I was confused when I couldn't find any of the food they were eating on there. It turned out the English menu wasn't a translation of the Vietnamese menu but was instead a load of different western dishes that they assumed the tourists would prefer to eat. Well, we didn't want those dishes, so we instead pointed at the dishes that were coming out and said we wanted to get them, whatever they were. This plan went well initially until Charles ordered us a plate of crispy fried frog; to my surprise, the meat was quite tasty, but there wasn't very much of it in comparison to all the bones and other inedible parts of the animal, so it's not a dish I think I would order again. By now it was getting late, and we had a rare treat of watching some of the locals attempting a drunken bar fight, which mostly involved not landing any blows, knocking over drinks and staggering around and falling over, but it was entertaining nonetheless and shortly after that we decided to call it a night, leaving Charles on his own to continue his drunken assault on the town.

***

The following morning there was no sign of Charles, which was a shame as we had quite an exciting outing on the itinerary this morning – a tour around the sights in the countryside near Hue, on the back of a fleet of scooters driven by some locals. On the face of it, this sounded like a potentially high-risk activity and in Hung's introductory speech back in Hanoi when explaining this outing, I presumed he was going to reassure us as to how professional and experienced the drivers are and that it is, therefore, a low-risk exercise, but that wasn't how he chose to calm our fears; instead, he had gone with:

'It's okay, you don't need to worry – they have insurance.'

Not reassuring. After travelling for a few minutes on the back of my scooter it was apparent I didn't need to worry as traffic was not too hectic and our entourage of two-man scooters wound their way through the streets at a relatively sedate pace, which I was unable to more precisely quantify as speedometer of my scooter was broken. During the initial briefing we had been shown the correct way to hug our driver, prompting a dirty laugh and a 'Ha! No reach-arounds!' comment from Shane, but I opted to hang on to the rear handles and was feeling confident I could survive the morning without falling off. A key attraction of the scooters was that they were able to go down all manner of alleyways and laneways which a car couldn't go down, so our route took us around some fascinating little back streets in the city before moving into the countryside and through small villages where we saw families eating their breakfast at roadside stalls and children playing in the streets. Arriving in the middle of a large area of paddy fields we passed by an amazing scene of a herd of about ten water buffalo taking a dip in the river before reaching a duck farm, which was mainly used for the production of eggs rather than meat. I don't know if it was just the time of day or if they are always at it, but the ducks seemed to be particularly over-amorous with a number of romantic interludes taking place in the water as we watched, including what I can only describe as a 'vertical duck three-way', which certainly hadn't been advertised in the brochure.

A little further out of town we made a stop at a local village where a morning market was taking place, giving Jackie, who was following the scooter group in a car, the opportunity to do yet more shopping. Wherever we had been on the trip so far, Jackie's sole focus had been on buying whatever she could get her hands on, including pottery, fridge magnets, multiple pairs of shoes, woven pictures, a photo of the group outside the citadel in Hue and all manner of food products. There was no sign of this compulsive shopping relenting, and I think she added another couple of pairs of plastic sandals at this stop to the stash. The market was quite rough and ready, with ladies in colourful pyjama-like outfits selling goose heads and other pieces of meat that looked to have only been recently removed from the animal, a selection of fish in small metal bowls of water, and one kind of fish, which I think was a snakehead, that didn't even have any water and just flapped around in the dry bowl. While the market itself was not the prettiest sight, the village in which it was located most certainly was, as it was set along the banks of a small river filled with lily pads and magenta lotus flowers, with small wooden canoes moored on its banks, where red lanterns hung from the trees alongside and an old wooden covered bridge completing the scene. The scene giving me one of my favourite photos of the whole trip.

From this village, the bike tour continued on through the largest cemetery in Vietnam, literally kilometre after kilometre of headstones, shrines and tombs of various shapes and sizes, before stopping at a look-out over the 'Perfume River'. After a pause here for some comedy group photos of us pretending to drive the scooters with the drivers on the back, we visited the tomb of the Emperor Tu Duc, who had ruled Vietnam from 1848 to 1883. The tomb was actually more of an estate, with a large complex of buildings set around a large lake where Tu Duc spent his retirement years and the tomb itself. The buildings were well maintained, decorated with some eye-catching orange and forest green ceramic motifs, making for an entertaining 30 or so minutes' walk around for the group – with the exception of Jackie, who didn't come into the complex and instead spent that time at the souvenir stalls outside the gates. Our lunch stop was at a Buddhist temple, and you already know from my experience in Koyasan they type of food that meant we were eating. Jackie was not impressed, having one mouthful of the soup that came out first and pushing it away in disgust with a 'Yuck!' This was followed by rice cakes, a vegetable curry and a vegetable pho, a selection which I enjoyed much more than the equivalent Japanese selection and which I got to eat a load off, as I was seated next to Jackie and I ended up eating all of hers too. After lunch we had one final instalment of what had ended up being a really fun scooter adventure, taking us to a riverside pagoda and temple complex from where we took a leisurely boat ride back up the river to the city centre, drinking beers while a lady tried unsuccessfully to sell us clothes and souvenirs – with even Jackie saying no!

After a four-hour bus journey the next morning, we arrived at our next destination of Hoi An. Hoi An was an important trading port back during the 16th to the end of the 18th century when nearby Danang became the new centre of trade, but this loss of interest in the city is now its appeal, as much of the heritage of those historical times has been preserved, giving the old town area a unique feel that has put it firmly on the tourist map. Hung led us on a walking tour of the historic streets which are now filled with textiles, ceramics, art galleries, coffee shops, bars and restaurants, interspersed with preserved historical buildings and temples. The walking tour ended at one of the town's famous tailors, Yaly, where many of the group were getting suits or dresses made, and I took myself off on a walk around town to kill some time before the excitement of another evening street food tour.

The tour started with a brief visit to a tiny bakery where a handful of bare-chested men in a small, hot room were working the dough into baguettes, which they were then baking in a giant oven in the corner, providing the shop next door with bread for their Banh mi, which is where we went next. Hoi An is another place Anthony Bourdain had visited on his Vietnam tour, and he had ordained this place, 'Banh Mi Phoung', as making the best example of a Banh mi he had ever eaten. While he is no longer with us, they were still trading heavily off his visit, with his photo and quote on the menu board and the sandwiches themselves served in printed wrappers again reminding their customers that Anthony thought their sandwiches were rather good – which they were. Were they as good as the ones in Hanoi with the lucky sauce? It was a tough call, to be honest as they were both delicious, so I might call the result of that contest as a draw. We hit the central market where there were a number of stalls each preparing one or two speciality dishes, stopping at one which was making 'Banh xeo', which was a pancake with herbs and prawns rolled up with a rice paper roll and eaten with a dipping sauce – the taste was superb, and the crisp bottom of the pancake gave the dish a great crunch to it, so this was another winner.

Moving on to a small restaurant in a side alley for one of the towns most celebrated dishes, the 'white rose', we were served up what was basically a dumpling that had been shaped into the form of a rose. The presentation was good, but I didn't think there was enough filling, meaning the overriding taste was just the dumpling itself which wasn't that exciting, though the restaurant did redeem itself by having *'Sound of Silence'* playing when we arrived. Seriously. Again! The final savoury stop of the tour was at a placemaking chicken rice, which was pretty much as described but the beautifully moist chicken and mix of fresh chilli and chilli sauce with which it was served, made a dish that seemed much greater than the sum of its parts and as a result, I saw off two large plates of it. The other highlight of this stop was my first traffic incident, with a scooter driving into the back of my leg as we entered the alley where the restaurant was located. Luckily, he got the brakes on sharpish, and I was left with just a slight sense of surprise and a tyre mark on the back of my calf rather than any serious injuries of note.

The tour concluded at one of the many coffee roasters in the old town where we had an excellent, strong, Vietnamese coffee. The coffee selection here included 'weasel coffee' for sale, something which I had been noticing a lot on our tour around the country and which I now had a chance to read about. I realised I had heard about this coffee before, using its other name 'civet coffee' and the rather unusual way it is produced, which involves making coffee from part-digested coffee 'cherries', eaten and defecated by the 'Asian palm civet'. The civets only choose to eat certain cherries, and their digestion process apparently has a favourable impact during fermentation which results in them shitting out 'coffee gold'. Or at least that's how it seems to be regarded by the extraordinary amount people pay to drink it. I had seen a cup of civet coffee for sale in the marina at Halong Bay for about $50 – who is paying $50 for a cup of coffee? Not me, I'll stick to my skim flat whites with undigested coffee beans thanks.

This was another thoroughly enjoyable and educational food tour, which we followed up with a walk around the city to enjoy the sight of it lit up with the hundreds of colourful lanterns which lined the streets and to have a few more beers. Over drinks, Shell, Rob and I decided that the fruit patterned shirts which we had seen all over the place, with their brash watermelon, pineapple and banana designs, were one of the highlights of the town and one which we should celebrate. We concluded the best way to do this, was to suggest that everyone in the group should buy a watermelon print garment of some description, whether that be a shirt, hat, skirt or pair of shorts and that we should all wear our outfit at our final dinner in Ho Chi Minh City. So that's what we did, by way of a message that I sent around the WhatsApp group advising them of the plan and which Shell followed up with a picture of the recommended watermelon print. Time would tell whether this idea caught on or not.

***

After a lazy day in Hoi An, we were on the road again, with a short bus ride to Danang airport with the pleasure of Hung on the microphone, talking to us about the idea of some of 'the naughty boys' in the group, to buy watermelon print outfits for our final dinner, an event that he was now rather over-excited about. The Danang airport experience came and went, and after a one-hour flight courtesy of my friends at Jetstar, we got our first look at Ho Chi Minh City, arriving to a grey day, passing by the skyscrapers in the city centre and over the network of wide rivers around the city, with its densely populated areas spreading out in all directions to accommodate the fourteen million people who lived here.

Our first stop of the day was to the War Museum, where I was expecting to see some similarly confronting material to my day out in Hiroshima and this indeed proved to be the case. The exhibition started with the history of the country before the Vietnam War itself, and as this wasn't something I had ever studied, this was a useful overview of a history that seemed to be mostly characterised by other countries invading, occupying and eventually being defeated by the Vietnamese. This cycle had started with the colonisation of the country in the mid-19th century by the French, who had remained in control until the Japanese occupation in the 1940s. After the Japanese had been defeated in WW2, President Ho Chi Minh declared Vietnam's independence from France, but the French decided to come back for another go, resulting in the First Indochina War which ran from 1945 through to the French finally being defeated in 1954, at which point the 'Geneva Agreement' was signed, dividing Vietnam into two countries; communist-led North Vietnam and the Republic of Vietnam in the South. In the later years of this war, the US had taken an increasing interest and had supported the French with money and weapons, as they were concerned about the potential further spread of communism into the region and the increased power base that would give to their main adversary at the time, the Soviet Union. After the French had been defeated, the US concerns escalated, and they joined forces with the Republic of Vietnam to fight against North Vietnam, starting the 19 years of conflict in Vietnam, Laos and Cambodia which became known as the Second Indochina War, or simply and more recognizably, the Vietnam War.

The exhibits chronicled the various stages of the conflict from the indirect US involvement at the start, the subsequent escalation of their involvement following the 'Tonkin Incident' in 1964 when they alleged the Vietnamese forces had pursued a US destroyer, through to the peak of hostilities in 1969 when the US had 550,000 troops deployed in the region, and then the Paris Peace Accords of 1973 and the eventual final departure of US military in April 1975. The narrative in the museum was written in an understandably one-sided manner with some very emotive language used to describe the actions of the Americans, so this probably wasn't the most balanced education of the events of the war. Putting the emotion aside, it did serve to build my knowledge of the conflict from a base of practically nil to one of now having some idea as to the events that occurred and the subsequent fallout.

After setting the scene of the conflict, we moved through a number of rooms with exhibits and photos from the front lines, both of the soldiers and of the civilians caught in the cross-fire, including perhaps the most famous photo from the war, depicting a young girl running away from her village in terror after the napalm attack had burnt all the clothes from her body. One of the rooms focused on the impact of the 'Ranch Hand' operation, in which the Americans had attacked the areas of the countryside where they believed the Viet Cong were holed out with a poison known as Agent Orange, in an attempt to drive the enemy forces out into the open. This poison infected the water supply of the area and caused great suffering not just for those who ingested it at the time but for the generations that followed, many of whom who were born with birth defects, deformities and disabilities as a result. On our journey back from Halong Bay to Hanoi, we had made a stop at a charitable organisation where people with disabilities, many of them from the Agent Orange, were provided support and jobs where they made woven pictures and other souvenirs to sell to the tourists, demonstrating the impacts of the war were still being felt here in many ways, even nearly fifty years later.

Like the Hiroshima museum experience, this was never going to be a comfortable way of spending my time, and I soon got to a point where I was feeling rather depressed and troubled by what I had seen, so feeling I had seen enough to understand the horrors of the conflict a bit better, I headed for the exit. After the group had re-gathered, we made another quick stop to look around the Notre-Dame Cathedral and the Central Post Office next door, attractions which made up what appeared to be a reasonably short list of things to see in the city, before moving on to a restaurant called 'Pho 2000' for lunch. This was another restaurant that was trading on a celebrity endorsement, as it proudly displayed a photo of Bill Clinton surrounded by their staff, who enjoyed a pho here many years before.

I had decided my hair and beard were once again out of control, and I couldn't even manage three more days to wait and get it sorted in the safety of a Sydney barber, and so I set off for a walk around town to a barber located near the main shopping area. After ten minutes of walking, I realised I had been looking at the map upside down, and my confident progress thus far had been in completely the wrong direction. It really was just a little bit sad I thought to myself, that after over one hundred days of solo travel around the world, I was still seemingly incapable of reading a map or getting anywhere without getting lost. The traffic was even more crazy than Hanoi with a lot more cars and trucks amongst the scooters, and the massive construction site that ran through the middle of the city for the new metro system meant it wasn't a very scenic walk, though I'm sure there are nicer areas, so I shouldn't write off the whole city based on this experience. After correcting my initial directional error, I managed to get to the barbers without further drama, and the guy did a really excellent job on both the hair and the beard, which raised my spirits significantly for the evening ahead. Unfortunately, my improved mood was dashed when we went out to have some drinks at the 'party street' near our hotel, which was full of identical-looking bars with western food menus and drinks masquerading as 'happy hour specials', which were in reality double or triple the price we had been paying for them everywhere else in Vietnam. Maybe I was a bit tired and cranky, and Ho Chi Minh City was getting the same short end of the stick that Seattle had received from me, but I just didn't find myself warming to the place.

***

My disappointment with the city mattered not the next day, the final day of the tour, as we were due to spend most of the day elsewhere, taking our final bus journey south to a Mekong Delta river tour. Another bus tour could only mean one thing, yes, Hung back on the microphone and being super random again. The general theme was once again corruption and this time he managed to weave in a story about one of his uncles who had moved to the USA to open a nail salon in Georgia after being embroiled in a corruption scandal at home and another story involving the Vietnamese intelligence agencies. He claimed they had tracked down a wealthy property developer who had skipped the country and moved to Germany under a cloud of corruption charges and upon locating him in the embassy there, had broken him out to bring him home to face charges. This tale sounded very farfetched unless the Vietnamese had an agent called Jac Baua at their disposal, so I felt compelled to go, and fact check the story online; the story was almost true in fact, but the Vietnamese agents had actually grabbed the guy while he was walking in a park, not hiding out in an embassy, so the story wasn't quite as 'black ops' as it sounded. That said, they still managed to sneak him out of the country under the Germans' noses, who weren't very happy about that, so it still went down as a decent heist for me, and I now believed Hung's claims that if you did something wrong, there is nowhere to hide from the Vietnamese authorities.

Back to the journey itself, it took us about 45 minutes to get out of the urban area passing by an extensive farming area with rice fields, coconut trees and dragon fruit plantations, all of which had scattered groups of men and women in conical hats tending to their crops. After about three hours we arrived in the Mekong Delta area, passing over bridges that spanned the many massive limbs of the river system, with a number of flat bedded vessels steaming up the middle loaded with sand and other aggregates, making their way from the coast up towards the city. A little further on we reached the smaller tributary where we boarded our boat, a simple wooden affair with rows of wooden chairs from where we took in the sights as we made our slow progress up the river. Most of the boats coming the other way had colourful eyes painted onto the front of the bow, apparently a legacy from hundreds of years ago when the crocodiles who lived in the river back then would be scared off by these eyes staring down on them. The pace of life looked to be a slow one here and one of the barges that passed by carrying a large load of timber was driven by a man who appeared to be asleep in a hammock suspended on poles at the stern of the boat. As we cruised along, our guide served us a plate of local fruit including familiar fruits such as mango and ladyfinger bananas, alongside others which had to be identified for us, including longans, which were a bit like lychees and not my cup of tea and jack fruit, which is difficult to describe but surprisingly tasty, particularly for a non-fruit lover like myself.

After crossing one of the wider stretches of the river where the chocolate coloured water was being blown into small waves by the wind, all of a sudden it felt like we were out at sea and we turned into a smaller channel to dock and disembark for the first stop of the day at a coconut processing factory. There were piles of discarded coconut husks all over the place, and they were making what seemed like an endless list of coconut product derivatives from the fruit. They had extracted coconut water from the younger ones, and coconut milk, cream and oil from the older ones. The solid products I saw included coconut powder, coconut flour, coconut sugar, coconut candy and even some clothes made from the fibres – it was amazing how many different applications they had found for coconuts. I am a big coconut fan both savoury and sweet, so this was a welcome stop for me, and I enjoyed some of the coconut candy, which Jackie, of course, bought, without taking out any more fillings from my teeth, which was a relief.

From the coconut estate, we walked to a narrow waterway nearby, where we were loaded into small traditional wooden canoes and rowed by some local ladies to a spot further down the river and then collected by tuk-tuks, which drove us for a further ten minutes to a local riverside restaurant. The lunch was a little bland in my opinion, even with the addition of a whole baked elephant-ear fish for the main course, though the drip coffee we had at the end did take out the accolade for the best coffee of the trip. After lunch, we were back onto the boat for the journey back up the river to catch the bus home. If I sound a little bit indifferent as I describe the events of the day, it's because it just wasn't that exciting, which was a shame given this was our final day out. On the bus home, it seemed I wasn't the only one who felt that way and the general consensus was that if we had our time again, we would choose to do the trip in reverse, ending in Halong Bay which had, almost without exception, been the highlight and a worthy final day outing. I have spoken before about random events that had saved previous dull days and today was no exception, with that event taking place about thirty minutes into the return journey when we passed a man on a scooter carrying ducks. When I say he was carrying ducks on his scooter, I mean he was carrying live ducks, and I would estimate that he had at least thirty of them, all of them carried in sacks which went around both side of the bike, with just their white heads and yellow bills popping out the top and they were looking around and quacking! It was an incredulous sight, and we yelled excitedly at the driver to slow down so we could all get a clear photograph as the guy drove past and then all waited impatiently to get on Wi-Fi so we could break Instagram with it later on.

The green shoots of recovery provided by the duck sighting bloomed further when returning to Ho Chi Minh City and congregating in the lobby for the final dinner with each member of the group dressed in their watermelon outfits, including Hung. The group photos provided him with much entertainment and happiness, and I am sure he would be proudly showing off to his fellow group leaders as soon as he got the opportunity. Our final dinner was at a restaurant called 'Koko', a charitable organisation set up to provide employment to disadvantaged people, which sounded not dissimilar to Jamie Oliver's 'Fifteen' restaurant chain. The food was excellent, and there was a great atmosphere to the meal from the combination of end-of-tour excitement and the novelty value and reactions from our fellow diners to our table of watermelons. Rob did a little speech to thank Hung for his efforts through the trip and present him with his tip and then it was time for another group activity which was not on the advertised itinerary but which I had been agitating for in a not too subtle manner since the start of the trip, a group outing for karaoke.

Not everyone was brave enough to come along, but we definitely had a quorum, with myself, Shell, Rob, Peter, Charles, Ines and Tania joining Hung, who had now reached peak levels of over-excitement, in a trip to a nearby glitzy looking establishment, where we laid siege to a number of sing-along favourites. I think there is probably some rule about 'what goes on at karaoke stays at karaoke', so I won't reveal all of the group's secrets, but rest assured there were worthy attempts at numbers from artists including Bon Jovi, Bruce Springsteen, Take That and Roxette, as well as an eye-catching singing 'AND' dancing routine to go with *'Gangnam Style'*. Lots and lots of fun and from a selfish point of view, for me, it felt like an appropriately ridiculous way to be spending the final night of my grand tour.

I decided in the morning my watermelon shirt could not possibly reach the lofty heights of the night before, and I left it behind in the room for a well-earned early retirement. And then it was time to pack my bags for the final time, say my goodbyes to the members of the group who were still around and take a taxi to the airport to catch my final flights to return back to normal life at home, whatever that was going to be…

Fin.

Summary – Vietnam

Kms travelled (air) – (Inc. HCM to Syd) – 9,010
Kms travelled (land) – 1,300
Number of Banh mi eaten – Five
Number of bizarre stories from Hung – Several
Number of Jackie's shopping trips – Fifteen.

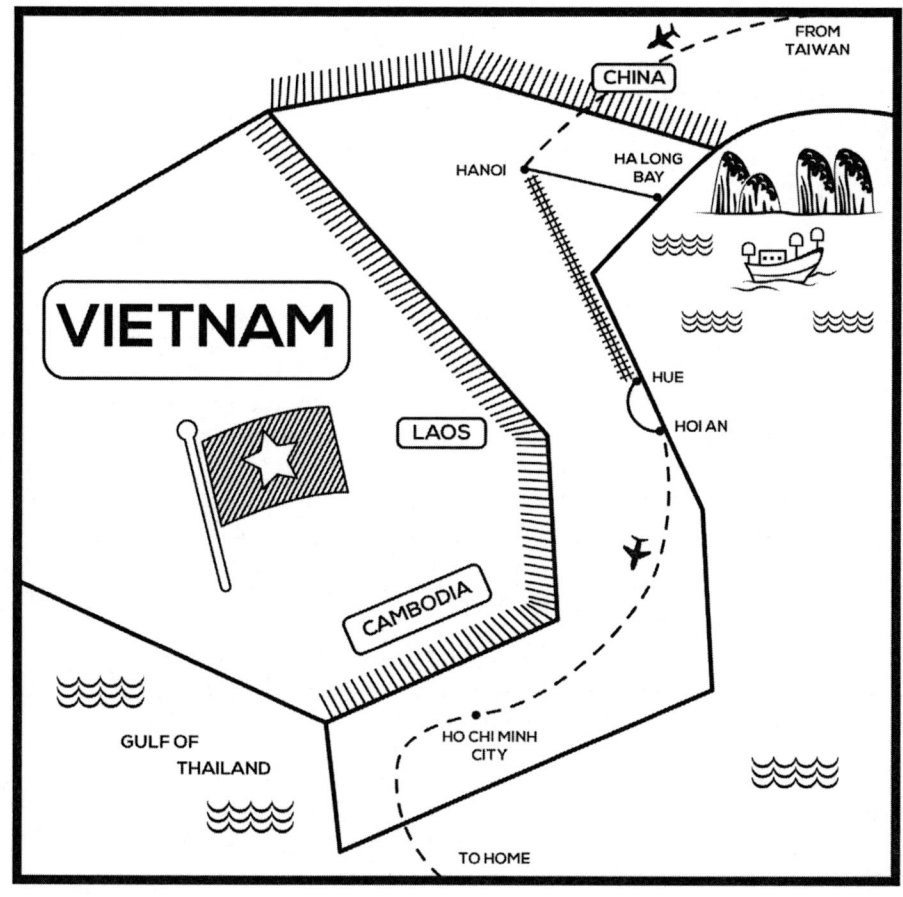

Epilogue

If you were watching the film adaptation of my book, at this point the screen would have gone black, and you would now be waiting for the bit at the end where the white text comes up to tell you the fate of the main characters. Actually, thinking about it, that's how they do it for serious films. For a more jolly tale like mine, they would probably present those updates over the top of a photo montage of each person they are referring to, maybe with some up-tempo feel-good Michael Buble number in the background and that's exactly the picture I have in my head now, as I ponder how to neatly summarise the events of the last four months. Yes, it's been a lot about the places I have visited, but more so it's been about the experiences I have had along the way and the eccentric supporting cast who found their way into my story. So who's in that montage? Well I think I'm a good shout to be in there somewhere, but the other pictures that come to mind in vaguely chronological order are:

- James in Richmond, standing in his doorway in a towel, looking me up and down in a questioning manner and saying, "Yes, I'm James?"
- Julio calling the Peru walking gang to order, flashing a beaming grin while clapping his hands together and saying, "So, family! Are we ready?"
- Scott from San Jose leaving his unhappy walking tour group standing in disbelief in the city centre before strolling home to watch some Netflix.
- Ramon from Antigua feeding tortillas to his enormous St Bernard before crashing through a window, still with an inane grin on his face.
- Victoria in Yucca Valley frantically making up the spare room for me, while sending me text messages as I sit in the darkness of the front garden.
- The lady in the San Francisco bar removing her teeth mid-conversation.
- Audra telling me in uncomfortable detail what was wrong with the sex she had on her last date.
- Wakiko in Kyoto chasing me into the shower each evening; and
- Hung delivering another hour-long monologue on a subject tenuously related to the topic he started on some time earlier.

And what are they all up to now? I have no idea, to be honest, but I'm confident most of them are bringing joy to other travellers making their acquaintance, intentionally or otherwise. And what about me? What does the movie say happened to me? That's a longer answer, so I'd better draw breath, and start a new paragraph.

I referred early on in proceedings to Emily's request that the book not be about me 'finding myself', but I knew that was never going to be the case, as I didn't feel like I was lost at the start. That's not to say there wasn't change for me, but I would characterise this more as 'rediscovering myself' as a single person, recognising differences in my behaviour in the absence of the filter I would apply as part of a couple, and recognising the differences between single me at 25 and single me at 40. Over the course of the four months, I had more 'ponder time' than ever before in my life, and while I wasn't getting any closer to discovering the meaning of life, I was using the time to explore some critical introspective matters. Like reflecting on what it said about me as a person that I wouldn't consider dating someone who had misused the words 'your' or 'you're' in their profile and whether that was something that I should try to change, or instead just celebrate?

The solo travel environment provided the opportunity for quiet thinking time but also pushed me into being much more sociable than I might usually have been, as I found myself making more effort in conversation with people, who in many cases would be unlikely to progress further than just a passing acquaintance. One of the open questions I had setting out on my journey, was whether I might find out I was a 'closet introvert' and want to explore the world in solitude, but the evidence of my actions along the way had put that thought to rest, for whether it be with dates, Airbnb hosts or complete randoms, I often found myself preferring to go on a hunt for a chat over spending time alone.

But hang on a minute, I hear you say, you were just behaving that way because you were trying to write a book and you needed to find some people who were more interesting than you and had some weird stories or behaviours you could re-tell in the book to keep us entertained? And you would have a point – I do recall thinking to myself along the way that the line was getting a bit grey as to whether I was actually 'talking' to people or whether I was in fact 'interviewing' them, and this was something I reflected on. I don't have an answer for you right now, but time will tell whether I behave in the same way when I am not keeping notes on my daily activities. I also felt a genuine step-change in how quickly I was able to build relationships with people when I was really concentrating on learning a bit about them right from the first conversation and not just going through the motions to pass the time, and I believe it is highly likely this is a change that will stick for me. There were other more predictable changes from a physical perspective, as spending four months out of the office and walking around rather a lot meant I lost a fair amount of weight and got my fitness to a level I would hazard to say I have not attained at any previous point in my life. This wasn't a fortuitous outcome, it had been a deliberate aim from the start of the trip so as to get to a healthy base from which to take on my 40s when keeping fit apparently gets progressively harder – or at least that's how the older members of my football team justify me having to do all the running anyway, so it must be true. For me, the most impressive statistic on the subject of my physical welfare was that I had made it through four months with no illness, only two 'digestion incidents' and two minor injuries, being the ankle roll in the Grand Canyon and the face plant at Hiroshima Station – for someone as accident prone as me, this outcome almost defies belief!

Looking beyond my own sentiments, I was also fascinated by the comments I received both from people I had spent time with along the way and messages from my friends back home on how they had experienced the journey with me. While going travelling in your younger years is a fairly well-trodden path, I think a lot of people I spoke to looked at me as something of a novelty item, first of all for the fact I was doing it at this stage in my life and, secondly because I was making the whole trip on my own. Once the conversations got past the novelty aspect, I found people were genuinely fascinated by what I was up to and more than a few people I spoke to said that they found what I was doing inspiring. I hope those people, and they will know who they are, were using that word in something more than a throw-away kind of fashion, and they will harness that feeling to go and do some travel, or even just challenge themselves to do something in their life a bit differently from the norm. For me, spending time in a world where the new norm was that there was no norm, was a fascinating experience and the thought that I actually get to create my new norm is exciting.

Right back at the start, I introduced my story by describing myself as being at a crossroads in my life, looking out into an unknown future from a relationship perspective, wondering whether I should be feeling more purpose in my working life and setting off on a 'big walk' to see if some time out and world travel would help me find the direction I was looking for. So did it?

Well, from a work perspective, I was not really going to learn much about what I enjoyed or otherwise, about my job by just not doing it for six months but I knew that would be the case. Work would still be there when I came home, and I could work through that side of things at that point in time, so my time away was more about having a bit of a refresher on myself, working through where it was that I found joy in life and then working out a plan to find some more of it. Although, I actually already had the answer to that before I even left Sydney Airport back in July.

When I had decided I was a bit unhappy at work over a year before, I had gone for a few catch-ups with the lovely HR leader from our team at the time, Sarah, who had challenged me with the obvious questions you ask people in that situation, "Well Alex, if you think you don't want to do this job, what do you want to do? What makes you happy?" and I gave her the following answer:

"I like to make people laugh. And I think I would like to write a book."

Sarah looked back at me and gave me a supportive looking smile, but I could tell that what she was really thinking was, 'Idiot!'

And she would have been right. I didn't realise it at the time, but I was talking about two different things here. Yes, I do like to make people laugh, but that's something you can do every day whatever job you do, and I have done quite a good job of doing that throughout my career, while also getting the job done that my clients are paying me to do. I'm the first to admit I'm not the best at what I do (still pretty good though...), but people like to work with people whose company they enjoy, and the joy I take from my work isn't just what I do, but also the fun had along the way and the relationships that endure after it is done. Whatever role it is I end up settling back into on my return I know I will carry on doing that.

The book point is different and one that was described quite eloquently by, well, actually, it was by me, back in Chapter One, when I told you that I had 'found myself yearning for a creative outlet outside of work', with 'outside of work' being the keywords here. Well, I already knew writing would be that creative outlet for me and arising from an unfortunate starting set of life circumstances, I found myself an interesting tale to tell and, more importantly, the time I needed to convert that tale into a book. To your credit, you have gamely managed to battle through to the closing moments – relax, the end is finally almost in sight.

The trip itself was always going to be a big adventure, but the book writing along the way took me in a direction I don't think I would have gone without it. I have commented already about making deeper connections along the way, but there was more to it than that. Everywhere I visited I paid a little bit more attention to the details, what I was seeing, how it looked, how the light was, what was the best word to describe the shade of whatever colour I was looking at, what were those people doing, what was that guy wearing, how did it make me feel – all of it in the hope I could explain it to others, but then also finding the unintended outcome of this was that I got to live each of those experiences, in the moment, with awareness and in a much richer way than I would have otherwise.

I had been on a mission to learn more about how others found passion in their lives and in their work and somewhere along the way, I had realised that my passion was right here. In taking a wild four months of adventure around the world, recording it in a jumble of notes on my iPhone and then sharing it with you in the book you have before you now.

Final Summary

Kms travelled (air) – 56,260
Kms travelled (land) – 12,485
Number of circumnavigations of the globe – One
Number of books written – One

Acknowledgements

Content contributors, both knowingly and unknowingly – Emily, Jane, Stan, Jo, Maria, Rachel, Kieran, Sunny, Skids, Cyrus, Louise, Armando, Julio, Chino, Audra, Angela, Tall, Powell, Dom, Becca, Belinda, Charles and Hung.

Airbnb hosts – Delyth and Luke, James, Mauricio, Jorge, Ellie, Raul, Vanessa, Scott, Greivin, Carlos and Alexandra, Evelyn, Licho, Java, Alvaro, Saul and Giselle, Sara and Mauricio, Albany and Juan, Cassie and 'Cassie's Mum', Edson, Victoria, Suzanne, Kc and Tater, Kemi and Paul, Everardo, Josh, Ben, Christina, Linda, Curtis, Jackee, Wakiko, Yoko, Takashi and Seiji.

Soundtrack – Spotify, Paul Oakenfold and Paul Van Dyk.

Social media and travel survival assistance – The inventors of Wi-Fi, WhatsApp, Facebook, Instagram, the Kindle, the iPad and the iPhone.